12-13-66

THE CONSUMER'S HANDBOOK

THE
CONSUMER'S
HANDBOOK

Edited by
Paul Fargis

HAWTHORN BOOKS, INC.
Publishers
NEW YORK

To
Beth and John

1389882

FOREWORD

The Consumer's Handbook has been designed to help consumers in two ways: to provide basic information on all aspects of homemaking and household management and to show the consumer how he can continually use this information to save countless time and money.

You, a consumer, are surely aware of the daily barrage of information on how, when, where and why to spend your hard-earned dollars. Radio, television, newspapers and magazines all provide advice to help you shop wisely. But *do* you shop wisely? Do you read consumer information and put it to practical use?

The chances are that you do not. According to a recent consumer survey, only three out of every 100 people make regular use of available consumer information. Obviously, then, something is needed which contains as much information as a consumer needs in order to make intelligent decisions. Everyone likes to save money and most of us like to do things in the easiest and most efficient manner. Therefore, if we can get all the facts in one source, the problem is greatly simplified. This is what we hope has been accomplished with *The Consumer's Handbook*.

A book such as this is never really the work of one individual. This particular book is basically the work of hundreds if not thousands of men and women who have contributed their experiences and writings in the service of your Government. The book could not have been compiled without the information supplied by the United States Department of Agriculture, the Government Printing Office and the many consumer service organizations.

Much of the information in these pages has been taken from *Consumers All*, a publication of the Department of Agriculture. We are very grateful for the privilege of using all the material from that book and from other sources. Because the articles have been edited, updated or rewritten, it is not proper to list their original authors. However, we do wish all the contributing experts to know that they have our sincere thanks. They are the real authors.

Paul Fargis
Chatham, Mass.

TABLE OF CONTENTS

FURNISHINGS

FOOD

CLOTHING

EQUIPMENT

OUTDOORS

TO OWN OR TO RENT

FOR SOME FAMILIES, ownership of a home savors of a love affair. They find exactly the right place in the right location. Homeownership has always been their goal. It will make them independent and respected.

For others, ownership has an economic value. A house is an inflation-resistant investment and a tangible incentive to save. Rents are too high and ownership is cheaper. Ownership improves their credit rating, or suitable rental properties are not to be had.

Others are less enchanted by ownership. They have neither time nor inclination to manage the upkeep of a house. They may find available rental properties best suited to their needs. They fear hidden or unexpected expenses sometimes connected with ownership and shrinkage of capital if property value goes down.

Others do not have or may never have the capital to buy a house. Renting makes adapting to changing family needs easier than owning. Because real estate transactions take so much time, the mobile one-in-five family wants no house to lessen its bargaining power for a new position or to lose mobility for other than occupational reasons.

But homeownership is not necessarily a little white cottage or a farm. Apartment ownership has developed through cooperatives (a share of an apartment complex) and condominiums (title to a specific apartment). Also, although not counted in the statistics, are owned mobile homes, usually sitting on a tract of rented land.

The decision to own or rent is related to stages in the life cycle that begin at marriage and extend some time after the dissolution of the family by death of one of the mates.

A typical sequence of changes upgrades shelter with increases in assets, age, and family needs. Net worth is highest after age 35. Homeownership is greatest after age 45, but does not begin extensively before age 25.

The residential cycle usually begins in a small, rented apartment.

The next step may be a larger apartment or the rental of a two-family house. After age 25—following the arrival of children—the family may buy a small new or used house and build up an equity. The family may sell this after about age 35 in favor of a large, new house.

Later demands of children call for expansion by remodeling it or buying another· and larger house. If finances permit, a custom-planned house may be built.

It may be the last house until old age and retirement indicate a smaller house; a condominium apartment to which specific title is held; a mobile home; or a rented apartment. The spouse remaining after the death of the partner may remain a while, but later may seek quarters with children or other relatives or in homes or projects for the aged.

Families move through the life cycle at varying rates and with varying numbers of moves. When changed residential status is not caused by migration for a new position or upgrading accommodations, turning points usually come during the expanding and contracting phases.

Changes in residence, rented or owned, entail changes, often abrupt and substantial, in allocation of family resources. Whether as rent, mortgage installments, taxes, or repairs, the residence claim is regular, and it is inexorable.

Homeownership is achieved oftenest

by means of mortgages. Three-fifths of the owner-occupied nonfarm homes were mortgaged in 1960.

The average time required to pay off a mortgage on a house is about 20 years, about the same as it takes to rear a child from infancy to maturity and slightly longer than the couple has together after the children have left.

If a family moves several times during this period, the feat of finally owning a home free and clear of debt is accomplished by enlarging the equity on succeeding houses.

LENDING INSTITUTIONS and homeowners alike have worked out several principles in regard to financing.

The attitude toward mortgages on homes has changed from something feared and liquidated quickly to "open-end" mortgages. These may be extended (without renewal expense) for additions to the house, education for the children, health maintenance, or other new financial needs.

It's an old rule of thumb (often used by lenders) that a buyer can afford a house that is two and one-half times his income. For example, if your salary is $9,000, the theory is that you should be able to afford a house worth $22,500.

But remember, as with all rules of thumb, this is a generalization. Individual circumstances will always have to be taken into account. Some families will have heavier debts or more dependents than others and therefore may not be able to carry the burden of a household mortgage.

So, consider that rule of thumb as a general guideline—nothing more. The rule was more valid several years ago when credit was cheaper, taxes lower, and salary deductions minimal. Presently, what you can afford will depend on your take home pay, not your gross income; the down payment you can afford, and your analysis of present and future financial commitments.

Be careful to shop around for the best buy from the types of lending institutions. Compare the advantages and disadvantages. Recently the magazine *Changing Times* gave ratings to the various types of home-loan institutions. Their ratings were based on an 18-city report to the Federal Home Loan Bank Board. On *conventional* loans they were rated as listed below.

What this obviously means is that you can get a good deal if you compare the rates of the lenders in your area and then base your decision on what you want or can get in terms of interest, length, and amount of down payment.

The lending institutions will show you prepared payment schedules which you can collect and compare against others. The payment schedules will show you how much you will be paying on interest and principal each month, the rates of interest, and the lengths of time for different types of loans.

Obviously, therefore, it is important and wise to start your shopping as far in advance as possible because the lender will want to judge your borrowing power. The financial picture you present of yourself is just as important as your careful shopping. Make sure you

RATINGS OF VARIOUS HOME-LOAN INSTITUTIONS

	Purchase Price	Interest Rate	Length of Loan	Down Payment
Insurance Company	high	lowest	longest	fairly high
Mortgage Company	medium	next to highest	long	low
Savings & Loan	low	high	medium	low
Savings Bank	medium	next to lowest	medium to long	high
Commercial Bank	medium	medium	short	high

present the best analysis of yourself as a mortgage risk, your expenses in relation to your income, and your present and future job prospects.

See the next section for more information about mortgages.

The ratio of the down payment to the purchase price is determined by available family financial resources and by lending policies of financing institutions. The lower the ratio, the more limited the choice of lenders.

A young family buying its first home often has little money. The only choice may be a loan insured or guaranteed by a Government agency but lent by the conventional lending institutions. Their houses must be new and built to certain standards. Their credit rating and prospects must be good.

For a house valued at 15 thousand dollars, they need only 450 dollars for a down payment, as they can borrow 97 percent of the property value as appraised by the Federal Housing Administration. If they want a house of higher value, they must have a larger down payment until at the maximum value, 30 thousand dollars, they need 3,500 dollars.

Other avenues are open to those who can make only a small down payment.

The second mortgage, formerly used to close the gap between a low down payment and the lender's requirements, has been largely replaced by the installment land contract. In this contract, a deed held in trust is a safeguard, but if the seller retains title, he may mortgage it.

Other lenders, whose policies permit loans of only 50 to 60 percent of appraised valuation, insure loans above this amount (up to 15 to 20 percent) with private mortgage insurance corporations. This relieves them of risk for amounts above their regular lending policy.

Besides the down payment, buyers need closing costs for a lender's initial service charge; cost of title search and title insurance; and charges for preparing, recording, and notarizing the deed and mortgage. Other costs prepaid at purchase are taxes and premiums for hazard and other insurance.

Although closing costs are low in some localities, they usually vary from 100 to more than 600 dollars.

WHETHER RENTING or buying, the annual cash-outlay-to-income ratio is important.

It generally ranges from one-eighth to one-third net family income, depending on the age of the family, income, and value placed in housing. Cash outlay may be rent alone. For homeownership free of debt, it includes taxes, maintenance, and hazard insurance. With a loan, it includes payments and interest in addition. The ratio is determined when renting by the amount the family is willing to forgo and when buying by the policy of the financing institution also. Some refuse loans when the cash outlay for housing is more than one-fifth of net income. Others feel that if approximately one-sixth has been paid for rent, one-fourth or a little more could be devoted to purchase, since both rent and savings are included.

When a squeeze from reduced income and increased housing expenses occurs, homeowners who use 30 percent or more of their income for housing expenses are likelier than others to have mortgages foreclosed.

There are, of course, exceptions to any of those ratios. Demands made on the net income differ from family to family and are affected by the size, age, and health of the family; stability of job and income outlook; amount of savings accumulated; and the importance of housing in the family scale of preferences.

Terms of home mortgages have lengthened substantially. Conventional institutions lend for 20 years or more. FHA insures mortgages on new homes for 35 years or 40 years for families displaced by urban renewal, Government purchase for water conservation, military, or other public purposes.

Long-term mortgages allow some families with relatively low incomes to become homeowners. They enable some to buy more expensive houses than would otherwise be possible. They may make it easier to sell a house when necessary, because buyers may be attracted by a long-term mortgage and a small cash down payment. Also, income tax deductions from interest paid can be made so long as such interest is paid.

The chief disadvantages of long-term mortgages are higher total costs and slow buildup of equity, as interest may exceed the principal payment for much of the life of the loan.

The rate of interest and length of term are determinants in keeping payments low. Lengthening the loan period is more potent than reducing interest rate but is more costly in the long run.

For example, total interest cost on a loan of 15 thousand dollars at 5.25 percent is 17,823 dollars for 35 years, but only 9,264 dollars for 20 years, a difference of 8,559 dollars.

With the rate at 6 percent, total interest is 20,623 dollars for 35 years and 10,793 dollars for 20 years, thus increasing the total interest by 2,800 and 1,529 dollars, respectively.

At the same time, it takes 22 years on the 35-year loan for more than half of the monthly payment to be applied to principal rather than interest and 7 years on the 20-year loan.

Given the desire to own, compare the costs. A loan of 15 thousand dollars at 6 percent costs 85.65 dollars a month—in all, 20,623 dollars in interest for 35 years. At the end there is an owned house, perhaps somewhat depreciated, but continuing with some rental value.

Rent at even such a low figure as 75 dollars a month totals 31,500 dollars—without homeownership. Nothing is left except the savings on 10.65 dollars, the difference between monthly payments and rent.

The decision to own or rent is yours, but there are costs either way, and they must be fitted into the budget.

BASIC FACTS ABOUT MORTGAGES

OF PRIME IMPORTANCE at the outset to you and the prospective lender is how much you can afford to pay for a home —whether your family pocketbook is large enough to meet the payments on the loan.

Three basic estimates are involved.

One is a realistic estimate of the income the family can reasonably expect to receive.

The second is the family's living costs and payments on other debts.

The third is the total housing expense, including taxes, insurance, maintenance, and loan payments.

In estimating future income, a family should consider income received during the past 4 or 5 years and the income prospects in the years ahead. Take into account the age of the family wage earners, their skills, the stability of employment, and the job opportunities in the area. Be realistic, not overoptimistic.

The largest expense of most families is living costs. Usually it is a rather rigid one. But if your family includes growing children, living costs—food, education, clothing, entertainment, and other expenses—also will grow.

Other expenses may have to be provided for. If you own a farm or a business, you need to allow for the cost of operation. The house itself will add costs you may not have had before, such as taxes, insurance, fuel for heating and cooking, utilities, maintenance, and repairs. Payments on existing debts must be met. You will have to allow for savings for education and retirement.

How much is left after deducting all these expenses from the hard-core income is the beginning point in determining how much you can pay on a home loan.

Various ratios have been suggested between a family's income and the highest price it can prudently afford to pay for a home. Rules of thumb used by some lenders range from two to two and one-half times the family's annual income, but these are only general guides.

You and your family must decide on the basis of the budgetary facts of your personal situation and the relative value you place on homeownership in comparison with other possible uses of your income.

WHEN YOU SHOP for housing credit, you

may encounter various terms to describe different types of loans, such as conventional, FHA-insured, and GI or direct VA loans.

Just about 80 percent of the financed homes in the United States are financed by conventional loans. A higher initial payment than the FHA or VA is usually required by conventional institutions and their interest rates fluctuate. The amount of the loan, however, is not as limited as an FHA or VA loan.

Both FHA and VA loans are advantageous only as long as they are in line with the conventional mortgage rates. If they fall too far below the conventional mortgage rates, then the lending agencies will not make such loans or will change special discounts.

Many potential homeowners assume that FHA and VA loans are granted by the government—that is, that the government is in the business of making loans. This, definitely, is not true. The loans all come from private lending institutions. What the FHA does is to insure that the lender will not lose on the money he has loaned. If you are a borrower, you pay a premium of $\frac{1}{2}$ percent of the loan amount annually for this insurance. With a VA loan (available to veterans of World War II and Korea) the Veterans Administration guarantees the lending institution a major amount of the loan if the veteran defaults—with the borrower in this case paying no insurance premium.

The rates, terms, and conditions depend on the local policies and practices of the lenders and, in the case of Government or Government-assisted loans, the statutory authorizations under which the loans are made or insured.

As mentioned in the previous section, shopping for the best available mortgage credit may save you money. The rates and terms at which you will be able to finance a home will depend on the house itself and on the family's financial position, income prospects, and credit rating.

How you arrange your mortgage and the rate of interest you secure can made a difference of several thousand dollars in how much your house actually costs.

A very important point to keep in mind is the fact that little or no down payment and longer terms than are actually needed are *not* necessarily advantages. The more money you put down and the less time you take to pay, the lower your ultimate total costs. But, a large down payment and a short term mortgage is not always possible, especially for young couples with a limited amount of cash and other pressing necessities. It might be a wiser idea for the young couple to take a longer mortgage in order to pay cash for other purchases and investments and to build their savings account to meet emergencies.

The extent to which the rate of interest and length of repayment affect monthly payments and the total amount of interest paid during the life of the loan for each 1 thousand dollars borrowed are:

Repayment period (years):	Monthly Payments of Principal and Interest	
	at 5%	at 6%
10.............	$10.61	$11.11
20.............	6.60	7.17
30.............	5.37	6.00

Repayment period (years):	Total Interest Paid During Period of Loan	
	at 5%	at 6%
10.............	$273.20	$320.00
20.............	584.00	820.80
30.............	923.20	1,160.00

Conventional loans are made by savings and loan associations, commercial banks, mutual savings banks, insurance companies and mortgage companies, individuals, and other lending agencies without the benefit of Government insurance or guarantees.

Interest rates on loans by conventional lending institutions may vary, but presently they range from $5\frac{1}{2}$ to $6\frac{1}{2}$ percent.

The terms vary with local policies and practices of the lenders. You can get information about conventional loans from the lender or from the real estate firm selling the home if the firm has made prior arrangements with a lender to finance the home.

FHA-INSURED HOME LOANS are made by

private lending institutions and insured by the Federal Housing Administration.

FHA insurance protects the private lender against loss if the borrower cannot repay the loan. To cover possible losses, the FHA charges a mortgage insurance premium of one-half of 1 percent a year on the average scheduled mortgage loan balance outstanding during the year. The premium is included in the monthly payments.

FHA-insured home loans are available only for the purchase of new or existing dwellings or the refinancing of the completed home if the home is built by the owner. They are not available to finance the construction of a home. Anyone interested in building his own home must arrange for interim financing during the construction period.

The seller or agent usually will be able to suggest a lender if the house meets FHA specifications. The lender will supply the necessary forms, help the applicant complete them, and, if he is willing to make the loan, submit the application to the Federal Housing Administration office serving the area to obtain a commitment to insure the loan.

The Federal Housing Administration will review the application, appraise the property, and analyze the applicant's ability to pay.

At the time of this writing, the interest rate on FHA-insured home loans is 6 percent. An additional one-half of 1 percent is added as a mortgage insurance premium.

A first lien is required. The FHA-insured loan must be secured by a mortgage that will give the lender first claim on the property if liquidation becomes necessary.

Besides the down payment, the borrower pays the settlement cost and other initial charges, including the FHA application fee and loan closing costs, such as recording fees and title examination. The charges may vary from one locality to another.

VA (GI) GUARANTEED home loans are made to eligible veterans by private lending institutions.

The Veterans' Administration enters into an agreement with the lender to guarantee only part of the loan but in such a way that the lender has little likelihood of loss. The interest rate is 6 percent. The repayment period may be as long as 30 years. A first lien is required.

The veteran who has selected a house and expects to finance it with a GI loan will need to get a certificate of eligibility from the Veterans' Administration. A lender will want to see that certificate, the house plans or sales contract, a financial statement, and an appraisal report of the property before committing himself to make the loan.

If a veteran wants to build his own home, he usually will need to arrange for interim financing during the construction period.

VA (GI) DIRECT home loans also are made by the Veterans' Administration to eligible veterans in areas where a shortage of credit for housing exists. Generally they are rural areas and small cities or towns where housing credit is not readily available.

Veterans who are interested in finding out whether their area is eligible should get in touch with the Veterans' Administration regional office or the local Veterans' Administration center.

The procedures are similar to those in getting a GI-guaranteed loan. The main difference is that the funds are furnished by the Veterans' Administration rather than by a private lender.

BUYING OR BUILDING a home and obtaining a loan to do so involves the execution of a series of documents to formalize and complete the purchase.

When a family has selected the home it wants to buy, the seller usually requires the buyer to sign a sales contract. Between execution of the contract and closing of the loan, usually the property will have to be appraised, evidence of title obtained, and a survey made if establishment of the property lines is necessary.

At the time the loan is closed, the note and mortgage will need to be signed, and the deed conveying title to the buyer will be executed and then recorded.

If the sale is on the basis of a long-term sales contract, the seller may retain title to the property until a specified amount of the debt has been paid.

A SALES CONTRACT usually is the first document you sign after you have selected the home you want to buy. Such a contract customarily requires a cash deposit as evidence of good faith.

When signed, a sales contract obligates the buyer to buy and the seller to sell, subject to any special conditions that may be specified.

A sales contract often provides that the contract is effective only if the seller can show satisfactory evidence of title and the buyer can qualify for a loan.

Sometimes a potential buyer may be able to obtain an option from the seller. The main difference between an option and a sales contract is that an option gives the buyer a specified period during which he can decide whether or not to buy the property.

Before signing a sales contract, you should read it carefully. The contract should be specific in its terms and state clearly the conditions of the sale and the responsibilities of the buyer and the seller. It should state that you, the buyer, will get a refund in case you are unable to get a loan or if the seller does not comply with the terms of the agreement.

If you do not go through with your part of the agreement, the contract may provide that you will forfeit your down payment.

EVIDENCE OF GOOD TITLE is necessary to assure that the applicant actually owns or will own the property and that there are no claims against it that would restrict its marketability.

Lenders usually require a title certificate or title opinion or title insurance.

A title certificate or title opinion usually is prepared on the basis of a search of the public records or the examination of an abstract by an attorney. The lender may require title insurance to protect his interest. The home-buyer may also want to purchase an owner's title insurance policy for his protection in case a defect in the title should develop.

A PROMISSORY NOTE is a personal promise of the borrower to repay the loan.

The note usually states the amount of the loan, the interest rate, and the repayment schedule. It also may include other provisions, such as penalties, prepayment privileges, and any special conditions the lender may wish to insert if the borrower agrees to them.

The note ordinarily is signed by both husband and wife. The original note is held by the lender. In the event the property is foreclosed, the lender may be able to hold the signers of the note personally liable for any deficit.

A bond is used instead of a note in some States.

THE MORTGAGE describes the note and, in case of default by the borrower, gives the lender the right to have the property sold and the sale proceeds applied on the debt.

The mortgage usually includes special conditions that apply should the borrower fail to comply with any of his agreements, such as making payments on the note and maintaining insurance and paying taxes on the property.

If the borrower defaults, the lender can declare the entire debt due immediately and foreclose on the property in order to collect the debt. An "open end" clause and "advance" or "prepayment privileges" are two items to ask for in your mortgage contract.

The "open end" clause gives you the chance to obtain additional funds on the same mortgage after you have paid part of it. This can be very helpful if you later wish to make improvements in your home or meet other financial obligations. Since your house will be the security on these additional funds with low mortgage interest it will be cheaper than a personal loan.

Prepayment privileges (sometimes termed a "right to repay" clause) enable you to increase your payments when your income allows it. If the penalty for this clause is low enough, then it is to your advantage.

The mortgage is signed by the owners of the property. Most lenders prefer that the property be in the name of both the husband and the wife. The mortgage must be recorded in the public records. This is notice to other parties that there is a lien on the property.

When the loan is repaid in full and the note and mortgage are satisfied, either the lender or borrower should have the mortgage satisfied or released on the public records. Other forms of lien are used instead of mortgages in some States.

The home the buyer wishes to purchase may have a mortgage on it that is satisfactory to him. If so, he may be able to make arrangements with the lender to assume the indebtedness.

The buyer should, however, have the title as well as the loan papers examined by a competent person to be sure that he knows exactly when he will become the owner and understands all of the other terms and conditions of the mortgage.

A deed is the document issued by the seller transferring ownership of the property to the buyer. The deed should be recorded in the public records.

SHOP CAREFULLY for your home, select the neighborhood you want, and be sure the house is one that you can afford and will meet your needs.

Shop for credit to obtain the best terms available.

If you plan to build, construction should not be started until you have arranged for financing. Once a lender has agreed to make a loan, you should proceed in accordance with the lender's requirements.

Obtain from the lender a complete, itemized list of all the costs you will need to pay at the time of closing the loan. The list should be dated and signed by the lender.

Read your contract carefully before you sign it. Check to see that it is specific on all important points. When you and the seller sign the contract, it becomes a legally binding agreement.

SMART WAYS TO GET AND USE CREDIT

INSTALLMENT CREDIT can be a help or a hindrance, depending on how you use it.

It has helped many families to furnish a home, buy a car, and meet all kinds of financial emergencies.

It also has caused many families worry, hardship, and loss.

You are urged to use installment credit by merchants who want to sell their goods and by banks and loan companies that want to lend their money. You are encouraged with promises of "loans on your signature," "no money down," and "very easy payments."

You easily can be carried away by such promises and you will be wise to learn the facts about installment credit, so you can make sensible decisions about it.

Consumers can get installment credit in a number of places. Retail merchants offer credit in the form of deferred payments for goods you take and use while you are paying for them. Banks, credit unions, finance companies, and small loan companies lend money, which you repay bit by bit.

WHEN YOU BUY goods on the installment plan, you have to pay out more than when you buy for cash. When you get an installment loan, you pay back more than you receive.

Consumer credit is a service with a price that can and should be shopped for. Many families are unaware of what they pay for it. Rates charged vary considerably from dealer to dealer, with the size of purchase under consideration, with the credit reputation of the purchaser, with the length of the loan period, with the organization or institution to which the purchaser will ultimately owe his payments—that is the dealer or retailer himself, a large commercial credit corporation, a bank, credit union, or other source—and with the laws of the particular State.

Charges for consumer credit necessarily cover more than interest on the unpaid balance. They cover such additional expenses to the seller or lender as the following: (1) cost of investigating the credit-worthiness of an applicant, (2) often, cost of life insurance on buyer for the period of the contract so that if he dies before completing payments, the seller can collect the balance from the insurance company, (3) cost of making out and processing the contract, (4) cost of bookkeeping and recordkeeping, (5) cost of making monthly or weekly collections, and (6) cost of allowing for delinquent payments and losses.

Some merchants and lenders charge more for credit than others. Charges for different kinds of loans differ, too. The credit rate is usually higher for small than large loans and for unsecured than for secured loans.

For example, the rate is higher when the lender has only your signature or promise to assure him of getting his money back (this is an "unsecured" loan) than when you put up a car, refrigerator, bonds, or some other security he can take if you do not pay.

LENDERS USE different methods of figuring credit charges on installment purcured than for secured loans.

There are two common methods.

One is to calculate the amount you owe for credit each time you pay an installment. It is figured as a percentage of the debt you owe at that time (the "unpaid balance"), so it gets smaller as the debt decreases.

The lender quotes the charge as a certain percentage of the unpaid balance per month. Notice that this is *per month* and not *per year*. If you want to know the rate per year, multiply the monthly rate by 12.

Some typical monthly and yearly rates are shown in the next column.

This method of calculating credit charges is generally used by credit unions and small loan companies. Retail merchants use it for revolving or budget charge accounts.

If the monthly rate is—	The rate per year (the true annual rate) is—
¾ of 1%	9%
1%	12%
1½%	18%
2%	24%
2½%	30%
3%	36%

Another way of figuring credit charges is to calculate the credit charge all at one time—when you get the loan or make the installment purchase. It is figured as a percentage of the total amount you borrow or the price of the item you buy.

The charge for the entire loan period is added to the loan by some lenders and subtracted from it by others. Then the total is divided into installments.

The lender may quote the charge as a certain number of dollars per 100 dollars per year—as 4, 5, or 6 dollars per 100 dollars.

Take a loan at 4 dollars per 100 dollars as an example. If the lender adds the charge ("add-on" method) you receive 100 dollars and pay back 104 dollars. If he subtracts it ("discount" method), you receive 96 dollars and pay back 100 dollars.

A credit charge of 4, 5, or 6 dollars per 100 dollars per year on these loans appears to be 4, 5, or 6 percent a year, and the lender sometimes quotes it that way.

Actually, however, since you do not have the use of the entire 100 dollars for a whole year, the true annual rate is much higher than that. In fact, it turns out to be about double.

The table on the following page shows the true annual rates on loans repaid in 12 monthly installments. (The rates would be slightly higher than these if you took longer to pay.)

Usually banks and sales finance companies use either the "add-on" or the "discount" method of calculating credit charges when they make loans for buying cars and other consumer durable goods.

The retail dealer usually figures your debt by the "add-on" method when you buy equipment or furniture on time. He is likely to quote you the total credit charge in dollars rather than the credit rate.

One more thing to note here: Lenders sometimes add more charges on top of the add-on or discount rates they quote. These may include charges for investigation of your credit rating, credit insurance, filing fees, and such. Watch for these extras, for they make the true annual credit rate higher.

Some of these look like very high rates to pay for credit. They look especially high when you compare them with the rate of interest you get on your savings. Think of this if you have savings you could use instead of credit.

PERHAPS YOU WILL find credit costs easier to understand if you see them in dollars rather than percentages.

Here is how the dollar cost of a loan on a new car worked out for one buyer —a fairly typical case. He brought a car priced at 3,075 dollars, received 375 dollars for his old car as a trade-in, and made a cash down payment of 700 dollars. He financed the rest of the cost through the dealer (who probably turned it over to a sales finance company), who added 149 dollars to cover insurance for the car. The buyer agreed to pay 24 monthly installments of 111 dollars.

Calculations to find out the dollar cost were:

(1)	Price of the car.............		$3,075
(2)	Value of trade-in...	$375	
(3)	Cash downpayment..	$700	
(4)	Total downpayment [(2)+(3)].............		1,075
(5)	To be financed on car cost [(1)−(4)].............		2,000
(6)	Car insurance...............		149
(7)	Total to be financed [(5)+(6)]......		2,149
(8)	24 payments of $111 each....................		2,664
(9)	Dollar cost of credit [(8)−(7)]................		515

This buyer paid 515 dollars more for his car than if he had bought it for cash. This is not an unusually large amount to pay for credit on a major purchase like an automobile.

Now let's look at another example of a less expensive, but still a major purchase. Let's say a refrigerator costs $300 and can be paid for by making a $12

TRUE ANNUAL RATES ON LOANS REPAID IN 12 MONTHLY INSTALLMENTS

		The true rate per year is—	
If the credit charge per year is—	*The quoted rate per year is—*	*For "add-on"*	*For "discount"*
$4 per $100.................	4%	7.4%	7.7%
$6 per $100.................	6%	11.1%	11.8%
$8 per $100................	8%	14.8%	16.1%
$10 per $100	10%	18.5%	20.5%
$12 per $100	12%	22.2%	25.2%

CREDIT RATES COMMONLY CHARGED BY DIFFERENT LENDERS

Lender	*True annual rate*	*Quoted rate*
Retail dealers (including mail-order companies) on—		
Revolving or budget charge accounts.	12% to 18%...	1% to 1½% per month on the unpaid balance.
Installment purchase of appliances, furniture.	12% to 20% (or more).	Usually quote dollar charge only.
Banks.....................	6% to 16%....	3% to 8% per year (or $3 to $8 per $100 per year).
Credit unions..............	9% to 12%....	¾ of 1% to 1% per month on the unpaid balance.
Small loan companies........	18% to 42%...	1½% to 3½% per month on the unpaid balance.
Auto finance companies......	12% to 24%...	6% to 12% per year (or $6 to $12 per $100 per year).

down payment and 12 monthly payments of $25.95 each. To calculate the dollar cost of credit we multiply the amount of each payment by the number of months. ($25.95 x 12 = $311.04). From that $311.04 we subtract the amount to be financed (the cash price minus our $12 down payment or $288) and we get $23.04 as the cost of the credit. Rather than the quoted price of $300, the refrigerator would actually have cost you $323.04!

Here is an example of how dollar costs can add up on smaller purchases. Many families equip their homes (or replace household equipment) by buying pieces one by one on the installment plan.

Let's say a family plans to buy a washing machine, dryer, refrigerator, electric range, and vacuum cleaner. Buying them from a mail-order company, one after the other, the family would pay about 200 dollars more for them on the company's installment purchase plan than by paying cash. The credit price would be about 1,260 dollars; the cash price, 1,060 dollars. By planning and saving ahead, the family could pay cash and save enough to buy another convenience—perhaps an air conditioner, a TV set, or a piece of furniture.

The table below gives the dollar cost of credit charges on a debt of 1 thousand dollars, at different credit rates. It shows how the cost mounts when you take longer to pay off a debt. Take a loan of 1 thousand dollars at an add-on rate of 6 dollars per 100 dollars per year as an example. The credit charge would cost you 60 dollars if you repaid the debt in 12 monthly payments, but 180 dollars if you took 36 months to pay it.

It will be to your advantage to choose as short a repayment period as you can manage the payments for.

Now YOU HAVE some information about where you can get installment credit and how much it costs.

The next problem is whether you want to get into this sort of thing at all. If you have in mind some particular thing to buy, you might think about such questions as: Could we pay cash for it without using too much of our savings? Is having it now worth the extra cost of buying it "on time"? Can we handle this much debt?

Perhaps you have read the rule of thumb that a family should not commit itself for installment payments amounting to more than 20 percent of its after-tax income.

The truth is that many families would be unwise to commit as much as 15, 10, or even 5 percent of their income to installment payments.

Some, on the other hand, might pay installments amounting to more than 20 percent of their income—for a time, at least—without hardship.

DOLLAR COST OF CREDIT CHARGES ON A $1,000 LOAN AT DIFFERENT CREDIT RATES, REPAID IN DIFFERENT NUMBERS OF INSTALLMENTS

Credit rate	Dollar cost of credit charges when number of monthly installments is—					
	12	18	24	30	36	42
"Add-on" rate (added to beginning amount of debt):						
$4 per $100 per year	$40	$60	$80	$100	$120	$140
$6 per $100 per year	60	90	120	150	180	210
$8 per $100 per year	80	120	160	200	240	280
$10 per $100 per year	100	150	200	250	300	350
$12 per $100 per year	120	180	240	300	360	420
Percent of unpaid balance:						
¾ of 1% per month	49	73	96	120	145	169
1% per month	66	98	130	162	196	230
1½% per month	100	149	198	249	301	355
2% per month	135	201	269	340	412	488
2½% per month	170	254	342	433	528	627

Each family has different financial resources, as well as different needs, wants, goals, future prospects, and management skills. These are the things that will determine how much installment debt they can handle.

Instead of searching for a rule to tell you how much installment debt you can safely assume, take stock of your own financial situation.

Have a family budget session to review your spending plan, your accounts, assets, and liabilities.

Considering these questions will help you to make a decision:

• How much do we have left from our income each month now, after we have paid all our living expenses, made the payments on our present debts, put the planned amount into our savings account, and taken care of other obligations? (It makes sense not to take on another installment payment larger than this amount.)

• Is it always easy to make the payments on our present debt? (If it sometimes means scraping and squeezing or skipping a payment, better think twice before taking on another debt.)

• How much do we have in savings accounts, bonds, or other funds we can easily draw on? (Unless it is enough to pay living expenses and keep up debt payments for at least a month or so in case of illness or layoff from work, go slow.)

• Will some debt be paid off soon, so we can use the money we now pay on that for installments on a new debt? (A "yes" here may be a go-ahead indicator.)

• Will another installment debt mean we have to postpone or give up some goal we have planned for? (If the answer is "yes," weigh the pros and cons carefully.)

Taking time to think things through like this may save you from the kind of impulse installment buying that gets families into trouble.

Every installment payment you promise to make has to fit into the budget somewhere. The time to make sure it does is before you sign on the dotted line.

ONCE YOU HAVE made up your mind to buy or borrow on the installment plan, keep the price you pay for credit as low as possible.

First, shop around for a good credit deal. If you are considering credit from a retailer, compare prices on the item you are buying as well as the credit charges. Sometimes merchants who sell on time charge more for the goods they sell.

Consider the following examples of different sources of credit and what you will pay at each:

Banks are the most common source and their most widely used types of loans are those for personal finance and for automobiles. The rate of interest for both types ranges from 4.5 to 6 percent.

Credit unions are organizations that are made up of people with a common interest. For instance, factory workers, fraternal associations, or church groups could form a credit union. Members of the credit union are charged a monthly rate—often as low as $3/4$ of 1 percent per month—on the balance owed. On the average, the true rate of interest amounts to 8 to 12 percent a year.

Small-loan companies usually charge 1.5 to 3.5 percent *per month* on the decreasing balance, depending on state laws and local competition. The true rate of interest would range from 18 to 42 percent. While small-loan companies do fill a need, they are one of the most expensive sources for money and should be used only as a last resort.

Department stores usually have two types of credit plans in addition to the regular charge account plan: the extended payment and the installment contract.

Under the extended payment plan, normally used for clothing and small items, you charge your purchase up to a certain limit and pay in monthly installments.

The installment contract requires a down payment and monthly payments for two or three years. You sign a contract for such credit and pay 9 to 10 percent interest. Such contracts are widely used for furniture and appliances.

In any case, be sure you are doing business with an established dealer or lending agency—one with a good reputation.

Do not be taken in by the unknown door-to-door salesman who offers to sell on the installment plan.

Make as large a down payment as you can without reducing your savings to the danger point.

Finally, make monthly payments as large as your budget will allow. This way, you can pay the debt in the shortest possible time and save dollars.

When you buy things on time or get an installment loan, you have to sign a contract. Be sure you get a copy. Keep it in a safe place so you can refer to it if you need to.

Before you sign the contract:

• Read and understand everything in it, including the fine print.

• Be positive that there are no blank spaces left when you sign.

• See that the contract tells exactly what you are buying; the purchase price, or the amount of cash you will receive from the loan; all the credit charges; the down payment and trade-in allowance, if any; the total amount you have to pay; the amount you have to pay for each installment; the number of installments to be made, and the dates due.

• Find out to whom you are to make the payments.

• Know what will happen if you cannot pay, and if you want to pay ahead.

• Know what the seller's responsibility is for maintenance, service, or replacement of the goods purchased.

Whenever you consider borrowing on credit, ask yourself these six questions and follow the rules that apply to each.

1) Is the purchase really necessary? Reserve the use of credit for items that are truly needed.

2) Can you avoid using credit? In particular, avoid the small uses of credit.

3) Are you getting the lowest rate of interest? If not, shop around for the best deal.

4) Are your monthly payments too high or costing too much by being too low? In general, try to pay back as quickly as possible.

5) Can a part of your savings be used instead of credit? A loan secured by your savings may have the lowest interest rate of all.

6) Are you borrowing more money than necessary? Borrow only what you need.

ONCE YOU HAVE MADE a credit deal, it's up to you to see that the installments are paid regularly.

If you fail to make the payments, the creditor can take the washing machine, car, or whatever it is you owe for. This means you lose the money you have already paid on it. In some States, you can be required to pay more, too, if the creditor cannot sell the washer or car for as much as you owe.

Your rating as a credit risk depends on how prompt you are in paying your debts. Because you may want credit again, it will pay you to keep this rating good.

THE FAMILY BUDGET

A BUDGET is something you make and remake until it works for you and you are satisfied with the results.

There is no magic formula.

But whatever form your budget takes, it must have three essential characteristics: reality, practicality, and an up-to-date outlook. If not, it will fail.

Budgeting does not mean pinching pennies and recording every cent spent.

It is a way to get what your family wants most, whatever that may be.

If you do not have money to pay bills when they are due or cannot accumulate enough for a vacation trip, a budget can ease worry about money and start you on a savings program.

Making and following a budget helps all members of your family to understand how and where to use money.

Various rules of thumb are sometimes quoted as guides. Examples are such statements as: "When a home is purchased with a small down payment, the price should be below 2½ times the annual take-home income." "Total housing costs per month should not exceed 1 week's take-home pay." "No increase in installment payments should be undertaken until the family has a reserve fund equal to at least one week's pay; a month's is better." "The last installment should be paid before the purchased item is used up or worn out."

Such statements are sound, but they are not tailored to an individual family. They are usually based on average family spending or on the working experience of financing agencies that deal with many families. Included among the many who make up the average is a wide range of individual cases. Some are younger families with better prospects of income increase; others have steadier jobs; some have better health or more skills; some are in a sounder debt position or have assets to draw on; some might be called house proud, others automobile enthusiasts; others are more willing to make different sacrifices; and many other special conditions could be mentioned.

THE FIRST STEP in making a budget is to set goals. Some goals are for the distant future. Some are for next year. Some are for right now.

Decide what your family's needs and wants are. List them in order of importance.

Add to the list—and also subtract from it the items that time makes unimportant.

Do not let long-term goals get lost in day-to-day demands. Too many porterhouse steaks this month may crowd out a new dishwasher next year.

Define your goals clearly. Then they will be easier to reach. An example: Long-term goals may be paying off the mortgage, establishing a fund to cover the children's schooling, or saving for retirement. Your goal for the next year may be a new car, a living room rug, an encyclopedia, a fine phonograph and records.

THE NEXT STEP is to estimate how much money you will have available to spend for the planning period.

The planning period may be a month, a year, or any period. A year is a usual time for which to plan, but you may wish to set up a trial budget for a shorter period to see how it works out.

Start by considering your income in two ways—before taxes and after taxes. Income after taxes is the true amount available to spend and save. Thinking only of the amount before taxes may lead you to buy more than you can afford.

Write down all income you expect to receive. Include wages or salary, net money earned from a business, interest from a savings account, dividends, and any extra money that may be earned from other work.

Then estimate your income taxes and subtract them from your total money income. Write the answer down. That is the figure to keep in mind in making the budget.

Now estimate your expenses. You can recall some expenses well enough to make an estimate. Checkbook stubs, receipts, and old bills are good reminders for some items.

For other items (food, clothing, household operation, recreation), a record of present spending to see where your money is going is more helpful.

You might buy a form for keeping records or draw up your own. Rule off a form on a sheet of paper or in a looseleaf notebook. Allow a separate column for each category of expense that you want to keep track of. Leave enough space to enter the items you bought and their cost. Add up the amounts at the end of a week or a month.

Keep the record for a month or two. Use it as a guide in estimating expenses in your plan for future spending. In the estimate, make any changes you think are needed in order to get the things your family needs and wants most.

AT THIS POINT you are ready to set up your plan. The plan needs to be based on your goals, income, and expenses.

Start by planning to save something for a purpose or toward a goal. Decide on an amount and treat it as you do any other bill that must be paid.

Budget experts strongly recommend that you build up an emergency fund for illnesses, repairs that unexpectedly become necessary, accidents, and such.

After you have an emergency fund, start saving for your other goals.

If saving for retirement is a longtime goal and a certain percentage of your salary is being withheld to be applied toward retirement, count it as part of your savings goal. Or if the social security tax is deducted from your paycheck, consider it as savings, too.

Some of your expenses occur once or twice a year or every month. Some of them have to be paid in definite amounts at definite times.

In setting up your plan for future spending, list the expenses that come up only once or twice a year, such as real estate taxes, insurance premiums, vacation, fuel, and perhaps certain debt payments. Divide these expenses by 12 and set aside the required amount every month. Thus you spread the cost and have money to meet them when due.

Next list the expenses you expect to be the same from month to month. Your rent likely will be the same. If you are buying a house, or a car, or furniture on the installment plan, your payments will be the same. You may have other obligations, such as contributions to church and relatives.

After you have estimated your savings and regular expenses, you are ready for the day-to-day expenses.

Estimate how much to spend for food and beverages, clothing, transportation, and all the other budget groups. Go back over the records you kept and see what you spent for each of the budget groups. You may decide you need to spend more on some and less on other groups.

Remember to allow some leeway for unexpected or forgotten items.

A personal allowance for each person that need not be accounted for is a good thing, we believe, even if it has to be small.

Now work in the items you and others in the family have listed as your immediate goals.

After your plan is completed, put it to use. This is when the work really starts! How firm will you be under the salesman's spell? Can you resist impulse spending?

If you are really interested in sound money management and want to form good buying habits, you will find a sufficient supply of consumer information available for your study.

Here are some general guidelines that may help you get the most for your money:

• Inform yourself about a product before you shop for it.

• Get over the idea that everything you buy has to be brand new. Secondhand furniture, for example, may be a good investment for young couples, especially if you are not permanently settled and are likely to move about considerably in the years ahead.

• Be alert to quality. Compare prices.

• Patronize seasonal sales at reliable shops. The so-called white sales offer towels, sheets, and other household textiles at substantial savings.

• Be knowledgeable in the use of credit. Know what it costs.

WITH THE INFORMATION you have now, you are ready to add the totals and compare your planned outgo with your estimated income for the planning period.

If your income covers your savings and expenses, you have no problem. Any surplus you can add to savings for future goals or use to satisfy some immediate wants and desires.

If, as more likely will be the case, you have planned for more than your income will cover, you will need to take a new look at all parts of your plan.

You will need to decide which of your wants are less important, important, and very important. Look at the day-to-day expenses. Try to trim them.

For example, you may be able to defer some of them, or substitute a cheaper item, or paint your house yourself instead of hiring someone to do it, or take advantage of free community services, or patch John's pants instead of buying a new pair.

Scan your regular expenses, too. Maybe you can reduce some of them. It may be better to move to a less costly house, get a cheaper car, or convert an endowment insurance policy to a cheaper form of life insurance. Look at these thing realistically—are they nearly as important as the really big things you want, such as security, education, and the means by which you attain your ambitions?

After trimming here and cutting there, if your budget still does not balance, you may want to consider ways of adding to your income.

A BUDGET PLAN

Item	Amount
Money income after taxes	$
Savings:	
Future goals and emergencies	$
Seasonal and large irregular expenses	
Regular monthly expenses:	
Rent or mortgage payment	$
Utilities	
Installment payments	
Other	
Total	
Day-to-day expenses:	
Food and beverages	$
Household operation and maintenance	
Housefurnishings and equipment	
Clothing	
Transportation	
Medical care	
Education and reading	
Recreation	
Personal and miscellaneous	
Gifts and contributions	
Total	
Total	$

ESTIMATES OF SPENDING BY CERTAIN FAMILIES

	Income after taxes	
	$4,000 to $5,000	$6,000 to $7,500
	Percent	Percent
Total	100	100
Savings	2	4
Personal insurance	5	5
Gifts and contributions	4	4
Total for current living	89	87
Food and beverages	24	21
Shelter (rent or mortgage interest payments and upkeep, insurance and taxes)	12	11
Fuel and utilities	5	4
Household operation	5	5
Housefurnishings and equipment	4	5
Clothing	8	9
Transportation	15	14
Medical care	6	6
Education and reading	1	2
Recreation	3	4
Personal and miscellaneous	6	6

IF THIS is your first budget, it may help to have some idea of how other families divide their income. The preceding table gives some estimates based on studies of spending by families at two income levels with three or four members.

The estimates show that a budget based on one set of percentages would not fit both income groups. Neither would one set of percentages fit all families in the same income group. Families have different needs and different desires.

For example, if your family prefers to live in a house with plenty of space, your plan may allow more of your income for shelter, fuel and utilities, and household operation, and less for some other items.

ONCE YOUR BUDGET is made, try it out.

It helps to keep records to see how the budget works. (Records are also helpful when it comes time to make out your income tax report.)

An easy way is to have a spindle on which to stick receipts and other notations of amounts you spend. At the end of the week or month, add up the amounts and record them. Or you may wish to continue using the same form you set up earlier to record your expenses.

Keep records simple—the simpler the better. Once you know where your money goes, you may not need a detailed account.

The object of your budget is to save money. And the best way to save money is to reduce the costs of the goods and services you buy. Here are some suggestions which should help yield big savings.

Pay now, save now. Whenever possible, pay in advance and don't get caught with high interest installment payments.

Watch the interest rate and shop around for the best credit buy.

Time your buying. Postpone your purchases until you can take advantage of sales.

Don't overbuy. You don't always need top quality so don't always demand it. Children's clothes, for example are quickly outgrown and need not be the most expensive you can find.

At the end of the budget period, compare what you actually spent with what you planned to spend. Were you fairly close? Were you satisfied with the results? Did you spend more than you planned? If so, why? Did you buy on impulse?

Your first try at budgeting may not be completely successful, but each time you try means improvement.

Even if your first budget is "perfect," it will need adjusting from time to time. For example, if you have a change in income, children are added to the family, or you move to a different community, you will find you need to adjust your budget.

Through a budget, however, you can plan to get your day-to-day needs and future dreams.

KNOW HOW TO BUY INSURANCE

THE LANGUAGE of insurance may be puzzling, but your decisions about insurance will be easier if you keep a few fundamentals in mind.

You should first know what insurance is supposed to do. Basically, it is to help protect you and your family against financial hardship due to hazard, accident, death, and so on. To rebuild your home after a fire, pay a large court judgment, or provide for your family if you die early may require more money than you have. Damage to your car or theft of property, however, may be less serious financially.

Knowing your risks, then, is important to selecting the right insurance.

Start by looking at your property and your family responsibilities. Think about the chance of various mishaps or events, which could cause major trouble and expense. It is wise to insure against them.

Do not insure against the little losses that will not hurt.

Few families can afford all the protection they need and should insure the greater risks first.

A little study before you see an insurance agent will help your money go as far as it can in fitting you with proper insurance. He will answer questions and advise you on details, but the final decision is yours. The kinds of insurance from which to choose seem limitless.

THE FOUR BASIC policies of life insurance are term, whole-life or straight, limited-payment, and endowment.

They differ mainly in whether the insurance is permanent or temporary and the extent to which savings, as well as insurance, are involved.

Your family responsibilities and goals and your pocketbook will guide you in your selection. The best insurance for you may be a combination of two or more types.

Term insurance is protection bought for a limited period or term, usually 5 or 10 years. Protection ends at the end of the term, and the policy has no savings or cash value no matter how long you pay. Because it is strictly for protection, the cost (premium) for young people is relatively low, but the cost increases with each renewal and becomes prohibitive at older ages. Some term policies do not permit renewal without a medical examination.

If you are younger than middle age and need every dollar's worth of protection you can buy, term insurance is good. It can provide stopgap protection for young couples, for example, until they are able to afford insurance to cover permanent responsibilities. Usually, however, it should supplement regular permanent life insurance. It is best used as additional protection for temporary periods of extra risk, such as when children are growing up or when debts are heavy.

Straight life insurance is commonest. Sometimes called whole-life or ordinary insurance, it runs for your lifetime. The premium depends on your age when you first take the insurance and stays the same each year. Part of the premium goes into savings (against which

you may borrow), and the cash value of the policy increases as the years go by. After the need for insurance is past, the cash value can be obtained for retirement or other purposes.

Straight life insurance is the least costly lifetime protection you can get. Usually it is the most suitable for young families. Taken out early, it will be the foundation of a permanent insurance program.

Limited-payment life insurance is similar to straight life insurance, except that you pay premiums only for a stated period, say 20 or 30 years or up to age '65. At the end of the period, the insurance continues as a paid-up policy and no more premium payments are required. It is designed mainly for people who do not want to pay premiums as they get older. The cash value increases faster than with a straight life policy, but it is more expensive for the protection received.

Endowment insurance is important for its savings features. Money accumulates faster than with other types of policies and at a certain date it is paid as income or in lump sum to the insured, and the insurance protection ends. Should the insured person die before that date, the insurance is paid to his beneficiary. Because savings are emphasized, endowments are the most costly way to buy insurance protection.

Each of the four kinds of life insurance has many variations and special features, and two or more kinds can be combined.

The so-called family income plan offered by most life insurance companies combines one of the permanent policies, usually straight life, with gradually decreasing term insurance.

For example, a young family covered by a 20-year family income policy of 10 thousand dollars would have that amount of permanent insurance. If the father dies within 20 years after he took out the policy, his family would also receive a stipulated monthly income during the remainder of the 20-year period—a period when income would be most needed.

Types of Life Insurance Policies

Approximate premium rates per $1,000 of each of four types of life insurance policies*

Bought at age	Term 5-year renewable and convertible	Straight Life	Limited Payment Life (Paid up at age 65)	Endowment 20-year
18	$ 8.65	$15.80	$16.90	$48.85
20	8.75	16.50	17.70	48.90
25	8.90	18.45	20.15	49.05
30	9.25	21.00	23.60	49.40
40	12.20	28.50	34.75	51.40
50	20.10	45.65	60.15	56.55

* Rates shown are approximate premium rates for life insurance protection for men. Rates for women are somewhat lower. Rates of participating policies (those offered by mutual insurance companies) would be slightly higher, but the cost would be lowered by annual dividends. Non-participating policy rates would be somewhat lower than those shown and no dividends would be paid.

THE WORDS used to discuss life insurance are often confusing to many people. It is a good idea to understand certain terms to better our understanding of the insurance vocabulary. Here are some simple definitions of basic terms:

Policy - a life insurance contract.

Beneficiary - the person named in the policy to receive the money when the insured person dies.

Premium - the regular amount you pay for your insurance.

Dividend - a return of a portion of the premium.

Cash Value - the money you get back if you give up your policy.

Face Value - the amount of insurance mentioned in the policy.

Maturity - when the face value becomes payable.

Grace Period - the time you have between the date the premium is due and the date the policy can be cancelled for nonpayment.

Loan Value - the amount you may borrow against the policy. (The loan value is usually the same as the cash value.)

Settlement Options - different ways that money from a policy can be paid by the insurance company.

Double Indemnity - payment of twice the face value in case of accidental death. (Usually available at a small extra cost.)

Convertible Term - under this type of policy, term insurance can be converted to another type, i.e., straight life.

How MUCH life insurance you should buy may depend largely on what you can afford. Young families seldom can buy all they need.

As an amount to aim at, however, figure the money you need to live on and pay sickness and funeral expenses. Then buy what you can, keeping in mind other sources of income you can fall back on, such as savings and social security benefits.

Figuring out how much insurance you need and how much you can spend for it will also help you decide the kind to buy. If income is extremely short, you might consider term insurance as a temporary measure. Transfer it to permanent, straight life insurance as soon as possible, however. Until your needs for basic protection are met, it is best to postpone taking out endowment or limited-payment life insurance.

Also, keep in mind that to protect dependents in a family, the income earner's life is the one to be insured. Hold off insuring the lives of children until you can afford to do so.

KNOWING HOW TO BUY insurance also can help you get the most for your money.

Usually it is best to buy policies of at least 1 thousand dollars and pay premiums quarterly, semiannually, or annually.

Premiums paid annually are less than those paid semiannually, and the semi-annual payments are less than quarterly payments.

Policies for smaller amounts, for which the insurance agent collects premiums weekly or monthly, are costly relative to protection received because of the extra expense to the company.

On the other hand, if group life insurance is available where you work, probably you should take it, as it is good, low-cost insurance. But consider it mainly as supplementing your regular insurance, because it may not protect you if you change jobs.

If you are careful you can generally save money on insurance. Here are some important points to keep in mind:

• Concentrate life insurance on the breadwinner in your family.

• The rate for each $1,000 of insurance is normally lower on policies of $5,000 or more.

• Don't pay premiums by the month unless your financial situation demands it. You can save about 8 to 10 percent by paying premiums annually. Never pay by the week: it is much too expensive in the long run.

• If you can, pay premiums several years in advance. You can usually get a good discount on such payments.

• Buy all the low-cost group insurance offered by your employer. Most group insurance, remember, is term protection ending when you leave the group but it is usually cheaper than equivalent private coverage.

• See if you qualify for "preferred risk" coverage. If you meet the health requirements, your rates might be lower.

• Look into insurance sold by savings banks in New York, Massachusetts, and Connecticut. They generally charge less than insurance companies.

• Buy mortgage insurance and other term policies, whenever possible, as riders tacked onto permanent policies. As a rider, such coverage will usually cost much less than if bought alone.

To make sure your policy provides for emergencies consider these points:

• Does your policy have a common disaster clause? This will prevent funds from going into a common estate and being paid to relatives who were not meant to take part in the policy.

• Do you have a second beneficiary in case the principal beneficiary dies?

• Do you have a premium waiver? Under the clause, the insured person does not have to pay premiums if he is totally disabled.

If savings banks, credit unions, fraternal organizations, or others sell life insurance in your area, check the features and cost of their policies.

When you take out life insurance, you may choose a settlement option, which specifies how the money will be paid to your dependents when you die.

The choice can be a lump-sum payment, monthly income payments, or only payments of interest until the full amount is needed. If one of these settlements is chosen by the insured person he may change it while he lives. His choice cannot be changed by the beneficiary after the insured person dies. But if he has not selected a monthly income settlement, his widow or other beneficiary may choose one at the proper time instead of the lump-sum payment. An insurance company makes no direct charge for this service.

The choices are also available to an insured person who lives to see his endowment policy mature and who wants to receive the face value plus interest as a retirement income. Or he may let it accumulate at interest for payment later as a lump sum or in installments to his beneficiary. The choices are also available with some limitations to those who cash their policies for their surrender value.

If you do not specify an option, your beneficiary usually can decide the method of payment at the time of your death. You may have to change settlement options and beneficiaries as time changes the financial requirements of your family.

That underscores the importance of reviewing your life insurance program every year or two to bring it up to date, for example, to include additional children.

If, after your policy is in force, you are unable to pay your premium within the grace period (1 month after the due date) your policy will ordinarily lapse. Some policies, however, include an automatic premium loan provision, under which the company will automatically pay the premium and charge it as a loan against your policy.

Your policy, unless it is a term policy, probably will also have nonforfeiture value if payments have been made for 1 to 3 years. You can turn in the policy and get its cash value or use the built-up values to obtain reduced paid-up insurance or obtain extended term insurance for as long as the cash value permits.

MANY FAMILIES protect themselves against the rising costs of sickness and hospitalization through health insurance. Policies generally cover three types of expenses—hospital, surgical, and medical. Insurance against loss of income because of illness or accident also is available. Further details are given in the following section on health insurance.

If you cannot afford health insurance for the entire family, consider it at least for the breadwinner. His sickness would mean loss of income as well as medical expenses.

It is important to read the health contract to know what benefits it includes, particularly if you are not in a group. Find out what operations and illnesses are covered and what hospital services are offered. Some families may want to be sure of maternity benefits. Older persons should check whether the policy can be canceled or benefits reduced at a particular age. Ask for one that is guaranteed renewable.

To learn more about health insurance, talk to your employer or to your insurance agent.

FIRE INSURANCE is needed for both the house and furnishings.

In most States, a so-called standard fire insurance policy contains terms that comply with State laws and regulations. This policy protects you against fire and lightning losses.

It is customary also to add extended coverage to protect against some other hazards, such as windstorms, hail, explosion, smoke, riots, and damage by aircraft and vehicles.

Many homeowners carry personal liability insurance as well as regular fire insurance. Under a liability policy, the insurance company agrees to defend you in court and pay damage claims in the event someone is injured on your property. Injuries or damage resulting from activities of anyone in your family also are covered. Some liability policies provide medical payments up to 250 dollars or more, regardless of your liability.

Most insurance companies sell a package, or homeowners', policy, which covers personal liability and fire and extended coverage insurance plus personal-property floaters which protect you against property damage and cases of what is called "mysterious disappearance." Policies for tenants also are available. Considerable savings in time and bookkeeping can be made by combining all this coverage in one policy. Such policies are usually cheaper than if coverages were bought separately. The savings can be as high as 26 percent of the cost of policies written separately. Some package policies, however, may include more protection than you want. Consult your agent about the policy that best meets your need. Companies usually have three basic home-owners' policies that differ in the extent of coverage.

SOME FAMILIES spend more for insurance on their automobiles than for coverage on all other property they own. An automobile may be stolen, wrecked, or burned, cause damage to other automobiles, and injure persons.

Liability insurance is most important. Some States require it. It protects you against financial loss that may result from property or bodily injury damage suits. As the number of automobiles on the highways increases, the chance of accident and injury rises. Court judgments of thousands of dollars are not unusual. Few automobile owners can afford not to insure against this big risk.

Automobile liability insurance is spoken of as 10-20-5, 50-100-5, and so on. The meaning of 50-100-5, for example, is maximum coverage in the policy of 50 thousand dollars for each injury, 100 thousand dollars for each accident, and 5 thousand dollars for property damage. The larger policies do not cost much more than the minimum coverages and usually are well worth the difference.

Insurance to cover medical expenses of passengers who may be injured in your car is also desirable. It is relatively inexpensive to buy. The maximum medical care insurance offered is customarily 2 thousand dollars per person.

Collision insurance protects the automobile owner from expense of damage to his own automobile in an accident. This type of insurance is relatively expensive, and many persons reduce the premium cost by agreeing to pay the expense of repairs up to, say, 50 dollars. It is called deductible insurance.

Comprehensive insurance covers damage to your car by a variety of causes, such as fire, lightning, flood, theft, and breakage of glass.

If you are buying the automobile on credit, the lender undoubtedly will require you to carry collision and comprehensive insurance. Damage to your own car, however, would not be so great a financial loss to you as would be a liability loss resulting from injury or death to someone.

CHOOSING the amounts and kinds of insurance that fit your needs will take study. Insurance problems will always be with you as your situation and responsibilities change.

That usually means choosing an insurance agent in whom you have confidence and with whom you can work out a sensible insurance program. The agents recommended by your friends, your banker, or your lawyer are likely to be the best for you.

HOW TO GET THE BEST HEALTH INSURANCE

STATISTICIANS can tell you how much medical care will cost in a year for the country as a whole, but they cannot predict which families will need to spend little and which will need to spend much.

Since most families will not know ahead of time what to expect in the way of medical bills, a twofold approach to fitting medical care into the family budget is best.

Plan to pay for run-of-the-mill and small expenses directly out of income.

Carry insurance to take care of unexpected and costly emergencies.

You may find also that occasionally you will need to draw on your emergency fund to backstop both your budgetary allowance for health care and your health insurance.

Most health insurance available today does not cover expenses for minor illnesses, preventive medical care, or dental care. These costs must then be taken care of directly out of your budget allowance for health care or out of your emergency fund.

In any case, you generally will save money by planning to pay directly for constantly recurring items.

It does not pay to insure against expenses that are a virtual certainty. If you do, you must pay not only these expenses but a share of the cost of running the insuring organization.

An exception to the principle that the expected, day-to-day expenses will cost you less if you pay them directly will be found in some organizations offering comprehensive prepaid care through their own staffs of physicians and supporting personnel. In such organizations, the savings possible through group practice may outweigh the bookkeeping and related costs involved in insuring.

While you may be ahead financially by paying directly for the run-of-the-mill health expenses, the charge you must pay for the protection against the unexpected that insurance provides is a worthwhile expenditure.

Through insurance you can reduce the costs of major illnesses and accidents to manageable proportions by spreading them over the years. Depending on the level of your insurance program, you can safeguard both your family's health and your savings.

Considerable diversity exists in the health insurance on the market today. To do a good job in providing for your family's health, you should find out what is available to you and then choose the type that gives the most protection for the amount you can afford to pay.

Health insurance can be divided into three broad categories: hospitalization with or without medical-surgical insurance; major medical insurance; and comprehensive service programs.

HOSPITALIZATION insurance provides stated amounts of protection against hospital charges. Medical-surgical insurance does the same against doctors' bills arising from illness requiring hospitalization and accidents.

Neither hospitalization nor medical-surgical insurance offers blanket protection. Both carry limits on the amounts of care covered (the number of days of hospital care or the number of doctor's visits, for example) and the types of care covered (the type of hospital room, laboratory and other services in hospital, and perhaps limitations on treatments for some diseases).

Both may also carry limitations on the total payment for covered services. If your insurance reimburses you for bills you have paid, the reimbursement will be in line with a schedule of allowances included with your policy.

Blue Cross and other service policies assure you of full payment for the hospital services specified, but Blue Shield guarantees full payment of doctors' bills only if your income is below specified limits.

MAJOR MEDICAL INSURANCE is more inclusive in coverage than hospitalization and medical-surgical insurance.

In addition to the coverage they provide, it includes physician's care for other illnesses, private nursing care, drugs, X-ray and laboratory examinations, physical therapy, prosthetic devices such as artificial limbs, and ambulance service.

But major medical insurance usually does not cover preventive health examinations, dental care, and eye examinations and glasses. It also provides limited coverage only for the treatment of tuberculosis and psychiatric disease.

Major medical insurance, a later entry to the insurance field, was designed to cover the upper level of risks left uncovered by hospitalization and medical-surgical insurance. Consequently it is written with a "deductible" clause requiring the subscriber to pay a specified amount before benefits begin. The deductible may range from 50 to 500 dollars per person covered.

Benefits are stated in terms of total cash indemnity to pay covered expenses and may range from 2,500 to 10 thousand dollars.

To encourage the subscriber to hold down expenditures, major medical insurance also includes a coinsurance provision that requires the subscriber to pay a stated proportion of all expenses above the deductible—usually 20 to 25 percent.

You may combine hospitalization and medical-surgical insurance with major medical insurance to get more coverage than either provides alone.

Hospitalization and medical-surgical will usually meet the deductible for major medical if illness requires hospitalization.

If hospitalization is not required, you will quite possibly have to meet the deductible directly before benefits begin.

COMPREHENSIVE SERVICE programs differ from other health insurance in the range of benefits offered and in the form in which benefits are provided.

These programs may fall short of being completely comprehensive (all have limitations on the total amounts of service and most have specific limitations on treatment of psychiatric diseases and tuberculosis), but they have a broader scope in that they generally provide all the benefits offered by the other two types of insurance, plus preventive care and care of illnesses not requiring hospitalization.

Comprehensive group practice programs' are organized on a clinic basis and provide care through their own staffs and to varying extents through their own facilities.

In contrast to the other types of insurance that permit the subscriber almost unlimited choice of hospitals and doctors (Blue Cross and Blue Shield subscribers must use member hospitals and doctors, but this requirement is not restrictive, since many hospitals and most doctors are members), comprehensive service programs limit the subscriber's choice to members of their own staffs and selected facilities.

Since a group policy always costs less than an individual policy providing the same benefits, you will want to give serious consideration to getting your health insurance as a member of an insured group.

The group forming the basis for this kind of insurance is most frequently the employees of a business concern, but any group not organized for the purpose of obtaining insurance and of sufficient size can be the basis for such a policy.

Depending on the size of the group, the insurer may require a specified pro-

portion of the whole number to subscribe.

If you or members of your family are not "good risks"—that is, if you have conditions that make it likely you will need medical care—group insurance has an additional advantage. You may be rejected if you apply for an individual policy, or the policy may restrict benefits for these conditions. A group policy, however, is available to all members of the group.

To avoid an overload of unfavorable risks, your opportunities to enroll under a group policy are usually limited to the time the policy is negotiated or you join the group, and to occasional "open seasons." So, do not wait until you need the protection of insurance to apply for it. If you wait, you may find you cannot get it or that the cost is much higher.

QUESTIONS TO ASK and items to check before you take on your policy:

• Have you checked with an authority on whether the policy benefits are too limited?

• Will the policy pay for nursing care, laboratory fees, ambulances, X-rays?

• Do you know what *all* your benefits are? Families sometimes pass up benefits that could be claimed.

• Compare the allowances for surgical fees, especially for the more common operations. How many days of hospital care are provided for?

• Until what ages are your children covered?

• Are maternity benefits included? Is the cost for this allowance too high?

• If you give up your job, can you arrange to convert from group to individual coverage?

• Don't be misled by attractive *maximum* benefits. The basic benefits for typical hospital illnesses are more important than high payments for highly unlikely illnesses.

SOME OTHER considerations in buying health insurance:

Make sure that your hospitalization or medical-surgical policy gives you the right to continue it as long as you keep the premiums paid. Such a policy will cost somewhat more than if the insurer has the right to cancel the policy for reasons other than nonpayment of premiums, but it is worth the additional cost. The reason for cancellation by the insurer would be your becoming a bad risk, and you then would find yourself without protection when you need protection most.

If age 65 is in sight, look for a policy that does not terminate on the anniversary following that birthday. Many do, and insurance taken out after 65 is likely to be more limited in the amount and kind of protection offered and much more expensive.

Of course, a policy you can carry after 65 will be somewhat more expensive than one that expires when you reach that age, but it will be worth the difference.

If, on the other hand, you are a long way from 65, do not pay extra for the privilege of carrying your insurance beyond that age. New developments in health insurance are still so frequent that there is little likelihood that youngsters will carry their present policy to age 65.

The recent social security amendments established a broad program of health insurance, known popularly as "medicare," for people 65 or older. This program is important for young people too, for they will have this protection in later years. But if you are already 65, or will reach that age soon, you especially will want to have the information on how these health insurance programs will protect you.

You can get hospital insurance and medical insurance even if you are not receiving social security or railroad retirement benefits, but to get them you must apply for them.

There are two kinds of health insurance under the Medicare program. Hospital insurance helps pay the bills when you are hospitalized. The program also provides payments for skilled nursing care and other services in an extended care facility after hospitalization, outpatient hospital diagnostic services, and home health services. This insurance is financed out of special contributions paid by people while they work, with matching contributions from employers, so that people will not have to pay for this protection when they are old and not working. Medical insurance helps you pay the bills for doctors' services and for a number of other medical items and services not covered under the hospital insurance program. The medical insurance program is voluntary. You decide whether to enroll for protection under the medical insurance program. You can have this important added protection at a low cost ($3 monthly) because the Federal Government will pay an equal amount toward the cost.

To get medical insurance protection, you must enroll for it within the period of time set out in the law. Even if you are already receiving social security checks, you will get medical insurance only if you enroll for it.

If you are 65 or over and are receiving monthly social security or railroad retirement checks, you are automatically on the rolls for hospital insurance benefits.

If you are not receiving social security checks, you will probably be eligible for hospital insurance protection, but you will need to apply to get it.

If you are 65 or older and without health insurance, look into the new policies developed by Blue Cross-Blue Shield and commercial insurers, especially those that supplement Medicare coverage. These policies are offered without regard to health status at premiums roughly comparable to those offered good risks.

To make this possible, processing expenses are held to a minimum by offering only limited choices and subsidizing this type of business both by absorbing its overhead costs and in other ways.

So far, the emphasis here has been on the protection available to you, and little consideration has been given to its cost.

Sufficient health care costs on the average about 115 dollars per person per year, including care in hospitals

AVERAGE MEDICAL CARE EXPENDITURES OF FAMILIES IN SELECTED CLASSES

	All families	Place of residence		
Family class		Urban	Rural nonfarm	Farm
All families...........................	$345	$362	$297	$310
Income class (income after taxes):				
$2,000–$2,999.....................	230	237	208	245
$3,000–$3,999.....................	272	280	241	296
$4,000–$4,999.....................	298	291	311	334
$5,000–$5,999.....................	346	347	345	338
$6,000–$7,499.....................	399	404	370	424
$7,500–$9,999.....................	475	486	427	434
$10,000–$14,999.................	589	585	641	493
Family size:				
1-person........................	168	173	151	126
2-person........................	351	371	303	282
4-person........................	409	428	357	353
6-person........................	349	379	284	349
Age of family head (years):				
25–34...........................	331	340	306	280
35–44...........................	365	385	309	324
45–54...........................	373	393	317	340
55–64...........................	364	381	336	290
65–74...........................	326	352	261	285

and costs of doctors, dentists, medicines, and other care. But an average, in this case, is not a good figure to follow, because you can never forecast serious illnesses. You might budget 345 dollars a year for medical care for a family of 3 and then end up with payments that are 10 times that amount. How, then, should you decide what type and how much health insurance you should have?

In deciding how much to carry, consider whether the cost of the insurance is reasonable for the protection offered; what the chances are that you will need the various elements of protection offered; and whether you can fit the premium into your budget without too great a strain on other important elements of family living.

Once you have decided on your insurance, you can decide how much to allow for those run-of-the-mill expenses that were discussed earlier.

Set the amount to cover what you might have to spend before your insurance begins to pick up the tab. Be sure that you have provision one place or the other for routine examinations and preventive services and dental and eye care.

If you are drawing up a budget for the first time and have not kept records of your expenditures in the past, you may be at a loss to know what your health care should cost you.

Some of the known factors that influence the amount spent are income level, family size, and the age of the head of the family. What you spend will not be affected much by where you live—city, small town, or farm—but will reflect your income level.

Up to a point, the larger your family, the more you can expect to spend on medical care. In large families, however, other demands on income force some reduction in spending for medical care.

You can expect to spend most for your family's medical care when you are between the ages of 45 and 54, which is also when your family will probably be largest. Your medical expenses will drop off somewhat thereafter, but not in proportion to the decrease in the size of your family.

Not all of your health needs must be met out of your own budget. Even though you are not indigent, you can expect some services from your local or state health department and from voluntary societies organized to combat the various chronic diseases.

To get the most from your health budget, once you have set one up, have a "family doctor"—one or more. You may have a general practitioner who will care for all members of your family, or you may have an internist for the adult members and a pediatrician for the children. Just be sure that someone knows the health status of your family.

If illness strikes and specialist care seems indicated, let your family doctor direct and advise you.

Do not hesitate to discuss costs with your doctors.

Providing for your family's health does not begin and end in the allowance for medical care in your budget. Nutritious meals, healthful living conditions, good habits of work, exercise, recreation, and rest in balanced amounts—all will help safeguard your family's health.

SMART WAYS TO SAVE ON CARS

A CAR is the most expensive item, next to a house, a family is likely to buy, what with the original cost, the upkeep, and the operating expenses.

There are ways, though, to save quite a few dollars every year.

Some facts:

The *average* family with a car (or cars) spends about 900 dollars a year for car expenses. That is *more* than is spent on shelter, clothing, medical care, or any other item except food!

The average price paid is about 3 thousand dollars for a new car and 900 dollars for a used car.

New cars are kept an average of 6 years; used cars, 4 years.

Every few years a family has to decide whether it is time to buy another car. The most economical time to buy generally is when your present car costs you more for depreciation, repairs, gasoline, and oil than a new one would.

A car depreciates at a slower rate each succeeding year. The cost of upkeep and operation, on the other hand, goes up as the car ages. The best time to

trade varies according to the use the car has had and the type of driver.

WHEN IT COMES to buying a car, the choice among sizes, models, and extras may not be easy to make.

The car you choose should fit your own needs and purse. At the same time, the selection of a car that buyers of used cars will want when you are ready to trade is one way to cut the high cost of depreciation and protect your investment.

If your family is small or you need a second car to drive to work, a low-priced compact may be the one for you. If you have several children, a standard-sized car may be better for you and worth the higher cost. If you cannot decide between these two sizes, consider one in the intermediate size—between compact and standard models in size, price, and operating costs.

As for body styles, the four-door sedan is the most popular. If you prefer a two door, the hardtop generally is considered a better buy than the regular sedan. You will get back most, if not all, of the extra cost when you trade in the hardtop. Station wagons (the four-door models) are always in demand among big suburban families. So narrow down your choices as much as you can before you even enter a showroom.

The extras can add several hundred dollars to the cost of a new car without adding much to trade-in value later. Judge them on their worth to you.

Radio, heater, automatic transmission, and power steering are among the accessories most likely to offer a fair return. An automatic transmission will add to the cost of running the car, because it takes more gasoline than a standard transmission. But, it might be worth the extra $200 also if you do a lot of gear shifting. All-vinyl upholstery looks good and is easy to care for.

Some accessories are nice to have but do not add much to the usefulness of the car. In general, you get back only a small part of their original cost. Among them are whitewall tires, tilt-type steering wheels, and power seats and windows.

Pick the right time to buy. Some of the best times are toward the end of the month, when salesmen and dealers are anxious to meet their quota; during slow winter months (February and March); and during sales contests.

Liberal discounts are generally given just before the new models come out but you may have a limited choice. Remember, too, that you will have an old model within a very short time, but that is less important if you keep your automobile a long time.

When trading your used car in for a new one, make sure you know the real value of your used car and the true list price for the new car. You will be in a better bargaining position if you are sure of the true dollar value for both.

Don't be afraid to take the offensive with the eager salesman. If you are a good bargainer (and the salesman expects you to bargain) you can probably get a better deal by haggling, plus careful shopping around.

It is perfectly legitimate for the salesman to try to sell you the most costly car he can. But some salesmen will resort to tricky or illegal tactics to win a sale. So be sure to watch out for the salesman who greatly overappraises the value of your trade-in and then proposes a more realistic price just before he's convinced you to buy. Then, too, watch out for the salesman who makes a verbal commitment for an "unbelievably low price" on a new car and then withdraws the commitment—again, just before you are about to take ownership—on the pretext that his sales manager would not approve the price he quoted. This trick is usually used when the buyer does not have a trade-in.

PAY CASH IF YOU CAN. No additional charge is made then for interest, investigation, recording, and so on.

If you must borrow money, make as big a down payment as possible and keep the financing period short. The appraised value of your trade-in car becomes part of your down payment.

If you are planning to finance, shop

for the lowest terms. To do so you need to have certain information: the cost of the new car; the trade-in allowance for your old car; any additional down payment; the amount of your loan; the amount of the monthly payment; and the number of payments required.

Multiply the monthly payment by the number of months you are to pay. Subtract the amount of your loan from this total. The remainder is the amount you will pay for the use of credit on your dealer's plan.

With that information, you can shop for the lowest financing terms. Go to lending agencies and compare costs. You will probably find it costs less to borrow directly from a bank or credit union.

MOST OWNERS have some form of insurance. When you buy auto insurance, you usually are buying several kinds of coverage in one package.

You can shop for the best insurance buy if you know the kind and extent of coverage you want.

Liability insurance gives you financial protection for bodily injury or property damage to others. State laws tell you how much to buy to fulfill the legal requirements. It is a good idea to buy more than the minimum amount required, if you can possibly squeeze out the extra cost. The additional cost is relatively small compared with the greater protection. Jury awards can be very high; judgments of 50 thousand dollars are not uncommon.

Comprehensive insurance provides for loss or damage to your car from a number of hazards—fire, theft, windstorm, glass breakage, and vandalism.

Comprehensive insurance becomes less important as a car grows older, if you can absorb the loss.

Collision insurance covers damage to your car from collision or upset, if you or someone else is at fault. This kind of coverage is expensive. To reduce the cost, it usually is written with an amount—50, 100, or 250 dollars—deductible. You pay for the deductible amount of the damages on your car, and the insurance company pays the rest.

The higher the deductible limit, the lower the premium.

If you consider yourself a reasonably safe driver or feel you can pay the first 100 or 250 dollars in case of an accident, you can cut the cost of your insurance with one of the higher deductibles. It may not pay you to carry this kind of coverage on an older car.

If you finance the purchase of a car, you will be required to carry comprehensive fire and theft and collision insurance to cover the full value of the car. Be sure you also have liability coverage.

You can also buy medical-payment insurance that pays medical and hospital bills should you or anyone riding in your car be injured. This kind of coverage may not be necessary if you have an adequate medical coverage through other insurance plans.

On other kinds of insurance, such as towing and uninsured-motorist coverage, you will need to decide how important they are to you in relation to the risk involved and the cost.

Car insurance rates vary from company to company. Some companies offer lower rates because they specialize in auto insurance, sell directly to the customer, or sell only to good risks.

GASOLINE is a big item in the operation of a car. A change from premium to regular or regular to economy gasoline can save you money on your car.

Unless the manufacturer specifies it, most cars do not need a premium grade. Some cars do just as well on one of the economy fuels.

Buy the lowest grade of gas that will give satisfactory operation in your car.

Develop good driving habits to get as much mileage as possible from the gasoline you buy: Avoid jackrabbit starts and sudden stops. Accelerate smoothly and with a light touch. Look ahead and slow down gradually. Maintain a steady speed. Travel at moderate speeds.

Another way to save on gasoline is to keep your car in proper running order: Have a tuneup periodically. Clean the spark plugs and make replacements when necessary. Check the carburetor occasionally. Keep the air filter clean.

When it comes to oil changes and chassis lubrications, it is best to follow the recommendations in the owner's manual. The new, longer periods between oil changes for new cars are a convenience and save money. To insure safe and reliable operation, though, it is still necessary to give your car the attention called for.

Do not overbuy on tires. You may need premium-grade tires if you do a lot of driving on rough roads, but the cheaper first-line grade should be adequate for most ordinary driving. Keep the tires inflated to the pressure the manufacturer recommends. Check the alignment of the front wheels. Make the necessary corrections. Good driving habits mean the most wear out of your tires and hold the cost down.

KEEPING YOUR CAR in good condition helps to cut depreciation to a reasonable minimum. The new paints used on cars may need less polishing and waxing than the old paints, but regular washing is necessary. Paint that is protected from the sun, sleet, and snow lasts longer and looks better. If you have a garage or carport, make a point of putting your car under cover.

Some of these savings may seem small. When you add them up, you will be surprised at how much you can save.

WHERE SHOULD YOU LIVE?

MOST OF US have not one but a number of homes in a lifetime.

Most of us, therefore, as we move from country to city or city to suburb or job to job or status to status, have choices to make every time.

Let the choice be a good one or at least a thoughtful one, for—even if you stay in a place only a short time—it can influence your and your family's well-being, sometimes even involvement and identity, and happiness.

A mistake, if you make one, can be corrected, but a mistake almost always leaves some kind of mark.

FIRST, THE COMMUNITY you choose.

Since no one can visit every community and every available new home in a given area, an excellent way to narrow down the prospects is through the classified section of the local newspaper. Armed with the real estate ads and a good metropolitan area map, you can drive through the areas you select for a quick preliminary appraisal.

Are the houses lined up like soldiers at attention without regard to such factors as their relation to the hot sun, protection from street noises and public view, and good drainage? Are streets monotonously gridironed, or are there curves and blind ends (cul-de-sacs) that eliminate or discourage through traffic and speeding? How about trees and landscaping? Finally, do the houses have a substantial appearance?

Before you make your choice, compare the costs of commuting in money, time, and fatigue with the advantages and disadvantages of space, privacy, and quiet for yourself and your family.

Do not overlook differences in public amenities and governmental services and in taxes and the costs of insurance and utilities.

Wherever you decide to live, you will be concerned with the policies of local government—in the country, with the county and school district; in town, with them and also with the services and policies of city hall.

Choose, if you can, to live within the jurisdiction of a government that has a master plan of zoning and development, legislation to support it, and an active review procedure to keep it alive and fresh.

During any period of expansive physical development stimulated by the effects of increases in population and metropolitanization, it is hard to foresee the future of a community or to influence its development. Without a plan, growth is chaotic and unpredictable.

Many families have built houses in the country only to find the city at their doorsteps sooner than they had expected. Many others have built or rented in city neighborhoods whose residential character becomes eroded by conversion to incompatible uses.

The best advice therefore is: Do not buy or build a house on land that has a potential for industrial, commercial, or multiple-housing development, except as a calculated investment.

Rather, seek a site protected by zoning.

You will find other advantages in legislation for city or county planning.

Visual quality—beauty and order—depends on the good will and sensibility of each property owner and the competence of his architect, but laws can control some of the influences that have contributed to the deterioration of the American landscape—signs, billboards, gas stations, and utility structures.

Some communities limit the location of billboards, refuse to accept standard designs for gas stations, and require that wires and pipes of utilities be put underground. Choose a community that does all that and is alert to the possibilities of more improvements like them.

LOCAL GOVERNMENT and public education are financed largely by taxes on privately owned property.

Tax rates and sometimes assessment practices vary among communities. But do not assume that communities with low taxes therefore are more efficient. Usually they simply provide fewer or inferior services.

Some communities try to attract industry in the belief that new factories are another source of nonresidential tax income to help defray costs of government and schools. An economic analysis of the tax impact of each potential industry on the community, however, should be made to set forth the new costs as well as the new revenues.

New families that will accompany an industry to a community must be taken into account, because, ironically, most families are tax liabilities—their share of governmental and school costs is greater than their contributions.

In the final analysis, the property tax has inevitable shortcomings, because it penalizes quality by rewarding shoddy developments with low assessments.

When you attempt to estimate the fiscal soundness of a city or county or your future tax costs as an owner of property within its jurisdiction, do not oversimplify the problem.

An example: Nothing is more important than excellent public schools. They are not easy to develop and are expensive. Usually they coexist with high property taxes, but differences in tax rates in communities with good schools and those with poor schools are seldom great enough to influence one's choice and are never worth the "savings."

Communities with good schools usually are stimulating in other ways, too. So, when you are looking for a place to live, look into opportunities for intellectual activity, libraries, museums, theaters, concerts, a little-theater group, an amateur symphony. Mutual interests foster friendships more than geography does.

Look also for a beautiful place, or one that at least is not ugly.

Visual quality, like a good school system, is not achieved quickly. It depends on long traditions of pride and long-continued programs of responsible public works. Street trees take years to mature. Established visual elegance in a residential community is literally priceless.

Consider also convenience to work, shopping, and schools in terms of distance and methods of transport, for a house for most families in this day and age is a center from which to commute to work and to acquire goods and services. Children commute to school. If for no other reason, anticipate traveling costs in order to know how much you can afford to spend for housing.

IN THE OLDER parts of established cities, you find multiple types—row houses or taller apartment buildings. These extend to outer parts of larger cities, where old townhouses, duplexes, and garden apartments (row houses scattered through the landscape rather than along streets), may be found. Suburbs now have duplexes, small apartments, and a renaissance of row houses, besides the traditional freestanding house, usually the only type found in the country.

Still another recent house form is the mobile home, or trailer. Presumably it was developed to accommodate a mobile and space-loving society, but trailers usually are parked in crowded courts without privacy. Their occupants tend to be no more mobile than families in apartment houses; they move about once every 2 years. Actually, trailers used as tract houses are not inexpensive, but they do avoid or minimize tax contributions for the support of schools and local government.

Homeownership used to be possible only in a separate house, duplex, or row house. The mobile home and the extension of the condominium to American apartments have extended the own-versus-rent choice.

It is possible to demonstrate that in a rising market it is more economical to own than to rent equivalent quarters. Owning, as opposed to renting, also has Federal (and sometimes State) income tax advantages, but renting and owning generally must be regarded as economic equivalents.

The choice should be made on other grounds—how long you expect to remain in a given locality and whether you wish to be involved in the maintenance, improvement, and accumulation of furnishings and equipment that accompany ownership.

How important are the intangibles of ownership? Much has been said about owned houses as prestige symbols. As psychologically satisfying as this may be, it is better to realize that true value lies in utility and soundness and in the satisfactions that derive from compatibility, privacy, and the expression of personality.

SOMETIMES A NEIGHBORHOOD is so attractive that it determines one's choice of community, but usually the community is selected first.

Transportation may influence the second decision as well as the first. So, inevitably, will the housing situation. If you are interested in a particular kind of house or lot or one at a certain price, you may find it only in a limited number of places.

But, assuming there are alternatives, how to proceed?

Some Americans think that every man ought to own his house. On the other hand, many families rent because of mobility. As a matter of fact, when moving into a new community, there is an advantage in renting for a while.

Many qualities, especially the intangibles that have to do with sociability, common interests, and climate, cannot be understood without experience. Renting in an unfamiliar community will give you a clearer idea of the kind of house you want and the neighborhood in which you would like to live.

Whether renting or buying, look first for visual character. It is even more important in the neighborhood than

in the community, because the neighborhood is closer to home.

Established neighborhoods have at least two advantages: You can examine the houses, and the landscape has had time to mature. Some of our best houses are very old, but middle-aged houses and neighborhoods tend to deteriorate.

Judge the viability of an established neighborhood before placing a new house there. If you don't trust your own evaluation, seek professional advice. New developments still under construction are harder to visualize, but plans can give some indication of their eventual completed appearance.

Houses for sale or rent and remaining lots in stable residential neighborhoods command higher prices. So does property in thoughtfully planned and sensitively designed new residential areas that can reasonably be expected to develop admirably.

Your choice is difficult: Whether to accept an area that is not and probably will not be developed attractively, or place a larger percentage of your investment in land and improvements to take advantage of a superior location, remembering that you will be able to do little to change the aspect of the neighborhood.

Look for a location where you can walk to stores and shops, school, and a park. That may be difficult, because much zoning legislation, in overreacting to 19th-century slums, has produced antiseptic neighborhoods, which by being unvaried are also unserviced. Well-designed and well-maintained multiple housing can be interspersed skillfully with smaller houses, and convenient shops are an advantage.

Incidentally, communities with too few service facilities often can improve their tax base simply by attracting the needed services.

Communities vary a good deal in the availability of facilities and programs for recreation. Do not overlook their importance for children.

Select a location that is free from unpleasant sources of noise, fumes, and dirt and not near a freeway, railroad, airport, or objectionable industry. Noise travels surprising distances on quiet nights. So do fumes and dust on breezy days.

Consider the views. If the terrain is hilly, the views are more extensive, but construction costs probably will be higher.

What does the street look like? Most streets are too wide. Narrower streets may be crowded now and then, but they hold down the scale of the neighborhood and so add to its character.

Streets are classified on the basis of expected traffic loads, and widths are proportional to the classifications. Select a site facing a street of the lowest classification, where the lightest traffic load is anticipated.

Purely local streets have advantages of relative quiet and safety. Subtly curved streets usually are more attractive than straight ones, but excessively curved patterns are puzzling to strangers and casual visitors.

What do the neighboring houses look like? Fences? Landscaping? What is the orientation of the lot?—can you take advantage of winter sunshine, yet keep out excessive summer sun? What is the direction of prevailing winds? Of prevailing storms? Are summer cooling breezes accessible? Is the lot readily drained? What is the character of the soil? Is it subject to movement, settling, slides?

After you have made a tentative on-site selection of neighborhood, find out at the city hall or county courthouse how it is designated on the master plan: Is it to be permanently residential and free from highways or overhead transmission lines? What will be its relationship to future developments— schools, libraries, transportation, recreation, and shopping and service facilities?

Look up the zoning regulations. Find out what you can and cannot do there, the restrictions on the house itself, and the kinds of activities that can take place in it. Can you have a separate house for your guests? Rent out a room? Practice a part-time profession or occupation? Build a swimming pool in the backyard?

Look into requirements for the setbacks of structures from lot lines so that you will understand possibilities for building or remodeling.

Ask whether there has been a recent flood in the neighborhood. If not, and if it has survived a severe rainy season, its drainage facilities are adequate unless subsequently overloaded by new developments.

Select a neighborhood that has underground electrical and telephone wires. Experience in California and elsewhere indicates that this can be done reasonably in new subdivisions.

Inquire about provisions for collecting trash and garbage.

Is there a water shortage, or is the supply adequate for house and garden? Are water softeners necessary?

Everyone runs some risk of buying or building in a neighborhood that soon deteriorates.

The best protection lies in planning and zoning, but master plans and zoning legislation can be changed. You probably can improve your chances by selecting a location near an attractive and compatible development, such as a college campus, golf course, or public park, which, oftener than not, exert stabilizing influences on nearby residential property.

If you follow these criteria and acquire a sensitively designed and soundly constructed house, property values probably will be sustained. A house that is no more expensive than the average in the neighborhood and perhaps a little less so is a conservative investment. But who then will uphold the value of the neighborhood? Which comes first, responsibility or security?

Now, THE HOUSE itself.

When one acquires a house, he is inclined to think of the enterprise as an investment. It is true that a house can be ostentatiously out of place in its neighborhood or too expensive for a given market to support, especially in small communities without diversified demands. But be careful to distinguish superstition from sound assumption.

Experience does not support common assumptions about the effects of ethnic homogeneity. When a minority group begins to move into a neighborhood, property values do not automatically decline. Sometimes they increase.

Of course, one should consider all the economic factors involved in the venture: The relative advantages of renting and owning; indirect costs, such as transportation; and all direct costs— the land and improvements, building, landscaping, furnishing, and operation (amortization, maintenance, taxes, and insurance).

Land costs usually are lowest in the country and highest in the central city and vary with the desirability of the location and the extent of its improvement.

Do not overlook the costs of site improvements. As a prospective property owner, determine your liability to the city or county for current or future work.

In town you will usually be committed by law to a proportion of the neighborhood costs. In the country you are freer, but it is harder to anticipate total development costs accurately.

Grading, utilities, and streets are expensive. Their costs do not vary much from community to community for comparable developments, but some communities have higher standards of design and construction. Usually they are in more desirable urban locations and entail lower maintenance expenses.

All things considered, it is better to live in a community that requires first-class utilities, drainage facilities, street construction, and street lighting, but not in one that uses highway lighting standards in residential streets. They do violence to residential quality.

At the other end of the process, think of landscaping and furnishing costs. Families often find themselves with inadequate funds for these items simply because they follow site and structure in the sequence of acquisition.

Insurance costs vary with the quality and proximity of fire and police protection, but differences in premiums do not measure the advantages of adequate protection.

The building itself represents the largest single expenditure. Many variables influence its cost. For families with reduced incomes, cost will be critical and the alternatives severely limited, but for many others, several choices will be available at similar prices.

At this point, turn to considerations other than price to find measures of value. Who else can understand precisely how important to you is an escape to an unspoiled stretch of wilderness or the sound of music or the company of friends?

The choice among house types and among individual examples of each is complex. Usually a single-family house offers the most privacy and an apartment the least. Duplexes and row houses fall between. However, tract houses with opposite bedroom windows at 10 feet are much less private than row houses with well-built party walls. Some apartments are far more private than others, depending solely on qualities of design and construction.

Many people prefer the sense of a small private world, which is possible in a well-designed and well-maintained house (but hardly in most apartments) and believe that separate houses are better places for children.

However, if your final decision is to rent an apartment, keep the following questions in mind when selecting your apartment:

• Will your budget be stretched by high rent? A general rule of thumb is not to spend more than one week's pay for rent.

• Does your landlord have a good reputation for care and maintenance?

• Must you pay for all utilities or only part of them?

• Is the neighborhood attractive and safe?

• Is there adequate public transportation nearby?

• If you own a car, is garage space available? Must it be rented or is it included with the apartment?

• Is the plumbing adequate and does it work well? How about the wiring? Is there enough to handle all your appliances? Does the apartment allow air conditioners?

Have the landlord agree to paint and repair the apartment before you move in.

And don't forget to check: the laundry facilities; closet space and shelving; lighting; window insulation; size of elevators and stairways (will your furniture fit through them?) ; fire escapes and play areas for children.

If you prefer not to live in an apartment or rent accommodations elsewhere, you face a number of alternatives: Whether to buy a lot and build a house, buy an existing house, or buy a new tract house.

Existing houses, new or old, can be examined before the purchase. Building a new house, on the other hand, presents the opportunity to achieve a uniquely personal environment, given competent professional design—at least an architect, and preferably also a landscape architect.

Many houses could have been conceived more economically had an architect designed them, but valid professional service entails costs and so does custom building. Select your architect carefully on the basis of his work —one who is interested and experienced in house design.

Select the builder carefully, too. Most people assume that competitive bidding is the only way to solicit a reasonable price. Sometimes it is, but limit the bidders to good contractors.

The best procedure, if you can manage it, and if your community is fortunate enough to have such men, is to select the best builder just as you selected the best architect. A man who takes a professional interest in his work usually quotes the same price whether he is bidding competitively or simply invited to build.

If your house is being designed for you, its form has limitless possibilities. Take advantage of the opportunities to make it truly original, but avoid exotic excesses, which disrupt visual harmony

in the neighborhood and can make it difficult to sell in some unforeseen future.

Prefabricated houses are available in some localities for erection individually. Some are well designed by good architects and less expensive than custom-designed houses of comparable size and construction.

The term "prefabrication" does not describe the quality of design or structure but simply the building process. Quality must be judged separately, as it must for houses built by conventional methods.

The more homes you look at, the more adept you will become in judging from the outside what you are likely to find on the inside. As you approach a house, note how it has been "sited"—that is, how it has been placed on its lot. Consider the orientation of large window areas. If the orientation is bad, heating and cooling costs will be unnecessarily high.

Ideally, a house in the northern hemisphere will have a southern exposure. Adequate roof overhangs will block out unwanted summer sun yet admit welcome winter sunlight to help heat the house. By comparison, east and west exposures receive six times more sun in summer, while the northern exposure receives little sun in summer and none in winter. Unfavorable orientation is sometimes unavoidable. When this is the case, the good designer can often compensate for this shortcoming.

Now look at the house itself. Do you like the general style and appearance? Architects say the least expensive home per square foot of floor area is a nearly square two-story house. Because it occupies less area, such a house can save in land costs, too. So beware of a style with shifts and breaks in the wall and roof lines.

Another popular design is the one-story house, which eliminates stairclimbing and can ease cleaning chores. This is especially important to mothers of young children.

The split-level adapts features of both of these designs to the siting problem presented by an irregular building lot.

You are the best judge of how a particular style of house meets the needs of your family. If yours is a growing one, keep in mind the possible need for future expansion. Some homes are designed to provide this at minimun cost.

Most people buy tract houses because repetitive construction processes reduce unit costs. If you buy a tract house, select one designed by a reputable architect. These are becoming prevalent and will be the rule if consumers insist upon quality; no builder puts up ugly houses he cannot sell.

Complain about shortcomings in design to the salesmen and do your fellow consumer a good turn. Some enlightened zoning legislation has given professionally designed subdivisions advantages—freedom in space organization within buildings and within neighborhoods. Seek such a community, because the quality of future residential developments there will be relatively high.

FEATURES OF A WELL-BUILT HOUSE

How CAN YOU TELL whether a house you are thinking of buying is well built?

First, get a copy of the plans and specifications. Compare what you can see of the house with what is shown on the plan. Often plans are revised during construction, for better or for worse.

Some general features are not structural but still may be important to you.

Among them are: Which way does the house face? Is the arrangement and size of rooms good? How about natural light and cross-ventilation? Do the rooms provide enough wallspace or storage space? Does the plan permit some flexibility of living arrangements?

These are partly matters of personal taste. If they satisfy your family's needs or preferences, they are good.

From this we go to the structural parts of the house—the foundation, walls, floors, ceilings, and roof.

START from the outside. Walk around the house.

Look at the foundation walls, which should extend at least 6 inches above the finished ground level. Watch for vertical cracks, which may indicate the structure has settled.

Hairline cracks in the concrete are due to volume changes and have no great significance.

If the concrete is uneven or honeycombed or has broken corners, it probably did not have enough cement or was carelessly placed in the forms—a sign of poor workmanship.

In block or stone walls, observe the character of the joints. Use a pocket-knife to pick at the mortar and see if it crumbles easily. If so, it is a sign that too much sand or a poor quality of cement was used. A nail driven into the joint will indicate whether the mortar is skimpy there.

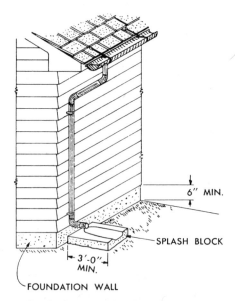

Good drainage features include slope from the house, splash block, and good downspouts and gutters.

If you wish to check the wall thickness, measure through a basement window.

Termites are a hazard to houses in much of the United States. Ask if there are termite shields or soil poison to protect against them.

If the house is built over a crawl space, look inside and check the girders and joists for signs of decay and for moisture stains on the floor framing.

Dampness in the crawl space may be due to lack of proper ventilation. The ventilators should be big enough and so placed that there is cross-circulation.

Whether there is a foundation wall or concrete slab on grade, the slope from the foundation at the grade line should be enough for rain to run off.

Basement window wells must drain readily. Water from the roof should be carried away by adequate gutters, conductors, and downspouts of noncorrosive material.

If downspouts are not connected to a storm sewer or other suitable outlet, splash blocks at the outlet will divert the roof water away.

Check basement window jambs and trim to see if they fit snugly against the masonry wall.

The sills of all windows should have sufficient pitch to drain water outward. Here is a place where decay may have occurred—probing with an icepick or small screwdriver will soon tell you.

AFTER A FINAL LOOK at the foundation walls to make sure the corners are even and walls are vertical, we can inspect the framed sidewalls.

They may be covered with wood or composition siding, shingles, brick, stucco, stone, or other types of enclosing materials. All are good if used properly.

Behind the covering is probably a frame of a 2- by 4-inch studs to which is nailed a sheathing material such as wood, plywood, or fiberboard.

If the siding has been painted, examine the condition of the paint. See if the paint film is dense and opaque, or if the wood is showing through. Check for any gloss on the surface. Painted surfaces that are dull and chalky indicate that repainting is necessary.

The horizontal lap siding should be laid evenly with correct overlap and tight butt joints. At the corners, the siding may be mitered or fitted snugly against vertical corner boards. An end of the siding board should not be exposed to the weather because it will soak up moisture.

Make sure the nails are of the noncorroding type and that the space between the nailhead and the face of the siding has been filled in before painting or staining. Simply scratch to find out.

Windows and doors should have a protective flashing of noncorrosive metal above them. They should be checked for weatherstripping.

Check the sills for sufficient pitch for good drainage. A drip groove under the sill will permit the water to drip clear of the siding.

You have now had an opportunity to form an opinion on the quality of workmanship that has gone into the outside walls. Neat foundation walls, good metal gutters and downspouts, snug-fitting woodwork, and provision for surface drainage all indicate the builder has made a conscientious effort to erect a house that will endure.

Signs that the builder has skimped are chipped or honeycombed concrete, loose mortar in the brickwork, large cracks between the ends of the siding and window or other trim, rust stains from an inferior grade of outside hardware and thin or flaked-off paint in a nearly new house.

Now GO INSIDE the house.

In the basement, look more carefully at the foundation walls, posts, and girders and at the floor joists if they are not concealed by the ceiling material.

The basement floor should be dry. Look for waterstains along the angle between floor and walls. Check to see that all holes where pipes come through the foundation wall and floor are properly cemented.

The basement floor should slope to

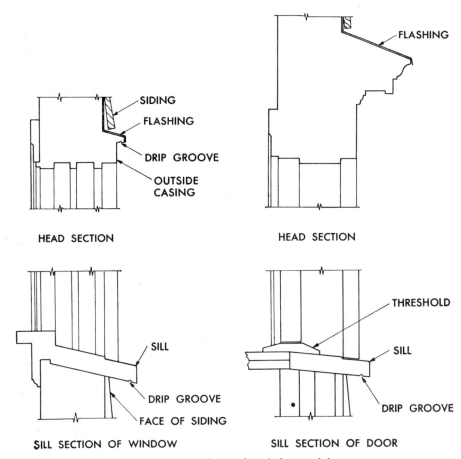

SIDING

FLASHING

DRIP GROOVE

OUTSIDE CASING

HEAD SECTION

FLASHING

HEAD SECTION

SILL

DRIP GROOVE

FACE OF SIDING

SILL SECTION OF WINDOW

THRESHOLD

SILL

DRIP GROOVE

SILL SECTION OF DOOR

Good construction in exterior windows and doors.

the floor drain to permit quick runoff. A concrete floor should have a hard, smooth surface without spalling, cracking, or dusting.

The joists that support the floor above rest on the foundation walls and are intermediately supported by wood or steel girders. These girders in turn are supported by posts or by division walls.

If wood posts are used, they should be set on a concrete base block above the finished floor level.

When wood girders are built up by nailing several members side by side, make sure the members are well nailed together and that joints are over a post or a division wall.

Check to see that the ends of wood

joints are not embedded in masonry or the concrete wall, as this practice may invite rot unless there is an airspace at the sides and end of the beam.

The wood joists should be spaced evenly, usually every 16 inches. Examine them for sagging, warping, or cross-breaks.

Look carefully at any joists that have been cut for heating ducts or piping. Notches or holes on the bottom edge or near midspan have the greatest weakening effect.

You may be able to see the grademark stamped on the joist, which will indicate the quality of lumber used.

Looking between the floor joists, you can probably see the subfloor. If it is of 1-inch boards, they should not be more than 8 inches wide and preferably laid diagonally to the joists.

Plywood often is used for subfloors. The 4- by 8-foot sheets should be laid with the face grain at right angles to the joists. Small knotholes on the undersurface of plywood subfloor are acceptable.

Check the area between the foundation wall and sill. Any openings should be filled with a cement mixture or a calking compound. The filling will lower the heat loss and prevent the entry of insects or mice into the basement.

MOST CONSTRUCTION in the living area will be hidden by various wall and ceiling finishes, but you can check the interior finish and such items as flooring, window or door trim, and other trim.

Examine the trim for any open joints, hammer marks, warped pieces, or rough nailing.

Over the door where the side casings meet the horizontal, the joint is often mitered. If this joint is tight, as all joints should be, you have a pretty good sign of careful workmanship.

Note, too, if the baseboard fits snugly against the flooring and the wall at all points.

Interior finishes are commonly of plaster or of such dry-wall construction as wood or composition materials.

You seldom see plaster cracks in a newly built home, because they develop slowly. In a house a year or more old, the absence of cracks indicates a well-built house. Of course, cracks can be concealed temporarily by wallpaper or a coat of paint.

Cracks extending diagonally from the corners of windows or doors may be signs of poor framing or that the house has settled.

If the nails that hold the dry-wall construction in place protrude (referred to as nail pops) from the face of the material, the framing lumber may have been at too high a moisture content at the time of installation. This problem can be corrected by redriving the nails, but you should take into account the cost of doing this renailing.

As you walk over the floors, notice if they squeak or seem too springy. If the floor joists are big enough and the subfloor has been laid correctly, neither fault should happen.

If the flooring is exposed, hardwood flooring or the harder species of softwood are usually preferred. If carpeting is used, the underlayment may be

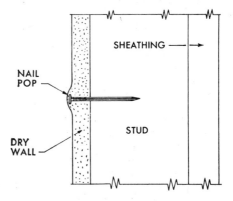

Nail popping in dry wall construction.

of any material that presents a smooth and firm surface.

Look carefully for signs of nailing. Flooring of a standard thickness is tongued and grooved and is blind nailed along the tongue so the nailing does not show. Small nailheads on the face or top of the flooring mean that a very thin flooring has been used.

Wood strip flooring normally becomes dry and cracks open between the strips in late winter in the colder States. These cracks, if they are not too wide, will close up the following summer.

Do not condemn floors in an old house simply because they are scratched and marred. Perhaps all they need is refinishing. If so, take this extra cost into account.

Perhaps the kitchen and the bathroom have tilework in the floor, on the wall, or wainscot. The tile floor should be smooth, without raised tile or depressed areas.

Wall tiles should fit snugly around all

windows, door trim, and around the fixtures. Joints should be calked tightly to keep water out.

Check the doors to see if they swing freely and close tightly without sticking.

Is there a threshold under the exterior doors to keep out snow and cold winds? Some of these doors may have metal weatherstripping.

Are the interior doors hung so as to clear your rugs? Do they interfere with other doors? Do they latch readily and stay latched?

Check all doors to see that they are not excessively warped.

Windows usually are of the double-hung type—the lower sash slides up and the upper one slides down.

Open and shut all windows to be sure they work properly and there is not too much play in the sash. The weatherstripping, if there is any, should not interfere with the ease of operation.

Raise the shades to assure yourself there are no cracked window-panes.

Check window woodwork and plaster for waterstains and signs of decay.

Note the kind of glass in the window. Is it clear and flawless, or does it distort objects seen through it? Also see if the putty that holds the glass is in good condition and is painted.

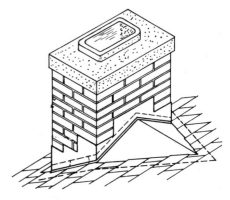

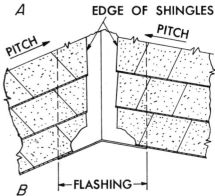

Correct flashing for A, *chimney and shingles and* B, *valley.*

CHECK the attic area for the thickness of insulation between the ceiling joists and to see if there is a moisture barrier on the room side of the insulation.

Also, check the attic ventilators. They should be open summer and winter. In summer, ventilation helps to lower the attic temperature. In winter, ventilation removes moisture that may work itself up through the ceiling and condense in the attic space.

Frost on the ends of nails in winter indicates insufficient ventilation and excess moisture.

Check the roof rafters or trusses to see that they are unbroken and that the framing joints are tight.

INSPECT as much of the roof as you can. For most types of shingles, the roof slope should be at least 1 to 2; that is, the roof should rise 6 inches in every foot measured horizontally.

Wood shingles and composition shingles are the most common types of roofing materials that you are likely to encounter. If you can, find out for how long the roof is guaranteed.

Check the flashing at the valleys and around the chimney. They are often the source of leaky roofs.

See if you can see roll roofing under the shingles at the eaves. If it is there, water held by small ice dams above the gutters will not work back into the wall and cause damage.

YOU MAY BE UNCERTAIN if the joints are big enough or if a crack in the wall or a stain in the plaster means serious trouble. If so, you should ask for professional help.

First inquire whether the suspected

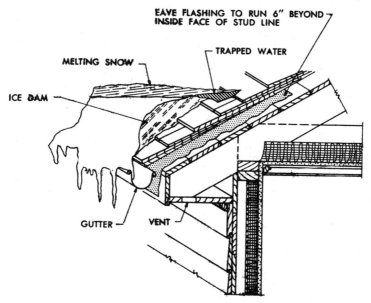

EAVE FLASHING TO RUN 6" BEYOND INSIDE FACE OF STUD LINE

TRAPPED WATER

MELTING SNOW

ICE DAM

GUTTER

VENT

Proper eave flashings prevent snow and ice dams.

defect conforms with the local building code.

Questions that are more complex or that cannot be answered by comparison with a published standard may require the services of an architect or engineer. Make sure you find a man who has a good reputation and is well qualified. The cost of his services may be small compared to the troubles that can arise from serious defects. Much helpful assistance on specific technical questions can be gained from such organizations as the National Association of Home Builders in Washington or from its local chapters in the larger cities.

SOME TIPS ON HOUSE PLANS

NOTHING is more important than careful planning when you build a house.

The house plan is a key part of planning. It helps you visualize ideas and needs, shows the relationships of the various parts of the house to the entire building, and is the means of showing others your thoughts and desires. In its finished form, it becomes a basis for financial negotiations and building.

A plan can be developed by modifying an existing plan or by using a step-by-step process in which you consider the various elements and then fit them together by trial and error—on paper rather than in construction. You save money, time, and worry when you are certain you have good plans.

Whichever your choice of procedure, your family's needs today and for several years must be considered first.

The family requirements are an expression of functional needs according to number, age, health, and occupations and include shelter from the elements, sleep, hygiene, food preparation, dining, recreation and entertainment, clothing care, study, business, and storage.

Resources and physical factors certainly will need to be considered before you make a final decision. Finances, building site, climate, utilities, experience of workmen, availability of materials, and local building codes are among the factors.

Features you will want to plan for

include adequate size of rooms and closets; a good traffic pattern; adequate natural and artificial light; convenient kitchens and other workplaces; sound and economical construction practices and materials; pleasing views; good ventilation and an adequate and economical system of environmental control; an efficient and effective plumbing layout; and interiors and exteriors that are pleasing to the eye yet durable and economical to maintain.

The services of an architect to assist in making these decisions and to develop a plan are desirable but not always economically feasible. Thus, an individual usually turns to stock plans and selects one that most completely satisfies his needs.

RECOGNIZING A GOOD interior floor plan will take a bit of practice, as any architect will tell you. But here are several basic questions you can ask yourself about any house.

Without going through any other room, can you go directly from:

living room to bathroom?
kitchen to dining area?
kitchen to bedroom area?
bedroom to bathroom (without being seen from other parts of the house)?
back or side door to kitchen?
basement to outside?

A house with a good floor plan will have living, sleeping, and working zones clearly separated from each other yet coordinated not only with the other areas but with the sun and the outdoor area.

KITCHEN: The Small Homes Council of the University of Illinois studied kitchens in more than a hundred housing developments and concluded that more than 90 percent had insufficient base cabinet storage, 77 percent had insufficient wall cabinets, and 67 percent had inadequate counter space.

In addition, a Cornell University study of efficient kitchen design recommended that the distance from refrigerator to sink to range should form a triangle with a walking distance of 12 to 20 feet. There should be counter space on both sides of the sink and alongside range and refrigerator.

Finally, the kitchen should be a bright, cheery place with proper lighting (good orientation will give the room bright morning sunlight), ventilation, and sufficient room to prepare a meal.

LIVING ROOM: Is it bright and airy? Is it large enough? Is it located so as to avoid heavy traffic? Look for extra touches of glamor in your living room, for this is the place where you will be entertaining friends and relaxing with your family.

DINING ROOM: Briefly abandoned by designers, the dining room or dining area is back, with new emphasis. Families who have lived in homes without dining rooms or areas are emphatic in stressing their importance. You should be able to reach the dining room directly from the kitchen, while the kitchen sink and dirty dishes should be screened from view. The number of persons you wish to serve, the type and amount of entertaining done, and your preferences for style of service and furniture will determine the number, size, and location of your dining areas.

Plan at least one major dining area large enough for family sitdown meals. It should be attractive, have a window if possible, be convenient to the food preparation area, and be directly accessible from the living room.

BEDROOMS: Are adult bedrooms big enough to hold a desk or vanity and chairs as well as bedroom furniture? Will your present furniture fit the new room? Children's rooms need adequate window area and enough room for study and play.

BATHROOMS: Consider your family's needs carefully when planning bathrooms. The location, size, and arrangement of your bathrooms—whether in a new or remodeled house—depend upon the uses to be made of them. The single bathroom in a small house may have to serve as a washup area for men coming in from work, as the place to bathe and change infants, and as the main laundry area or the area for hand-laundering.

Bathrooms should be centrally located and have plenty of storage space. Today, extra bathrooms are much in demand and will prove an important resale feature later.

FAMILY OR "REC" ROOM: The family or recreation room today is an important part of living for many families, since it lends itself to the ease and informality that go with today's increased leisure time and larger families. So make sure you have what you want, as well as what's necessary for your family's pleasure.

LAUNDRY: In one-story homes, a laundry near the kitchen and bathroom is ideal, but it should not be located where food is being prepared. There should be adequate storage for soap, detergents, etc.; counter space for sorting; and space enough for ironing. The clothes dryer should be located on an outside wall and vented; this is a must. Utility rooms in two-story and split-level homes should have similar facilities, while a clothes chute to the laundry area can be a boon.

STORAGE: There never seems to be enough storage area. As someone has said, a house without adequate storage is like a coat without pockets. The Southwest Research Institute made a study of the storage problem and laid down a number of rules for good storage. There should be: a clothes closet near the main entrance; storage in the living room for books, records, and fireplace wood; enough kitchen cabinets; dining area storage; utility area storage for laundry necessities; built-in bathroom storage; a large closet in each bedroom; outdoor storage for garden tools and summer furniture, especially in a one-story home. There should be a total floor area for general storage of not less than 30 square feet, exclusive of closets; 50 square feet is considered good.

WORKMANSHIP: The general level of workmanship, or "finish," is an important index of the overall quality of construction. All woodwork should be smooth, clean with neatly mitered joints, and no nail holes should be unfilled or evident. Doors and windows should fit well and should be properly weather-stripped. Bathrooms should be well finished with durable fixtures. The electric service should be able to meet the simultaneous demands of all electrical appliances and provide sufficient power to meet future needs as well. There should be plenty of switches and outlets. To check plumbing, turn on all faucets, flush the toilet at the highest house level, and watch for a water pressure loss; there should be none.

Masonry should be free of mortar and paint stains, and all mortar joints should be filled. Full mortar joints are the key to weather-tight brick walls. Tooled mortar joints press the mortar tightly against the brick and produce the best resistance to rain penetration.

The water heater should carry a 10-year guarantee, the furnace should be neatly installed with good ducting work if it is a hot air system. The basement (if any) should be checked for dryness. Wet walls or floors should be regarded as serious defects.

Minor revisions are practically unavoidable, but they should be made with care. Any change in one part of the plan may adversely affect other parts of the plan—and the result may be a disappointment. A discussion of the changes with experienced homebuilders can be helpful.

Stock plans are available through the State agricultural extension services and from various private sources, such as suppliers of building materials, magazines, and private plan services.

The Cooperative Farm Building Plan Exchange of the Department of Agriculture and the States provides many of the plans that are distributed within the States.

A few one-story plans are included here to give you a general idea of what to look for when inspecting sketches and plans. You should note that a complete set of working plans is more correctly called a set of working drawings and should include floor plans; foundation plan; elevations of various sides; elevations of kitchen and other interior details; the electrical outlet locations; a cross-section of the entire house; and sections of critical details, such as fram-

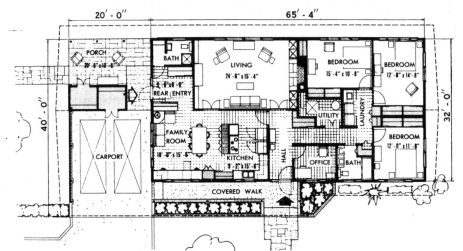

This perspective and diagrammatic floor plan aid a prospective user in determining whether he should order the complete set of plans (working drawings). It features a convenient area for Dad and the kids to hang their clothes and wash up when coming in from the field and play. The living room is free from cross traffic. Another feature that is desirable is the proximity of the kitchen to both entrances. Any plan should be carefully studied for convenience in moving from one room to the other. This plan meets the desire of some homemakers to have the laundry area convenient to the bedrooms and bath. This plan also fills the need for an office in the house.

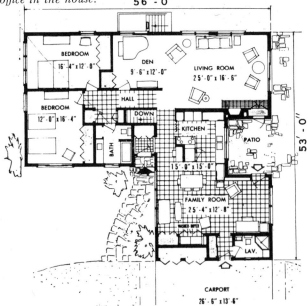

This house was planned around the kitchen. The central location of this kitchen lends itself to convenient indoor-outdoor living by linking together living areas and affords spaciousness for entertaining large groups. Bedrooms are large and are isolated from the living area. A third bedroom could be provided by adding a partition between the den and living room. When bedrooms are added, the adequacy in size of the dining area and the number of baths should be checked against the family's needs. The dining space in this plan would be adequate for a three- or four-bedroom house.

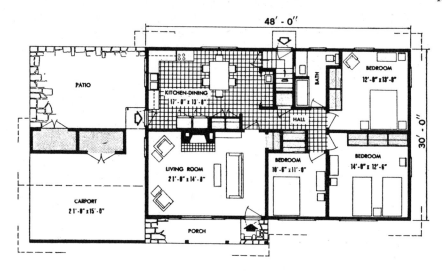

The rectangular shape of the house is economical and permits good use of all interior space. The spaciousness of the kitchen-dining area allows this room to be used for family activities. Rooms and storage areas are large. A living-room width of more than 13 feet provides greater versatility in placement of furniture. Notice the value of spotting furniture on the floor plan. The beds can be placed under the window of the front bedrooms as these windows are well above the floor. Look for window placement in your plan. These high, front windows also aid in gaining privacy, although natural light will be reduced.

ing and windows. It is usual also to have a set of supplementary specifications.

MATERIALS AND PLANS

WHEN A HOUSE is being designed, it is well to consider first the lot, so that its slope, trees, and other features can be made part of the plan.

Local regulations in many communities control the type of house to be built to make sure it conforms generally with houses already constructed.

It is good practice to follow the general architectural style of existing houses. In a community of low ramblers, for example, a two-story house should be planned so that it does not detract from the general appearance of the neighborhood.

In planning a new house, consider also the future needs of the family. To get future bedrooms, you might select

a one-and-one-half-story house rather than one of one story, but with the plumbing, heating, and electrical work only roughed in on the second floor. Thus, at small extra cost, space is at hand for extra rooms.

It is usually not possible to figure accurate costs until the contractor submits his estimate, but you may use an approximate figure of 10 to 16 dollars a square foot of living space as an initial guide.

Bear in mind, though, that cold winters, types of outside finish, a garage and porch, type of interior finish and flooring, the number of baths, a fireplace, the amount of millwork inside, and many other factors can change the basic costs a great deal.

You may get a better estimate of what your investment will be by asking about the cost of a nearby house of the general type and size you have in mind.

THE WOOD FRAME HOUSE is easy to erect. It is adaptable to many types of exterior finishes. It can be insulated easily and is relatively low in cost.

All-masonry houses are common in some localities in the South because they resist termite damage. Builders of masonry houses in the North need to consider matters of moisture and insulation. You can take the general type of construction in your area as an index of which is the most practical.

Because the wood frame house has such general use, most of the following descriptions apply to it.

First, the foundation.

If you select a slab foundation so as to have only one floor or because of a high water table, remember to include space for laundry, heating, and storage, which often are placed in the basement. Insulation is required in cold climates.

A crawl-space house has the comfort of a wood floor system, but it also requires additional area for laundry and storage and often for the heating plant. Floor insulation is required.

Often a ground cover, such as polyethylene or roll roofing, is needed to reduce problems caused by moisture in the soil.

A house with a basement can take advantage of a sloping lot that allows for full-size windows in basement rooms.

A full basement is a logical choice if ground water is not a problem and the house is in a cold climate where footings must be below frostline regardless of the type of house. Floor insulation is not normally required. A wood floor system and space for storage, a laundry, and the heating plant are a few of the advantages of a house with a basement.

A concrete slab is most adaptable to resilient-finish flooring, such as asphalt or vinyl tile. A woodblock floor can also be used.

Wood flooring often is used for houses with crawl space or basements. Beams and posts at the center of the house carry the joists. A subfloor gives a rigid platform for construction of the rest of the house. Sandwich or stressed-skin panels may be used for floors, but they are difficult to obtain in some localities. They are panels with thin facings, such as plywood, glued to a light inner wood

framework (stressed skin) or to a core of foamed plastic or paper honeycomb (sandwich).

The wall in the conventional wood frame system consists of spaced studs, exterior sheathing, and a suitable interior and exterior finish. Bracing against wind is provided by diagonal wood sheathing, diagonal braces, or large sheets of plywood or fiberboard.

The post-and-beam system with light intermediate panels sometimes is used for contemporary designs.

Roof systems frequently consist of the conventional rafter and ceiling joist or the wood truss. A sheathing of plywood or boards supplies a base for wood or asphalt shingles or other types of roofing materials.

One advantage of a truss system is that it needs no interior supports and so gives freedom in the location of walls.

An adequate overhang at the eave and gable improves the appearance of most styles of houses and protects the walls from rain and sun.

Roof slopes are determined somewhat by the architectural style of the house. A Cape Cod house may have a steeply sloped roof and dormers that can be adapted to present or future development of the second floor. A ranch type or a rambler usually has a much lower pitch. A contemporary house may have a flat or low-pitch roof, a barrel vault, or a folded plate roof design.

A barrel vault design consists of a series of half-round forms supported by interior beams and posts. A folded plate design is a series of inverted V-forms, supported in a manner similar to a barrel vault roof.

The slope of the roof usually governs the type of roofing used, whether of asphalt or wood shingles or of a built-up construction.

THE CHOICE OF MATERIALS for a house naturally affects the total cost.

We begin with the foundation and continue in the same general order that the materials are used.

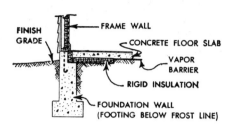

Section through wall of typical floor slab house.

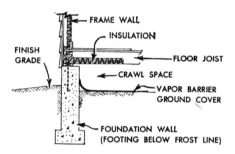

Section through wall of typical crawl space house.

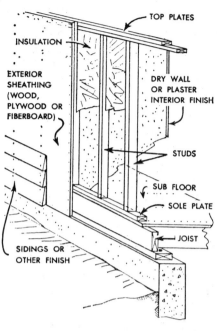

View of wood frame wall.

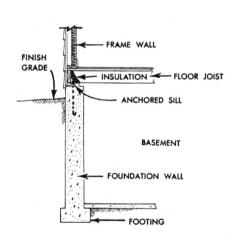

Section through wall of house with basement.

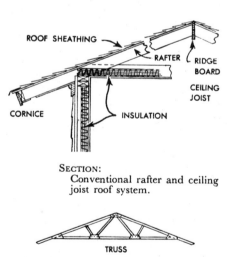

SECTION:
Conventional rafter and ceiling joist roof system.

Wood frame ceiling joists and rafters.

A well-poured concrete wall is stronger and resists penetration of moisture better than a concrete block wall without treatment. A wall of con- crete block has better insulation but must be waterproofed properly.

For a wood frame floor, tables are available to assure correct joist sizes by wood species for various spans and spacings.

Subfloors may consist of diagonally laid boards or of plywood. Either provides a good base for strip finish flooring, but a plywood base is normally required for resilient tile or other types of flooring that use adhesive for installation.

Where damp conditions prevail, as in bath and kitchen areas, it is good practice to use Exterior Grade (waterproof) plywood.

Required sizes of wood frame members to use for ceiling and roof are available in span tables.

Wall and roof sheathing is commonly wood boards, plywood, or fiberboard. Boards are used horizontally for walls and roofs, but diagonal corner braces are required for the walls to provide rigidity. No bracing is required when boards are used as diagonal wall sheathing.

Plywood is used also for wall and roof sheathing. When sheets 4 by 8 feet or longer are placed vertically on walls, with perimeter nailing, the house normally is rigid enough. If siding or shingles are to be nailed to this plywood, it should be one-half or five-eighths inch thick for the walls and three-eighths or one-half inch for the roof.

Fiberboard sheathing twenty-five thirty-seconds inch thick (or one-half-inch-thick medium-density fiberboard) commonly is used without bracing when placed vertically with perimeter nailing. When used horizontally or in 2- by 8-foot sheets, however, fiberboard and other similar materials need supplemental bracing.

In post-and-beam construction, filler wall panels usually are used between the posts. The roof can consist of 3- by 6-inch or 4- by 6-inch matched wood decking or laminated fiberboard, which also provides insulation and serves as interior finish.

Local codes sometimes specify which type of roofing materials are to be used. For moderate-to-steep roofs, wood shingles or shakes and asphalt shingles often are used, although slate and tile are

popular in many places.

For flat or very low slopes, built-up roofs normally are used. They consist of several mopped-on layers of felt paper topped with a gravel finish. Some of the new plastic films, such as polyvinyl fluoride, are used as roof coverings over plywood.

In selecting the roofing, consider the initial cost and the probable life of each type. A built-up roof costs slightly more than an asphalt shingle roof. Wood shingles also cost more than asphalt shingles, but their life is considerably greater.

As to exterior finish and millwork:

A wood window and frame may be had in such styles as double hung, where two sashes slide past each other vertically; the casement type, which opens as a door (usually outward because of better weather resistance); the awning type, which swings outward at the bottom; and fixed sash, as insulating glass in a stationary frame.

Windows and doors should be in keeping architecturally with the style of the house. A colonial design may require a double-hung or casement window cut into small lights. A rambler may take advantage of groups of the awning-type window in stacks and in double and triple widths.

Most wood sashes and frames are dipped in a water-repellent preservative, which resists moisture penetration and decay and forms a good base for subsequent costs of paint.

Storm windows or combination storms and screens are good investments in cold climates. A storm window or insulated glass reduces heat loss and minimizes condensation on the inner glass surface during cold weather.

Exterior doors normally are of a panel type or a solid-core flush type. The use of a storm or combination door is recommended in cold climates.

Select the exterior siding or covering material to accentuate the architectural features of the house. Wood materials available vary from bevel siding to vertical boards and battens with smooth or rough-sawn surfaces. Plywood with paper facings provides a good paint base. Also available are the newer plastic-faced plywoods that are said to require no refinishing for 15 years or more. Grooved or face-treated plywoods are adaptable to stained finishes.

Exterior coverings also include wood shingles and shakes installed individually or as a prefabricated section, prestained or painted. Medium-density fiberboards, primed or plastic coated, are available in packaged units. Metal, cement-asbestos, or other nonwood covering materials can also be obtained in a variety of finishes, as can the many masonry veneers, such as brick and stone, which are adaptable to wood frame structures.

Other exterior millwork used for the house includes trim and molding for the cornice and gable ends, shutters, and similar items. Many are standard millwork items and should be used whenever possible, as variations requiring special machining increase the cost.

All exterior wood finish should be free of knots, sap streaks, or flat grain, which reduce the life of the paint film.

INTERIOR FINISHING includes wall finishes, millwork, and flooring.

Thermal insulation usually is installed in the walls after rough-in work for heating and wiring has been completed. Insulating blankets or batts are made of wood fibers, cotton, or mineral or glass fibers.

Because the difference in their insulating value per inch of thickness is small, selection may be based on cost or upon the efficiency of the vapor barrier.

Foamed plastics having good insulating qualities are available and often are used for perimeter insulation or as insulation and plaster base for a concrete block wall.

Interior walls and ceilings ordinarily are plastered or have a dry-wall finish. Plaster commonly is used on a gypsum lath base with a sand finish or a putty (smooth) finish for kitchen and bath.

Dry-wall finishes are available in sheet or other forms. They include gypsum board with taped and filled joints, wood or prefinished plywood paneling, plastic-coated hardboards, and fiberboards in a number of finishes and sizes.

Advantages of dry-wall construction are that installation time is reduced from the conventional plaster finish and no moisture has to be removed. The plaster wall is more resistant to impacts, and the surface can be leveled readily.

Interior finish and millwork includes door and window trim, baseboard and shoe, interior doors, stairway assemblies, and fireplace mantels.

Perhaps the most important factors in the selection of those materials are the species of wood and the correct architectural details. For example, the selection of a painted panel door for a traditional interior indicates the use of molding, mantels, and other millwork in keeping with this style.

Millwork that is to be painted often is white pine, sweetgum, or similar species. A natural or stained finish commonly is used on such species as oak and birch. The denser species, such as oak and birch, are more resistant to denting than the pines and other softwoods but usually cost much more.

Floor coverings may consist of strip or woodblock flooring with an unfinished or prefinished surface in oak, maple, birch, beech, and other species.

Resilient flooring, such as vinyl, linoleum, cork, and rubber, also is available.

Ceramic tile, slate, and similar floors may be chosen for the bath and entryways where the presence of moisture would harm other materials.

IF YOU HAVE little or no knowledge of construction, seek the advice of a friend who has built a house and is somewhat more familiar with home-building.

Many lumber companies have planning services from which you can get advice and details of costs.

Contractors are usually willing to give suggestions and allow examination of homes they have completed.

The time and care you spend on planning before construction begins will repay you in many ways.

HOW TO STOP WOOD DECAY

WOOD ROTS when minute plants—fungi —feed on it.

Fungi, like all plants, need the right conditions of moisture, food, and temperature to grow.

Wood absorbs or gives off water vapor when the relative humidity changes. Dry wood cannot absorb enough water vapor from the air to support active decay. Liquid water, as rain, tapwater, or condensate, must be added before any great amount of decay occurs.

Any wood subject to wetting should be naturally decay resistant or treated with a wood preservative.

Redwood, cedars, and bald cypress have high resistance to decay. Douglas fir, longleaf pine, and eastern white pine have moderate resistance. Only the dark heartwood of all of them is resistant; the light-colored sapwood of these, or any other wood, will decay if wet.

A decay-susceptible wood used under a high hazard must be impregnated under pressure by a commercial treating plant. Lumber that has been pressure treated with creosote, pentachlorophenol, or one of the inorganic salts is available in most cities.

Ask your lumber dealer about local sources and the preservative that is best for a particular need.

Water-repellent preservatives are particularly valuable for siding and other woodwork exposed on the surface of a building. They also restrict entry of rain into joints.

Water-repellent preservatives often must be applied on the job by dipping, brushing, or spraying. When you apply them after construction, brush or spray all joints thoroughly.

If you buy dip-treated lumber, retreat all surfaces exposed when the lumber is cut to size.

To prevent decay in houses, use dry lumber relatively free of stain and mold. The fungi that are responsible for stain and mold make wood porous, so it wets more easily.

Stained lumber often has the beginnings of decay that you cannot see. The infections remain alive, but dormant, for years in dry lumber. Decay again starts when the wood is rewetted. Bright, kiln-dried lumber is preferable.

Some parts of buildings should be made of naturally decay-resistant or treated wood. This need varies with design and climatic zone.

Condensation is likely in crawl spaces with wet soil in winter in places with average January temperatures below 35° F. and in summer in air-conditioned houses in hot climates.

The soil in crawl spaces should be dusty dry. If it is not so with normal drainage, cover the soil with 6-mil polyethylene sheeting or 55-pound roll roofing. The seams need not be overlapped. Soil covers are effective in keeping crawl spaces dry.

Well-spaced vents through the foundation also will keep wood dry. If vents are closed during the winter and the soil is moist, however, use a soil cover.

Except for poles and piling, no wood should be in contact with soil. Siding and trim should be at least 6 inches above grade. The amount of clearance in crawl spaces is not important so long as it is big enough to permit inspection.

Remove all wood forms and grade stakes used in pouring concrete steps, porches, slabs, and foundations.

Decay in siding, trim, windows, doors, and other parts of exterior walls results mainly from rain seepage into joints. Good roof overhang is the best prevention.

Some ways in which walls can be protected are: Place trim over the ends of drop siding and metal corner caps over bevel siding. Use only lightweight breathing papers under wood siding. In warm, high-rainfall areas, avoid sheathing if feasible, because it favors moisture accumulation; when sheathing is needed, a good roof overhang is important. Use water-repellent preservatives on all joints or prime the backs and ends of siding with a lead paint.

Some types of condensation lead to decay. In cold climates (average January temperatures of 35° or below), install an effective vapor barrier on the warm side of walls and ceilings below unheated attics to prevent winter condensation.

Kitchens, laundries, and unheated attics should be well ventilated.

In hot climates, condensation may occur under floors over wet crawl spaces of air-conditioned houses. Dry out the crawl space and cool only to moderate temperatures.

SERIOUS DECAY damage is most often due to one or more of the following errors in construction or maintenance:

• Undrained soil and insufficient ventilation under houses without basements.

• Wood such as grade stakes, concrete forms, or stumps left on or in the soil under houses.

• Wood parts of the house in direct contact with the soil, especially at dirt-filled porches.

• Wood parts embedded in masonry near the ground.

• Use of unseasoned or infected lumber.

• Sheathing paper that is not sufficiently impermeable to moisture vapor.

• Inadequate flashing at windows, doors, and roof edges.

POOR PRACTICE   GOOD PRACTICE

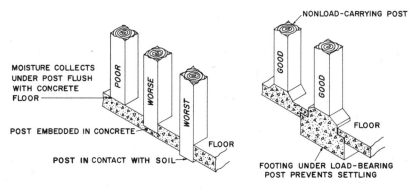

Wood posts on concrete basement floors.

POOR PRACTICE   GOOD PRACTICE

Wood floors on concrete slabs. Waterproofing membranes may be placed either in, under, or on top of the slab.

• Poor joints around windows and doors and at corners, and inadequate paint maintenance.

• Lack of rain gutters and/or roof overhang.

• Unventilated attics.

• Roof leaks; leaks around shower-bathtub combinations, kitchen fixtures, and laundry rooms.

• Failure to use preservatively treated or naturally durable wood where moisture cannot be controlled.

WHAT SHOULD YOU DO when you find decay?

Periodically inspect attics, basements, crawl spaces, and exterior woodwork for signs of wetting. Make corrections before decay requires replacement.

On painted wood, look for paint peeling at joints, rusty nails, and stain coming through the paint as signs of rain seepage.

Keep gutters and downspouts clean and free of leaks.

Inspect attics and crawl spaces in early spring and crawl spaces again in late summer in air-conditioned buildings.

If you find damp wood, dry out the crawl space or attic.

When you find signs of rain seepage in siding and trim, brush or spray a water-repellent preservative into the joints. Replace the siding boards with horizontal splits. Calk joints of wood to the masonry. Reseal joints in gravel stops as often as necessary to prevent leakage.

If decay spots occur frequently in siding as a result of wetting by rain, the cheapest correction is to cover it with asbestos-cement or cedar shingles. Follow the manufacturer's recommendations.

In cold climates, winter condensation may be involved, however. In that event, covering the siding will increase the trouble unless it is corrected by applying a vapor seal on the inner wall.

Suspect condensation in winter if a general paint failure is expressly troublesome on north walls and dark stains develop from moisture seeping out from under the siding.

Replace steps and porchs, when decay occurs, with decay-resistant material—naturally decay-resistant or treated wood, concrete, brick, stone, and metal.

ACTION AGAINST TERMITES

GROUND-NESTING TERMITES occur throughout the United States. They flourish in the South Atlantic and Gulf Coast States and California.

Their chief food is cellulose obtained from wood, as in the woodwork of buildings.

One way to thwart the immense damage they do is to construct buildings properly.

Another way is to treat the soil near foundations and under concrete slabs with chemicals.

Action against them begins with knowing what they are.

Termites are social insects, which live in colonies or nests in the soil, from which they obtain moisture.

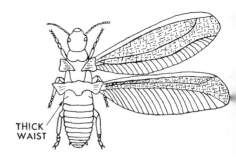

Winged reproductive termite.

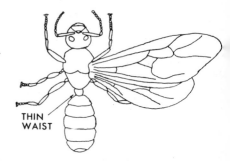

Winged reproductive ant.

The adult workers and soldiers are wingless, grayish white, and similar in appearance. The soldiers have much larger heads and longer mandibles, or jaws, than the workers.

The workers are the ones that destroy wood and are usually seen when a piece of infested wood is examined.

The reproductives, or sexual adults, have yellow-brown to black bodies and two pairs of long, whitish, opaque wings of equal size.

They often are mistaken for ants, but the reproductive forms of true ants have two pairs of transparent wings of unequal size. Termites have thick waistlines. Ants have thin waistlines.

The first signs of an infestation may be the swarming of larger numbers of winged reproductives from a building or their discarded wings on the floor beneath doors and windows or the presence of flattened earthen shelter tubes over the surface of foundations.

Often you cannot see the damage on the surface of the wood. You have to look inside.

The workers build galleries within the materials they attack. Occasionally they honeycomb timbers completely and leave little more than a thin shell. Grayish specks of excrement and earth cover the inside of the galleries.

Subterranean termites (ground nesting) do not reduce the wood to a powdery mass or push wood particles to the outside, as do some other wood-boring insects.

Termites enter buildings through flat earthen shelter tubes that the workers construct over the surface of foundations; through cracks and joints and around plumbing in concrete slabs; and through wood that connects the soil with the woodwork of the building.

SOME PREVENTIVE MEASURES:

• Remove all tree roots, stumps, and other wood debris from the building site before construction starts. Remove grade stakes, frame boards, and scraps of lumber. If no wood is left in or on the soil, the danger of an infestation is reduced.

• Prevent moisture from accumulating in the soil under a building. Slope the soil surface so that moisture will drain away from the building.

• Choose carefully the kind of foundation. Poured concrete foundations properly reinforced are best. If hollow blocks or brick foundations or piers are used, cap them with at least 4 inches of reinforced poured concrete or fill the top course of blocks and all joints completely with concrete to prevent attack through poor mortar and through hollows in blocks.

• The beams and girders of buildings with crawl space under them should be at least 12 inches above the ground. The bottom of floor joists should be at least 18 inches above the ground. Make the outside gradeline at least 6 inches below all exterior woodwork.

• Provide good ventilation underneath buildings with crawl space.

Water emulsions of any of these formulations will give many years of protection:

Aldrin, 0.5 percent; chlordane, 1 percent; dieldrin, 0.5 percent; and heptachlor, 0.5 percent. These chemicals are sold as concentrated solutions which can be diluted with water to the desired concentrations.

Apply 4 gallons of the water emulsion per 10 linear feet to the soil along the inside and outside of perimeter foundation, along interior foundation, and around the places where plumbing comes through the slab. Apply 1 gallon per 10 square feet as an overall treatment.

REMEDIAL MEASURES if your house is infested with termites:

• Remove all scraps of wood, form-boards, and other debris containing cellulose from under and near the building.

• Remove any wooden units, such as trellises, that connect the ground to the woodwork of the building, and replace them so as to break those contacts.

• Replace structurally weakened sill, joists, flooring, and such with sound material.

• Fill voids, cracks, or expansion

joints in concrete or masonry with cement or roofing-grade coal tar pitch.
• Provide drainage and ventilation.

THE CHEMICALS USED to prevent attack can be used also to control existing infestations. The buildings with crawl spaces very often can be treated easily and effectively in these ways:

Dig trenches 6 to 8 inches wide around all piers and pipes and along both the inside and outside of all foundation walls. For poured concrete foundations, the trench need be only 3 to 4 inches deep. For foundations of brick and of hollow block masonry, it should be at least 12 inches deep. Where the footing is more than 12 inches deep, use a crowbar, pipe, or rod to make holes about a foot apart, and extend them from the bottom of the trench to the footing. This will prevent termites from gaining hidden entry to the building through voids in these types of foundations. Never dig the trench below the top of the footing.

Pour the chemicals into the trench at the rate of 4 gallons per 10 linear feet for each foot of depth. If the trench is deep, apply the chemical to alternate layers of about 6 inches of oil.

To treat basements, dig a trench 6 to 8 inches wide and about a foot deep along the outside wall and close to it. Then with a crowbar, pipe, or rod, make holes about a foot apart from the bottom of the trench to the footing. Pour the chemical into the trench at the rate of 4 gallons per 10 linear feet for each foot of depth from grade to footing; alternately replace and treat 6-inch layers of soil.

DRYWOOD TERMITES and powder-post beetles also attack the woodwork of buildings. Their damage may be mistaken for that caused by subterranean termites.

Drywood termites occur most abundantly in southern Florida and along the coast of California. They do not require contact with the soil as do the subterranean forms.

Their damage can be recognized by the clean cavities cut across the grain in comparatively solid wood and the presence of slightly compressed pellets in the cavities. Some of the pellets are pushed outside through small openings and often form piles on surfaces below.

Localized infestations can be controlled by injecting 5 percent DDT, 2 percent chlordane, or 5 percent pentachlorophenol in No. 2 fuel oil into the cavities or by thoroughly brushing the surface with one or more applications.

POWDER-POST BEETLES occur throughout the United States. They attack both softwoods and hardwoods. The adult insects are seldom seen.

The whitish larvae, or grubs, work within the wood and reduce it to fine or to coarse powder, which is packed in the galleries or pushed to the exterior through small holes. The presence of this dust on the surface usually is the first sign of an infestation.

You can control local infestation by brushing or spraying the infested places thoroughly with 5 percent DDT, 2 percent chlordane, or 0.5 percent dieldrin in No. 2 fuel oil or deodorized kerosene. More than one application may be necessary if the infestation is deep seated.

If infestations of drywood termites or powder-post beetles are spread through a building, fumigation is the most practical method of control.

The service of a licensed pest control operator is required for fumigation.

All the chemicals mentioned are poisonous to people and animals. Handle them carefully. If the chemicals accidentally come in contact with skin or eyes, wash the skin immediately with warm, soapy water and the eyes with plenty of water or with a solution containing a teaspoonful of boric acid per glassful of warm water.

GOOD LIGHTING

GOOD LIGHTING adds to the beauty, cheer, comfort, convenience, safety, and value of your home.

It helps you move about and work rapidly and safely, do tasks when and where you wish, protect eyes from strain, and relax or concentrate.

To obtain those benefits, you need good task (or local) lighting and general background lighting—each helping the other—to attain proper levels and balance for usual activities.

For most tasks, soft, diffused light from a fairly large or long source helps avoid spotty or line reflections and harsh shadows, but fine handsewing or detailed hobby work may require some strong, direct, additional light to bring out details.

Choose and place local task lighting equipment in relation to eye levels— seated or standing. Average eye heights are 40 to 42 inches for women and men seated in lounge chairs and 61 to 64 inches when they are standing.

Workplaces must be well lighted, but when the general lighting is good, local light is needed only on the task you are doing.

The place where you do the work is important, too. For example, you can make good use of a task light (because of reflection) by placing a desk, sewing center, or workbench against a wall or in a corner.

Areas near the task should not be brighter than the task area and should not be less than one-third as bright if the task is to take long. If desk tops are dark, say, light-colored blotters, which reflect light, help get this relationship.

WHEN YOU choose lights, consider color effects as well as the amount of light.

Many bulb and tube finishes enhance cool or warm colors, but some affect the output of light considerably.

Choose white or warm white tubes and inside-frosted and white bulbs for the most efficient light, and deluxe warm or cool white tubes or tinted bulbs to bring out colors of furnishings.

Avoid daylight tubes or bulbs unflattering to skin, food, and furnishings.

Color is an important aid to light. For ceilings, choose white (for work areas), near-white, or pale tints.

Elsewhere, light-to-medium ranges reflect light fairly well and make rooms seem larger.

Dark colors absorb and waste light, as dust and dirt do. Dark-light contrasts, shiny finishes, and glare are an-

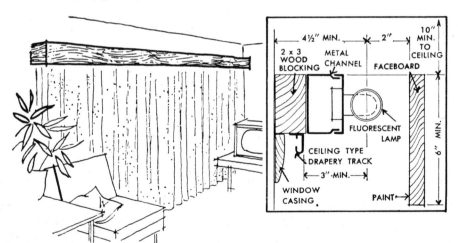

Valances are usually used at windows with draperies. The valances provide up-light, which reflects off ceiling for general lighting and down-light for drapery accent. When closer to ceiling than 10 inches, use closed top to eliminate annoying ceiling brightness.

High wall brackets provide both up and down light for general room lighting. Used on interior wall to balance window valance both architecturally and in lighting distribution. Mounting height may be determined by window or door height, should never be less than 65 inches unless used as low bracket over buffet, 60; sofa, 55-up; bed, 52; range, 58; also 15-18 inches above desk, centered over work.

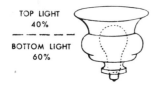

TOP LIGHT
40%

BOTTOM LIGHT
60%

CLM GLASS DIFFUSER "flared-top; crown"

Blown white glass—10% more light than best bowl diffuser; most diffused light on reading surface. Shields bulb at top.

Top	*Bulb Wattage*
8 in.	50–100–150, 50–200–250
10	100–200–300, 50–100–150

Shade: 9–10 inches up at center depth, 16–18 in diameter.

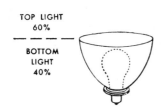

TOP LIGHT
60%

BOTTOM LIGHT
40%

GLASS OR PLASTIC BOWL "open-bowl; bowl-shape"

Thin white glass best: 20% more light than thickest pressed glass. Plastic bowl is cheaper but heat may discolor it if bulb wattage is high.

Top	*Glass*	*Plastic*
6 in.	100w	75–100w
8	150w	100–150w
9¼	200w	150w
10	300w	200–300w
11½*		50/150w

*Shade-bowl, mesh disk.
Shade: 6–10 inches deep; 10–18, bottom diameter.

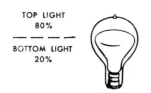

TOP LIGHT
80%

BOTTOM LIGHT
20%

R–40 WHITE INDIRECT BULB IN WIDE HARP

Whiteness and large size (5-inch across) help diffuse light and direct much up to ceiling, adding to general lighting. Uses: Casual reading, short-time studying, most types of sewing. Harp change is easy. Bulb comes in 150, or 50–100–150 watt.
Shade: 8–10 inches up at center depth, 13–18 in diameter.

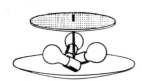

PLASTIC DISK DIFFUSER

May have metal disk or plastic disk over bulb. Plastic or fiberglass disk is below bulb(s), 1 inch above bottom of shade for most light. 1-socket (3-step type if 3-light bulb used): 150 or 200 watt, 50–100–150 watt, 50–200–250 watt. Multi-socket (3-step): 3 bulbs, 60w each.
Shade: 6–8 inches deep; 14–18, bottom diameter.

Undershade diffusers soften and spread light in portable lamps and in fixtures of open-bowl or disk types. Better Light Better Sight study lamps, introduced in 1965, use inverted metal cone reflectors or prismatic refractors to improve lighting further for close-seeing tasks.

noying and can make even simple tasks more difficult.

Portable lamps or special-purpose fixtures that direct light over task areas provide light for close work. Well-designed types contribute to balanced lighting around tasks and add to the overall effectiveness of room lighting.

For long-range value, economy, and comfort, give consideration to the types and location of fixtures and portable equipment. They should be fairly near the ceilings, walls, objects, or people that you are trying to light. Well planned and balanced lighting in each room creates a harmonious decorative

effect throughout the house.

Off-center and suspended equipment brings light close to the task and adds decorative interest but may limit the rearrangement of furnishings. Hanging heights range from 30 to 36 inches over a dining table to 48 inches above laundry centers or workshop benches.

Just as daylight needs some window treatments for full effectiveness, artificial light needs improving devices. Some of these are bulb finishes, bowls, globes, shades, shields, louvers, and reflectors. They enlarge the source, conceal it, soften or diffuse the light, reflect and direct it, and increase its amount where needed.

Dimmers and step switches let you dim or brighten light. Adjustable positioning devices also are useful. These include reels or pulleys with counter-weights to raise or lower fixtures and wall lamps; adjustable height shafts in floor and table lamp bases; and various swing-arm and other swivel devices or flexible shafts that bring light closer to work or help you to position it to decrease reflected glare or shadows on your work.

A number of materials make equip ment attactive and efficient. Many light-diffusing plastics and white or milky glass, for example, are superior to etched or clear glassware. Also good are laminated combinations of fabric, plastic, fiberglass, or paper. Fabrics, stitched (not glued) for washability, are satisfactory for lampshades and fixture shields.

GOOD FIXTURES for all style periods are available. Large or long ones are good buys that should maintain their value, since they follow room proportions and couple low brightness with a wide light spread.

Recessed fixtures require thoughtful handling; near-white ceilings, lighted from below, and fairly light floors can dispel gloom. One such fixture should be used for each 40 to 50 square feet.

Especially good are inconspicuous fluorescent types. For local light, low brackets and built-in soffits—over sinks, buffets, sofas, and desks—bring the light close to the subject. For general lighting, window valances, ceiling cornices, coves, and other ceiling units produce an overall lighting effect to balance local lighting.

Small to medium rooms require 3 to 8 feet of shielded tubes when they are used with a ceiling fixture, or 6 to 16 feet without one. Large rooms with no ceiling fixture should average about 1 foot of tube for each 15 square feet of floorspace—roughly 16 to 20 feet of tubes for large living rooms. Use 1.5-inch (T-12) tubes unless space demands tubes 1 inch (T-8) in diameter.

Large panels and luminous ceilings with tubes installed between ceiling beams are practical in work areas and elsewhere if they have dimmers. Plastic diffusers in building dimensions, suspended on hangers below the tubes, make a smooth, easily maintained installation. In building or remodeling, balance high initial costs against other costs of ceiling finishing, fixtures, and future maintenance.

The main problem with flourescent lighting is choosing all fixtures of the right size and quality, because you cannot change the light output later, as you can with incandescent types. Ask about radio-interference suppressors, sound rating, starting speed, and dimming possibilities before you buy fluorescent fixtures.

WELL-STYLED LAMPS, all appropriately spaced, can add to the attractiveness of a room while meeting the requirements of task lighting.

The marks of good lamps are: Bulbs located low in the shade; undershade device to reflect, refract, or diffuse the

FOR PERSONAL GROOMING
Bathroom or dressing room soffits are designed to light user's face, hair. Therefore, cover bottom opening· with highly diffusing material which will scatter light over face, top of head. Wide bottom opening (14–18 inches) helps also. Light-colored countertop or sink reflects light under chin.

light; broad, white-lined shades open at the top; harmonious shades; and good proportions that are neither squat nor gigantic.

Thin, long, portable lamps fit into tight places, under cabinets, and in, on, or behind furniture or room dividers. Average one lamp for each 40 to 50 square feet of floorspace.

COMMON incandescent bulbs are inexpensive, relatively hot, small, high-brightness sources. Their average life is 750 to 1 thousand hours. Ratings of 1,200-2,500 hours sacrifice some light output for longer life.

Bulb failures occur early when house voltage exceeds V-rating (115-130), as marked on the bulb, or the bulb overheats in a small or poorly ventilated fixture, or if it receives rough service or unusual vibration.

At extra cost, you can buy three-light or high-low bulbs to change light levels, and large bulbs with special finishes to lower brightness.

Comparatively, fluorescent sources—tubes, circles, or square panels—give greater light spread at lower brightness. They emit 3 to 4 times as much light and last 6 to 10 times as long as incandescent bulbs. They also feel cooler. Their average life of 7,500 hours balances against a higher initial cost. Frequent starting shortens the life of fluorescent tubes, however.

WHEN YOU BUY a new house or redecorate an older one, you often can offset the expense of adequate lighting equipment with a little ingenuity in modernizing or making equipment.

To obtain portable equipment inexpensively, consider buying assembly kits for study, wall, and vanity lamps or improving poor lamps.

Lamp improvers include large R-40 (5-inch diameter) white indirect bulbs and wide harps; threaded holders and bowls, or disk diffusers; shade risers; miscellaneous oil-lamp converters; and shade or disk materials.

Spray paint in color or metallic finishes gives old equipment a new look or new efficiency, as when you spray paper or metal lampshade liners white.

Fixture improvers include special fixture bulbs, candle shades, screw-in adapters, plastic converters, or diffusing lanterns (12 to 24 inches across), and other shielding material.

For help on how to improve, make, or choose equipment and where to put it, consult your power distributor, home extension agents, homemaking and shop teachers, and lighting dealers and distributors.

When buying equipment, rely on the labels of "UL" (Underwriters' Laboratories, Inc.) for safety testing, "ETL" (Electrical Testing Laboratories, Inc.) for quality testing for certified equipment programs: BLBS (Better Light Better Sight Bureau)—study lamps with reflectors or prismatic refractors under shades; CBM (Certified Ballast Manufacturers)—fluorescent ballasts; CLM (Certified Lamp Makers)—lamps, often special-order item; RLM (Reflector Lighting Equipment Manufacturers)—reflectors designed to specifications of the RLM Standards Institute, Inc., and used in workrooms with whitened-bowl or silvered-bowl bulbs and for outdoor equipment.

For further information on home lighting, booklets are available at a low cost from the American Home Lighting Institute and the Illuminating Engineering Society.

When you have met lighting needs for safety—outdoors, entries, stairs, halls, hazardous work—and for eyesight protection at main activity locations of all family members, you can concentrate on accent lighting, say, picture lighting, or decorative wall panels, garden lighting, and other delights of light for living.

A GUIDE TO WIRING

To ADEQUACY, convenience, and safety of electric wiring, you should add a fourth requirement when you buy or plan a house—expandability, to take care of future needs.

It is best to have a professional electrician install the wiring in your house, but some knowledge of the functions and capabilities of electric systems will help you when you contract for the installation and help you use electricity safely and economically.

To meet all your needs for electricity, you should have enough lighting and general-purpose outlets and circuits to spread the load evenly.

The National Electrical Code, a recognized authority, has given guidelines as to needs and safe practices, although the code requirements in your own locality may differ in some details.

To be fully adequate, the minimum lighting in a house is 3 watts to the square foot of building area. The location of outlets is important.

Receptacle outlets on 15- or 20-ampere branch circuits must be spaced no more than 12 feet apart, so that no point on the wall measured along the floorline will be more than 6 feet from an outlet.

Outlets in the kitchen, laundry, pantry, dining room, and breakfast room should be equally divided between two or more 20-ampere branch circuits. This provision is required of kitchen outlets. Many homeowners have each kitchen outlet installed on an individual circuit. That increases costs of installation, but the extra convenience is worth the difference.

For safety, all outlets should be grounded. Grounding-type outlets permit the connection of parallel-blade, two-wire cords and plugs used on appliances, as well as three-wire plugs for cords that connect devices that must be grounded.

Ceiling outlets for lighting should be centered in bedrooms, dens, kitchens, dining and living rooms, halls, passageways, and stairways.

Lights in bathrooms are placed above mirrored cabinets and overhead in shower stalls. Work areas in kitchens, laundries, and home workshops need light directly over task areas.

Overhead lighting is recommended in basements and recreation rooms.

Outlets for lights are desirable over or alongside each outside entryway to the house and for floodlights around the dwelling.

Outlets for the switch control of lights are placed in the wall about 48 inches above the floor at the lock side of entrances.

Three-way and four-way switches are needed to control lights from two or more locations. These may be at entry points to the living room, dining room, kitchen, at the top and bottom of stairways, and at inside and outside entrances to the basement and recreation room. Switch control for outside floodlighting outlets may be desired in the master bedroom.

At least one receptacle outlet for floor or table lamps in the living room should be controlled by a switch, when ceiling outlets are not used. Here, silent-type or mercury switches may be desired.

Receptacle outlets should be installed in the wall, 18 inches above the floor in bedrooms, living room, den, and dining room. They should be no more than 12 feet apart. Additional outlets take care of varied arrangements of furniture.

One wall outlet in the dining room should be above table height to connect portable cooking or warming appliances at the table.

In kitchen and work areas, receptacle outlets should be 8 inches above the worktable level. Clock outlets in kitchen and workshop areas do not need a switch.

Weatherproof outlets are desirable on the driveway side of the house and on the opposite side about 4 feet above ground.

Additional weatherproof outlets may be needed in outside walls of the house for patios or porches.

Bathrooms may require an outlet for a heater. The frame of electric space heaters must be grounded for safety. Receptacles for electric shavers and the like may be incorporated in the lighting fixture over the mirror.

Switches and receptacles of specification grade work better and last longer at only a slight increase in cost.

Thought should be given to the

proper selection of wire sizes in circuits throughout the home. General-purpose circuits and lighting circuits, for instance, require No. 12 (copper) wire or more. The wire sizes are increased wherever heavier loads for larger appliances and equipment are expected.

In the kitchen and workshop, individual circuits for each receptacle provide minimum interruption in the use of appliances. Circuits of 120 volts are a minimum requirement there. They include outlets for the iron, automatic washer, garbage disposer, dishwasher, roaster, waffle baker, food freezer, and the like.

Individual power circuits of 240 volts are needed for such major appliances as an electric range or tabletop cooking unit, wall oven, clothes drier, space heater, and large air-conditioning equipment.

Both fuses and circuit breakers provide acceptable protection against overloading. Only the procedure used to restore interrupted service varies. A blown fuse must be replaced with a new one of like capacity.

Circuit breakers require the operation of a toggle switch to restore a circuit connection after the cause of the interruption has been removed.

The cabinet door of each load center has a table of numbered circuits. Your wireman should list on this table exactly which area or individual appliance is served by each circuit. In addition, at least two 120-volt and one 240-volt spare circuit spaces should be allowed for future circuits.

Examples of methods used to calculate required circuits, feeders, and main services may be found in the *National Electrical Code,* a copy of which may be obtained at small cost from your State fire insurance rating bureau.

Other helpful guides may be had from the Industry Committee on Interior Wiring and from the National Electrical Manufacturers Association, 155 East 44th Street, New York, N.Y., 10017.

Finally, require your wireman to have his work checked and inspected for safety by an authorized inspector and furnish you with a copy of the certificate of approval.

KEYS TO ECONOMIC HEATING

BENJAMIN FRANKLIN once wrote: "In traveling I have observed that in those parts where the inhabitants can have neither wood, nor coal, nor turf without excessive prices the working people live in miserable hovels, or are ragged and have nothing comfortable about them. But when fuel is cheap (or where they have the art of managing it to advantage) they are well-furnished with necessaries and have decent habitations."

Fortunately in our country cheap heating is available but the "art of managing it to advantage" is not very well understood by the American consumer.

The methods you use to heat and cool your house depend largely on how comfortable you wish to be and how much you can afford to spend.

Central heating or complete house heating systems provide the comfort most Americans want. They are a good investment in all but the lowest cost houses and in warm climates. Thermostats make their operation almost automatic.

FORCED-WARM-AIR systems with blowers to circulate the air mechanically are the most popular. The type with ducts distributes filtered air to all rooms and provides uniform temperatures in a properly built house.

Furnaces for warm-air systems, using gas, oil, or electrical resistance heaters, heat quickly. This is a desirable feature for heating on chilly fall and spring mornings.

A basement is the best place for the furnace. If only crawl space is available, a horizontal type of furnace may be hung under the floor; there should be plenty of room to get to the furnace to service and repair it.

Automatic oil heating systems with

ducts usually cost 800 to 1,500 dollars installed in the average three- or four-bedroom house. Gas-fired and electric furnaces may cost less.

Electric furnaces need no vents and require no maintenance other than servicing the fan, motor, and filters.

The installed costs of heating systems vary according to type of fuel, the duct system, climate, and labor rates.

When you compare installed costs, do not forget to include the cost of a larger capacity electrical system if one is needed for an electric furnace.

Do not buy too small a furnace because of a slightly lower price; you will not get the quick heat desired at times, you may use more fuel in the long run, and the heat exchanger may not last so long.

On the other hand, too large a furnace is inefficient and may not provide even temperatures.

Get a reputable dealer to figure the size you need.

In most central warm-air systems, the air is filtered through inexpensive replaceable or washable filters.

Electronic air cleaners remove pollen, fine dust, and other irritants that pass through ordinary filters and thus are especially desirable for persons with respiratory ailments. In the most efficient type, particles in the air are electrically charged before the air passes between closely spaced electrically charged plates. The cost installed, with automatic washing and drying of the cleaner, runs about 600 dollars, or perhaps 25 percent less without the automatic feature.

Compact oil or gas forced-warm-air furnaces may be installed on the floor of the house in a closet or other recess at less cost than a central system with furnace in the basement.

Some have ducts running through the attic to discharge heated air through a diffuser in the ceiling of each room. The ducts should be tight and heavily insulated to save fuel.

Others have no ducts, but discharge the heat from a large register at the top of the furnace. This type is somewhat similar to a circulator heater with

fan and heats best in an open-type plan where few partitions interfere with circulation throughout the house.

Without cold air return ducts, temperatures are less uniform. The cold air is drawn along the floor from the cooler outside walls, and floors may be cold. This applies also to circulator heaters even when equipped with electrically driven fans.

Furnaces mounted on the floor of the house may be noisier than basement installations, as the furnace is closer to the occupants.

If you plan to build a house with a concrete floor, you can use a downdraft furnace and form the ducts into the concrete floor. Provide openings for registers along outside walls. This system gives a warm floor and satisfactory heating.

HOT WATER SYSTEMS provide uniform heat, especially with baseboard convectors or a piping system in the floor.

They are compact and require little space for the piping. Two-pipe systems are best. In houses with basements, they eliminate ducts, which may interfere with headroom and any plans to finish the ceiling.

The baseboard convector is a hollow unit that looks like a baseboard and replaces the wood baseboard on outside walls. Cool air at the floor is warmed by passing over finned tubes in the unit.

Heating is fairly quick in the modern hot water systems, now often called hydronic systems. Boilers are small, and the hot water is circulated quickly by an electrically driven pump. The cost using baseboard convectors is slightly higher than a good forced-warm-air system.

HEATING the entire house electrically is economical only in communities where rates are low.

Some power suppliers have rates as low as 1 to 1.3 cents per kilowatt-hour (kw.-hr.) above a specified minimum power usage. Seasonal costs of heating vary in different climates.

Your local power supplier can give

you typical costs and may give you a guaranteed maximum cost per month or annually.

Baseboard heaters or cables in the ceiling are especially satisfactory for heating the entire house. They provide uniform temperatures and are noiseless. Usually these types are controlled by a wall thermostat in each room.

Some housewives object to the baseboard type because they interfere with floor-length draperies.

Baseboard and ceiling cable installations usually run from 50 to 75 dollars a room.

Electric wall heaters with or without fans and with self-contained thermostats sometimes are used, but may not provide uniform temperatures except in small rooms.

Heat pumps, which heat in winter and cool in summer, are becoming more popular. They cost less to operate in winter than when heat is supplied entirely by electrical resistance heaters.

Consult your local power supplier before adding large electric heaters or installing a complete system. You may need larger service entrance wiring and distribution panel.

YOUR HOUSE must be properly insulated to get comfortable, uniform temperatures and comfortable heating bills.

Four inches of insulation in the ceiling and 3 inches in walls is the minimum recommended for most types of heating.

Electricity costs more per unit of heat (British thermal unit, or B.t.u.) than other fuels. If you use electrical heating, place at least 6 inches of insulation in the ceiling and 4 inches in walls and in floors with vented crawl space.

Some manufacturers stamp their insulation with an "R" value. A high "R" value means thicker, better insulation. For electrical heating, use an "R" value of 19 in ceilings, 11 in walls, and 13 in floors as a minimum.

In the colder climates, more insulation is desirable, particularly in ceilings. In new construction, be sure that there is insulation around the perimeter of concrete slab floors on grade.

Vapor barriers are essential in most areas of the country; otherwise, moisture passing through the construction from inside to outside may condense that reduces insulative value and eventually causes the insulation and structure to deteriorate.

Some insulation batts and blankets are made with vapor barriers, but it is almost impossible to seal all joints. Have an additional barrier placed between the inside finish and the insulation. Use polyethylene· film, metal foil, or duplex kraft paper with asphalt between laminations.

Have all joints sealed, even around light switches and electrical outlets, with special tape.

Some paints on interior surfaces are fairly effective. Two or three coats of alkyd gloss, semigloss primer-sealer plus enamel, or rubber-resin lacquer paint are needed.

Cover the ground of a crawl space with heavy plastic film, roll roofing, or other vaporproof material to reduce transfer of moisture from the ground to the wood floor above. Asphalt-saturated building felt is not effective.

You should also weatherstrip windows and doors and calk cracks between the frames and the siding or masonry walls to reduce air leakage.

Flexible weatherstripping of felt, rubber, or plastic may be easier to install on doors than interlocking metal or spring metal friction types but may need replacing oftener.

Storm windows and doors are essential in cold climates. For example, about 14 times as much heat goes through a single pane of glass per square foot as a wood frame wall with 3 inches of insulation.

Thus, if the house has large areas of glass, the total heat loss is high even with insulated walls unless the loss is reduced by use of storm windows or double-pane insulating glass.

You feel colder, too, with the single thickness of glass, because the body radiates heat to the cold glass surface.

Glass storm windows present problems of breakage and of storage in summer. Storm windows of plastic film are cheaper and light in weight, but the plastic has limited life. They must be handled carefully to avoid puncturing.

Storm windows must fit tightly. If they leak air, you lose the effectiveness of the dead-air space formed between the windows.

HUMIDITY CONTROL in the house is difficult.

The average person is comfortable if temperatures are within 70° to 75°F., and the relative humidity is between 25 and 60 percent.

Because high humidities may cause condensation on windows and sometimes cold walls in winter, humidity of less than 40 percent is desirable.

Exhaust fans operated occasionally in the bathroom, kitchen, and laundry room help remove moisture.

Condensation can be reduced if the heating system is designed so that warm air sweeps over window areas. Tight storm windows help solve the problem.

Electrically driven dehumidifiers are helpful in winter and summer if the humidity is too high. They reduce mildew and dampness during summer, especially in basements where moisture tends to condense on the cooler walls and floors.

Keep windows closed when dehumidifiers are operating.

If the humidity is not high enough in winter, use a humidifier in the furnace if you have a warm-air heating system.

Some humidifiers have absorptive plates that extend into the airstream from the humidifier water pan. The plates need replacing occasionally. The mechanical atomizing type of humidifier is better but is more expensive.

Vapor barriers in the construction and tight doors and windows will help retain moisture in the house.

COOLING YOUR HOUSE

SOME TIPS that will help you keep your house cooler in summer:

• Orient the house (if you are building) with its long axis east and west if possible. If you do not plan to have mechanical air conditioning, make certain of good cross-ventilation and orient the house to take advantage of prevailing breezes.

• Arrange shrubs and hedges so they will not shut off the breezes.

• Avoid large glass areas in east and west walls, where they are harder to protect against sun.

• Shade the south windows with wide eaves or overhangs.

• Shade the house with deciduous trees and shrubs (which lose their leaves) and let in sunshine during the winter.

• Use awnings over the windows or louvered bar screens if it is not feasible to have trees or overhangs for shade.

• Use light-colored roofing materials, light paint on exterior walls, and light-colored shades and draperies or curtains.

• Insulate the house if it is not already insulated. Use the same thicknesses of insulation for cooling as for heating.

• High-pitched roofs are cooler than low-pitched ones.

• Avoid large paved areas next to the house because they may reflect the sun's rays into the house.

WINDOW OR ATTIC FANS may be used where nighttime temperatures drop sufficiently to cool the house. A *good* room fan has large blades, turns at about 1,000 r.p.m. (it may have a speed adjustment), operates quietly, and has an oscillating mechanism. It will cost from $35 for a table model to $50 for a 7-foot, pedestal floor model.

Attic and window fans exchange inside air for outside air. You can use them for night cooling, or whenever the temperature inside your home is greater than the temperature outside. When you have cooled your house at night, keep the windows and doors closed during the next day for as long as it is cooler inside than out.

You will find that window fans are easier to install than attic fans—no

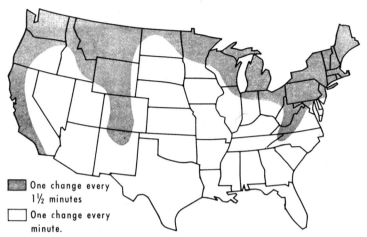

One change every
1½ minutes

One change every
minute.

Minimum air changes recommended for fan cooling.

construction is required—but you will also find that they are usually noisier.

Fans are rated by the amount of air they move in cubic feet per minute (c.f.m.). But there are several different tests for determining that rating and therefore a single fan may have as many as four different c.f.m. ratings from four different tests.

Determining the size of the attic or window fan you will need for your house requires the help of an engineer (some retail firms provide this service). The air inlets and outlets, the horsepower of the fan motor, and the revolutions per minute of the fan blade must be taken into consideration. You can, however, determine the approximate size yourself and probably get satisfactory results.

To determine the size fan you will need to—

Find the volume of the area you want to cool. Multiply the length of the room by the width. Then multiply that by the height.

If you live in the shaded area of the accompanying map, divide the volume by 1.5. This will give you a minimum c.f.m. requirement. If you live in the unshaded area, your minimum c.f.m. requirement will be the same as the volume you want cooled.

Pick a fan that has a c.f.m. rating higher than your c.f.m. requirement—

a larger rating will allow for slight differences in test procedure and efficiency.

If you choose a fan that is driven with pulleys and a belt, rather than one that is driven directly by the motor, the size of the pulleys can be varied slightly to adjust the amount of air moved. Models with two- and three-speed motors are also available.

Normally, a ⅛-horsepower, 30- to 36-inch attic fan will provide 40 air changes per hour for the average 3-bedroom house. This is sufficient ventilation in the shaded area. Such a fan will cost from $60 up.

A larger attic fan is required in the unshaded area—a ⅓- or ½-horsepower, 36- to 42-inch fan that will normally provide 60 air changes per hour for the average 3-bedroom house. It will cost from $70 up.

Window fans are usually smaller. They range in size from 20 to 30 inches. The 20-inch size is the most popular and it will generally provide about 23 air changes per hour for the average 3-bedroom house. Twenty-inch window fans cost from $20 up.

You can also remove accumulated attic heat during the day with an attic fan. Often an attic is 25° hotter or more than outside. Even if the ceiling of your house is insulated, this additional heat will warm your house.

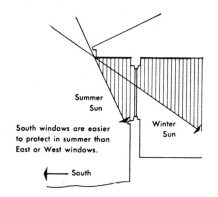

Roof overhang keeps out summer sun and lets in winter sun.

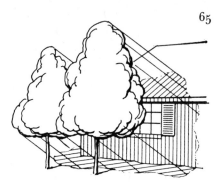

Shade from trees and large shrubs help keep house cool. Use trees that lose leaves in winter to let sun in.

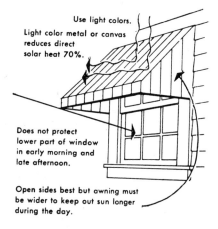

Awnings help keep house cool.

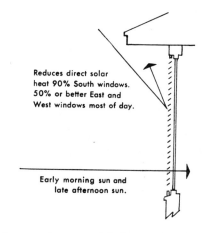

Louver or bar screens help keep out heat from sun.

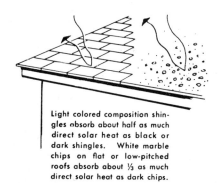

Light colors on roofs and walls reflect heat from the sun.

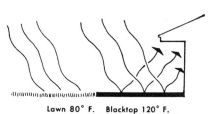

Large paved areas adjacent to house absorb and reflect sun's heat into house.

When you remove attic heat with an attic fan during the day, close the attic off from the rest of your house.

Otherwise the fan will draw hot outside air into your house.

Suppose you decide to cool your

One method of installing an attic fan.   Gable louvers or other openings must be large enough to let air escape from attic.

home with water or air conditioning, but wish to ventilate the attic anyway. A fan—smaller than an attic fan—will do that; it should be capable of changing the air in the attic at least once per minute, and should operate continuously when the temperature in the attic exceeds 110°. It may be controlled by thermostat, time clock, or manual switch. Such a fan will cost about $50.

Cooling with fans has some disadvantages. Dust and pollen are likely to be drawn into your home. Fans are noisy. The cost of a good fan plus installation may be as much as a room air conditioner. And remember, a fan will cool your house to only approximately the temperature of the outside air.

AIR CONDITIONING by mechanical refrigeration is the only certain method of obtaining uniformly comfortable conditions in summer in places.

The air is cooled and moisture is removed so that the lower humidity provides greater comfort, especially in humid climates.

Not all air conditioners dehumidify adequately during humid, muggy weather. The result is that the cool air they put out feels clammy. This clamminess can be reduced, to a certain extent, by operating a dehumidifier when you operate your air conditioner.

The aged, those with heart ailments, babies, and persons affected by dust and pollen often are helped by this type of air conditioning. Less noise from the outside may be an additional benefit.

Houses should be insulated, relatively tight, and protected against the sun as much as possible to obtain effective, economical cooling.

ROOM AIR CONDITIONERS mounted in windows are generally less expensive than central systems but provide less uniform temperatures. Most units are noisier than well-designed central systems and shut out some light from the windows in which they are installed. Part of the house can be air conditioned initially and additional units added as funds permit.

Conditioners of small capacity operate on 115 volts, but larger ones require 208 or 230 volts; you therefore may need additional wiring.

Shade the units on the outside to protect from direct sun heat if possible.

The reverse-cycle or heat-pump types of air conditioners, either room units or central systems, heat in winter and cool in summer. They are more expensive than conditioners that cool only. Auxiliary electrical resistance heating is needed in all but the warmer climates.

CENTRAL AIR-COOLING units can be installed in some hot air systems and thus utilize the same ducts for distributing cool air through the house. The ducts

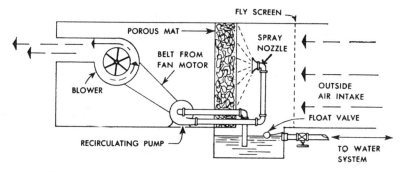

Evaporative coolers may be purchased for use in hot, dry climates.

must be insulated.

Hot air systems with small delivery ducts, such as 3-inch diameter, are not fully satisfactory for air conditioning. The higher air velocities required for cooling need more power and create undesirable noise.

New forced-air-cooling systems may be installed in the basement, hung from the ceiling in central halls where the ceiling heights permit, or placed in the attic.

Existing hot water systems with upright forced-air convectors in the rooms may be adapted for cooling by adding a chiller to cool the water pumped through the system.

Gas air conditioners, as well as the all-electric type, are available.

Most residential units, including heat pumps, have air-cooled condensers, but some are cooled by water where an adequate supply is available at low cost or where a cooling tower may be used. The water-cooled type is more efficient. The cooling tower should be located away from the house; it is noisy.

INSTALLATION COSTS vary considerably depending upon the temperature, exposure to sun, size and construction of house, and labor rates.

The cooling unit may add as little as 500 to 600 dollars to the cost of a new house if it is included in the heating system.

A central system installed separately from the heating system in an existing house may cost as much as 400 to 500

dollars per ton of refrigeration (a ton of refrigeration equals 12 thousand B.t.u.'s per hour—most units are now specified in B.t.u. capacity).

The cost should be less if installed in an existing heating system where ducts or piping can be used for cooling.

Where temperatures do not usually exceed 95°, an air conditioner rated at 6,000 B.t.u.'s per house will cool a room with 100 to 230 square feet of floor space. Where temperatures exceed 95° but do not exceed 100°, an air conditioner rated at 6,900 B.t.u.'s is required to cool the same area.

Approximately 1 kilowatt-hour of electricity is required to remove each 6,500 B.t.u.'s with an electrical air conditioner. This is the same amount of electricity that is required to operate ten 100-watt light bulbs for 1 hour.

Operating costs for mechanical air conditioning vary greatly because of many factors involved. With low electricity rates, a good average for warm climates might be 30 dollars per ton of refrigeration per season when uniform temperatures are maintained throughout the season.

PRIVATE AND RESTFUL BEDROOMS

TIME WAS WHEN a bedroom was only a bedroom. Now, thanks to the efforts and thinking of home economists, architects, and homemakers, it is coming into its own, as befits the room where we start and end each day, spend a third of our time, keep our personal possessions, and find a haven of rest and privacy.

In the bedroom, greater convenience comes from designing separate areas with enough space and furnishings for sleeping, dressing, and other activities —studying, reading, writing, lounging, sewing, hobbies—that may take place in the bedroom.

If space is limited, plans for sleeping and dressing are first.

For sleeping and napping you need a bed or beds that are comfortable and large enough; a surface or storage place for articles near the bed; a light source over or near the bed for each person for reading or emergencies; some control of natural light, as with draperies or blinds; adequate ventilation; and quiet. The room should be away from noisy areas or insulated against noise.

For dressing and undressing you need a mirror to see yourself full length; seating for putting on shoes and hose; clothes storage facilities grouped for each person; a dressing table with storage and a well-lighted mirror, and adequate artificial and natural lighting.

THE NUMBER of occupants, the number and types of activities, and the furniture needed determine the size of the bedroom.

A guide to size: Very small, 80 to 110 square feet, one bed; small, 120 square feet, the minimum for twin beds; medium, 140 square feet; large, 190 square feet or more.

Some suggestions about arrangement:

Group the furniture by activities, as sleeping, dressing, and study.

Place the bed for good air circulation but away from drafts, street lights, and morning sunshine.

Locate the dressing area near the bedroom entrance or bathroom.

Keep traffic lanes open, short, and direct.

Place the dresser so that adequate light falls on the person dressing and not on the mirror.

Place the large pieces of furniture and rugs parallel to the walls of the room.

Place the writing unit to provide enough light, free from glare.

THE FOUNDATION for restful sleep is a comfortable bed.

Each sleeper needs at least 38 inches of bed width and a bed length 9 inches longer than he is. A standard double bed is 54 inches wide by 74 inches long; that width, divided equally, allows each bedmate only 27 inches—the width of a baby's crib. A person more than 5 feet 5 inches tall finds the standard length too short for comfort.

Oversize beds and twin beds on swingaway frames attached to a king-size headboard are becoming popular. The larger bed does not necessitate a

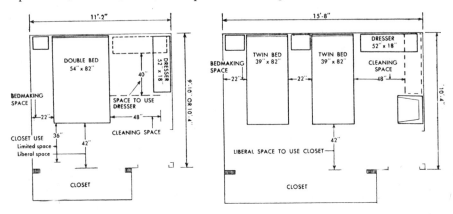

Two floor plans of bedrooms that show space recommendations for specific activities and the relationship of the space to items of bedroom furniture.

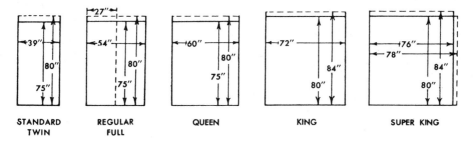

| STANDARD TWIN | REGULAR FULL | QUEEN | KING | SUPER KING |

Mattress sizes.

larger bedroom. A bed 70 by 80 inches in a small bedroom allows more space than separate twin beds. Coverings to fit the larger sizes are available.

THE THREE BASIC mattresses are innerspring, solid, and latex or urethane foam.

An innerspring mattress may have 180 to 850 or more coiled springs enclosed between two layers of insulating materials, such as sisal, and padding, usually of cotton. A large number of springs does not, however, insure a comfortable and durable mattress. The quality of steel and the shape and size of the coils used for the springs are more important than the number.

The borders of the mattress should be prebuilt or reinforced so that they will not sag or break down from sitting on the bed.

Foam mattresses are about half as heavy as innerspring mattresses. If they are of high density and 4 to 6 inches thick, they are equal to innersprings in comfort and durability.

WHEN YOU SELECT a mattress, check for strong, securely fastened handles; enough padding so that innersprings cannot be felt through the padding; ventilators on each side for air circulation; neat, firm stitching; and durable ticking.

Heavy 8-ounce ticking of twill weave is recommended for long wear.

It makes little difference whether the top of the mattress is tufted, quilted, or plain.

A cross-section of the mattress is usually available at the salesroom for you to inspect.

Before you buy, lie down on the mattress and test its buoyancy and firmness. It should support every part of your body equally and not sag at points of greatest weight. If you prefer, ask the salesman to stretch out on the mattress; then stand back and observe carefully if sagging occurs. Buy from a reputable dealer.

THE BEDSPRING, the foundation for the mattress, provides one-third or more of the total resilience.

At least 90 percent of the bedsprings sold are box springs. These consist of securely tied springs, mounted on a wood base frame, padded, and covered with ticking.

Most of the criteria that apply to mattresses apply also to bedsprings.

A CHEST of drawers provides space for folded articles and other personal possessions. Look for sturdy construction, dustproof drawers that are smoothly finished and slide easily, and handles that are easy to grasp.

Chests are available with special storage features, whose usefulness and flexibility you should evaluate in relation to their cost.

Most homemakers feel a need for more storage space in bedrooms than they have. A further need may be for making better use of available space.

Every closet should have enough space for the wardrobe of the person or persons occupying the room (3 to 5 linear feet for each person) ; a depth of 24 to 30 inches; doors that open almost the entire length and height of the closet for convenience in reaching articles; and planned storage, so that articles are easy to see, easy to reach, and easy to grasp. Frequently used items should be most accessible.

A rod or rods should be placed so that garments clear the floor by 6 inches. Recommended heights are: Robes and other long garments, 72 inches; dresses and coats, 58 to 63 inches; shirts, jackets, and skirts, 45 inches.

Shelves should be adjustable or placed to meet varying storage needs. Distances recommended between shelves are 7 inches for shoes and 8 to 10 inches for hats.

Closets should have good light and possibility of airing.

Of the two general types of closets, walk-in and reach-in, the reach-in closet is the more popular and economical use of space.

A single-hung door is economical and satisfactory for a walk-in closet. The back of it can be utilized for books, racks, mirrors, shelves. Such a door limits accessibility of a reach-in closet—a serious handicap if the closet is more than a foot longer than door width. Space must be allowed for the door to swing.

Double swinging doors permit good accessibility if they are the width of closet. Their backs can be utilized. Their disadvantages are that they need space to swing, and the storage of heavy items on them may cause the doors to sag.

Sliding doors require no floorspace for swing, but only half of the closet is accessible at one time. They may warp or stick. Their backs cannot be utilized.

Accordion-folding doors require no swing space, give good accessibility, and occupy a small part of door space when they are open. They occupy an inch or two of closet depth when they are open, however; the door back cannot be utilized; and a poor track mechanism may cause difficulty in opening and closing them.

Bifold doors give good accessibility and require little floorspace for doors to open. Their sliding mechanism may stick and require frequent adjustment. Door backs cannot be utilized.

GENERAL LIGHTING for the bedroom may be provided by ceiling fixtures or structural lighting, or both.

Ceiling fixtures should be large enough (15 to 17 inches in diameter for a small room or one of average size). The shielding material should diffuse light evenly so that "hot spots" are avoided. The low ceilings in to-day's houses suggest shallow fixtures with three to five lamp bulbs mounted horizontally. Fixtures mounted flush with the ceiling or inset do not collect dust and insects.

Structural lighting, in the form of valances, cornices, or wall brackets, may be used with ceiling fixtures or instead of ceiling fixtures. A cornice across a closet wall provides light within the closet and general light.

Wall switches controlling general lighting should be installed on the latch side of the door. Also desirable is an additional switch within reach of the bed

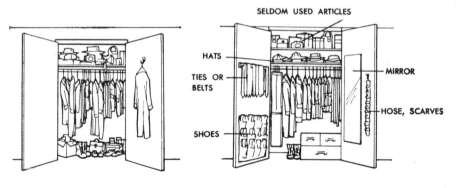

TYPICAL USE OF CLOSET   PLANNED USE OF CLOSET

SELDOM USED ARTICLES

HATS
TIES OR BELTS
SHOES
MIRROR
HOSE, SCARVES

or a master control switch near the bed to control selected lights inside and outside the house.

Light for reading in bed may be provided by table lamps, ceiling-mounted adjustable fixtures, wall lamps, or wall brackets.

If a double bed is used, provide a light for each person.

For makeup, light is needed on both sides of the face at face height whether you are sitting or standing. Two lamps or two wall-mounted fixtures are good. Fixture shields or lampshades should be white or off-white and translucent, so that maximum light falls on the face.

How TO PROVIDE for all the bedroom activities of children and at the same time provide for their changing needs is quite a problem.

Some people maintain that children's bedrooms should be equipped with inexpensive child-size furniture, which will be replaced. Others believe the furnishings should be flexible enough in use and permanent enough to survive the growing and changing years.

Probably the best solution is a combination of the two, since the requirements for furnishings are different at each stage of a child's development.

The nursery should be near the master bedroom. A crib, chest, and dressing equipment are necessary. A chair for the mother is desirable.

Any surfaces accessible to chewing babies should be treated with lead-free paint. The furniture should be free from sharp edges and other safety hazards.

A night light is a convenience in checking on the child without disturbing him.

At the preschool age, the child outgrows the crib. The new bed may be one that will last him until adulthood. At this age, the child is exploring spaces and shapes. He needs free floor-space for play and open shelves so that he can reach his toys easily. A childsize table and chair provide space for games, puzzles, and crayons.

Wall- or ceiling-mounted lights re-

duce the safety hazard of breakable lamps and trailing cords.

The rod in the closet should be low enough for the child to hang up his own clothes. Grooves should be provided for raising the rod as the child grows.

The child of school age needs a table or desk with good light for study. Toy shelves continue to be useful and often become places to keep hobby materials and collections.

WHEN TWO CHILDREN share a room, each needs an area for his own interests and privacy. Children enjoy having friends visit them, and the school-age child's room needs some provision for overnight guests.

The teenager's room should allow for individual expression. Some teenagers want a bedroom that looks like a sitting room. At this age, a girl should have a dresser or dressing table with mirror, storage, and adequate lighting.

A teenage boy also needs a well-lighted mirror and places to store his clothing and books and to display or work on hobbies.

The bedroom has an important function. It is a private and rest area where you find a retreat for self-expression without infringing upon others. Its character may take any direction that suits you as long as it meets your needs.

LOOK AT YOUR LIVING ROOM

THE LIVING ROOM is a family room, and it calls for well-chosen furnishings and backgrounds for them, easy-to-maintain surfaces, adequate size, provision for storage, utilities, and a convenient location.

As to location: The main entrance to the house should give easy access to the living room. It should have some parking space nearby. For guests, it should be the most easily reached entrance. This main entrance should be separated when possible from the main living area, however.

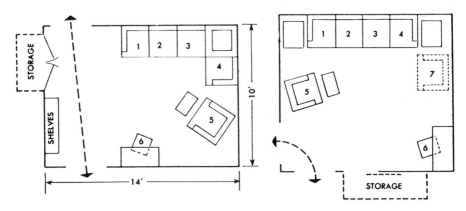

Placement of doors controls traffic through living area.

DOORS LEADING to the living room should be placed so that the room does not become merely a passageway across furniture groupings. Doors placed on the short side or at corners near such a sidewall help control the traffic through the living space.

Social routing into a residence usually is first to a reception room, the foyer; a cloakroom, the closet for wraps; the major social places for groups; to the minor social areas for hobbies or small group activities; to the dining or serving room; and sometimes to the bathroom or powder room for guests.

This movement of family and guests should be separated from sleeping and study rooms. In practical design, it seldom can be entirely separate, but hallways, rows of closets, different floor levels, and the like are features that achieve such separations.

AT LEAST 144 square feet is recommended for a living room. A square room 12 feet by 12 feet is more flexible than a room 10 feet by 14 feet 6 inches.

Any dimension less than 10 feet is not desirable, because furniture cannot be placed suitably for conversation and games.

Generally, however, a rectangular space has a more pleasing proportion than a square one. For a living room of liberal size with minimum furniture,

196 square feet is recommended. A dimension of 14 feet for the shorter room wall accommodates six persons in various group and individual leisure-time pursuits.

Liberal storage space for supplies used in the living area—card tables, folding chairs, records, books, games, cards, and the like—can be provided in a space about 8 feet long, 2 feet deep, and 6 feet 6 inches high.

Coat closets should be 2 feet 6 inches deep in the clear. Rods should be 2.5 inches below a shelf, if there is one, and high enough so that coats miss the floor by at least 6 inches. Dress wraps for a family of four require a rod 2 feet 2 inches long. Additional rod length of 2 to 3 feet should be added for hanging guests' wraps.

Space allowances need to be added to the floorspace mentioned for features such as fireplaces, built-in cabinets for television sets and record players, and pianos.

Regular and decorative fireplaces take 3 to 18 square feet of additional floor area.

Upright and grand pianos usually need 9 square feet (spinet) to 28 square feet (parlor grand), plus a seating allowance of 6 square feet.

FURNITURE ARRANGEMENTS should be planned with this in mind:

• For television viewing: A distance of at least 1 foot from the screen for each inch of screen size over 7 inches; for example, for a 19-inch screen, allow a viewing distance of 12 feet. Provide seating within a 120-degree angle for screen viewing.

• For four persons seated around a card table: 10 feet by 10 feet to walk past four persons seated in armless chairs, as in serving at a card table.

• For viewing slides and home movies: At a 40-inch screen—11 feet minimum distance from the projector; at a 60-inch screen—17 feet minimum distance from the projector.

• For conversational groups: Chairs for four to six persons, utilizing about 10 feet by 10 feet. Place chairs and tables close enough so that a seated person can reach a table.

• For bookcases: Clearance of 36 inches in front of shelves at floor level.

It is good to make a floor plan to scale and try out various arrangements for furniture. Consider space requirements and location in relation to swing of doors, views, and such structural details as fireplaces and alcoves.

Enough space is needed so that every person who uses the living room is comfortable. A person seated in a chair uses 30 inches of free space in front of the chair. A person walking behind a chair or beside a piece of furniture will use 16 inches when he edges past and 24 inches when he walks past a seated person. You use only 22 inches seated at a desk, but 36 inches in the clear for space to use the desk, arise, and be seated.

ADEQUATE DAYLIGHT in the living room may be had by allowing space for windows equal to about one-fourth of the floor area.

The sun is the primary source of light for daytime. Its light is scattered in its passage through the atmosphere and thereby creates a secondary source, the sky.

The relative amount of outside illumination depends on the position of the sun as well as the atmospheric conditions.

The amount of daylight in living rooms also is affected by the placement of glass areas, the finishes of walls and ceilings, and the draperies, curtains, and shades at windows. In general, the upper half of a window admits diffused light from the sky; the lower half, from the ground and nearby shrubbery, which are much darker than the sky.

FOR ARTIFICIAL LIGHT, indirect or semi-direct light sources should be selected to provide general illumination. One light source in the living room should be operated by a wall switch on the latch side of the main entrance door.

Multiple switches are convenient if doors are more than 10 feet apart. An exterior light should be controlled by a switch inside the entrance.

Wall switches normally are mounted 48 inches above the floor.

Totally direct light might be chosen for decorative accent, as on a painting, a planter, or a piece of sculpture. A shield may be needed to keep direct glare from the viewer's eyes.

Lights in cornices, valances, and shielded wall brackets provide good general light in living rooms. They can be used to balance daylight in a large room.

Pleasing effects can be created by using recessed down lights to wash entire walls. They are placed in the ceiling 1 foot from the wall and mounted 3 to 4 feet on center. The source of light needs to be correctly placed to eliminate glare and to produce a maximum amount of diffused brightness.

Along continuous walls, duplex electric outlets should be placed no farther apart than 12 feet, and wall space between doors should have a duplex receptacle if the wall length is 3 feet or more. Special outlets for television, room air conditioners, and clocks also may be needed. Dimmer switches give flexibility for decorative lighting. Floodlights in the ceiling may be installed to light music at the piano. Recessed light in ceiling cavities can be chosen above davenports or other furniture groups.

Portable lamps permit flexibility in the amount and the location of supplemental light. The light from lamps should be diffused for reading and study. White, eggshell, or ivory shades give the maximum light. All shades should have a white lining. All light sources should be shielded to avoid direct glare. The socket base should be 45 inches to 48 inches above the floor.

WOOD finishes, which emphasize the natural pattern and color of wood in walls, floors, and furniture have become popular. Smooth, dull surfaces usually are chosen for wall finishes.

Wood trim around doors, windows, and arches usually is finished in nearly the same value and hue as the walls. Ceilings are usually lighter—white, off-white, or a tint of the wall color.

Besides floors of wood, we have floors of resilient materials, such as linoleum and vinyl sheet goods or tiles. In addition, decorative floor treatments may be wall-to-wall carpets and rugs.

Large surfaces of one color in muted hues make small spaces appear larger. In general, we can say that pleasing effects in interior design can be achieved by repetition of a basic color.

Harmony in color can be had by adding two or more different colors in lesser amounts than the background color. In achieving color balance, bright colors are used in lesser amounts than the dominant background hue. Pictures or patterned textiles often can be used to tie together a color scheme for a living room.

THE PLACEMENT of hot-air registers and return ducts in the living room needs special attention.

Narrow openings in floors and baseboard and overhead openings for warm air are more desirable for living rooms than are large, nearly square floor openings.

Most of the specifications call for bathing the outside walls with warm air and maintaining a difference of not more than 4 degrees in the temperature at floor and ceiling. Cold-air returns need to be left free of low furniture to be satisfactory.

Curtain and drapery panels should not cover the outlets for air.

Windows and exterior doors should be weatherstripped. Ideally, fixed glass areas should be double glazed. An even temperature at sitting and floor level is especially desirable in the living area.

BATHROOMS: TIPS AND PLANS

WHEN YOU PLAN the bathroom, it is wise to consider your present family needs and anticipate future needs.

The amount of money you can spend, whether you are building a new bathroom or remodeling an existing one, may determine the results.

Give attention to every detail of location, arrangement of fixtures, storage, lighting, and safety.

The bathroom, if there is only one in the house, should open into a hallway that makes it easily accessible to all rooms. Its entrance should not be visible from the front door or the living room. It should be placed so that children in daytime can reach it from the back door without going through other rooms.

If there are two bathrooms or an extra half-bath or lavatory, an economical plumbing layout is to have them back to back or, in a two-story plan, one bath may be directly over the first-floor bathroom.

A GOOD ARRANGEMENT within a bathroom also is important.

We usually think of bathrooms with three fixtures—basin, bathtub, and toilet.

Compartmented or divided bathrooms can provide privacy for two or more persons at the same time and require less space than two rooms. The sink may be placed in one compartment with the tub and toilet in the other.

When space is lacking for two baths, it may be possible to use one tub to serve two bathrooms, or the bathroom may be divided into a series of separate rooms—one for the toilet, one for bathing facilities, and the remaining space for dressing and grooming.

The simplest and least expensive bathroom arrangement is one with all fixtures and plumbing pipes on one wall.

Greater convenience and better appearance may sometimes be achieved, however, by having fixtures on two or more walls and may sometimes offset the additional cost of piping. A washbowl placed near the window will have good light. It may be unwise to put the tub under a window because of drafts and because the window is difficult to open and close.

Leave enough floorspace around fixtures for comfortable use and accessibility. Space allowances around fixtures are shown in drawings on the next page.

The figures take into account the use and cleaning of bathrooms and provide slightly more space than the standards generally used.

Note that for a sink that is placed next to a wall, we allow 18 to 20 inches between the center of the basin and the wall to allow for the arm movements required for shaving and grooming.

The size, color, material, and style of bathroom fixtures affect their cost. It is wise planning to buy the best fixtures you can afford.

Vitreous china is considered to be the best material for bathroom fixtures.

Porcelain-enameled cast iron and pressed steel are cheaper and can be used for tubs and sinks. Stainless steel is used for washbasins designed for built-in installation. Reinforced plastic also is used for lavatories, tubs, and shower stalls.

Washbasins can be purchased with round, oval, square, triangular, rectangular, and D-shaped bowls. Some models are made to be hung on the wall with special brackets or hangers. Others are intended to be installed in a countertop. Legs of china or metal can be added to some designs for extra support. Corner basins are available for use in small rooms.

Install the basin at a height—say, 33 to 36 inches from floor to rim—that is convenient for adults.

THREE GENERAL TYPES of toilets are manufactured for home use—the siphon jet, reverse trap, and the washdown.

The siphon jet, the most efficient, has a quick and relatively quiet flushing action. The trapway is at the rear of the bowl, and the water surface is extra large.

Reverse trap bowls are like the siphon jet but have smaller water surface and trapway. Less water is required to operate them.

The washdown, the simplest in construction, is the noisiest. Its trapway is in the front of the bowl.

The standard toilets stand on the floor. Wall-mounted fixtures are neat, and it is easy to clean around and under them. They require special hangers or carriers.

RECTANGULAR BATHTUBS, for recessed or corner installation, usually are 4.5 5, or 5.5 feet long and 29 to 32 inches wide. The 5-foot tub is the one most generally used.

Square bathtubs also are available. The smaller receptor type adapts well to a tub-shower combination where space is limited. The height of receptor tubs is about 12 inches. Other tubs are 13.5 to 16 inches high.

A shower head over the tub is the most economical way to add a shower. If the fittings are installed at the time the bathroom is built, the pipes for the shower can be concealed in the wall. Shower heads usually are made of chrome-plated brass with swivel joints for directing the spray. The shower head usually is 6 feet 2 inches from the floor.

The rod for a shower curtain should be at a height of 6 feet 6 inches.

Shower stalls can be built on the job or bought in prefabricated form. Factory-built units of porcelain-enameled steel or reinforced plastic are the easiest and quickest to install. They range in floor size from 30 by 30 inches to 36 by 36 inches to 34 by 48 inches.

PROVIDE FOR PLENTY of storage space for bathroom linens, toiletries, cosmetics, and other items.

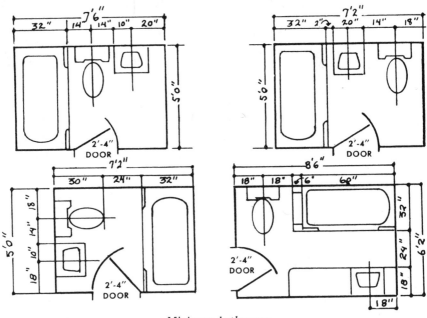

Minimum bathrooms.

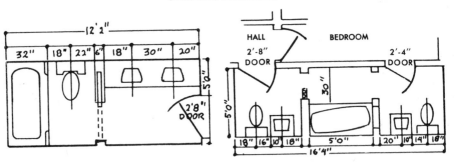

Compartmented bathrooms.

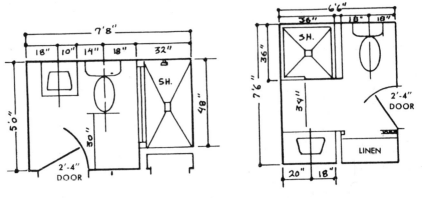

Bathrooms with shower stalls.

Cabinets for medicines and toilet articles usually are mounted above the wash basin. They have sliding or hinged doors, may have built-in lighting fixtures and outlets, and come in different sizes.

For medicines and other items that should be kept away from children and half-asleep adults, it is wise to have a separate cabinet or a compartment within the cabinet that can be locked.

A convenient height for the cabinet is 69 to 74 inches from the top of the mirror to the floor.

Two shelves 12 inches deep and 18 inches wide, with between-shelf clearance of 12 inches, are adequate for storing 12 bath towels and 12 washcloths.

A hamper for soiled clothing is a convenience.

Space for storing linens and bathroom supplies can be had even in a small bathroom. Two likely places are under the basin and over the toilet closet. Leave at least 12 inches between the top of the tank and a cabinet hung above it, to give access to the tank when it needs repairs.

Adequate light, properly placed, is essential. For shaving and makeup, light should shine on the face and not on the mirror. A ceiling fixture above the front edge of the sink and one light on each side of the mirror will illuminate the face without shadows. The side lights should be 30 inches apart.

Select light fixtures for bathrooms with white diffusers. Use white bulbs or shades, because tinted ones distort colors.

One fixture usually is adequate in a small bathroom. In large bathrooms, general illumination and area lights are needed.

One way to distribute light evenly is to have a luminous ceiling. These plastic-paneled ceilings can be installed in existing bathrooms.

Remember to install a grounded outlet at the sink, at a convenient height for electrical appliances that may be used there.

Ventilation must be provided for all bathrooms. Fans are often used. Most automatic bathroom fans operate at only one speed, but some have as many as five.

For small bathrooms, exhaust fans combined with heater and lights are a good choice. They can be installed with one switch, but separate switches are perferred if such an installation is permitted by codes and ordinances.

Make certain that light and ventilating fan switches are out of reach of anyone in the bathtub or shower or anyone using a water faucet.

Lights with pull cords are dangerous and should not be used in bathrooms.

BATHROOMS used by the handicapped and the elderly need extra consideration. Safety, convenience, and ease of maintenance should not be forgotten.

Doorways may need to be wide enough to accommodate a wheelchair or crutches.

The door locks should be of the type that can be opened from either side.

Beware of slippery floors. Wall-to-wall carpeting with nonskid backing is preferable to scatter rugs.

Install grab bars in tubs and shower stalls in places easy to reach whether one is sitting or standing. They must be mounted securely to the studs—a grab bar that pulls away from the wall under a person's weight is worse than none at all.

Grab bars on each side of the toilet make it easier for handicapped and elderly persons to sit down and rise safely.

Bathtub rubber mats, with suction cups, should be placed in the bottom of the tub to prevent slipping while the user is sitting or standing.

Night lights add to safety.

EFFICIENCY IN YOUR KITCHEN

YOUR KITCHEN is your workshop, office, and studio. At times it is also a place for eating and recreation.

My advice is: Make the most of it; make it attractive and efficient and the way you want it to be.

As to efficiency, think of your kitchen as having four work centers—places to mix and serve and the range and sink —each of which has its equipment, appliances, counter, and storage space for the supplies and utensils.

The mix (or food preparation) center is most convenient if it is between two pieces of major equipment—sink and range, range and refrigerator, or refrigerator and sink. The counter, 24 inches deep, should be 36 to 42 inches wide unless it extends into a corner; then 24 to 36 inches of frontage is enough.

You may wish to provide under-counter knee space so you can sit comfortably to work. You can store an adjustable posture stool, if it has a fold-down back, in this space.

A pullout cutting board that is adjustable to 26-, 30-, and 34-inch heights would provide a lower, more comfortable surface for certain mixing jobs and serve as a snack counter for children.

Stored at the mix center should be all the spices, flavorings, flour, sugar, measuring equipment, bowls, mixer, and baking pans you use there.

An efficient range center, convenient to sink and mix counter, includes a freestanding or built-in-range or built-in surface cooking units and wall oven. Provide counters 12 to 24 inches wide on both sides of the surface cooking area and to one side of built-in ovens. These surfaces should withstand the heat of utensils taken directly off the range or out of the oven.

To insure enough elbowroom, avoid placing major cooking appliances in a cramped corner. Allow at least 16 inches between the center of the nearest front cooking unit and a wall or piece of high equipment, the same clearance as between the center front of a built-in oven and an adjoining wall. For space in which to stand, allow at least 14 inches between the center of a front cooking unit and a turn of the counter.

An electric wall oven should be installed so that the bottom of the in-terior is about 32 inches above the floor. The most frequently used rack positions are at about counter height, a comfortable lifting position for most women.

Likewise, place a gas oven so the broiler rack is about 28 inches from the floor and the lowest oven rack is at 37 inches.

Serving dishes, platters, trays, un-cooked cereals, seasonings, pans, and small utensils used at the range should be stored at this center.

THE SINK probably is the most continuously busy work center of the kitchen.

A counter 24 to 36 inches wide to one side of the sink provides adequate space for stacking soiled dishes; 18 to 36 inches is needed to the other for draining clean ones.

Provide at least 14 inches of clearance between the center of the sink bowl and a turn of the counter for standing.

Most women like a double-bowl sink, one side of which is a shallow bowl, about 3.5 inches deep, and has the drain and food waste disposer set back of center. This arrangement provides a convenient height and enough knee space so you can sit at the sink to work.

An undercounter dishwasher placed to the right or left of the sink or at right angles to it should be close to the dish storage cabinet as well as to the sink. A portable dishwasher may be stored elsewhere and rolled to the sink for use. A permanently installed dishwasher occupies 24 to 30 inches of base-cabinet storage.

Soap, dishwashing supplies, and such foods as potatoes and onions should be stored here. Provide a place also for utensils for cleaning, cutting, and straining food, a can opener, paper towels, and clean and damp dish towels.

There should be a convenient and sanitary receptacle for trash at the sink center.

AT THE SERVING CENTER, close to both sink and dining areas, should be the items that go directly to the table, including dishes, glassware, tableware, linens, and accessories.

Ready-to-eat foods (like cookies, crackers, and dry cereals), and table appliances, including toaster, coffeemaker, and waffle iron, belong here.

A serving cart, especially if you have a place to store it, is a handy addition to any kitchen for serving and cleaning up.

THE AMOUNT of dining area you will need, whether it is in a dining room, dining L, family room, or the kitchen, is determined by the number of persons to be served; the size and pieces of furniture, including table, chairs, server, and cabinets; and clearances for passage and serving.

Allow 21 to 24 inches of table space for each adult. The smallest table at which eight adults can sit comfortably is 40 inches by 72 inches. The smallest for six adults is 36 inches by 60 inches. A round table 42 inches in diameter seats four, and one 48 inches in diameter accommodates six.

The space you need around the dining table depends somewhat on how you serve meals.

The minimum allowance between the edge of a freestanding table and a wall or piece of furniture is 32 inches. That much space is needed for a person to seat himself or rise from the table, but it does not give enough room for a person to pass behind occupied chairs to serve the meal or clear the table. Add 4 inches—making a total of 36— if you wish to allow for one person to edge past another seated at the table. Add 12 inches—a total of 44—for serving.

Built-in tables and benches in an alcove require less space than freestanding furniture but are less convenient for seating and serving. An arrangement with chairs on one side of the table and a built-in bench 22 inches deep on the other is preferable to one with two built-in benches.

A dining counter, 20 inches deep, may be considered for informal meals. The number you wish to serve should determine the length of your counter.

To find the length, multiply 21 inches (the minimum width of each place setting) by the number to be seated.

A dining counter should be 30 inches high if chairs with seats 18 inches high are to be used. A depth of 20 inches should be allowed beneath this counter for legroom.

If stools 24 inches high will be used, your counter height must be 36 inches, with footrests 6 to 8 inches high. Knee space at least 14 inches deep should be allowed under this higher counter.

IN A LARGE kitchen many women like to include a planning desk, food freezer, and laundry space.

Planning kitchen storage is worth while if it is done thoughtfully. Tools, foods, supplies, and utensils used oftenest should be stored in drawers and bins and on adjustable sliding and revolving shelves and perforated hardboard at heights between 28 and 64 inches from the floor. Large, heavy, seldom-used items store best below this; small, lightweight pieces can go above.

The standard 12-inch-deep wall cabinet holds all dinnerware except large serving pieces. They and small trays and baking pans may be stored neatly between vertical file partitions, which are slanted to accommodate their size or placed in a deeper cabinet —above a built-in oven, for example. Adjustable shelves are good.

Wall cabinets should be hung not more than 15 inches above the counter. Shallow cabinets that are 5 inches deep and have sliding doors may be installed under wall cabinets as convenient storage for small, often-used supplies and equipment.

Sliding shelves and pullout bins and drawers increase the usability of base cabinets and should be easy to pull, even when loaded. Bread, cake, and cookies may be stored in metal-lined drawers. Vegetables keep best in ventilated bins.

Special planning is necessary to utilize corner spaces in wall and base cabinets in the kitchen. One of the best ways is to install wall, base, or floor-to-ceiling cabinets with shelves that

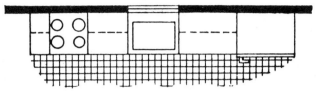

STRAIGHT LINE KITCHEN

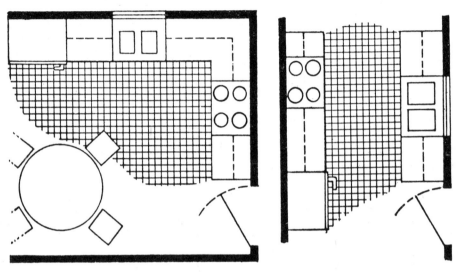

L-SHAPED KITCHEN   PARALLEL WALL KITCHEN

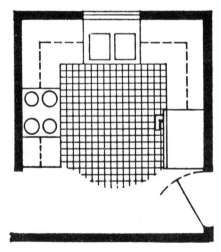
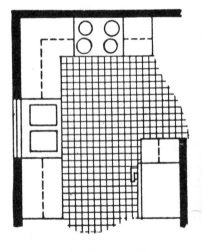

U-SHAPED KITCHEN   BROKEN-U KITCHEN

Five basic kitchen arrangements.

revolve individually or as a unit.

If base and wall cabinets are used as room dividers, the corner may be used from the adjoining dining area for linens, silver, and table appliances placed on sliding shelves and in drawers.

If you want a modern, built-in look, you will need to know the exact dimensions of appliances to be installed, so that the cabinets can be built or arranged to accommodate them.

If your cabinets are built by a cabinetmaker, they can be made to fit your space exactly without the use of filler strips.

Manufactured base cabinets in metal or wood come in widths from 9 to 48 inches on a 3-inch module. They are 36 inches high and 24 or 25 inches deep. The toe space at the bottom is 4 inches high.

Manufactured wall cabinets in widths and finishes to match the base cabinets are 12 or 13 inches deep and 15, 18, 25, 30, or 33 inches high. The doors should be no more than 12 inches wide, so they do not project dangerously beyond the front edge of the counter when they are opened.

The space between the top of the wall cabinets and ceiling may be enclosed so dust cannot accumulate there, or it can be used to store infrequently used items.

CERTAIN GENERALIZATIONS apply to almost all kitchens.

Allow 4 feet 6 inches to 5 feet 4 inches between facing counters and appliances—the space needed for two persons to work and pass each other.

Try to locate doors so that major traffic lanes do not go through the work area. A passageway at the end of an island or counter should be at least 3 feet 6 inches wide.

Refrigerators and wall ovens should be located at ends of a work counter, but preferably not so that their doors open into a doorway.

Provide 15 to 18 inches of counter space at the latch side of a refrigerator and at least 16 inches of clearance between the latch and a turn of the counter for standing.

The placement of doors, windows, and adjacent rooms puts most kitchens in one of five basic arrangements.

Straight-line arrangements fitted into alcoves or behind folding doors are suitable only for minimum kitchens. For work areas and storage to be adequate, these arrangements become too long to be efficient.

L-shaped kitchens tend to divert traffic out of the work area, provide a convenient location for dining or laundry, and have less walking distance between work centers than straight-line kitchens.

Although parallel-wall kitchens save steps between work areas, they often have doors at each end inviting traffic.

Well-planned U-shaped kitchens are compact, save steps, and are out of the way of traffic lanes. Special planning is needed, however, to make corner spaces in wall and base cabinets convenient for storage.

Broken-U kitchen arrangements frequently fit well into combination rooms such as kitchen-dining, kitchen-family, or kitchen-work rooms.

One duplex electric outlet for every 4 feet of counter is recommended, with a minimum of one outlet for each counter where portable appliances are likely to be used. Special-purpose outlets are located in places where appliances are permanently installed.

In addition to good, general, fluorescent or incandescent ceiling fixtures, area lighting is desirable at the sink and other work centers as well as at the dining table or counter. Fixtures beneath wall cabinets reduce annoying shadows on work surfaces.

This, the most expensive room in the home, is where the homemaker and family spend a considerable amount of time. Planning carefully for the kitchen you want takes time. It is time well spent.

WHAT YOU SHOULD KNOW ABOUT BASIC DESIGN

LOOK about you.

Look carefully at the things you take for granted—your house, its furnishings, and the yard. Possessions such as these—hundreds of them—create the backdrop of one's life.

If we select our possessions precisely, if they are carefully designed to meet the needs most important to us, if they are attractive and timely, they will ease the physical problems of living, stimulate our thinking, and lift our spirits.

On the other hand, possessions that enter our lives haphazardly may produce tensions that undermine family living.

A room crowded by frilly fabrics can smother its occupants. Jarring color combinations and obstacle-course furniture arrangements may evoke unpleasant responses without our realizing why.

Good taste should not imply a narrow process of selection. What is good for one individual or household at a given time is not necessarily good for another.

One family leads an active life, with an emphasis on what is happening at the moment. This concept expects energetic youngsters to damage and wear out the house and its contents. Things are considered expendable. It justifies buying for the short term.

A second family buys the best and expects its members to take great care to safeguard things for the future or even the next generation.

Yet another family has a middle-of-the-road outlook. Realistic life expectancies are attached to material possessions of moderately good quality, and respect for property is encouraged.

As we begin to understand the importance of design, we may wish for some convenient rules whose application automatically would bring the positive effects of good design into our homes.

If we define "design" broadly, we may say with Joseph Albers that it is "to place and organize, to order, to relate and to control . . . in short, it embraces all means of opposing disorder and accident."

Design is comprised of certain elements—line, space-form, color-light, and texture.

It means consciously ordering these basic ingredients to bring the end product into line with our deepest needs.

It does not mean placidly accepting what already exists or seems most readily available.

LINE may be described as stretching a dot. It is essentially the boundary of form—the edge of things.

SPACE-FORM must be considered together. Space is the void within which we move. Form is existing mass which interrupts space, creating its boundaries.

Shape usually denotes two dimensions, length and width. Form indicates three items—length, breadth, and depth.

COLOR-LIGHT also must be treated as two sides of the same coin.

Color has been defined as the hue of light reflected from an object. We can have no color without light, but we know that light also plays an important part in our perception of form and texture.

The hue is important. So are the amounts of darkness and brightness and the location of colors in relationship to each other.

TEXTURE is the way a thing feels or looks as it might feel.

Our appreciation of texture comes to us through both our eyes and our sense of touch.

UNDERSTANDING each element of design takes time and experimentation. Once you are acquainted with them, though, you are ready to consider how the components fit together.

First you ask yourself, "What do I hope to accomplish?" When you have the goal in mind, the process of ordering the elements becomes manageable.

Suppose you have decided to buy a man's chair. What will be your major considerations? Comfort? Ease of maintenance? Durability? Appearance? Cost?

Such questions must be examined in turn. Is this chair one that will provide good support as well as squirm space? Will working or puttering clothes soil the fabric easily? Will it support considerable weight and give a sturdy appearance?

When you have decided on the most important qualities, you still have to decide how they may best be obtained and retained.

As the chair must meet the needs of its owner, so must it relate well to objects around it. Because it will be large, finding enough space for it may be a problem. The new purchase should not overwhelm other furnishings in the room.

If it is constructed of wood and fabric, the two should share some qualities to establish unity, yet vary enough to contribute vitality to the overall design of the chair. Lines probably should express solidarity and masculinity.

THE PRINCIPLES of design become useful tools in a concrete situation.

Proportion means that we are concerned with establishing a pleasing relationship between parts.

An item appears well proportioned when the size and shape of its parts are neither varied to the point of chaos nor repetitious to the point of boredom. Finally, does the chair help to make the room a unified whole?

Balance is a principle that urges us to study relative weight.

Is an otherwise heavy chair supported by spindly, fragile-appearing legs?

Will a massive piece disrupt the balance of a room by making it seem uncomfortably lopsided?

Broad lines, thick forms, and unbroken surfaces contribute a sense of weightiness.

Slender lines, shallow forms, and broken surfaces produce the opposite effect.

Balance is not entirely a matter of apparent weight. A colorful, active painting may be important enough to counter large areas of heaviness in other parts of a room. A sense of equilibrium is created through the careful combination of weight and the power of attraction.

Emphasis, a third principle, encourages us to give one element—color, texture, form, or line—dominance. It is the counterpart of harmony.

Emphasis stresses differences rather than similarities. The spirit of the principle is also served when we choose an article understated in every respect to help calm an overlively room.

Rhythm refers to the suggestion of movement produced intentionally by the use of design elements. Do strong vertical lines sweep our glance along? Do spindles in the back of a straight chair form a pleasant pattern of alternation?

The principles of design are concerned, in the end, with quantities of harmony and contrast.

We must often compromise as we struggle with their application. A long-felt wish for something red may bow to the fact that a bright color would overemphasize an already large piece.

We may like the maintenance features of a vinyl covering, but we may be unwilling to accept the textural attributes of hotness in summer and coldness in winter.

Other compromises often stem from the fact that most homes serve the needs and preferences of a number of people.

Our carefully selected chair should offer an experience in beauty as well as comfort, in interest as well as durability.

THREE ESTHETIC TESTS for good design —unity, intensity, and vitality—are offered by Victoria Ball in her book, *The Art of Interior Design*.

The test for unity is twofold.

First, the parts of the chair must be brought together in a way that expresses a sense of oneness. No single part of the chair should be uncomfortably conspicuous in relation to any other.

By the same token, the chair must be an integral part of the unity of the room. If this sense of unity exists, the chair seems to be unquestionably right.

If the first condition is met, we will experience intense, conscious satisfaction with the effect we have achieved.

Finally, because of its rightness, the chair will attract and hold our interest, generating in our relationship with it a vitality that will make it as enjoyable a decade hence as it is today.

Learning to furnish a home well is not easy. It takes practice and the determination to keep trying.

The main requirement is a willingness to observe what is about us and think about what we see—about things and about their relationship to each other.

If we find the decisions we have made were not, after all, the best of all possible ones, there is no cause for discouragement. Study and planning provide an important part of our education for living.

HOW TO SELECT FURNITURE

THE DAY you visit the furniture stores to make some of the most important purchases of your life, you will spend considerable money for items that you must be friendly with for the next 20 years or more.

You must choose them with care to satisfy your taste, to fill the functional needs of your home, to select well-built, low-maintenance items, and to avoid high cost.

Here are a few suggestions.

First, consider the wood furniture to be used inside the house.

Chairs, tables, chests of drawers or chiffoniers, beds, and similar common pieces should be strong, good looking, of proper size, and easy to take care of.

Preferences for different species of wood come and go, but the old stand-bys of walnut, cherry, pecan or hickory (you cannot tell them apart), maple, birch, and oak are the native hardwoods that will always be used in furniture of good taste.

Each of those woods can be finished in its natural color, darkened with stain, or made almost blond by bleaching. They are all strong and have distinct grain patterns.

Other native hardwoods, such as gum, poplar, and cottonwood, have little grain pattern but can be stained to resemble other hardwoods and often are used in combination with the more expensive hardwoods.

Mahogany, the major foreign hardwood, will maintain its popularity because it has a pleasing, warm grain, can take a dark or light finish, and shrinks and swells less than almost any other wood with changes in humidity.

Other foreign tropical hardwoods, such as luan, crabwood, and utile, resemble true mahogany in texture and properties and have been used more and more for fine furniture.

Yellow and white pines are used in early-American chairs, beds, tables, corner cupboards, and odd pieces of furniture. Pine is acceptable for such items, but it is not considered a fine furniture wood.

If an eager salesman assures you that a table is made of solid, genuine, virgin white oak from a mountaintop in eastern Kentucky, bear in mind that the geographic origin of the species of wood (and even the species itself) is not the most important factor in selecting a piece of furniture.

If the wood is from one of the recognized and accepted furniture species and it pleases your fancy, then look closely at the grain of the wood, the construction of the piece, and the finish. That is really more important than the kind of wood.

The way a tree grows causes the grain of wood. It is the fiber direction and not the figure in the wood. If there is much cross-grain or slope of grain, beware.

Furniture parts that require strength, such as chair arms and legs, bedposts, and table legs, should have straight grain, or they may fail.

Drawer fronts, tabletops, and mirror frames should have straight grain, or they may warp with changes in humidity.

When you have satisfied yourself that the grain direction is all right, then look at the general construction of the piece.

First look for clean lines, properly smoothed edges and corners, and the absence of protruding annoyances.

Be sure that the piece rests firmly on the floor, with no leg or corner riding high.

Inspect the piece in a fairly strong light at an angle of 15 to 30 degrees to pick up irregularities in construction or finish. This angle of light will show you shadows of things that you may ordinarily overlook.

Now comes your most important and probably the most difficult inspection job. You should find out how the joints are made.

Because most joints are hidden, you may have to rely on the salesman. Ask him if he can furnish you with a factory drawing of the furniture construction.

Each of the joints shown in the drawing is suitable for some uses. None is suitable for all uses.

The weaker joints are the butt joint, the rabbeted joint, and the tongue-and-groove joint. They are not suitable for chair arms, table legs, bedposts, and similar items in which very high strength is required. These joints would be suitable for inserted panels in the sides and backs of dressers and for edge gluing furniture core material (center of plywood-type construction), and sim-

ilar applications in which high strength is not demanded.

The dovetailed joint is used commonly and is highly satisfactory for fastening drawer corners or for practically any use where two boards or panels join at a right angle.

The properly made dovetail joint will not come apart without breaking the wood. The dovetail joint is used in dresser drawers of almost all fine furniture.

The doweled joint and the mortise-and-tenon joint are used to connect chair arms, posts, and rails; parts of beds that demand high strength; and in many other similar applications. When well made, one is about as good as the other.

Even the best-made corner joints on chairs and tables must stand concentrated loads, and a good furniture manufacturer will often back up these joints with hidden metal braces or with triangular glue blocks of wood.

If glue blocks are used on the underside of tables and chairs, look closely to see that they fit tightly on all sides.

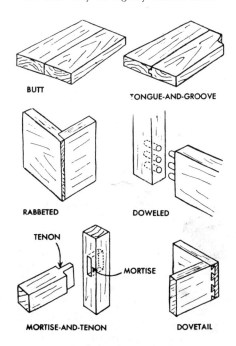

BUTT

TONGUE-AND-GROOVE

RABBETED

DOWELED

TENON

MORTISE

MORTISE-AND-TENON

DOVETAIL

Basic furniture joints.

If they are not snug and tight. they will do little good.

AFTER CHECKING on the furniture joints, look at all fastenings and hardware.

Good furniture is put together with glue and screws, not nails. See that all screws are drawn up tight and that all glue joints are tightly closed, with no telltale gaps that indicate poor workmanship.

Then check all drawer pulls and other hardware to see that they are properly fastened and tight. Nothing can be more disheartening than to have the drawer handles start coming off soon after the furniture is in your home.

If you are buying a table with dropleaves or one that slides open to insert extra leaves, ask the salesman to turn it upside down so you can see that the hardware is fitted properly and tightly.

Dropleaf tables should have a long, piano-type hinge or three or more hinges at least 3 inches long.

Veneered furniture made around the turn of the century was put together with glues that failed in high humidity. Some people still believe that veneered furniture is not so good as solid furniture. That is not true. Furniture today is almost always glued with water- and mold-resistant glues. Veneers seldom peel off.

An advantage of veneered furniture is stability, because the layers of wood and veneer are so balanced that you get less change in dimension with changes in humidity than you would with solid wood.

Another advantage is the beautiful figure that can be obtained in wood veneer by slicing burls or logs at angles and arcs not possible by conventional sawing of lumber.

One caution, however: Veneered parts should have an odd number of plies or layers—three, five, seven, or nine—with the grain direction of adjacent plies at right angles so that they will be balanced around the central core. An even number of layers may result in warping.

One of the best ways to become an expert on what to look for in furniture is to visit a furniture repair shop and look at the failures that are being repaired and the parts that have stood up under long usage. You can learn more in an hour this way than by reading several books.

IF THE LINES suit your taste and the construction meets your standards, find out what kind of finish was used.

There are many good finishes of varnish, lacquer, and synthetic resins. All are good if properly applied.

Ask for a guarantee that the finish will not waterstain under sweating glasses or discolor under a warm dish. That is especially important in dining and coffee tables. Many finishes are resistant to water, alcohol, and other things that may be spilled.

The most important thing that can be said about finishes is that the furniture should have some type of finish on all exposed wood parts, whether they are on the underside, inside a drawer, or inside the case.

That is advisable because moisture from the air moves into wood—even through the best finish—and causes wood to swell. If more moisture moves in one side than the other, the wood will swell unevenly and cause warping and tight drawers and may cause glue joints to open up or the wood to split.

When furniture goes into a very dry place, the opposite happens, and the shrinking of wood parts in furniture can cause just as many problems as swelling.

An even application of a good finish on all surfaces will usually give long, trouble-free service.

REGARDLESS of the type of furniture you buy, look for the manufacturer's name. It will be on the underside, on the back, or perhaps inside a drawer.

It will be there if he is proud of his product. He will back up his product if you should have any trouble. You may lose a drawer pull, or break a mirror, or have some part fail. Most good furniture manufacturers keep a supply of spare parts for several years for the furniture they make. They want your furniture to look its best—it's their best advertisement.

SMART WAYS TO REFINISH FURNITURE

A GOOD JOB of refinishing furniture is well worth the invested time, patience, and effort if the piece is of good wood, sound construction, and good design.

For removing old finish you need a good commercial remover; clean cans, wide-mouth jars, or old bowls for the remover; a pure bristle brush 3 to 4 inches wide (many removers dissolve synthetic bristles); a wide putty knife or spatula with filed-off corners to prevent scratching; medium (oo) steel wool; toothpicks, orangewood sticks, or match stems for carvings; heavy cord or a small, stiff bristle brush for grooves in turned legs; excelsior, old burlap, or other coarse material; soft, lintless rags; denatured alcohol or pure gum turpentine or both for the final cleaning (alcohol is most readily purchased under trade names for shellac thinners or solvent); old papers to protect floor and other surfaces; a box or can for wastepaper; and old clothes and rubber gloves.

It is essential that you work in a well-ventilated place. Some fumes are deadly in a closed room. Some of the materials are flammable. There should be no open flame, such as pilot lights and water heaters, near the workspace.

COMMERCIAL REMOVERS are of three general types—nonflammable semi-liquid, rinse-away-with-water, and liquid (with and without wax).

The nonflammable semiliquid removers are considered safe under normal conditions. They may be used on vertical surfaces when necessary. They do not raise the grain of the wood. They do not evaporate rapidly and may be left longer on hard, stubborn finishes without drying out. They do not burn the wood. They may be used on veneers.

The rinse-away removers as a group are the most expensive. They usually work quickly and easily, but they may burn the wood. The water used in rinsing may raise the grain, soften old glue in joints, and loosen veneer.

The liquid removers are the least expensive. They are effective on horizontal surfaces but too hard to control on vertical surfaces.

Most liquid removers are flammable. Some contain wax, which retards evaporation. All traces of the wax must be removed with a solvent before a new finish is applied.

Use the remover generously. Allow plenty of time for it to work. Except when you are removing several thick coats, you will hope to remove most of the finish with the first application. This means that the remover has been applied liberally enough and has had enough time to penetrate to the wood and lift the finish.

Do not disturb the finish until you are ready to scrape it off. Quite often stain from the old finish is rubbed into the wood by an impatient person who agitates the remover as it is working. It is better to scrape or wipe the entire surface and apply a fresh coat of remover.

Work on one surface at a time. Be careful not to let remover run down on an adjoining surface that has not been cleared. Such runs often produce stains, which are hard to remove. It is a good idea therefore to begin at the bottom and work up.

Remove finish from carvings with a small, stiff brush, round toothpicks wrapped with oo steel wool, or other objects that will not scratch the wood.

Grooves on turned legs can be cleaned with ravelings from burlap or other heavy cord.

After all finish is removed, scrub the entire piece with denatured alcohol or turpentine and oo steel wool. Rub with the grain of the wood. Use alcohol and turpentine in a well-ventilated area and away from open flame. Both are flammable, and the fumes are unsafe.

Often an old, hard, thick finish is resistant to the remover. Light sanding with medium or coarse sandpaper will cut the surface of the finish so that the remover can get through.

Nearly all quick-drying, easy-to-polish furniture waxes contain silicones. If silicone-bearing waxes have been used on the furniture, scrub it well with gum turpentine before and after removing the finish. Silicones retard the action of removers and also make the wood resistant to a new finish.

MATERIALS for gluing include glue (good-quality cabinetmaker's glue); clamps or strong cords; vinegar; and a small, stiff brush to apply the glue.

Glued joints loosen because of excessive heat or moisture or poor fit.

Since new glue sticks better on clean

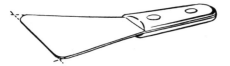

A wide putty knife or spatula with corners filed off to prevent scratching.

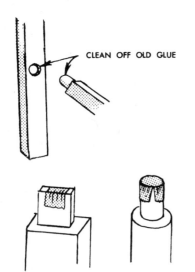

CLEAN OFF OLD GLUE

If some pieces are loose, glue strips of soft cotton cloth over the ends to make them fit.

wood, scrape off old glue. Be careful not to scrape off any of the wood.

Wash all glue out of the pores with warm vinegar. Wash away all vinegar with water. Dry thoroughly. Be sure joints fit tightly, or they will not hold.

Apply glue to both edges of wood to be joined. Clamp or tie together, using a tourniquet or clamps to hold them firmly. Wipe off excess with a damp cloth. Allow the furniture to dry the full time suggested on the container.

If the wood surfaces to be glued are very smooth, slashing with a knife will help the glue hold better.

Dampening with water will open the pores, but allow the wood to dry well before applying glue.

Both the glue and the wood should be warm (about 75° F.).

FOR REMOVING STAINS, the liquid household bleaches commonly used in laundering clothes often are effective. Apply them full strength or slightly diluted. Sponge off with clean water.

Or, for stains, you may use a saturated solution of oxalic acid (1 teaspoon of powdered oxalic acid or 2 teaspoons of crystals dissolved in a cup of hot water) or a solution of 2 ounces of oxalic acid crystals and 2 ounces of tartaric acid dissolved in a quart of hot water. Mix in a glass container.

These solutions should be marked *poison.* Avoid inhaling the fumes and the fine dust that comes from sanding.

Repeated applications may be necessary to remove some stubborn stains. Wipe the entire surface with the bleach to avoid light spots.

The action of these solutions should be stopped with a tablespoon of ammonia in a quart of water.

Commercial wood bleaches also are available.

Dents or bruises (not gouges) caused in solid wood by a heavy blow can be raised with steam. Do not use steam on veneer.

Steam may be applied with a steam iron used over several thicknesses of heavy, colorfast fabric, preferably wool. Or a dry iron may be used with damp cloth or four or five thicknesses of damp brown wrapping paper.

Several applications may be necessary before the steam swells the wood enough to bring it up to the surrounding level.

Because steam opens the pores of the wood, the surface must be sanded thoroughly to "repack" the grain; otherwise the area may absorb stain too rapidly; color will be uneven.

THE FINISH is no better than the smoothness of the surface on which it is applied.

The amount of sanding required to prepare the surface depends largely on how well the piece was sanded originally, the type of remover you use, and the thickness of veneer.

On an old piece, you will not want to sand through the patina—the mellow appearance that comes with age—but the surface must be smooth. If water was used in removing the finish, extra sanding is required.

Take care not to sand through thin veneer.

Garnet, silicon carbide, and aluminum oxide finishing papers are more expensive than the regular flint sandpaper, but they are sharper, last longer, and come in finer grits.

Regardless of the type you use, brush the sandpaper from time to time to prevent the sanding dust from clogging the surface. A lightweight metal brush or stiff utility brush may be used.

Use a fine-grit sandpaper on a fairly smooth surface. On a rougher surface, begin with medium grit and work to fine for the final sanding.

Wrap the sandpaper around a block of wood about 3 by 4 by 1 inches or a new, firm synthetic sponge, or use a hand sander.

Power sanders make the work easier, but orbital sanders should not be used except on wood with a pronounced grain running in different directions.

Keep the surface of the wood dusted as you work. If you have used bleach, wear a mask made of several thicknesses of cheesecloth to avoid inhaling dust.

After sanding until the wood is smooth to the touch, wipe it with a damp cloth. This will raise loose grain "whiskers." Allow it to dry for a few minutes and then rub with 3/0 (000) steel wool. Repeat this process if necessary. Brush the dust from crevices and carvings.

Remove all traces of dust with a tack rag. Tack rags may be bought at automobile supply or paint shops, or you may make your own. Wash a lightweight, lintless fabric several times. (Closely woven cheesecloth is excellent.) Squeeze out most of the water. Wet with turpentine. Add enough varnish to make the surface of the cloth yellow. Squeeze out excess moisture, refold, and squeeze again. Fold raw edges in to the center as the cloth is used. It should be damp enough to pick up dust but should leave no trace of moisture on the wood. Store in a closed jar or aluminum foil to prevent drying.

IMMEDIATELY BEFORE any staining is done, be sure to sponge with water and remove "whiskers" with 3/0 steel wool or very fine finishing paper.

Test the stain on the same kind of wood as the furniture to be finished. Check the color in daylight after it is dry.

Brush the furniture with equal parts of oil and turpentine before applying the stain in order that the latter may be absorbed evenly. Be sure to coat the end grain with this mixture or with a mixture of 1 part shellac and 5 parts denatured alcohol. Rub shellacked surfaces with fine sandpaper or steel wool before applying stain.

Apply the stain with a brush or cloth. Let it stand 2 or 3 minutes. Then rub it with a soft cloth. Use a circular motion to insure an even color. Let the stain dry at least 36 hours before sanding.

After staining a piece of furniture, be sure to protect the color against the operations that follow. Seal the stain with a commercial or home-mixed sealer.

New sealers now on the market greatly simplify the finishing process. Sealers have been developed to fit almost any type of finishing desired.

For best results when using two or more finishing coats on the sealer, use a medium-to-low solid sealer. If there is only one finish coat, a medium-to-high solid sealer is best.

For a homemade sealer, mix 1 part shellac and 5 parts denatured alcohol. Apply with a brush to seal the color. Use this also to seal the filler on hardwoods.

USE A PASTE wood filler to obtain an extremely smooth surface on new, open-grain woods, such as oak, mahogany, and walnut.

Buy a filler of the desired color, or tint it to match the wood (or stain) by using colors ground in oil.

Be sure not to let filler harden on the surface of the wood.

FINISHES include penetrating wood seal, oiled finish, shellac and wax finish, varnish, paint, and enamel.

Penetrating wood seal is highly satisfactory for the amateur. It makes an excellent finish for furniture, floors, and woodwork. It is easily applied and maintained and is easy to retouch. Many seals may be had in various colors. Use a pigment stain if a clear seal is to be applied over the stain.

Penetrating seals vary in composition, penetrating characteristics, and durability. One kind has the characteristics of an oil finish. Another penetrates the pores of the wood and hardens level with the surface. A third forms a surface coating. The seals of the first and second kinds are the most practical.

For an oiled finish, have the furniture free from dust. Brush on a coat of 2 parts boiled linseed oil and 1 part turpentine. Let stand 15 minutes. Let the wood absorb all the oil it can take. Wipe off the excess oil with a clean cloth. Be careful to clean all crevices; otherwise the oil will harden and will have to be removed with varnish remover.

Using a soft cloth, rub with the grain of the wood for 5 to 15 minutes or until a hard, lustrous surface results.

Repeat the application of oil and the rubbing at intervals of not less than 2 days until all dull spots disappear and a uniform clear luster results.

Apply oil once or twice a year to keep the finish in good condition.

For shellac and wax finish, have the furniture free from dust.

Brush on a coat of pure shellac diluted to half strength with alcohol. Allow this to dry thoroughly. Then rub down to the surface of the wood with fine steel wool.

Repeat coats of shellac until all pores of the wood are filled.

Rub down each coat until only the shellac that penetrated into the wood remains. When rubbing down a finish, use care not to cut through the edges.

After the final coat has been rubbed down, place paste wax in several layers of cloth and apply with circular motion. After 20 minutes, polish with the grain of the wood.

Use a folded cloth for polishing.

For hard wear, tabletops may be finished with a coat of shellac thinned one-half with denatured alcohol, followed by two coats of furniture varnish.

Be sure the tabletop is perfectly clean and dry before you apply the first coat. Allow to dry thoroughly (at least 48 hours) before applying second coat. Several days would be better, especially if the weather is the least bit damp.

Rub each coat with 000 steel wool or fine sandpaper to remove glassy shine. Rubbing between coats is necessary to form a base for the next coat.

Rub the last coat with a pumice stone and oil or water, using a felt pad for rubbing. Or rub with very fine steel wool and linseed oil. Always work with the grain of the wood. Use a satin-finish varnish to eliminate some of the rubbing on the final finish.

Varnishing should be done in a room as free from dust as possible. If a dining room table is varnished in the dining room, keep the doors closed and avoid sweeping in or near the room until the varnishing job is complete. Dust sticks readily to varnish and mars the attractive appearance of the surface.

When paint or enamel is to be used as the finish, sometimes it is not necessary to remove all of the old finish. The surface must be smooth—free of dents and rough edges from chips in old finish—however.

A primer or undercoat is used before applying paint or enamel. This may be white or tinted to approximately the color of the finish. After the primer is dry, rub with steel wool or fine sandpaper. Wipe free of all dust. Two or three coats of the desired finish are applied over the primer. Sand between coats to make "tooth" for the paint to hold. Always dust carefully.

Alkyd-base enamel is the best paint for wood. It may be bought as high gloss, semigloss, or flat. The high gloss is the most durable, but it is less attractive and is used only if the furniture is to receive extremely hard use.

MANY PAINT companies sell "antiquing" kits. If only one piece of furniture is to be finished in this way, a kit may be cheaper than buying the needed supplies.

The general procedure is to paint the furniture, as outlined, with a flat enamel of a color lighter than the desired final finish. The glaze will make it darker.

You may either buy a glazing liquid from your paintstore or mix your own in either of the following proportions: 1 part clear varnish, 3 parts turpentine, and one-half part color ground in oil (more or less as desired); or 1 part boiled linseed oil (purchase boiled oil), 3 parts turpentine, and one-half part color ground in oil.

It is best to mix the color with a little turpentine before adding to the mixture.

If you have painted or enameled the surface in a light color, raw Turkey umber or burnt sienna will be a good choice for a brown glaze. On a surface that is painted in a dark color, such as green or red, thin lampblack oil paint is effective.

THE BASE PAINT SHOULD be lighter and brighter than the final finish you want. For instance, white enamel as a base under a glaze tinted with umber will be light tan or cream when it is finished, depending on the amount of color used. Any color, including gold, may be used. Make a sample before you begin work on your furniture. The base finish may be a transparent finish. The bare wood may be stained, sealed, and varnished before the glaze is applied.

Apply the glaze with a brush or folded cheesecloth. While it is still wet, wipe off with dry cheesecloth. Start wiping at the center and wipe toward the edges. Do not remove all of the glaze from grooves and carvings. A dry brush is helpful in completing the blending. If some areas are to be highlighted, wipe them lightly with some turpentine.

An unsuccessful glaze may be removed while it is still wet by wiping with turpentine.

Allow the glaze to dry 3 or 4 days. Apply two coats of satin-finish varnish. When the varnish is perfectly dry, rub with 000 steel wool; then wax.

CARING FOR WOOD FLOORS

THE SECRET of good floors lies in your understanding of the nature and limitations of the finish you select and how you take care of it.

Two kinds of wood are used for flooring. Softwoods include fir and pine. Among the more durable hardwoods are birch, ash, and oak.

Knowing the difference will help you decide on the finish.

The four main steps in finishing floors are smoothing the surface, applying a filler for certain woods, applying a stain to unify the color, and selecting and applying the finish.

A smooth surface is essential. First, make sure nails are sunk slightly below the surface of the floor. Then sand.

Use a heavy floor sander, an edger for sanding around baseboards, on the steps, and other hard-to-get-to places, and correct grit sizes of sandpaper to fit sander and edger.

A first and second roughing cut are made on old floors that have uneven boards or heavy coats of paint or varnish. These two steps are not necessary on new floors or floors in good condition.

Worn shellac on an otherwise smooth floor may be removed by mopping with a commercial cleaner, which must be used according to directions. The floor must be buffed with steel wool until smooth and allowed to dry thoroughly before applying the new finish.

During the cutting process in sanding floors that have an old coat of finish, the finish heats, and the large spaces between the abrasive grits fill up with melted material. When the sandpaper becomes filled, it will leave a dark line on the wood. At this point, remove the paper and put a fresh sheet on the drum of the sander.

During the first roughing cut, guide the sander diagonally at an angle of about 45 degrees in a direction opposing path about 2 or 3 inches. Use a forward and backward motion to eliminate high spots and to remove paint and varnish accumulation. Use grit No. (coarse) 4 or 3½ open coat.

For the second roughing cut, guide the sander diagonally at an angle of about 45 degrees in a direction opposite to the one in the first roughing cut. Use grit No. (coarse) 4 or 3½ open coat.

Two smoothing cuts are necessary on all floors to remove scratches and produce the desired final condition.

For the first smoothing cut, use smooth lengthwise strokes in the direction of the boards or with the grain of wood. Use grit No. (medium) 2 or 1½.

For the second smoothing cut, use smooth lengthwise strokes in the direction of the boards or with the grain of wood. Use grit No. (fine) 2/0 or 1/0.

After sanding, remove all dust with a broom or a mop dampened lightly with turpentine.

FILLERS are of two kinds.

Natural fillers are colorless and transparent.

Colored fillers are opaque and usually dark brown or black in color; they are commonly named for the wood on which they are to be used, as walnut or cherry wood fillers.

Fillers come in liquid and paste forms.

Open-grain woods have large pores, which must be filled to obtain maximum beauty and service. Close-grained woods do not necessarily require fillers when the finish to be used is varnish or shellac. Use a transparent filler if one is needed. You can omit the filler and use three coats of penetrating seal.

STAIN is used to change the color of the wood and to bring out its grain.

Staining is not necessary if the color of the wood in the floor is satisfactory.

A clear finish will darken a floor slightly—a point to remember when you decide on the use of a stain. If you use a stain, it should be an oil stain.

Instead of using stains, you may add color during the application of a wood sealer. Suitable oil stain may be mixed with the first coat of sealer, or you can buy wood sealers that already contain the color.

WOOD FINISHES are of three general kinds—penetrating (sealers); transparent (shellac and varnish are used most commonly); and opaque (paint or enamel).

Penetrating sealers, of the light-body, hard-drying oil type, sink into and seal the pores of the wood. They are recommended as being the most durable under heavy traffic when they are waxed regularly. They resist chipping, scratching, ordinary stains, and water spotting. They have a soft, satiny gloss, which wax increases and protects. They are easy to apply.

Paste fillers are optional for most brands. They dry quickly to a clear finish or stained effect. They may be patched without visible trace and can be maintained indefinitely without removing previous coats of seal. They can be used either as a complete finish or as an undercoat for a surface finish.

They have limitations, however. They can be applied only on well-sanded, bare wood or on previous sealer finish. Blemishes from poor sanding are not covered by the finish. They should be kept waxed. They need more than one coat to give a satin finish.

A floor sealer with a heavy body and resin content differs from the light-body oil type in that it is less durable, penetrates the wood partially but leaves some coating on the surface, gives a high gloss without waxing, buffing with steel wool produces a low gloss, and can also be used on concrete or terrazzo. It will scratch under heavy traffic.

Transparent film finishes (shellac and varnish) suit the needs of people who wish to let their floors go as long as possible without special attention.

Opaque finishes (paint or enamel) can be used to finish wood floors. Such a finish will hide the grain of the wood entirely. Hardwood floors inside buildings therefore are seldom painted.

An opaque finish provides colors that are not attainable in transparent finishes.

None of the transparent finishes resists weather well enough to last very long out of doors. Good floor paint or enamel are more durable for porches.

Pour the seal into a shallow pan and apply with a long-handled lamb's-wool mop or lint-free rags, first across the grain, then smoothing out in the direction of the grain of the wood.

Let the seal penetrate until it becomes tacky (15 minutes to 2 hours, according to the characteristics of the sealer).

A correct interval between applying the sealer and buffing it is important. If you allow too little time, the sealer may still be too fluid to buff properly. Determine the interval you need by tests on samples of flooring.

Wipe off the excess with a clean, dry cloth. Buff with No. 2 steel wool and brush clean.

If you apply it carefully, one coat of sealer may be enough, but a second coat is generally recommended.

When the second coat is dry, use steel wool and buff as you did after the first coat. If you are not satisfied with the finish, apply a third coat. Wax and polish.

When the floor shows wear along paths of travel, remove the wax and patch with a floor seal. The patching does not show.

Conventional floor varnish has several advantages. Good varnishes give a durable protective coating if they are waxed and maintained properly. The finish will last if it is revarnished before it wears through. Varnish is tougher and more resistant to water and scratches than shellac and fairly resistant to stains and spots. Varnishes have several degrees of gloss.

When you apply varnish, use only floor varnish and apply with a clean, wide brush. The room should be at 70° F. or somewhat warmer, with plenty of fresh air.

First spread a brushful of varnish in a small space, with the grain of the wood. Then stroke it across the grain. Finally, brush it lightly with the grain again. Do not restroke areas that you have covered previously.

Allow at least 16 hours before you apply the second coat of varnish. Sand lightly, remove dust from the floor, and apply the second coat of varnish.

If filler was applied, two coats of varnish will be enough. Use three coats when the filler is omitted. Let dry 24 hours after the last coat of varnish. Then wax and polish.

Shellac dries rapidly and shows little change in color with age.

Use clear shellac (1 gallon of pure shellac thinned with 1 quart of No. 1 alcohol). Apply with a wide brush. The first coat on bare wood requires 15 to 20 minutes to dry. When dry, rub lightly with fine steel wool or sandpaper. Dust the floor to remove all particles. Apply the second coat and let dry for 2 to 3 hours. Again, rub the floor lightly with steel wool or sandpaper. Then dust the floor. Apply the third coat. Allow the floor to dry for 3 or 4 hours, wax and polish.

Floor paint and enamel come in a

variety of colors and are easy to apply. They coat the surface of wood and cover discoloration and blemishes in the floor.

Paint wears off and scratches quickly. It is difficult to patch without detection. Repeated coats form a buildup that must be removed for a satisfactory refinish. Paint chips and peels when several coats have been used. It is slippery when waxed. One should use only types of paint made specially for floors.

On new floors or floor that has just been sanded, or least two coats of floor paint or enamel are necessary. The first coat should be thinned with paint thinner according to the manufacturer's directions. Subsequent coats usually should be applied unthinned. Each coat should be allowed to dry at least 16 hours before the next coat is applied or before the floor is open to traffic.

THE CARE of floor finishes depends on the amount and kind of traffic they receive. Finish wears off rapidly on floors near outside doors, where water may be tracked in, for instance.

The durability of floor finishes can be improved by keeping them waxed. An application of wax every 4 to 6 months may be enough in many homes, but more frequent applications may be necessary where traffic is heavier.

Well-waxed floors are easy to keep clean by dry mopping or an occasional polishing with an electric polisher.

Wax tends to make floors slippery unless the wax layer is kept very thin. Wax is usually less slippery on floors finished with sealers.

Wood floors with fine finishes should never be scrubbed with water or unnecessarily brought in contact with water, except in connection with removing old wax or when refinishing floors. Sweeping or dry mopping should be all that is necessary for routine cleaning.

A soft floor mop kept barely dampened with a mixture of 3 parts of kerosene and 1 part of paraffin oil is excellent for dry mopping. When the mop becomes dirty, it should be washed in hot, soapy water, dried, and again dampened with the mixture. Commercial preparations are available for this purpose also.

Rubber burns (from friction between rubber footwear and the floor) that cannot be removed with the mop may be removed by rubbing lightly with fine steel wool moistened with turpentine or paint thinner.

Stains on a floor finished with a sealer can be sanded by hand, patched with fresh sealer, and then buffed with fine steel wool. Patching on varnished or shellacked floors may not blend so well.

Wax prevents stains, scratches, and general deterioration. It also gives a luster that adds to the beauty of the floor. Many manufacturers have added information to labels about rebuffable water-base waxes that may be applied and polished by machine.

Remove the old wax from the floor before you apply a new coat of floor wax. The kind of wax tells you the method to use in cleaning the floor, for it is the wax that determines the rest of the cleaning method.

Wax is not a hazard if you use it correctly. If there is too much wax, the result is a soft, smeary coat that may cause falls. Polish wax to a high gloss, because the more shine, the less slip.

Falls are apt to be caused by what comes between you and the floor, such as spilled liquids, loose rugs, foreign materials, or uneven floors.

JUDGING QUALITY IN CARPETS AND RUGS

MOST OF US select carpets and rugs on the basis or their color, design, and durability.

Ideas of early weavers of what makes a beautiful and useful carpet continue to influence machine-made ones. Those weavers balanced esthetics and durability. Rugs centuries old are still in use.

The oriental carpet is a handwoven fabric which has a pile knotted in during the process of making. The warp and pile generally are wool. The number of knots to the square inch (100 is a good average for an ordinary rug) indicates the fineness of the pile.

The leading types of orientals are named for the small villages and nomadic tribes of their origin. Often quality (luster, compactness of pile, and clarity of design) is associated with the names.

Rugs more than a century old are rare and expensive, but many 30 and 40 years old are available. Their colors have softened and the pile is polished. Often they are reasonably priced.

Used orientals sold in stores have been cleaned and carry a label stating their condition, such as excellent, good, fair, or poor.

Some American carpet manufacturers are making excellent reproductions of fine old orientals.

Early Spanish rugs, like the orientals, are knotted by hand. Spanish designs are used in machine-made rugs and in imported hand-knotted ones.

Aubusson and Savonniere are two famous types of French rugs. Machine-made rugs with designs based on them are made today.

The first power looms produced narrow fabrics, 27 inches wide. These widths were sewn together for room-size rugs. Later looms were made to produce widths of 6, 12, 15, and 18 feet. These widths are known as broadloom. Broadloom is sold by the square yard.

Wilton carpet, regarded as a standard of high quality, is noted for sharply outlined patterns and textures.

The Axminster weaving is like the hand-knotted carpets in that each tuft of yarn is inserted independently into the warp. There is almost no limit to patterns and colors. The back is stiff and can be rolled only lengthwise, not crosswise.

The velvet weave is the simplest of all carpet weaves. The pile is woven over wire. Knife blades at the ends of the wires cut the pile yarn as they are withdrawn. When the pile is not cut, it is known as looped pile.

A major advance in carpet manufacture was development of tufting, a high-speed method. It evolved from the hand tufting of bedspreads. With wide, multineedle machines, face yarns are sewn through the backing of woven jute or canvas. The finished carpet is passed over a latex roller, which coats the back to lock in the tufts. A secondary scrim backing sometimes is attached to the carpet.

WOOL has been the most widely used material for carpets for centuries. It is graded usually by the count system, which is based on fineness (40's, 50's, 60's, and so on) and designates the number of hanks of yarn 560 yards each that can be spun from a pound of wool top.

Carpet wools usually are coarse, wiry, harsh, and strong. Three major characteristics desired in carpet wools are wearing quality (abrasion resistance), resilience (springiness), and luster (brightness).

COTTON was the first fiber to be used in tufted carpets. Cotton broadlooms were colorful and widely accepted for wall-to-wall carpeting, but there was a difference in quality. Rapid soiling and frequent cleaning caused loss of color. Cotton carpets resisted abrasion well. Cotton broadlooms of good quality were pleasing with bedroom furniture and furnishings.

Research on synthetic carpet fibers progressed rapidly. Rayon followed cotton in the tufting industry.

Today five groups of synthetics are used in broadlooms. They are classified by their general name and usually with the brand name and company. The classification, brand, and name of the company is one reason for so many different words used in advertising them.

The general names of synthetics are acrylic, modacrylic, nylon, polypropylene, and rayon.

The brand and company names, for example, for the acrylics include Acrilan by Chemstrand; Creslan by American Cyanamid; Orlon by E. I. du Pont de Nemours; and Zefran by Dow Chemical.

The fibers of the pile alone do not determine the quality of the carpet. The backing is of major importance. The face yarns are damaged if it gives way.

Jute, the most widely used fiber in backings, is a vegetable fiber imported largely from India. The quality varies.

Cotton can be a flexible and strong backing. Some of the finest woven carpets have cotton backings. Cotton is more expensive than jute.

Kraftcord, a "cellulose fiber yarn," often is used for filling or bulking for binding tufts in Axminster carpets.

Research has started on synthetic backings. Most of those mentioned in advertisements as a replacement for jute are polypropylene.

For the wear life of the pile of a carpet, exclusive of color, the amount of fiber on the face of the carpet is important. The dense pile fibers support each other. In high-pile carpets with tufts spaced far apart, the pile falls to the side. It takes longer to wear pile down from the tip than from the side.

Regardless of the fiber you are buying, examine the carpet for denseness of pile. Bend back the face and look into the back. See how close the rows of tufts are placed. In a woven carpet, you can see the rows from the back. In a scrim-covered tufted carpet, you cannot see them from the back.

A CARPET is a background space in a room. It should recede in appearance and stay on the floor. If it is bright in color, it will appear to advance—come toward you.

A plain carpet, near the color of the walls, will make a room appear larger.

Carpets are usually designed to blend well with many styles of furniture. Plain carpet can be attractive with many.

Shading (dark or light spots) in plain carpets is caused by foot pressure and the lay of the pile pointed from the light. Shading appears in the best carpeting.

Wear, spots, and foot tracks show less on patterned carpet than on plain. Pattern may become tiresome unless it is excellent in design and color.

The final choice of color for a carpet should be made in the room where it will be used.

The price of a carpet is based on the cost of production of the fibers of the pile and backing; styling, design, and color; construction; and sales promotion and distribution. Variation in one or more may mean wide price ranges and differences in the quality of carpet within the range.

THE CARE given a carpet in use may lengthen its years of service.

Wall-to-wall carpeting must withstand wear in traffic lanes. It cannot be removed to distribute the wear on different surfaces.

Establish a routine for care and follow it. Base the routine on the amount of wear the carpet receives.

For weekly care, give it a thorough vacuuming, especially the dark surfaces under or around furniture. Remove spots immediately. Wipe up spilled water before it reaches the backing.

Precautions to be taken should include: Keep proper moisture in a room (40 percent to 50 percent relative humidity) to lengthen the life of the carpet and prevent the shedding of fibers; avoid walking on it with high-heel shoes to avoid cutting the pile and backing fibers; use small rugs at entrances in rainy or snowy weather; and do not shake or beat a carpet when you clean it.

SUGGESTIONS FOR FIREPLACES

IF YOU WANT a fireplace in your new home, if you want to "sit by the fire and take hold of the ends of the earth" (as Ralph Waldo Emerson wrote), the first thing to do is plan its place, design, and size as you begin to plan the house itself.

Your architect, if you have one, will offer his experience and skill as to proportion, size, location, and design of the fireplace so that it is in harmony with the rest of the room and fulfills the functional requirements.

You will, of course, have many ideas, but in selecting the most suitable type and design you are on surest ground if you choose a simple fireplace, use locally available materials, and install it according to tested principles.

You need not make it too fancy. The small house may have a fireplace, in keeping with its scale, that is as charming and comfortable as the pretentious rambler, which has a contemporary fireplace so built that the fire in it can be seen from two or three sides.

A fireplace should harmonize in detail and proportion with the room in which it is, but safety and utility should not be sacrificed for appearance.

Its position in the room should be coordinated with the location of the chimney, of course, so as not to spoil the exterior appearance of the house.

Also, there should be an area of comfort that is not affected by the coming and going of other persons in the room.

Consider the size of the opening, as heat radiated from a fireplace comes mostly from the heated brickwork that surrounds the fire.

For example, a fireplace 30 inches wide, well filled with fire, has greater heating efficiency than a 48-inch fireplace with the same fire. Openings usually are 2 to 6 feet wide.

The kind of fuel to be burned may suggest a practical width. For example, for cordwood (4 feet long) that is cut in half, an opening 30 inches wide is desirable. A narrower opening can be used for coal.

The height of the opening can range from 18 inches for an opening 2 feet wide to 40 inches for one that is 6 feet wide. The higher the opening, the more chance there is of a smoky fireplace.

In general, the wider the opening, the greater the depth. A shallow opening throws out relatively more heat than a deep one, but holds smaller pieces of wood.

In small fireplaces, a depth of 12 inches may permit good draft, but a minimum depth of 16 inches is recommended to lessen the danger that brands fall out on the floor.

Suitable screens in front of fireplaces minimize the danger of brands and sparks.

The chimney also must be soundly engineered. It should be designed and built so that it produces sufficient draft to supply enough fresh air to the fire and to expel smoke and gases of the fire.

ALL FIREPLACES are constructed in much the same way, regardless of design.

The construction of the foundation footing for chimneys with fireplaces is like that for chimneys without fireplaces. The footings must rest on firm soil below the frostline.

The fireplace hearth should be of brick, stone, terra cotta, or reinforced concrete at least 4 inches thick. It should project at least 20 inches from the chimney breast and should be 24 inches wider than the fireplace opening (12 inches on each side).

The hearth can be flush with the floor, so that sweepings can be brushed into the fireplace, or it can be raised.

A common practice, especially in contemporary design, is to raise the hearth to various levels and extend its length as desired.

If there is a basement, a convenient ash dump can be built under the back of the hearth.

In buildings with wooden floors, the hearth in front of the fireplace should be supported by masonry trimmer arches or other fire-resistant construction. Wood centering under the arches used during construction of the hearth and hearth extension should be removed when construction is completed.

Building codes generally require that the back and sides of fireplaces be constructed of solid masonry or reinforced concrete at least 8 inches thick and be lined with firebrick or other approved noncombustible material.

The jambs should be wide enough to provide stability and be pleasing.

For a fireplace opening 3 feet wide or less, the jambs can be 12 inches wide, if a wood mantel will be used, or 16 inches wide, if they will be of exposed masonry. For wider fireplace openings, or if the fireplace is in a large room, the jambs should be proportionately wider.

Fireplace jambs often are faced with ornamental brick or tile.

No woodwork should be placed within 6 inches of the fireplace opening. Woodwork above and projecting more than 1½ inches from the fireplace opening should be placed not less than 12 inches from the top of the fireplace opening.

A lintel must be installed across the top of the fireplace opening to support the masonry. For fireplace openings 4 feet wide or less, one-half by 3-inch flat steel bars, angle irons 3½ by 3½ by ¼ inch (or specially designed damper frames) may be used. Wider openings require heavier lintels.

If a masonry arch is used over the opening, the jambs must be heavy enough to resist the thrust of the arch.

The drawing on the next page shows the construction of a typical fireplace, and the table gives recommended dimensions for essential parts of fireplaces.

Proper construction of the throat area (*ff*, in the drawing) is essential.

The sides of the fireplace must be vertical up to the throat, which should be 6 to 8 inches or more above the bottom of the lintel.

The area of the throat must be not less than that of the flue. The length must be equal to the width of the fireplace opening and width will depend on the width of the damper frame (if a damper is installed).

Five inches above the throat (at *ee*, in the drawing), the sidewalls should start sloping inward to the flue (*tt*).

A damper consists of a cast-iron frame with a hinged lid that opens or closes to vary the throat opening.

Dampers are not always installed, but they are recommended, especially in cold climates.

With a well-designed, properly installed damper, you can regulate the draft; close the flue to prevent loss of heat from the room when there is no fire in the fireplace; and adjust the throat opening according to the type of fire to reduce loss of heat.

For example, a roaring pine fire may require a full throat opening, but a slow-burning hardwood log fire may require an opening of only 1 or 2 inches. Closing the damper to that opening will reduce loss of heat up the chimney.

A damper also permits you to close or partly close the flue to prevent loss of heat from the main heating system. When air heated by a furnace goes up a chimney, an excessive amount of fuel may be wasted.

Dampers of various types are on the market. Some are designed to support the masonry over fireplace openings, thus replacing ordinary lintels.

Responsible manufacturers of fireplace equipment usually offer assistance in selecting a suitable damper. It is important that the full damper opening equal the area of the flue.

A smoke shelf prevents downdraft. It is made by setting the brickwork at the top of the throat back to the line of the flue wall for the full length of the throat. The depth of the shelf may be 6 to 12 inches or more, depending on the depth of the fireplace.

The smoke chamber is the area from the top of the throat (*ee*, in the drawing) to the bottom of the flue (*tt*). As indicated, the sidewalls should slope inward to meet the flue.

The smoke shelf and the smoke-chamber walls should be plastered with cement mortar at least one-half inch thick.

A proper proportion between the size (area) of the fireplace opening, size (area) of the flue, and the height of the flue is essential for satisfactory operation.

The area of a lined flue 22 feet high should be at least one-twelfth of the area of the fireplace opening. The area of an unlined flue or a flue less than 22 feet high should be one-tenth of the area of the fireplace opening.

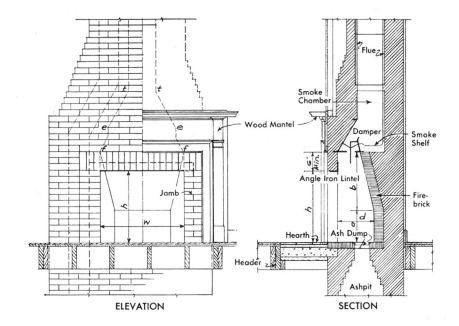

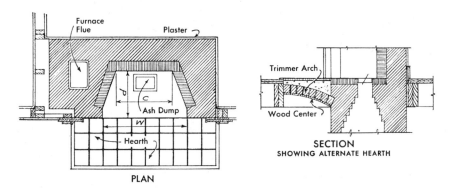

Construction details of a typical fireplace. (The letters indicate specific features discussed in the text.) The lower right-hand drawing shows an alternate method of supporting the hearth.

From the table, you can determine the size of lining required for a fireplace opening and the size of opening to use with an existing flue.

MODIFIED FIREPLACES are manufactured fireplace units.

They are made of heavy metal and designed to be set in place and concealed by the usual brickwork or other construction.

They contain all the essential fire-place parts—firebox, damper, throat, and smoke shelf and chamber. In the completed installation, only grilles show.

Modified fireplaces have two advantages.

Because the correctly designed and proportioned firebox provides a ready-made form for the masonry, there is less chance of faulty construction and more chance of a smokeless fireplace.

Properly installed, well-designed units heat more efficiently than ordinary

RECOMMENDED DIMENSIONS FOR FIREPLACES AND SIZE OF FLUE LINING REQUIRED
(LETTERS AT HEADS OF COLUMNS REFER TO THE DRAWING)

Size of fireplace opening			Minimum width of back wall	Height of vertical back wall	Height of inclined back wall	Size of flue lining required	
						Standard rectangular (outside-dimensions)	Standard round (inside diameter)
Width	Height	Depth					
w	h	d	c	a	b		
Inches	Inches	Inches	Inches	Inches	Inches	Inches	Inches
24	24	16–18	14	14	16	8½ x 8½	10
28	24	16–18	14	14	16	8½ x 8½	10
30	28–30	16–18	16	14	18	8½ x 13	10
36	28–30	16–18	22	14	18	8½ x 13	12
42	28–32	16–18	28	14	18	13 x 13	12
48	32	18–20	32	14	24	13 x 13	15
54	36	18–20	36	14	28	13 x 18	15
60	36	18–20	44	14	28	13 x 18	15
54	40	20–22	36	17	29	13 x 18	15
60	40	20–22	42	17	30	18 x 18	18
66	40	20–22	44	17	30	18 x 18	18
72	40	22–28	51	17	30	18 x 18	18

fireplaces. They circulate heat into the corners of rooms and can deliver heated air through ducts to upper or adjoining rooms.

The use of a modified fireplace unit may increase the cost of a fireplace, although manufacturers say that the labor, materials, and the fuel it saves offset any additional cost.

You need not use a unit merely to insure an attractive, well-proportioned fireplace. You can build an equally attractive and satisfactory masonry fireplace if you plan carefully.

Even a well-designed modified fireplace unit will not operate properly if the chimney is inadequate.

ALONG with their beauty, pleasure, and comfort, fireplaces may have hazards and shortcomings.

Formation of creosote in the chimney is common and is likelier in cold than in mild climates. Green wood may contain as high as 40 percent water; dry wood, 15 to 20 percent. Wood burned slowly gives off acetic and pyroligneous acid, which in combination with water or moisture form the creosote.

Creosote is hard to remove. When it ignites, it makes a hot fire, which may crack the masonry and char adjacent timbers.

The safest method of removal is to chip it from the masonry with a blade or straightened-out hoe attached to a pipe or handle. A heavy chain drawn up and down the flue walls sometimes is effective.

When creosote is removed, care is necessary not to knock out mortar joints or to break the flue lining.

Large amounts of salt thrown on the fire in the grate or fireplace will extinguish a chimney fire.

A fire in a fireplace flue can be checked in its intensity and frequently extinguished by first quenching the fire on the hearth and then holding a wet rug or blanket over the opening so as to shut off the air.

A fireplace that smokes should be examined to make certain that the essential requirements of construction have been fulfilled. If the chimney is not stopped up with fallen brick, and the mortar joints are not loose, note whether nearby trees or tall structures cause eddies down the flue.

The flue area should be not less than one-twelfth of the area of the fireplace opening. To determine whether the fireplace opening is in correct proportion to the flue area, hold a piece of sheet metal across the top of the fireplace opening and then gradually lower it, making the opening smaller until smoke ceases to enter the room. Mark the lower edge on the sides of the fireplace. The opening may then be reduced by building in a metal shield or hood across the top so that its lower edge is at the marks made during the test.

Another way to reduce the opening is to raise the hearth by laying one or two courses of brick over the old hearth. The sides may be made narrower where further reductions are necessary.

Another cause for smokiness is lack of ventilation for the interior. New calking and weatherstripping techniques now can make a house so tight that there are few air inlets to provide air for draft such as fires need; the result is that the unlighted fireplace becomes an inlet for outdoor air necessary to fuel-burning equipment that needs oxygen. Then when the fireplace is lighted, the draft down the chimney is likely to drive smoke into the room. Opening a window an inch or two may let in enough oxygen so the fire will burn satisfactorily.

FOOD TO SATISFY

WE EAT FOOD to live, grow, keep well, and get energy for work and play. It is easy to learn to choose the kinds and amounts of food that help us achieve those purposes.

The accompanying daily food guide, which puts needed foods in four groups, is the beginning.

If you choose the specified amounts of food from each of the groups, you will have a good foundation, but you will want additional foods to complete your meals and to meet your need for food energy.

The number of combinations you can make is almost unlimited, so varied and abundant is our supply of food.

How much of these other foods you should eat to maintain a desirable weight will depend on your age, sex, size, activity, and state of health.

Several examples will help to illustrate the use of the food guide in planning the diet.

SUSAN, 16 years old, attends a secondary school that participates in the national school lunch program. She allows little time for breakfast, but takes time to change her dress two or three times and fix her hair before she can face the world for the day.

"Breakfast makes me fat," she says, but to mollify her mother eats a little food before she leaves for school.

Susan eats the school lunch because the students are not permitted to leave the school grounds at noon. She could bring a bag lunch from home, but her parents insist that she have a warm meal. If cake, pie, or ice cream is served, she generally substitutes a piece of fruit she brings from home. (Menus are published a week in advance.) Susan requests and receives small portions.

Susan goes with friends after school to a soda fountain. She is hungry. She feels noble because she has eaten little all day. So she splurges on an ice cream creation (793 Calories).

At dinner, her parents are annoyed because she eats so little—she is again worrying about her weight. At bedtime, she raids the refrigerator.

The nutritional needs of teenage girls are great, and their emotional and psychological needs also are great. A girl may suspect there is inconsistency, maybe a lack of understanding, in this.

Susan, for example, knows she should eat a balanced diet. Like most teenagers, she wants to keep a slender figure and believes mistakenly that a balanced diet will make her fat.

So Susan tries to cut down or cut out the foods that have the nutrients she needs. Then she nibbles on foods that supply little besides calories or food energy. She does not gain weight, but she shortchanges herself nutritionally.

A teenager is more apt to make better choices of food if her daily routine pattern is not seriously involved— little time for breakfast; a stop after school at the soda fountain; a late evening snack.

By following the daily food guide, Susan can meet her daily nutritional needs without altering her activities very much. She can even eat the cake, pastry, or ice cream served in the school lunch if she chooses her snacks wisely.

A day's menu for a moderately active teenage girl like Susan may be:

Breakfast—orange juice, buttered toast, and skim milk.

School lunch—salmon loaf with cream sauce, green peas, bread and butter, perfection salad (jellied vegetable with French dressing, an apple, and whole milk.

At the soda fountain—ice cream soda. Dinner—meat loaf, baked potato, spinach, bread and butter, cup custard, and iced tea.

Evening snack—cheese and crackers and iced tea.

If you check the food guide, you see that the suggestions for the bread-cereal group were met in the day's menu with four slices of enriched bread and four crackers eaten during the day.

Susan had four glasses of milk or milk equivalent—milk for breakfast and lunch, cream sauce for lunch, cup custard for dinner, ice cream (in the soda), and cheese in the evening snack.

Fish for lunch and meat loaf for dinner provided two servings of meat.

The four servings of vegetables and fruit were peas and apple for lunch and baked potato and spinach for dinner. The orange juice for breakfast provided the vitamin C. The spinach for dinner is one of the dark-green vegetables that are valued sources of vitamin A.

The other foods added made the meals interesting and satisfying to Susan and provided approximately the 2,300 Calories of food energy a teenage girl of average activity needs daily.

A boy is different. His need for food energy—3,400 Calories for the moderately active boy—is greater than the girl's. He is not inclined to worry about his weight. He therefore eats more food and fares better nutritionally.

The food guide is a good way to check his meals to make sure he has enough of the foods included in the four basic groups.

GRANDMOTHER CARUSO came to the United States some years ago, but she likes best the food she had in the old country. Her daughter-in-law, with whom she lives, cooks many of the foods that Grandmother enjoys but has added many American dishes.

Grandmother prefers spaghetti and macaroni with various meats, seafood, or cheese and served with a rich tomato sauce. She likes fruits and vegetables. If she has raw vegetables, she usually serves them with oil and vinegar. If she cooks them, they are often served with a sauce. Her meals are not complete without Italian bread and coffee. She will eat the American-type prepared cereal and occasionally the milk puddings her daughter-in-law prepares for the children. When unfamiliar foods are served, however, she is inclined to make her meal of a macaroni dish, bread, and coffee.

The doctor has advised her that she should eat a greater variety of food and that she should watch her weight. He has frowned on the variety of spaghetti and other pasta dishes served with rich sauces she eats and on her preference for vegetables served with tomato and cheese sauces.

Grandmother has visions of her remaining days being filled with tasteless, uninteresting meals. The more she thinks of it, the more difficult it is to eat the food she believes she must have.

She occasionally can eat the food she enjoys, meet her nutritional needs, and keep her food energy down to the level suggested for women of her age. She will have to eat smaller portions than is her custom, however.

A day's menus for Grandmother Caruso may be:

Breakfast—orange juice, cornflakes, skim milk, Italian bread, enriched, coffee with milk and sugar.

Lunch—minestrone (vegetable soup with pasta), boiled beef (from soup), Italian bread, enriched, apple, cheese, coffee with milk and sugar.

Dinner—chicken, spaghetti, tomato sauce, mixed salad (romaine, tomato, green pepper, hard-cooked egg, oil and vinegar), Italian bread, enriched, tapioca pudding, coffee with milk and sugar.

A check of the menus with the food guide shows that Grandmother's need for foods from the bread-cereal group were met with three slices of Italian bread and a serving of cornflakes.

An elderly person needs two cups of milk daily. Grandmother's need for milk was met with the half cup of milk she used in coffee during the day, the half cup served with her breakfast cereal, the cheese in her lunch, and the

A DAILY FOOD GUIDE

VEGETABLE-FRUIT GROUP

FOODS INCLUDED

All vegetables and fruit. This guide emphasizes those that are valuable as sources of vitamin C and vitamin A.

Sources of Vitamin C

Good sources.—Grapefruit or grapefruit juice; orange or orange juice; cantaloup; guava; mango; papaya; raw strawberries; broccoli; brussels sprouts; green pepper; sweet red pepper.

Fair sources.—Honeydew melon; lemon; tangerine or tangerine juice; watermelon; asparagus tips; raw cabbage; collards; garden cress; kale; kohlrabi; mustard greens; potatoes and sweetpotatoes cooked in the jacket; spinach; tomatoes or tomato juice; turnip greens.

Sources of Vitamin A

Dark-green and deep-yellow vegetables and a few fruits, namely: Apricots, broccoli, cantaloup, carrots, chard, collards, cress, kale, mango, persimmon, pumpkin, spinach, sweetpotatoes, turnip greens and other dark-green leaves, winter squash.

CONTRIBUTION TO DIET

Fruits and vegetables are valuable chiefly because of the vitamins and minerals they contain. In this plan, this group is counted on to supply nearly all the vitamin C needed and over half of the vitamin A.

Vitamin C is needed for healthy gums and body tissues. Vitamin A is needed for growth, normal vision, and healthy condition of skin and other body surfaces.

AMOUNTS RECOMMENDED

Choose 4 or more servings every day, including:

　1 serving of a good source of vitamin C or 2 servings of a fair source.

　1 serving, at least every other day, of a good source of vitamin A. If the food chosen for vitamin C is also a good source of vitamin A, the additional serving of a vitamin A food may be omitted.

The remaining 1 to 3 or more servings may be of any vegetable or fruit, including those that are valuable for vitamin C and vitamin A.

Count as 1 serving: ½ cup of vegetable or fruit; or a portion as ordinarily served, such as 1 medium apple, banana, orange, or potato, half a medium grapefruit or cantaloup, or the juice of 1 lemon.

MEAT GROUP

FOODS INCLUDED

Beef; veal; lamb; pork; variety meats, such as liver, heart, kidney.

Poultry and eggs.

Fish and shellfish.

As alternates—dry beans, dry peas, lentils, nuts, peanuts, peanut butter.

CONTRIBUTION TO DIET

Foods in this group are valued for their protein, which is needed for growth and repair of body tissues—muscle, organs, blood, skin, and hair. These foods also provide iron, thiamine, riboflavin, and niacin.

AMOUNTS RECOMMENDED

Choose 2 or more servings every day.

Count as a serving: 2 to 3 ounces of lean cooked meat, poultry, or fish—all without bone; 2 eggs; 1 cup cooked dry beans, dry peas, or lentils; 4 tablespoons peanut butter.

MILK GROUP

FOODS INCLUDED

Milk—fluid whole, evaporated, skim, dry, buttermilk.

Cheese—cottage; cream; cheddar-type—natural or processed.

Ice cream.

CONTRIBUTION TO DIET

Milk is our leading source of calcium, which is needed for bones and teeth. It also provides high-quality protein, riboflavin, vitamin A, and many other nutrients.

AMOUNTS RECOMMENDED

Some milk every day for everyone.

Recommended amounts are given below in terms of whole fluid milk:

	8-ounce cups
Children under 9	2 to 3
Children 9 to 12	3 or more
Teenagers	4 or more
Adults	2 or more
Pregnant women	3 or more
Nursing mothers	4 or more

Part or all of the milk may be fluid skim milk, buttermilk, evaporated milk, or dry milk.

Cheese and ice cream may replace part of the milk. The amount of either it will take to replace a given amount of milk is figured on the basis of calcium content. Common portions of various kinds of cheese and of ice cream and their milk equivalents in calcium are:

1-inch cube cheddar-type cheese	= ½ cup milk
½ cup cottage cheese	= ⅓ cup milk
2 tablespoons cream cheese	= 1 tablespoon milk
½ cup ice cream	= ¼ cup milk

BREAD-CEREAL GROUP

FOODS INCLUDED

All breads and cereals that are whole grain, enriched, or restored; *check labels to be sure.*

Specifically, this group includes: Breads; cooked cereals; ready-to-eat cereals; cornmeal; crackers; flour; grits; macaroni and spaghetti; noodles; rice; rolled oats; and quick breads and other baked goods if made with whole-grain or enriched flour. Parboiled rice and wheat also may be included in this group.

CONTRIBUTION TO DIET

Foods in this group furnish worthwhile amounts of protein, iron, several of the B-vitamins, and food energy.

AMOUNTS RECOMMENDED

Choose 4 servings or more daily. Or, if no cereals are chosen, have an extra serving of breads or baked goods, which will make at least 5 servings from this group daily.

Count as 1 serving: 1 slice of bread; 1 ounce ready-to-eat cereal; ½ to ¾ cup cooked cereal, cornmeal, grits, macaroni, noodles, rice, or spaghetti.

OTHER FOODS

To round out meals and to satisfy the appetite everyone will use some foods not specified—butter, margarine, other fats, oils, sugars, or unenriched refined grain products. These are often ingredients in baked goods and mixed dishes. Fats, oils, and sugars are also added to foods during preparation or at the table.

These "other" foods supply calories and can add to total nutrients in meals.

half cup of milk in the tapicoa pudding at dinner.

Her need for two servings of meat was met with beef at lunch and the chicken and hard-cooked egg at dinner.

The four servings of fruits and vegetables were met with orange juice (her vitamin C need was met here), apple, the vegetables in her soup at lunch, and in her dinner salad.

These menus will supply the 1,600 Calories of food energy recommended for the elderly woman. Grandmother will need to keep her portion of minestrone to 1.5 cups and her portion of spaghetti to 1 cup, served with a quarter of a 2-pound broiling chicken if she is to keep her food energy at the level of 1,600 Calories.

JOHN DOE, middle aged, is a strictly meat-and-potatoes man. He dislikes fancy salads, especially gelatin salads, and most casserole dishes. He will eat coleslaw and occasionally a tossed green salad, but he prefers his vegetables served as such—either cooked or raw.

He enjoys food. His doctor thinks he has reached the point where he enjoys eating more than exercising. His doctor has advised him to keep an eye on his physical condition, including his weight.

The prospect of foregoing the foods he enjoys most and the beer in the evening as he watches the ball game on TV does not appeal to Mr. Doe. He tried cottage cheese salads with crackers and milk for lunch; he even tried the highly advertised formula diets. After a few days, Mr. Doe concluded he could not work on such food. He decided he might as well be dead as persecuted and returned to his old pattern of eating whatever struck his fancy without giving a thought to the food combinations that made up his daily total intake of food.

Mr. Doe could meet his nutritional needs with foods that he enjoys, have his occasional glass of beer and a snack in the evening, and still keep his food energy intake to the recommended 2,600 Calories for a man of his age and activity.

A day's menus for Mr. Doe may be:

Breakfast—grapefruit, bacon and scrambled eggs, toast, coffee with milk and sugar.

Lunch—stuffed green pepper (rice and meat) with tomato sauce, coleslaw, roll and butter, apple crisp, milk.

Dinner—swiss steak, mashed potatoes, glazed carrots, roll and butter, coconut custard pie, coffee with milk and sugar.

Evening snack—a can of beer, crackers, and cheese.

Mr. Doe's need for food from the bread-cereal group was more than met with two slices of toast for breakfast, rolls for lunch and dinner, and the rice in his lunch.

Two scrambled eggs for breakfast and swiss steak for dinner provided the two servings of meat or meat equivalent recommended in the guide.

Green pepper, cabbage (coleslaw), glazed carrots, and grapefruit made up the suggested four servings of fruits and vegetables. Grapefruit supplied the needed vitamin C and carrots the vitamin A.

Mr. Doe got his two cups of milk or milk equivalent in the milk he had for lunch, the custard of the pie, and the cheese in his evening snack.

Susan, Grandmother Caruso, and Mr. Doe are illustrations of the fact that with a reliable food pattern and a willingness to eat and enjoy the wide variety of food available in this country, you can eat what you need, like what you eat, and, barring accidents, expect to live to a pleasant old age.

CALORIES AND WEIGHT

YOUR WEIGHT as an adult reflects how well you balance the energy—or calories—provided by the food you eat and that used by the body for work, for leisure activities, and for other needs.

Your weight stays the same when calories from food balance those used by the body.

You lose weight when you get fewer calories from food than the body uses.

You gain weight when you get more. These facts point the way for weight control. Control the amount of food you eat, or your physical activity, or both so that the balance of calories is in the direction desired.

Children, of course, are expected to gain weight as they grow, but they should not gain more than is in keeping with normal growth.

A FIRST STEP in determining the number of calories needed to control your weight is to find out the best weight for you. Generally, the weight that is desirable for you in your midtwenties is the best weight for later years, too.

Take a woman of average height—5 feet 4 inches tall. She probably should weight somewhere between 112 and 132 pounds. This range in weight takes into account the fact that bone structure and muscular development vary from person to person.

If this woman has an average frame, her desirable weight probably should be near the middle of the range, about 122 pounds. If she has a large frame, her weight probably should be between 122 and 132 pounds, and if her frame is small, between 112 and 122 pounds.

The range for a man of average height (5 feet 9 inches tall) is 141 to 169 pounds.

Height is measured without shoes and weight is without clothing.

BODY SIZE influences the amount of energy or the number of calories required from food.

For example, a man 25 years old whose activity is average and whose desirable weight is 150 pounds, needs 2,850 Calories a day to maintain that weight. One whose desirable weight is 180 pounds needs 3,250 Calories.

(The large Calorie, spelled with a capital C, is the measure commonly used in expressing the calorie need of individuals and the energy value of food.)

Physical activity is a big factor in determining calorie needs. The calorie allowances shown in the table are for individuals of average activity.

When a person is very active, the number of calories required may be as much as one-fourth higher than when activity is average. Inactivity, on the other hand, reduces calorie needs.

Average activity might be described as spending 8 hours a day asleep; 6 hours in activities while sitting, such as reading, driving a car, eating, watching television; 6 hours in activities while standing, such as personal care or moving from one room to another; 2 hours in purposeful walking, largely out of doors; and 2 hours in sports, exercises, and light physical work.

Age also affects calorie needs. A woman of average activity who weighs 130 pounds required 2,100 Calories a

DESIRABLE WEIGHT FOR HEIGHT FOR ADULTS

	Height (without shoes) Inches	Weight (without clothing) Pounds
Men:		
	64	122–144
	66	130–154
	68	137–165
	70	145–173
	72	152–182
	74	160–190
Women:		
	60	100–118
	62	106–124
	64	112–132
	66	119–139
	68	126–146
	70	133–155

CALORIE ALLOWANCES FOR ADULTS OF AVERAGE PHYSICAL ACTIVITY

	Desirable weight Pounds	Calorie allowance		
		25 years	45 years	65 years
Men:				
	110	2,300	2,050	1,750
	120	2,400	2,200	1,850
	130	2,550	2,300	1,950
	140	2,700	2,450	2,050
	150	2,850	2,550	2,150
	160	3,000	2,700	2,250
	170	3,100	2,800	2,350
	180	3,250	2,950	2,450
	190	3,400	3,050	2,600
Women:				
	90	1,600	1,500	1,250
	100	1,750	1,600	1,350
	110	1,900	1,700	1,450
	120	2,000	1,800	1,500
	130	2,100	1,900	1,600
	140	2,250	2,050	1,700
	150	2,350	2,150	1,800
	160	2,500	2,250	1,900

day when she is 25 years old, 1,900 Calories when she reaches 45, and only 1,600 Calories at 65 years.

As adults grow older, fewer calories are required to keep the body functioning, and older people usually are less active physically than they were in earlier years.

To lose a pound of body fat, there need to be about 3,500 fewer Calories in the diet than the body uses.

If you want to lose 1 pound a week, your food should provide an average of 500 Calories a day fewer than are required to maintain weight (7 days 500 Calories=3,500 Calories). For example, if you maintain weight on 2,300 Calories daily, this figures out to be 1,800 Calories a day for a reducing diet. If you have been gaining weight on the amount of food you customarily eat, you will need to cut down by more than 500 Calories a day.

A way to help create a shortage of calories while controlling your food intake is to increase physical activity. To illustrate: An extra half hour spent daily in purposeful walking and 30 minutes less spent sitting means that for an average-sized man or woman about 45 additional Calories will be used up. In a year's time, the calorie equivalent of 4 to 5 pounds of body fat will be expended.

If the shift is made from sitting to daily exercises, sports, or light physical work, the man would use up about 90 Calories more, the woman about 60 Calories more. That would be the equivalent in calories in a year to about 9 pounds of fat for the man and 6 pounds for the woman.

For many persons, particularly for those whose calorie needs are low to begin with, it probably would be best to increase activity *and* to reduce calorie intake below the level needed to maintain weight.

When diets have fewer than 1,200 Calories, it is difficult to get the minerals and vitamins needed from foods. With an increase in activity, calorie intake would not need to be reduced as much to bring about a weight loss.

If you are considerably overweight,

you probably should reduce. Check with your doctor before you begin, to learn if you are in good enough physical condition for reducing. If you are, he can tell you how much weight to lose, the number of calories to include in your diet every day, and if exercise or other extra physical activity is desirable.

If you are only a little overweight, you may only need to watch your diet to avoid putting on more weight.

To PLAN a diet for weight control, you need to know the number of calories your daily food should supply.

Once you know what your calorie need is, you can refer to tables or charts listing calorie values of foods and make selections that will total to the desired number of calories. But it is wise to have a food guide as well as a table of calorie value as an aid in choosing food. Then you will be sure to include the kinds of foods in meals that are important for nutrients, such as proteins, vitamins, and minerals.

The Daily Food Guide, which has been included in earlier pages, suggests that you have two or more cups of milk a day; two or more servings of meat, poultry, fish, eggs, or occasionally dry beans, dry peas, or nuts; four or more servings of vegetables and fruits, including a daily serving of citrus fruit or other source of vitamin C and a serving every other day of a dark-green or deep-yellow vegetable for vitamin A; and four or more servings of whole grain or enriched breads and cereals—plus additional foods to round out meals.

For a quick check of your food selections, the following calorie values can be used. In some instances foods have been grouped together, and a single calorie figure is given. However, if you customarily have little variety in what you eat of the kinds of foods grouped together, it would be best to find and use a more complete table giving calorie values for individual foods.

Milk should not be eliminated from the diets of those who wish to lose weight. It is an important food that contributes more toward total nutrient needs for the number of calories involved than many other foods. Research has shown that the diets of teenage girls who eliminate milk from their meals are often short of needed calcium.

Some of your milk can be in the form of cheese or ice cream. Skim milk and buttermilk and cheese made from skim milk are lower in calories than other types of milk and cheese.

Calories

1 cup fluid skim milk or buttermilk....	90
1 cup fluid whole milk..............	160
1 ounce creamed cottage cheese.......	30
1 ounce of most cheeses other than cottage cheese	105
½ cup plain ice cream.............	150
1 large glass chocolate ice cream soda..	455

The calorie values for meat, poultry, fish, and eggs that follow do not include the calories from fat that might be used in cooking such as when these foods are fried. And it is assumed that meat has been trimmed of visible fat; otherwise the calorie figure would be higher.

For example, on an average, a 2-ounce serving of beef pot roast that includes both fat and lean would add 165 Calories to the diet. The figure listed for 2 ounces of cooked lean meat is 130 Calories.

Calories

2 ounces of cooked lean meat or poultry without bone....................	130
2 ounces bologna, frankfurters........	170
2 ounces cooked fish................	105
2 ounces cooked shellfish............	60
1 large egg.......................	80
½ cup cooked dry beans or peas......	135
2 tablespoons peanut butter..........	190

Vegetables vary quite widely in the number of calories furnished.

5 Calories
 1 large leaf lettuce, 4 small radishes, 6 slices cucumber, 1 large stalk celery, ½ medium green pepper
20 Calories
 ½ cup cooked or canned vegetables like asparagus, snap beans, beets, broccoli, brussels sprouts, cabbage, carrots, cauliflower, greens, pumpkin, summer squash, tomatoes or turnips—or 1 small tomato
65 Calories
 ½ cup cooked or canned vegetables such as parsnips, peas, mashed potatoes and winter squash

90 Calories
 ½ cup cooked or canned lima beans or corn, 1 large ear of corn, 1 medium potato
110 Calories
 1 small sweetpotato

Vegetables vary quite widely in the number of calories furnished.

If you add butter, margarine, or bacon drippings to cooked vegetables for flavoring or if you fry vegetables, their calorie count would be higher than the figures given. For example, one-half cup of mashed potatoes without fat gives 65 Calories; one-half cup of hash-browned potatoes supplies 225 Calories.

Sauces added to vegetables would also increase their calorie value and so would dressing eaten with salads.

For fruits, use the following calorie figures:

40 Calories
 ½ cup unsweetened or artificially sweetened canned fruit
50 Calories
 Raw fruits in the portions indicated—1 small apple, banana, orange, pear; 1 large peach; 2 plums; ⅔ cup berries; ½ cup pineapple; ½ medium cantaloup or grapefruit
60 Calories
 ½ cup of most fruit juices
105 Calories
 ½ cup fruit canned in sirup

Sugar and cream eaten with fruits increase their calorie value.

When you select breads and cereals, choose those that are whole grain or enriched. Although they are not any lower in calories than the others, they are more nutritious.

Calories

1 slice bread, regular slice............	60
1 slice bread, thin-sliced............	45
1 ounce of most ready-to-eat cereals...	105
⅔ cup cooked breakfast cereals........	95
⅔ cup cooked cereal products such as macaroni, spaghetti...............	105

Toast supplies the same number of calories as the slice of bread does before it is toasted.

There are also other foods that are commonly eaten as a part of meals, as additions to foods in cooking or in preparation for the table, or as snacks. They include desserts, such as pies,

CALORIES PROVIDED BY SOME "OTHER" FOODS

		Calories
Desserts		
Cooky	3-inch cooky	120
Doughnut, cake	1 doughnut	125
Cornstarch pudding	½ cup	140
Cupcake, iced	1 medium	185
Pie, such as apple, cherry, mince	⅓ of 9-inch pie	350
Chocolate layer cake	2-inch wedge from a 10-inch cake	445
Cream		
Half-and-half cream and milk	1 tablespoon	20
Coffee cream	1 tablespoon	30
Heavy whipping cream	1 tablespoon	55
Fats, oils, and related foods		
Butter, margarine	1 teaspoon	35
Other fats, oils	1 teaspoon	40
Boiled salad dressing	1 tablespoon	30
French dressing	1 tablespoon	60
Mayonnaise	1 tablespoon	110
Sugars and sweets		
Sugar	1 teaspoon	15
Jams, jellies, honey, sirup	1 tablespoon	55
Marshmallows	3 or 4	90
Hard candy	1 ounce	110
Caramels	3 medium	115
Fudge	1 ounce	115
Chocolate creams	2 or 3	125
Milk chocolate, plain or with almonds	1 ounce	150
Beverages		
Ginger ale	8-ounce cup	70
Regular cola-type drink	8-ounce cup	95
Beer, 3.6 percent alcohol	8-ounce cup	100
Whiskey, 90-proof	1½ ounces	110
Miscellaneous		
Olives, black	2 large	15
Pretzels	5 small sticks	20
Popcorn with added fat	1 cup	65
Potato chips	10 medium	115
Gravy	2 tablespoons	35
White sauce	¼ cup	110

cakes, cookies, puddings; butter, margarine, cooking fats and oils, salad oils and dressings; cream; sugars and sweets; fried tidbits; soft drinks and alcoholic beverages. These foods often account for the "extra" calories in a diet. Cutting down on them is an excellent way to cut down on calories without shortchanging the body of its other needs.

In choosing a diet for weight control, select first the foods suggested by the Daily Food Guide, Count the calories these selections furnish and subtract the total from your calorie quota. In this way you will know how many calories you can afford to have come from "other" foods.

For example:

	Calories
1⅔ cups skim milk.....................	150
½ cup cottage cheese.................	120
3-ounce serving cooked lean meat.....	195
1 large egg............................	80
½ cup greens.........................	20
½ cup orange juice...................	60
½ cup beets..........................	20
1 small tomato.......................	20
3 slices enriched bread...............	180
1 ounce ready-to-eat cereal..........	105
Total........................	950

If your daily quota is 1,200 Calories, you have 250 Calories left to come from additional choices. Some of the remaining calories probably will be used for a spread for the bread. Other choices may include more fruit and vegetables or meat, for example, or an occasional treat. With a quota larger than 1,200 Calories, a greater variety of selections would be possible.

Learn to enjoy the natural flavor of foods. Calories can be saved by avoiding added fat, sugar, sauces, cream, and so forth. For variety, foods can be seasoned with spices, herbs, vinegars, or tart fruit juices.

Eating regular meals each day is a good idea. Skipping breakfast or lunch leads to nibbling and an unplanned snacking and may cause you to exceed your calorie allowance.

Snacks can be a part of a diet for weight control, though, if they are planned. Save on calories from meals to allow for them. Or a piece of fruit, milk, or a simple dessert saved from mealtime can be eaten between meals.

You may find that small meals along with between-meal snacks planned to fit within your calorie allotment may work better for you than eating the customary three meals daily.

Once you have reached your desirable weight, continue to choose foods with an eye on their calorie content so that you will not go back to old eating habits that resulted in unwanted pounds.

Keep in mind that it is the calories in excess of your need that make you fat— not any one food.

NONSENSE ABOUT NUTRITION

ONE CONSUMER in 19 spends 50 dollars a year on unnecessary or falsely represented vitamin products and so-called health foods. All told, this type of consumer deception costs consumers more than 500 million dollars a year.

More than money is involved, however. Ignorant and unscrupulous promoters may distort the facts and claim benefits against diseases or symptoms that are not caused by dietary deficiencies of vitamins and minerals, and persons who may have serious medical problems are tricked into making their own diagnosis and thus delay getting proper attention.

Laws have been made to help pro-tect the health and pocketbooks of consumers.

The Food and Drugs Act and the Meat Inspection Act of 1906 established the responsibility of the Federal and State Governments to protect consumers by barring foods that are hazardous, adulterated, or misbranded. The 1906 Food and Drugs Act has now been replaced with the Federal Food, Drug, and Cosmetic Act, passed by the Congress in 1938.

Before the Food and Drugs Act was passed, a variety of chemical preservatives and dyes that could be hazardous to health were being used indiscriminately in foods. The law prohibited the practice. Since then, levels of safety for all additives to foods must be established before they may be used.

At one time, the reported sales of "Vermont maple syrup" exceeded the production capacity of that State by about 10 times.

Another example of an adulterated food was butter that contained other fats, such as lard. These products were not harmful, but they were not what the consumer believed they were.

Today, all foods entering interstate commerce must have labels that inform the purchaser of the contents.

THE FOOD LABEL must tell what is in the package. It must not be false or misleading in any particular. Important court decisions have done much to explain this point. Labels which are literally true have been held to be misleading because of what they failed to tell the buyer, or because the product was not what the consumer expected when she selected it by its common or usual name.

Now let us take a look at food standards. Three kinds of standards may be established: (a) Definitions and standards of identity, (b) standards of quality, and (c) standards of fill of container. Most fresh and dried fruits and vegetables are exempted from the standards-making provisions.

Up to now most of the standards have been standards of identity. This type of standard is intended to establish or define what a given food product is—in other words, what the consumer expects to receive when she selects food by its common or usual name. The standard sets the minimum figure for the valuable ingredients and may set a ceiling on an ingredient such as water. For example, the standard of identity for fruit preserves and jellies requires not less than 45 parts of weight of fruit or fruit juice to each 55 parts of total sweetening ingredients. This ratio was established on the basis of a long record of consumer understanding and trade practices in making these products.

The definition and standard of identity for cheddar cheese illustrates another kind of pocketbook protection for the consumer. Cheddar cheese must contain at least 50 percent milk fat (moisture-free basis) and not more than 39 percent moisture. Such maximum moisture and minimum fat requirements insure the consumer against paying cheese prices for excess water. A product which imitates a standardized food but does not meet the requirements of the standard is legal only if it is clearly labeled *"imitation,"* unless it has an identity of its own.

A standard of quality has been set for each of a number of canned fruits and vegetables. These are minimum standards only and establish specifications for such quality factors as tenderness, color, and freedom from defects. Under these standards, if a food does not meet the quality specifications, it must be labeled "Below Standard in Quality," followed by the statement "Good Food—Not High Grade," or a statement showing in what respect the product fails to meet the standards, such as "excessively broken," or "excessive peel," and so on. Tests are made to determine whether a product meets the official requirements.

The definition and standard of identity define what the product is and set floors and ceilings on important ingredients; and the standard of quality provides for special labeling for any product which is not up to the usual expectations of the consumer in quality, but is nevertheless a wholesome food.

Standards of fill of container are just what the name implies—they tell the packer how full the container must be to avoid deception of the consumer and to avoid charges of "slack filling." They are particularly necessary for products that may shake down or settle after filling or which are composed of a number of units or pieces packed in a liquid. In addition to cereals and crackers, such standards have been formally established for some canned fruits and vegetables, tomato products, and seafoods. Informal guidelines for fill of container have been issued for many other foods. For the packer, they answer the question of what is good manufacturing practice that is practical within the limitations of packing machinery and the peculiarities of the product. For the consumer, they help to fight a kind of deception that once was much more common—the selling of air or water or "space" in a container which could and should have held a larger amount of food.

Standards may also provide that a food labeled as "enriched" actually has been improved by the addition of significant amounts of vitamins or other nutrients. The standard-making authority often works toward an important nutrition objective, as in the case of standards for enriched bread, flour, cornmeal, macaroni products, rice, margarine, and evaporated milk. However, the basic purpose of the standards is not the nutritional improvement of these or any other foods, desirable as that might seem. Rather, the purpose is prevention of the consumer confusion that would arise if each competing manufacturer were to claim that his particular food was enriched in some special and superior way. The standards for these enriched foods also insure that the amount of enrichment is substantial—not just a trifling addition put in solely for advertising purposes.

The law requires the labeling to be truthful in what it says about the product; on the other hand, food standards require the food to be what the label says it is, namely the article the consumer expects to receive when she reads the label for it.

In general, manufacturers are not required to state the ingredients on the labels for standardized foods, except that presence of any artifical flavoring, artificial coloring, or chemical preservative must be declared. The common or usual name on the label of a standardized food, is, in effect, a statement by the manufacturer that the composition of his product will be what the consumer expects. It is therefore not ordinarily necessary for the label to state all of the ingredients. But the standard itself may specify which, if any, of optional ingredients should be declared on the label so the consumer will be fully informed. An example of an optional ingredient important to the consumer is the type of syrup used in canned fruits. The packer may choose to use light, heavy, or extra heavy syrup, or he may pack his fruit in water to meet special demand. He must state on the label the style of pack he uses.

The major ingredients of nonstandardized foods should ordinarily be listed in the order of predominance by weight, to avoid consumer deception. However, the law does not specifically require quantities of ingredients to be stated.

The final and necessary step that the consumer must take to benefit from these activities of both industry and Government, however, is to read and use the information on the label.

THE AMERICAN CONSUMER has become health conscious, diet conscious, vitamin conscious, mineral conscious, weight conscious, protein conscious, and fat conscious, but his ability to deal with all of these concepts may be limited.

He is aware that there are important nutritional factors and developments, but his knowledge does not permit him to distinguish always between sound nutritional advice and nutritional nonsense.

Words such as vitamins, minerals, protein, polyunsaturated fat, enriched, and fortified are rained upon him daily so that he feels much happier if he sees one or two of these words on the label of any food he buys.

At the same time he is constantly being told that if he wishes to enjoy good health, he must "improve" his diet with some type of supplement.

As a result, it is not surprising that some consumers find it difficult to make a rational choice of their foods.

It is of interest to note that several organizations that are foremost in spreading nutritional nonsense almost invariably have a stake in the sale of so-called natural foods and vitamins.

THE METHODS of promotion are so similar that the four chief selling points have been dubbed "the four myths" of nutrition.

These are:

The myth that almost all diseases are due to improper diets. The claim is made that chemical imbalance in the body because of a faulty diet is the primary reason for almost all diseases. The consumer is told that to correct this imbalance he must consume quantities of certain food supplements in addition to his regular diet.

The proponents of this myth fail to state, however, that there are extremely few diseases in the United States today that are caused by dietary deficiencies. The American food supply is unsurpassed in volume, variety, and nutritional value. By patronizing all departments of a modern supermarket, the American consumer can easily supply all of his nutritional needs. In fact, he actually must go out of his way to avoid being well nourished.

Another myth is that soil depletion causes malnutrition. The nutrition nonsense purveyor, or faddist as he is commonly called, claims that almost all of our farmland has now been so depleted of minerals that our nutritional needs cannot be met by plants grown on such land and animals fed on crops grown on such soil. In order to counteract this "nutritional sterility," according to the faddist, one must supplement his usual food intake with a manufactured concoction containing all of the nutrients alleged to be missing from the soil.

What is not mentioned is that the

composition of the soil has little significant effect upon the composition of the plants grown on it. Certain soil elements are needed for growth and reproduction of the plant, and the plant will not grow or reproduce unless these are available. Thus the quality of the soil on which food is grown has a definite effect on the quantity of the crop but very little on the nutritional quality of it.

That commerical food processing and cooking destroys the nutritive value of foods is another myth.

Foods such as white flour, refined cereal, canned food, and even pasteurized milk are condemned by the food faddist. He bemoans the supposed extensive loss in vitamins because of warehousing, storage, and exposure to daylight and insists that there is nothing left of any nutritional value after the food has been cooked.

In effect, the food faddist would seem to want us all to become grazing animals eating only foods *au naturel.* He overlooks the fact, however, that grazing animals have digestive systems quite different from the human digestive system.

He does not tell you that modern food processing methods have been designed to produce foods of high nutritional value. Fruit and vegetables are canned or frozen at the peak of their nutritional value, and flour, bread, milk, and margarine are all nutritionally improved in accord with recommendations of authorities on nutrition.

A certain percentage of raw fruit and vegetables is desirable in the diet, but most of our common foods usually are served cooked because they are more palatable and because they are more easily digested.

The fourth myth is that most Americans suffer from "subclinical" deficiencies and therefore must supplement their diets with various concoctions. A "subclinical" deficiency is merely one that has no observable symptoms. Thus, almost any ailment from falling hair to tired blood could be called a "sub-clinical" deficiency because of a lack of sufficient vitamins and minerals in the diet.

The person with chronic aches and pains finds this an especially appealing argument. Even though his physician has examined him and told him there is nothing wrong with him, he "knows" that there is. So when a dietary supplement salesman says there are certain vitamin deficiencies that doctors cannot detect, our friend falls right into the trap.

What the consumer should realize is that no normal person can go through a small part of his life without experiencing an occasional wornout, tired feeling. There is no more basis for believing that this is due to a "subclinical" deficiency than attributing it to the number of children in one's family—although that could well be the cause of that tired feeling—or the phase of the moon. If such feelings persist, of course, the advice of one's physician should be obtained.

IN THE SPHERE of nutrition misinformation the complete protection of the consumer through law enforcement alone is not possible.

The consumer himself must assume the responsibility for learning the facts about nutrition so that he is in a position to make a wise choice among the many items he encounters in the marketplace.

Many organizations are concerned with carrying effective nutrition education programs to the consumer. In addition to the Food and Drug Administration, other groups active in this are the Department of Agriculture, the American Medical Association, the National Better Business Bureau, the American Home Economics Association, the American Dietetic Association, the American Public Health Association, and the Nutrition Foundation.

The basic fact that our farming and food processing industries have provided the consumer with an unequaled variety of wholesome and nutritious food was corroborated with information obtained from studies of the Food and Drug Administration.

The studies were made on market-basket samples collected from grocery stores in five major United States cities in 1961 and 1962. They showed that the average moderate-income diet recommended by the Department of Agriculture contained an abundance of nutritive value when prepared and cooked by usual home kitchen procedures.

The studies originally were planned to discover how much strontium 90 and cesium 137 were present in the daily diet. They were extended to include analyses for pesticide residues and protein and vitamin content.

Analytical examination of these diets as prepared for eating showed that in all cases the amounts of protein, vitamin A, thiamine, riboflavin, niacin, vitamin B_6, and vitamin B_{12} were well above the amounts required for good nutrition.

This certainly refutes the claim of the purveyors of food misinformation that the foods available at the grocery are of no nutritional value and that in order to achieve proper nutrition it is necessary to purchase specially grown foods or specially formulated diet supplements.

The study again shows that persons in good health who eat a variety of foods have no need to worry about dietary deficiencies. *Foods, not pills, are the best sources of vitamins, minerals, and other nutrients.*

The studies also showed that the pesticide residues present in the diet were well within safe tolerance limits.

They further showed that the radioactivity present was well within the amounts considered by the Federal Radiation Council as acceptable for lifetime consumption.

To PROVIDE some guidelines for consumers, several products and practices consumers should beware of are listed here.

• *"Shotgun" formulas.* Food supplements that contain dozens of different ingredients are designed to impress the gullible. More than 40 recognized essential nutrients are required for metabolism in the body, but less than half that number are recognized by experts in nutrition as being appropriate for supplementation of the diet.

• *Loaded formulas.* Many dietary supplements contain amounts of vitamins and minerals that are many times the quantities that can possibly be utilized by the body. The uninformed consumer thinks that because he is getting more of certain substances, the product must therefore be better for him—if a little is good, more is that much better.

Actually, the body requires only certain amounts of the essential nutrients for proper functioning. Any excess, with the exception of the fat-soluble vitamins A and D, is not utilized.

• *Natural and organic foods.* These are foods that are supposed to be grown and produced without the aid of chemical fertilizers, pesticides, or food additives of any type.

It is questionable, however, whether very many are actually grown and processed in the manner represented. They are frequently a very expensive source of nutritional factors that are readily available in ordinary foods that cost much less.

The human body cannot differentiate between vitamin C from an orange and vitamin C prepared synthetically. They are identical chemical compounds and will be so used in the human body.

There is certainly no justification for paying premium prices for "natural" vitamins when the source has nothing to do with their value to the body.

• *Miracle foods.* Many common foods are offered by self-styled "experts" as cures for various serious conditions other than nutritional deficiencies. Examples are carrot juice for leukemia, apple vinegar as a general cure-all, garlic pills for high and low blood pressure, lecithin for heart disease, powdered grapefruit for diabetes, and royal jelly for sexual rejuvenation.

While the overall nutritional status of an individual will determine to a great extent his susceptibility to various diseases, no one food can be considered a cure or treatment for such diseases. One's physician is the only safe source of advice for proper treatment.

• *Reducing products.* It has been shown time and again that the most effective reducing plan is the ability to push yourself away from the table before you eat too much.

Because they do not have sufficient willpower, many persons look for willpower in a pill, capsule, or elixir.

Most reducing products that can be bought without prescription today are merely food supplements along with which there is a diet plan. If the diet plan is followed, with or without the food supplement, one will reduce calorie intake and therefore lose weight.

• *Mail-order products.* Mail-order literature is particularly noted for the prevalence of exaggerated claims, especially in the area of nutrition.

• *"Doorbell doctors."* House-to-house peddlers of food supplements are merely salesmen and are not qualified to discuss and give advice about health and dietary problems. Such advice should be obtained from one's physician.

• *Health food lecturers.* Some sincere and many not-so-sincere persons are self-styled nutrition experts who offer one or more free lectures on health and nutrition as a come-on for a paid series that follows. Such a person usually has something to sell—a line of "natural" foods, special cooking utensils, or false and misleading literature, all at fantastic prices. The forewarned consumer can recognize such a person immediately.

• *Popular books on nutrition.* The advice not to believe everything one reads is especially pertinent in the field of nutrition.

Many popular books on nutrition do contain good information, but many give medically and nutritionally unsound advice and encourage self-diagnosis, Thus, all too frequently, the unwary and uninformed resort to self-diagnosis, and a medical problem remains unchecked.

BE SMART WHEN YOU BUY FOOD

YOU PROBABLY CAN feed your family better and cut your grocery bill if you do some planning—perhaps with paper and pencil—before you go to the store.

The Daily Food Guide printed earlier will help you fit meals to your family's requirements.

From it, you will learn the number of servings of food in four groups—milk, meat, vegetables and fruit, and bread and cereals—that will provide the main part of the day's nutrient needs. In each of the groups, supermarkets offer many items with different price tags.

The family's approval is important. No food is a bargain or a body builder if it is not eaten. Keeping waste to a minimum is a big step toward keeping food costs down.

Consider also your own time schedule. Almost every homemaker has to budget time as well as money. The convenience foods save the time of cleaning, squeezing, peeling, mixing, and sometimes even cooking.

As to their cost, compare that and the cost of preparing an equal amount of a similar product at home. You will find that some convenience foods cost about the same or less than similar foods prepared at home.

Examples may be frozen and canned orange juice, biscuit mix, cake mixes, and instant coffee. Others, such as frozen and ready-to-eat biscuits, rolls, cakes and pies, ready-to-eat cereals, and dehydrated and frozen potatoes, may cost more than similar products that you clean, peel, mix, and cook at home. You may find these services well worth the extra cost, particularly if your time is limited.

Since you think of food needs, preferences, time, and storage facilities as well as cost, you may have to compromise as you plan menus. For example, you decide to find time to make inexpensive breakfast rolls that the family likes. Joe's favorite T-bone steak gives way to the pork roast advertised as the weekend special. You forgo cantaloup until the price is lower. On the other hand, you spend a little more for a company meal, and you get the small and more expensive boxes of raisins rather than the 1-pound box because they are handier for packed lunches.

A list made from menus that you have planned and that takes into account the food on hand makes shopping easy. It can help you avoid the pitfall of impulse buying—the out-of-season fruit and the costly, ready-prepared items or snacks that add little to the diet and much to the grocery bill.

Do not hesitate to adjust the list to make way for specials and other suitable items that offer price advantage when you compare prices at the store.

How much meat to buy for dinner? How many servings will come from a pound of fresh beans, a No. 2½ can, or a frozen package? The food shopper with an eye to thrift and good management learns to buy carefully just what she can use.

The following figures can help you decide how much to buy, and when reading market ads, you can use these figures to help decide what are real bargains.

Meat, poultry, fish

MEAT

	Amount to buy per serving
Much bone or gristle	½ to 1 pound
Medium amounts of bone	⅓ to ½ pound
Little bone	¼ to ⅓ pound
No bone	⅕ to ¼ pound

POULTRY
ready-to-cook
Chicken:

Broiling	¼ or ½ bird
Frying, roasting, stewing	About ½ pound
Duck	About 1 pound
Goose	About ⅔ pound
Turkey	About ½ pound

FISH

Whole or round	¾ to 1 pound
Dressed, large	½ pound
Steaks, fillets	⅓ pound

Vegetables and fruits

	Size of Serving	Servings Per Pound
FRESH		
Asparagus		
Cut	½ cup	4
Spears	4-5 stalks	4
Beans, lima	½ cup	2[3]
Beans, snap	½ cup	5-6
Beets, diced	½ cup	4[2]
Broccoli	2 stalks	3-4
Brussels sprouts	½ cup	4-5
Cabbage:		
Raw, shredded	½ cup	7-8
Cooked	½ cup	4-5
Carrots:		
Raw, shredded	½ cup	6-7[2]
Cooked	½ cup	4[2]
Cauliflower	½ cup	4
Celery, cooked	½ cup	5
Collards	½ cup	4
Eggplant	½ cup	5
Onions, cooked	½ cup	4
Parsnips	½ cup	4[2]
Peas	½ cup	2[3]
Potatoes	½ cup	3-4
Spinach	½ cup	2-3
Squash	½ cup	2-3
Sweet potatoes	½ cup	3
Turnips	½ cup	4[2]
Apricots	2 medium	5
Berries, raw	½ cup	4-5
Cherries, pitted, cooked	½ cup	3
Plums	2 large	4
Rhubarb, cooked	½ cup	3

[1] As purchased.
[2] Without tops.
[3] In pods.

For apples, bananas, oranges, and pears, count on about 3 (medium size) to a pound; peaches, 4 to a pound.

DRY

Dry beans	½ cup	11
Dry peas, lentils	½ cup	10-11

CANNED

		Per Can
8-ounce can	½ cup	2
No. 2 can	½ cup	4-5
No. 2½ can	½ cup	6-7
No. 3 cylinder (46-oz.)	½ cup	11-12

FROZEN

	Size of Serving (9 to 16 oz.)	Per Package
Broccoli:		
Spears	2 stalks	3-5
Chopped	½ cup	3-5
Cauliflower	½ cup	4-5
Corn, whole kernel	½ cup	3-5
Peas	½ cup	3-5
Others	½ cup	3-6

Cereals and cereal products

	Size of Serving	Servings per Pound
Flaked corn cereals	1 cup	18-24
Other flaked cereals	¾ cup	21
Puffed cereals	1 cup	32-38
Cornmeal	½ cup	22
Wheat cereals:		
Coarse	½ cup	16
Fine	½ cup	20-27
Oatmeal	½ cup	16
Hominy grits	½ cup	20
Macaroni and noodles	½ cup	17
Rice	½ cup	16
Spaghetti	½ cup	18

When shopping, go first to the meat counter to select the main-dish items. The price per pound is of little help in comparing costs of meat for a meal, because some cuts contain only edible meat, while others contain fat, gristle, and bone. Try to buy a cut for the servings of cooked lean meat it provides and learn to spot the packages that give the servings needed for a family meal—or for more meals as planned. Compare the costs of amounts needed for a meal to see which cuts are the best buys.

Examples of cost of some popular cuts of meats are shown below. Prices are recent ones from a Washington, D.C., store. For this comparison, one serving equals a 3-ounce serving of cooked lean meat. You may serve more or less than that, depending on the amount one of the family wants or the size of pieces, such as chicken parts, chops, or steaks.

| | Price per pound | Cost of | |
		1 serving	4 servings
Hamburger, regular......	$0.54	$0.14	$0.56
Haddock, fillet..	.49	.14	.56
Beef liver, frozen.......	.65	.16	.64
Chicken, fryer..	.39	.16	.64
Special price.	(.29)	(.12)	(.48)
Turkey, roaster.	.45	.19	.76
Chuck roast, bone in......	.59	.27	1.08
Ham, whole....	.69	.30	1.20
Leg of lamb....	.79	.33	1.32
Pork roast, bone in....	.69	.35	1.40
Special price..	(.49)	(.25)	(1.00)
Round steak, bone out.....	1.29	.40	1.60
Sirloin steak....	1.29	.50	2.00
Special price.	(.99)	(.39)	(1.56)
Pork chops.....	1.09	.56	2.24
Lamb chops....	1.49	.69	2.76

An average serving of cooked lean meat at this store would have cost as little as 14 cents and as much as 69 cents if chosen from these selected items. Specials, such as those given for chicken, pork roast, and sirloin steak, may bring expensive cuts within your budget limits or make inexpensive items even better buys.

Regardless of cost, you can get about the same food value from equal-size servings of cooked lean meat from different types and cuts of meats. Exceptions are frankfurters, sausages, bacon and some meats with breaded coatings. Amounts of these meats usually served may cost less than servings of average size of other meats but do not give as much in food value.

Eggs, often used as alternates for meat, usually are good buys in terms of nutrients.

OTHER SAVINGS can be made on purchases of milk.

Let us say yours is a family of four— two adults and two teenagers—and you use 21 quarts of milk a week, the minimum suggested in the guide. By making a few changes in the way you buy and use milk, you could make the following approximate savings each week in the Washington, D.C., area at present:

$0.63 by getting your milk in half gallons at the store, not through home delivery. In some places, one can save even more by buying the gallon rather than the half-gallon container.

$0.63 if you buy skim milk instead of whole milk in half gallons at the store.

$1.64 if you mix one-half nonfat dry milk (reconstituted) with one-half whole milk bought in half gallons at the store.

$3.26 if you use all nonfat dry milk instead of whole milk bought at the store.

You could save 2 cents each time you use a cup of evaporated milk (reconstituted) in place of a cup of whole milk, or 4 cents if you use a cup of nonfat dry milk (reconstituted) instead of a cup of whole milk.

Reconstituted nonfat dry milk and fluid skim milk have only a little more than half the calories of whole milk— an advantage to weight-watchers but a disadvantage to persons needing more food energy. The vitamin A value in the fat of whole milk is lacking in these more economical nonfat products unless the manufacturer adds it.

A VEGETABLE or fruit may be expensive or not depending somewhat on the item, season, and supply and whether it is fresh, canned, frozen, or dehydrated. If it is canned, frozen, or dehydrated, the brand, type of process, and seasoning affect the cost.

Costs of a serving of selected vegetables and fruit, fresh, frozen, canned, and dehydrated—some 80 all told—were compared in another Washington supermarket.

(One serving was counted as one-half cup of vegetable or fruit or a portion as ordinarily served, such as a medium apple, banana, orange, potato, half a medium grapefruit or cantaloup.)

Costs varied from less than 3 cents a serving of fresh carrots, cabbage, or potatoes to more than 10 cents a serving of fresh tomatoes, asparagus, navel oranges, strawberries, or pears.

Note that all these examples (both the cheapest and the most expensive) are fresh products, rather than frozen, canned, or dehydrated.

Fresh fruit and vegetables are a tonic to dreary meals, and choosing them with care is important to the economy-minded shopper.

Prices change markedly from season to season for many items. Use these fresh foods generously when they are in peak supply and when they are offered at a good price.

Consider the condition of perishable fruit and vegetables and the facilities for storing at home in deciding how much to buy.

A can or a package of frozen fruit or vegetable or two cans or two packages sometimes are a little less or a little more than a family's appetite requires. Try to buy the container that best fits the needs for a meal (or more, as planned) and serve larger or smaller portions.

You may well compare the cost of the container of frozen or canned products and the cost of the amount of fresh produce needed for a meal. An example, for a family of four, may be: A pound can of peas (18 cents), a 10-ounce package of frozen peas (19.5 cents), and 2 pounds of fresh peas (38 cents).

In making such comparisons among different kinds of fruit and vegetables on the cost basis alone, differences in nutrient content are not considered. To be safest on this count, choose a variety of fruit and vegetables, making sure to include a good source of vitamin C daily and a good source of vitamin A every other day.

Cost comparisons among some good and fair sources of vitamin C as listed in the food guide, at recent prices in a Washington store, are given. One serving of a good source or two servings of a fair source are suggested daily. Therefore, costs are given for one serving for good sources and for two servings for fair sources.

Similar comparisons of costs of servings of good sources of vitamin A are:

Good sources of vitamin C:	Cost of 1 serving
Orange juice, canned or frozen concentrate	$0.05
Orange, navel, fresh	.06
Grapefruit:	
Segments, canned	.07
White, fresh	.06
Broccoli, fresh or frozen	.07
Strawberries:	
Frozen	.11
Fresh	.14

Fair sources of vitamin C:	Cost of 2 servings
Cabbage served raw	$0.03
Tomato juice, canned	.05
Tomatoes, canned	.09
Potatoes, cooked in skins	.09
Kale, frozen	.09
Sweetpotatoes, cooked in skins	.10
Spinach, frozen	.12
Tomatoes, fresh	.19
Watermelon	.38

Similar comparisons of costs of servings of good sources of vitamin A are:

Good sources of vitamin A value:	Cost of 1 serving
Carrots	$0.03
Kale, frozen	.04
Sweetpotatoes	.05
Spinach, frozen	.06
Apricots, canned	.06
Broccoli, fresh or frozen	.07
Winter squash, fresh	.08

BREAD AND CEREALS are an important part of each day's food because they give worthwhile amounts of many nutrients as well as food energy. They are well liked. They are easily fitted into meal plans. Many cost only a penny or two a serving.

To put these pennies to best use for

good health, make sure that they are spent for whole-grain or enriched products.

Three and one-half loaves of unenriched white bread, costing about 75 cents, are needed to give the amount of thiamine (one of the B vitamins) in a loaf of enriched white bread, costing 21 cents, or a loaf of whole wheat bread, costing 24 cents.

Specialty breads, such as French, Italian, or raisin, often are not enriched. Check the wrapper to be sure.

Enriched spaghetti, macaroni, and noodles are superior to unenriched products in food value and sometimes cost less.

Parboiled rice is more nutritious than white milled rice. Even though parboiled rice costs more per serving, it is by far the best buy in food value.

Many ready-to-eat cereals give as much in nutrients and cost only a little more than cooked cereals. Small packages, coatings of sugar, special flavorings, and dry-freeze products add to the cost of the ready-to-eat kinds.

ASIDE FROM the four groups of foods, many other items find their way to your grocery cart, such as salad dressings, spreads for bread, sugar, beverages, pudding mixes, gelatin desserts, catsup and mustard, salt and pepper.

As a general rule, these foods add only calories (not necessarily nutrients) and spice to your meals. Calories and spice are needed, but in moderate amounts.

Sugar, sweets, fats, and oils often are used with other foods—sugar on cereals; margarine, butter, jam, and jelly as spreads on bread; and shortening for frying meat and seasoning vegetables and in salad dressing.

The cost of food energy from sugar and fat varies widely. One hundred Calories from granulated sugar may cost only a penny but as much as a dime from fancy candy. You get 100 Calories for less than a penny from margarine and other vegetable shortenings or for 2 cents or more from butter and fancy salad dressings.

Furthermore, weight-watchers will do well to forgo large amounts of sugar and fat in favor of other foods that give other nutrients needed for good nutrition.

What about savings from quantity buying? Be careful! The big economy size may mean only big waste at your house. If it can be used without waste, however, food in the large can or package is usually a good buy, but not always.

How can you tell? This is where the arithmetic comes in.

Look on the container for the net weight. It may be in small print, but it will be there. Divide the price on the container by the weight in ounces to find the cost of 1 ounce of food. The container with the lowest cost per ounce is the best buy.

For example, cornflakes are packaged in eight 1-ounce individual packs (32 cents), an 8-ounce pack (16 cents), and an 18-ounce pack (27 cents). By dividing the price by the number of ounces, we find the cornflakes in individual packs cost 4 cents an ounce; in the 8-ounce package, 2 cents an ounce; and in the 18-ounce package, 1.5 cents an ounce.

"Who cares about a 2-cent saving?" you may ask. But your family of four eating cornflakes every morning could save 70 cents a week by using the 18-ounce pack rather than individual packs.

So keep the following food cost-cutters in mind:

• Checking weekly specials in food-store advertisements.

• Preparing a grocery list before you shop.

• Comparing costs and buying food in the form—fresh, frozen, or canned—or the weight of package—that gives the most servings for the money. To make an intelligent choice among brands of the same product, test different ones to see which one gives the greatest quality and number of servings for the money.

• Shopping carefully for low-cost foods within each food group.

• Using grades in making your food

purchases. Government grades will enable you to be sure of the quality of the food you buy, and you are then better able to compare prices asked.

• Taking advantage of seasonal abundances. These foods will be at their peak of quality, and sometimes will be offered at lower prices.

• Limiting perishable food purchases to amounts that can be used while they are in top quality.

• Preventing food waste by proper storage and by cooking methods that conserve nutrients.

• Considering family likes and dislikes when food shopping. Thrifty food buys pay off only if your family eats and enjoys the food.

Here are suggestions that may help you get more food value for your dollars:

When buying meat, consider the amount of lean meat in the cut, not the cost per pound. Some cuts contain bone, gristle, and fat waste. For example, ground beef and beef short ribs may cost the same per pound, but ground beef will give twice as many servings or more per pound as short ribs. Bacon, which is largely fat, is one of the most expensive foods you can buy in terms of protein value.

Chicken and turkey have a large proportion of bone to lean, but are often bargains compared with other meats. Fish is high in nutrients; often low in cost.

Eggs are usually a less expensive source of nutrients than most meats.

Beef, lamb, and pork liver give unusually high nutritive returns for money spent.

Study bread labels before you buy. Choose bread for weight and food value, not by the size of loaf. Look for bread that is whole-grain or enriched, and that contains milk.

Buy packaged cereals or any other packaged food by weight, not by the size of the package. To compare prices, first look for the weights listed on the labels and note the prices. Then figure the costs for an ounce or a pound.

Ready-to-serve cereals in multipacks of small boxes may cost two or three times more per ounce than the same cereal in a larger box. Sugar-coated, ready-to-serve cereals and those with dry-freeze fruit cost more, per ounce, than many common, unsweetened ones, and furnish more calories, but less other food value.

Cereals you cook yourself (particularly the kinds that take longer to cook) are nearly always less expensive than the ready-prepared ones.

Baked goods made at home usually cost less than ready-baked ones.

Choose the type of pack or grade in a canned product that is appropriate to your cooking method. It is thrifty to buy canned tomatoes of low market grade for stews and sauces. A can of solid white meat tuna costs more than the same size can of grated light meat tuna. You may prefer the solid pack for a salad and the grated pack for casseroles and sandwich fillings.

Consider your time and the quality of the finished product in deciding between convenience foods (those with more than usual services added) and unserviced ones. Compare prices to see if it pays to prepare a product yourself from basic ingredients. Sometimes it does not. How much you enjoy cooking and how much time you can spend will influence your choice.

SAVING ON PLENTIFUL FOODS

You CAN SAVE up to 6 percent of your weekly food bill by buying meat, poultry, eggs, fruit, and vegetables when your local market has them in good supply and features them as sale items.

That means a sizable saving in a year. It is wise therefore to be flexible with your meal plans and serve the items that are in biggest supply.

Improvements in harvesting methods, packaging, transportation, and storage have extended the traditional season for most foods. But—especially for fresh fruit and vegetables—there is still a major harvest season when they are most plentiful in your locality.

Favorable weather or other crop and marketing conditions can bring about bumper harvests that overstock normal marketing channels. When there is a big supply of fresh produce on the market, prices tend to go down. That is the time to buy fresh fruit and vegetables.

For example, you may be tempted to serve fresh tomatoes and sweet corn in December, but unless they are in plentiful supply you may pay 15 cents a pound more for tomatoes and 30 cents more for six ears of corn in December than in peak harvest periods.

Another advantage is that fresh foods bought at harvest peak may be highest in flavor and nutritive value. A processed food in heavy supply probably was frozen, canned, or packed at the peak of quality.

Seasonal supply charts are good guides, but you should remember that they are guides and that supplies can vary year to year. Some years there is a short crop, and contrary to chart indications, the supply is limited.

Other years, the words "seasonally abundant" fail to describe the king-size harvests that exceed normal demands and may well cause problems of marketing. When that happens, the price to the grower drops, sometimes to levels below his cost of production.

At times you may have overbought something or purchased just the right amount but could not use it as you planned. On a large scale, that can happen to a producer who harvests a larger crop than he expected or has the crop ready for market ahead of or behind schedule, and his deliveries overlap with those from other sections. Just like you, he has to revamp his plans to avoid waste. He tells people about the abundance.

This information becomes readily available to the consumer through newspapers and magazines, retail merchants' advertisements and displays, and radio and TV broadcasts.

An instance: Beef was especially plentiful during 1964. The producers, who raise these animals and feed them for market, had achieved the highest level of beef production ever recorded in this country. Beef was listed as a plentiful food.

Excellent beef was available in abundance in markets everywhere at good prices and considerable savings.

By buying and eating 'beef, consumers helped move a food abundance through the normal channels of trade, to the benefit of producers, packers, the food industry, and consumers, who were able to stretch their food budgets while "beefing up" their menus.

HERE ARE some suggestions about the use of plentiful foods.

For some, turkey still means Thanksgiving and Christmas, but turkey now is available all year. Consumers willing to change their buying habits take advantage of summer turkey sales and serve turkey in new ways—stuffed and roasted, broiled, barbecued, fried, or served cold in sandwiches or salads.

The next time turkey is featured, do not look at the calendar but rather in the cookbook. Generally you pay less per pound for the larger turkeys, a 20-pound tom being cheaper per pound than 10-pounders. You get more meat in proportion to carcass on the big ones. Just be sure you can manage a big turkey.

Try this: Ask the meatman to saw a frozen turkey into halves or quarters. Wrap the pieces individually and place them in your homefreezer as soon as you can.

Modern methods of producing and processing keep the number of broiler-fryers that come to market in rather abundant supply all year. Grocers like to offer special sales on them to alternate with specials on other meats. If you find broilers on special sale, you may be able to save as much as 20 to 30 percent. Put them in your freezer.

Instead of roasting chickens, buy whole broiler-fryers of 2.5 pounds or more for stuffing and roasting. You may be able to save 10 cents a pound, or more.

For stewing, get a large broiler-fryer and simmer it to tenderness. The cooking time will be less, because these are young, tender birds, Stewed broiler-fryers are excellent in soups, stews, and casseroles.

The prices of beef vary because of greater demand for certain cuts, like porterhouse, rib, sirloin, and round steaks, as compared to chuck, brisket, plate, neck, and shank meat. Because ground beef usually is prepared from less popular cuts, it costs less.

Lean for lean and fat for fat, however, all cuts of beef are about the same in nutritional value. Variations in calories are related to the amount of fat that interlaces the lean meat. A well-balanced diet needs a certain amount of fat for proper digestion and utilization of the goodness in all foods.

Knowledge of the different cuts of beef helps one in buying beef. The demand for steaks and rib roasts is exceptionally high in some seasons. For example, summer cookouts create a heavy demand for steaks and barbecue meats. If roasts go on sale then, buy one, even if it is summer, or stock your freezer with several roasts.

Buying larger cuts of beef when they are featured can be a wise purchase, too. The trick is to have the meat cut into portions to suit your family needs. A rib roast five ribs thick may be too large for an average family; ask the meatman to remove the shortribs, cut off two or three rib steaks, and leave the two-rib roast. You now have the makings for three meals: A braised shortrib dish, broiled rib steaks, and a rib roast for a special dinner.

Small- and medium-size eggs sometimes sell for as much as one-fourth less than the large and extra-large size in the same grade, especially in late summer and early fall.

Always compare prices of eggs of different sizes within the same grade to see which is the best buy. It does vary. The size does not affect quality, but it does affect price. You should always judge egg quality by the grade, not by the size. There are Grade A Extra Large, Grade A Medium, and Grade A Small eggs as well as Grade B Extra Large, Grade B Medium, and so on.

To determine which eggs are the best buy, divide the cost of a dozen eggs by the number of ounces a dozen eggs weigh. That gives the cost per ounce, which, multiplied by 16 (ounces), gives the cost per pound of the dozen eggs. The minimum weights per dozen are: Extra Large eggs, 27 ounces, or 1 pound 11 ounces; Large, 24 ounces, or 1 pound 8 ounces; Medium, 21 ounces, or 1 pound 5 ounces; Small, 18 ounces, or 1 pound 2 ounces.

For example, if Extra Large Grade A eggs sell for 86 cents a dozen, the price paid per pound is 51 cents. If Small Grade A eggs sell at 58 cents a dozen, the price per pound is 52 cents. The Extra Large eggs would be about 1 cent a pound cheaper. If, however, the Small Grade A eggs sell at 40 cents a dozen, the price per pound is 36 cents, or 15 cents a pound cheaper than the Extra Large Grade A eggs at 51 cents a dozen.

Fresh, frozen, canned, and dried fruits and vegetables are the mainstay of menus. The increase in processed foods makes it important for each consumer to keep a watchful eye on food advertisements. For many times the abundant supply is a processed food item rather than the fresh product.

Citrus fruit, root vegetables, cranberries, and apples generally are plentiful and more favorably priced in fall and winter. Fresh berries, melons, peaches, plums, and garden produce are in generous supply and lower in price during the late spring to fall harvest months. They are usually lowest in price in your community when it is harvesttime in the nearest growing district. Advances in transportation, however, make it possible for all to share in an abundant harvest miles away.

Budgets and appetites respond when plentiful fruits and vegetables are included in the shopping lists.

For example, if lettuce goes up in price (perhaps because of weather conditions that cut the size of the crop), consider using cabbage or endive for the salad or have a relish tray salad of carrot, green pepper, and celery.

Fresh oranges and grapefruit are most reasonably priced in January into April. In summer, the family can still enjoy citrus products in canned or frozen form. Many grocers feature frozen and canned orange, grapefruit, and lemon products in summer. Watch the advertisements so you can keep your freezer and cupboards well stocked.

You can also get vitamin C from tomatoes, raw cabbage, and some of the dark-green vegetables that may be in plentiful supply.

When a fresh product comes on the market at the beginning of its harvest season, it may be higher in price than it will be after the harvest has been underway for awhile.

For instance, tomatoes may start coming onto the market in quantity in May, and prices may start dropping. But lowest prices usually do not come until midsummer, sometimes in August, when the harvest is at its peak.

Keep checking the advertisements and keep a watchful eye on the various produce items when shopping, if you plan to buy in quantity for canning or stocking the freezer.

Canned and frozen foods often are bargains when grocers make their end-of-year inventory. January sales on odd lots of canned goods, discontinued lines, or lines that are moving slowly are good for stocking the cupboard.

Sometimes case-lot promotions are conducted in February and March. Fall by-the-case sales also are worth watching, especially if there is a generous new pack of the fruit or vegetable. It is important for the last year's pack to be moved in order to make room for the new. Sales of frozen food also gain momentum then.

Take advantage of special sales of salad and cooking oils. Buy by the quart, half gallon, or gallon for use in many ways, like these:

Add 1 tablespoon salad oil per layer when whipping up a package cake mix. The result is extra lightness.

Brush gelatin and candy molds lightly with oil before using. The molded creations will come out easily.

To keep macaroni, rice, noodles, and spaghetti separated during cooking and also to keep water from boiling over, add a tablespoon of oil per cup of boiling water.

Cakes, cupcakes, and breads will have evenly browned, unbroken crusts when the pans are brushed lightly with vegetable oil and then dusted lightly with flour before the batter or dough is added.

USDA GRADES: AID TO SHOPPERS

Shopping for food today is much more complicated than it used to be. Most grocery stores have a bewildering array of foods; and you probably find it difficult to select the particular variety or quality you want.

Your solution may be to buy a particular brand, or a food that carries on official grade mark. The U.S. Department of Agriculture offers a shopper's aid in the form of U.S. grades for consumers. You are probably familiar with some of these grades—U.S. Grade A or AA for eggs, for instance.

USDA (United States Department of Agriculture) grades for food are a dependable, nationally uniform guide to quality and a means of making valid comparisons of quality and price.

Beef, lamb, butter, poultry, and eggs are the products most likely to carry the USDA grade shield.

This official emblem of quality is not so widely used on other foods, although it is available for use on many others.

The food that carries the USDA grade shield—usually with the designation U.S. Grade A or AA, or (for meat) U.S. Choice—measures up to a definite standard of quality, as determined by a Government grader who has examined it. It is clean and wholesome.

Processors and packers who wish to employ Government grading services and have their product carry the USDA grade shield must meet strict requirements for plant sanitation and operating procedure.

Meat and poultry must be inspected

for wholesomeness if they are to be graded.

Federally graded meat is easy to identify. It bears a grade stamp which consists of a shield enclosing the letters "USDA" and the appropriate grade name, such as Prime, Choice, or Good.

This stamp is registered in the U.S. Patent Office and only an official grader of the U.S. Department of Agriculture is authorized to use it.

Another purple stamp you may see on meat is round in shape and bears the legend "U.S. Insp'd & P'S'D." This is the symbol of Federal meat inspection and assures you that the meat was wholesome at the time it was inspected. Federal inspection is compulsory for meat shipped in interstate or foreign commerce. All meat federally graded must first be inspected for wholesomeness.

Products with the shield are not the only ones graded. Your grocery store may do most of its buying on the basis of USDA grades. Wholesale grades, such as U.S. No. 1, marked on containers of fresh fruit and vegetables often carry through to the retail level. Look for them on consumer packages of such commodities as potatoes, onions, apples, and citrus fruits.

THE DEPARTMENT OF AGRICULTURE performs three functions that have to do with the quality and wholesomeness of food—standardization, grading, and inspection.

Since food, as a product of Nature, comes in varying degrees of quality, some way of sorting it out—grading it —is needed.

Standards for grades of quality cannot be quite so precise as measures of quantity. They are based on the attributes of a product that determine its value and its usefulness.

For instance, consumers have said they want tenderness, juiciness, and flavor in a beefsteak. In order to develop standards for grades of beef, then, it is necessary to identify the factors that indicate how tender, juicy, and

flavorful the meat from a particular beef carcass will be.

The standards for beef accordingly take into account the amount of marbling (fat interspersed within the lean), the color, firmness, and texture of the meat, and the age of the animal.

Standards for each product describe the entire range of quality. The number of grades for a product depends upon its variability. It takes eight grades to span the range of beef quality, for example, but only three are required for frying chickens, since their quality varies less than beef does.

Specialists in the Department of Agriculture have developed and published grade standards for more than 300 farm products.

They develop new ones as they are needed and revise the established ones to reflect changes in production, use, and marketing practices.

The standards are widely used by processors and packers for their own quality-control programs. The use of the Department of Agriculture grading services, often operated in cooperation with State departments of agriculture, is voluntary, unless required under State or local law or an industry program. They are provided on a fee-for-service basis, not at Government expense.

Inspection for wholesomeness, on the other hand, is a Department service that is required under Federal law for meat and poultry destined for interstate or foreign trade and therefore is provided at Government expense. Inspection in this sense does not relate to the quality of the food—only to its fitness for human food.

Here, for use as a shopping guide, is a summary of the kinds of products graded, the grade names, and an explanation of what the grades mean in each case.

SIX KINDS OF MEAT are graded: Beef, veal, calf, lamb, yearling mutton, and mutton.

The grade names, U.S. Prime, U.S. Choice, and U.S. Good, can apply to all, except that mutton is not eligible for the Prime grade. There are lower grades for each of these meats, also, which differ slightly in terminology but are not likely to be seen in retail stores.

The next three lower grades for beef, U.S. Standard, U.S. Commercial, and U.S. Utility, may appear on occasion on retail counters. A store usually carries only one grade—the one it has found pleases most of its customers.

U.S. Prime, the top grade of beef, is produced from young and well-fed beef-type cattle. Meat of this grade is liberally marbled. Roasts and steaks are tender, juicy, and flavorful. Most of the supply of Prime beef is sold to restaurants and hotels.

U.S. Choice is the grade preferred by most consumers and is widely available at retail. It is of high quality and usually has less fat than Prime beef. Roasts and steaks from the loin, rib, and top round in this grade are tender and juicy. Other cuts, such as those from the bottom round or chuck, which are more suitable for pot roasting or braising, are juicy and have a well-developed flavor.

U.S. Good grade beef is lean but of fairly good quality. Although cuts of this grade lack the juiciness and flavor associated with a higher degree of fatness, their relative tenderness and high proportion of lean to fat please many thrifty shoppers.

U.S. Standard grade beef has very little fat and a mild flavor. It lacks juiciness but is relatively tender, since it comes from young animals.

U.S. Commercial beef comes from older cattle and therefore lacks tenderness. Long, slow cooking with moist heat is required for most cuts to develop the rich, full flavor of mature beef.

VEAL is produced from animals that are 3 months or less in age; calf from animals between 3 months and 8 months old. The higher grades of veal, U.S. Prime and Choice, are more thickly fleshed than the lower grades and have a higher proportion of meat to bone.

Also, they have more fat and therefore are more juicy and flavorful. No grade of veal, however, has enough fat intermingled with the lean to make cooking with dry heat practical. Moist heat is needed to insure juiciness and development of flavor. Calf is intermediate between veal and beef in its texture, flavor, and tenderness.

MEAT produced from sheep is divided into three classes, according to its age when slaughtered—lamb, yearling mutton, and mutton.

Most of the sheep produced in this country are marketed as lamb. Because lamb is produced from young animals, most of the cuts of the higher grades are tender enough to be cooked by dry heat—roasting, broiling, and pan broiling.

Yearling mutton comes from animals between 1 and 2 years old. It is produced in limited quantities, but is preferred by some people because it is more flavorful than lamb. Chops and legs of the higher grades are tender enough to be cooked by dry heat.

Mutton, which comes from mature animals, lacks natural tenderness and should be braised or pot roasted.

SIX KINDS OF POULTRY are graded: Turkey, chicken, duck, goose, guinea, squab.

The grade names are U.S. Grade A, U.S. Grade B, and U.S. Grade C.

Poultry grades are based on the conformation, or fleshing, of the bird—the proportion of meat to bone; the finish—the amount of fat in and under the skin, which tends to keep the meat moist and tender while cooking; and the absence or degree of defects such as cuts, tears, and bruises.

The "class" of the bird, which will appear on the label, is a guide to tenderness and to the appropriate cooking method. "Class" is indicated by the words "young," "mature," or "old," and by such terms as "broiler," "roaster," "stewing hen."

Much of the poultry produced is graded and is identified at retail with the USDA grade shield. Usually only U.S. Grade A is identified. Lower

Below is a guide to cooking time. Quality of meat, size and shape of roast, and its temperature at the start all affect the time required. If you use a meat thermometer, insert it so the bulb is at center of thickest part of meat and does not touch bone or fat.

Kind and cut of meat	Ready-to-cook weight	Approximate roasting time at 325° F.	Internal temperature of meat when done
Beef			
Standing ribs:	*Pounds*	*Hours*	*° F.*
Rare................	6 to 8......	2 to 2½......	140
Medium...........	6 to 8......	2½ to 3......	160
Well done........	6 to 8......	3⅓ to 4½....	170
Rolled rib:			
Rare................	4 to 6......	2 to 3........	140
Medium...........	4 to 6......	2½ to 3¼....	160
Well done........	4 to 6......	3 to 4........	170
Rolled rump......	5........	3 to 3¼......	160 to 170
Sirloin tip........	3........	2 to 2¼......	160 to 170
Veal			
Leg................	5 to 8......	2½ to 3½....	170 to 180
Loin...............	5........	3............	170 to 180
Rolled shoulder...	3 to 5......	3 to 3½......	170 to 180
Lamb			
Leg................	6 to 7......	3¼ to 4......	180
Shoulder..........	3 to 6......	2¼ to 3¼....	180
Rolled shoulder...	3 to 5......	2½ to 3......	180
Pork, fresh			
Loin...............	3 to 5......	3 to 4........	185
Shoulder..........	5 to 8......	3½ to 5......	185
Ham, whole........	10 to 14....	5½ to 6......	185
Ham, half.........	6..........	4............	185
Spareribs.........	3..........	2............	185
Pork, cured			
Cook-before-eating:			
Ham, whole.......	12 to 16....	3½ to 4¼....	160
Ham, half........	6..........	2½..........	160
Picnic shoulder...	6..........	3½..........	170
Fully cooked:			
Ham, whole.......	12 to 16....	2 to 3........	130
Ham, half........	6..........	About 1½....	130

grades are seldom, if ever, labeled as such.

You can use the following rough guides for amounts of poultry (at ready-to-cook weight) to purchase per serving:

Chicken:
Broiling or barbecuing .... ¼ to ½ bird
Frying, roasting, stewing about ½ pound
Duck .... about 1 pound
Goose .... about ⅔ pound
Turkey .... about ¾ pound.

And below is a guide to roasting poultry.

EGGS ARE GRADED for size and for quality. There is no relation between size and quality.

Grade B eggs have a thinner white, which spreads over a wide area when broken. The yolk is rather flat and may break easily.

The term "Fresh Fancy Quality" is used only on eggs that have been produced under a special quality-control program designed to insure freshness as well as high quality.

Official egg sizes are based on weight per dozen, not size of the individual egg, although variation of sizes of individual eggs within a dozen is limited by the standards. Minimum weight of a dozen Large eggs is 24 ounces; Medium, 21 ounce; Small, 18 ounces, and so on. There is a 3-ounce difference between each weight class.

Kind of bird	Ready-to-cook weight	Large bread-crumbs for stuffing	Approximate roasting time at 325° F. for stuffed, chilled bird
	Pounds	*Quarts*	*Hours*
Chicken:			
Broilers or fryers...........	1½ to 2½	¼ to ½	1¼ to 2
Roasters..................	2½ to 4½	½ to 1¼	2 to 3½
Capons..................	4 to 8	1¼ to 1¾	3 to 5
Duck.....................	3 to 5	½ to 1	2½ to 3
Goose...................	4 to 8	¾ to 1½	2¾ to 3½
	8 to 14	1½ to 2½	3½ to 5
Turkey:			
Fryers or roasters (very young birds)...........	4 to 8	1 to 2	3 to 4½
Roasters (fully grown young birds).................	6 to 12	2 to 3	3½ to 5
	12 to 16	3 to 4	5 to 6
	16 to 20	4 to 5	6 to 7½
	20 to 24	5 to 6	7½ to 9

The grade names for quality are Fresh Fancy Quality or U.S. Grade AA, U.S. Grade A, and U.S. Grade B.

For size, the names are U.S. Jumbo, Extra Large, Large, Medium, Small, and Peewee.

The two higher grades of quality have a large proportion of thick white, which stands up well around a firm, high yolk. They are delicate in flavor.

OF THE DAIRY PRODUCTS, butter, Cheddar and Swiss cheese, and nonfat dry milk are graded.

A quality-control program and "Quality Approved" rating is available for process cheese, cottage cheese, sour cream, and buttermilk.

Grade names: U.S. Grade AA, U.S. Grade A, and U.S. Grade B for both butter and Cheddar cheese. They are the same for Swiss cheese, except there is no U.S. Grade AA. (There is also a Grade C for Cheddar and C and D grades for Swiss cheese.)

Grades for nonfat dry milk are U.S. Extra Grade and U.S. Standard Grade.

The higher grades of butter have a pleasing and desirable sweet flavor and are made only from cream that has such flavor. Grade B butter is generally made from selected sour cream and therefore lacks the fresh flavor of the top grades.

The top grades of cheese indicate desirable and consistent flavor, body, and texture, as appropriate for the type of cheese, which in Cheddar includes sharp, mellow, and mild. Labeling of cheese with the U.S. grade shield is not widespread, though much of it is graded at wholesale.

The U.S. grade shield on a package of nonfat dry milk is assurance of dependable quality and compliance with sanitary requirements. It is also assurance, in the case of "instant" nonfat dry milk, that the milk powder will in fact dissolve instantly.

MOST FRESH FRUIT and vegetables are packed and sold on the wholesale market on the basis of U.S. grades. There are standards for 72 different kinds. Thirteen "consumer standards" have been developed for use at the retail level but are seldom used.

The typical range of grades used at wholesale for fresh fruit and vegetables includes U.S. Fancy, U.S. No. 1, U.S. No. 2. There are sometimes grades above and below that range. For instance, grades for apples are U.S. Extra Fancy, U.S. Fancy, U.S. No. 1, and U.S. Utility. The "consumer grades" are, generally, U.S. Grades A, B, and C.

Grades for fresh fruit and vegetables are determined on the basis of the product's color, size, shape, degree of maturity, and freedom from defects. Defects may be those caused by dirt, freezing, disease, insects, or mechanical injury.

GRADES have been developed for a great variety of processed fruits and vegetables, canned, dried, and frozen, and a number of related products, such as peanut butter, jams, jellies, pickles, olives, honey, and orange juice crystals.

The usual grade names are U.S. Grade A or U.S. Fancy; U.S. Grade B or U.S. Choice or U.S. Extra Standard; U.S. Grade C or U.S. Standard. There are few exceptions to this pattern.

U.S. Grade A (or Fancy) indicates an excellent quality in processed fruit and vegetables, uniformity in size and color, virtual freedom from defects, and the proper degree of maturity or tenderness. This grade is suited for special uses, as in desserts or salads, where appearance and texture are important.

U.S. Grade B is a good quality, just as nutritious as the top grade, but the product may be less uniform in size and color and less tender and free from blemishes. Most processed fruit and vegetables are of this grade. It is quite satisfactory for most uses.

U.S. Grade C indicates fairly good quality. The product is just as wholesome and may be as nutritious as the higher grades.

Only a limited amount of processed fruits and vegetables and related products are marked with the U.S. grade shield, which means that a Government grader has examined the product and certified that it is the quality stated.

Hundreds of processors, however, employ the grade standards in packing and selling processed fruit and vegetables. They may use the grade name, without the "U.S." in front of it, on their labels, even though the product has not been examined by a Government grader, as long as the quality actually is as good as indicated by the grade name.

If the quality does not measure up to the grade claimed, the processor is liable to prosecution under laws on mislabeling.

MILLED (white) and brown rice, dry edible beans, peas, and lentils are graded.

The grades are: For milled (white) rice, U.S. Grades 1, 2, 3, 4, 5, and 6; for brown rice, U.S. Grades 1, 2, 3, 4, and 5; for beans and peas, U.S. Grades

U. S. GRADES AT A GLANCE

Product	Consumer Grades		Wholesale Grades *			
	1st Grade	2d Grade	1st Grade	2d Grade	3d Grade	4th Grade
Beet Greens	U. S. Grade A	. . . .	U. S. No. 1	. . . .	. . . .	. . . .
Potatoes	U. S. Grade A Large U. S. Grade A Medium to Large U. S. Grade A Medium U. S. Grade A Small	U. S. Grade B Large U. S. Grade B Medium to Large U. S. Grade B Medium U. S. Grade B Small	U. S. Fancy	U. S. No. 1	U. S. Commercial	U. S. No. 2
Broccoli (Italian Sprouting)	U. S. Grade A	U. S. Grade B	U. S. Fancy	U. S. No. 1	U. S. No. 2	. . . .
Brussels Sprouts	U. S. Grade A	U. S. Grade B	U. S. No. 1	U. S. No. 2	. . . .	. . . .
Carrots	U. S. Grade A	U. S. Grade B	(Topped carrots) U. S. Extra No. 1	U. S. No. 1	U. S. No. 2	. . . .
Corn (Husked, on the cob)	U. S. Grade A	U. S. Grade B	(Green corn) U. S. Fancy	U. S. No. 1	U. S. No. 2	. . . .

FRESH FRUITS AND VEGETABLES

Cranberries	U. S. Grade A	. . . . . .	. . . . . .	U. S. Commercial	. . . . . .	. . . . . .
Kale	U. S. Grade A	U. S. Grade B	U. S. No. 1	U. S. Commercial	. . . . . .	. . . . . .
Parsnips	U. S. Grade A	U. S. Grade B	U. S. No. 1	U. S. No. 2	. . . . . .	. . . . . .
Spinach Leaves	U. S. Grade A	U. S. Grade B	U. S. Extra No. 1	U. S. No. 1	U. S. Commercial	. . . . . .
Tomatoes	U. S. Grade A	U. S. Grade B	U. S. No. 1	U. S. Combination	U. S. No. 2	U. S. No. 3
Turnips	U. S. Grade A	U. S. Grade B	(Topped turnips) U. S. No. 1	U. S. No. 2	. . . . . .	. . . . . .
Celery	U. S. Grade AA	U. S. Grade A (3d Grade— U. S. Grade B)	U. S. Extra No. 1	U. S. No. 1	U. S. No. 2	. . . . . .
Apples	None	None	U. S. Extra Fancy	U. S. Fancy	U. S. No. 1 / U. S. No. 1 [1] Cookers / U. S. No. 1 [2] Early / U. S. Hail Grade [3]	U. S. Utility

[1] Same as U. S. No. 1 except for color.
[2] Same as U. S. No. 1 except for color, maturity and size.
[3] Same as U. S. No. 1 except for hail injury.

* Partial listing of commodities for which there are wholesale grades to show how these grades compare with consumer grades.

U. S. GRADES AT A GLANCE

Product	1st Grade	2d Grade	3d Grade	4th Grade	5th Grade
MEATS					
Beef	USDA Prime	USDA Choice	USDA Good	USDA Standard	USDA Commercial [1]
Veal	USDA Prime	USDA Choice	USDA Good	USDA Standard	USDA Utility [2]
Calf	USDA Prime	USDA Choice	USDA Good	USDA Standard	USDA Utility [2]
Lamb	USDA Prime	USDA Choice	USDA Good	USDA Utility	USDA Cull
Yearling Mutton	USDA Prime	USDA Choice	USDA Good	USDA Utility	USDA Cull
Mutton	....	USDA Choice	USDA Good	USDA Utility	USDA Cull
DAIRY PRODUCTS					
Butter	U. S. Grade AA (U. S. 93 Score)	U. S. Grade A (U. S. 92 Score)	U. S. Grade B (U. S. 90 Score)	....	....
Cheddar Cheese	U. S. Grade AA	U. S. Grade A	U. S. Grade B	U. S. Grade C	....
Swiss Cheese	U. S. Grade A	U. S. Grade B	U. S. Grade C	U. S. Grade D	....
Nonfat Dry Milk	U. S. Extra Grade	U. S. Standard Grade	....		
Cottage Cheese	No Grades—May be marked USDA "Quality Approved"				

Poultry	U. S. Grade A	U. S. Grade B	U. S. Grade C		
Eggs	Fresh Fancy Quality U. S. Grade AA	U. S. Grade A	U. S. Grade B	U. S. Grade C	
Milled Rice	U. S. No. 1	U. S. No. 2	U. S. No. 3	U. S. No. 4	U. S. No. 5
Brown Rice	U. S. No. 1	U. S. No. 2	U. S. No. 3	U. S. No. 4	
Dried Beans	U. S. Choice Handpicked U. S. No. 1	U. S. No. 1 Handpicked U. S. No. 2	U. S. No. 2 Handpicked U. S. No. 3	U. S. No. 3 Handpicked	
Dried Peas	U. S. No. 1	U. S. No. 2	U. S. No. 3		
(and related products) [3]	U. S. Grade A (Fancy)	U. S. Grade B (Choice or Ex. Std.)	U. S. Grade C (Standard)		

POULTRY & EGGS

RICE, BEANS, AND PEAS

PROCESSED FRUITS AND VEGETABLES

[1] Three lowest grades are USDA Utility, Cutter, and Canner.
[2] Lowest grade is USDA Cull.
[3] Grades used for these products are usually as listed here, but there are some exceptions.

1, 2, and 3; for lentils, U.S. Grades 1 and 2.

For dry beans there are also special handpicked grades that are adapted to use at retail. They include U.S. No. 1 Choice Handpicked, U.S. No. 1 Handpicked, U.S. No. 2 Handpicked, and U.S. No. 3 Handpicked.

The grades for rice are based on such factors as the absence or degree of defective kernels (broken kernels or those damaged by heat, water, or insects): mixed varieties (which may affect cooking qualities); and objectionable foreign material. General appearance and color also are considered.

Grades for beans, peas, and lentils are based on factors such as color and absence or presence of defects, foreign material, and beans, peas, or lentils of different classes.

Grades for all of these products are widely used in the trade but seldom appear on retail packages. Some packages of rice are marked with the grade name.

WHOLESOME MEAT AND POULTRY

YOU ALREADY KNOW—or take for granted —that you can buy federally inspected meat and poultry products with confidence that they are wholesome.

You can also be sure that they are truthfully labeled. If you make a habit of reading the label, you can learn what you are paying for and put the information on the label to work for you.

The law requires that the label on a federally inspected meat or poultry product carry five items of information:

• The true name of the product, such as frankfurter, beef pot pie, kosher salami, or chicken cacciatore.

• A list of the ingredients, beginning with the one greatest in weight or volume.

• The name and address of the processor or distributor.

• The weight, if it is shown, must be accurate.

• The inspection stamp or mark.

ALL MEAT products prepared under Federal supervision must carry a "U.S. Inspected and Passed" stamp, and poultry products must carry the "Inspected for Wholesomeness" mark.

On meat, you may see this stamp (abbreviated to "U.S. INSP'D & P'S'D"), in purple on large cuts, although often the butcher trims it off at the retail market. (This purple color is safe; you need not trim it off).

On fresh poultry and uncooked frozen poultry, the stamp usually is attached as a tag to the wing of the bird, printed on the plastic film wrapper, or on the wrapper enclosing the giblets.

On prepared foods, such as frozen meat dinners, bologna, or chicken pies, the mark of inspection is printed on the package, can, or label.

This stamp, whether on fresh or prepared meats, tells you that the animal or bird was healthy; the carcass and all its parts were examined individually; other ingredients, if any, are wholesome; and the product was handled in a clean plant, under sanitary conditions. The Federal inspector in the plant makes sure that the labels are used properly.

How CAN THE LABEL help you get what you pay for?

Chile con carne, a cooked-meat product, is an example. If it is a federally inspected product, it must contain at least 40 percent meat on a fresh-weight basis. You can be sure that the inspector in the plant saw to it that the batch of chile met that requirement.

Since the meat is cooked, it would be hard for you to identify the kind of meat used if you had to depend on your own taste after it had been seasoned with chile and other spices. The Federal inspector is in the plant to make sure that if the label says beef, and if it has no other meat listed in the statement of ingredients, the chile does not contain meat from the head or heart.

Sometimes head, cheek, or heart meat are used. When they are, they cannot exceed 25 percent of the total meat, and they must be identified in the ingredients statement on the label. These are wholesome, nutritious meats, but generally less expensive than the beef cuts you may use at home. The statement of ingredients can help you judge the product that best suits your taste.

If the label says, "chile (or chili) con carne with beans," the meat content is less than in "chile con carne." Regulations specify that this product, if it bears the mark of Federal inspection, must contain at least 25 percent meat on a fresh-weight basis.

Whatever chile you decide to buy, if the Federal stamp is on it, you can know that ingredients other than meat are limited, too.

THE LABELS on other products can help in the same way.

For instance, you can learn whether frankfurters are all beef, all meat, or meat with cereals or contain nonfat dry milk or other additives.

You can find out what kind of meat is in the bologna of your choice, the salami, luncheon loaf, and any other kind of sausage or meat food product that comes from a federally inspected plant.

As to poultry, the label on one of the new frozen products—for example, turkey roll—tells whether the roll contains all breast meat, white and dark meat combined, or all dark meat. This information helps you to suit your taste and your pocketbook.

Federal regulations for both meat and poultry products limit the amounts of other ingredients used in their preparation, although these limits vary with the item.

In frankfurters, for instance, ingredients such as cereals or nonfat dry milk are limited to 3.5 percent of the weight of the finished product, regardless of whether those ingredients are used individually or in combination.

You can see why this is an important area in which Federal inspection offers you protection. Products, like frankfurters and chicken croquettes, that are made by grinding, chopping, and mixing, afford opportunity for the excessive use of the less-expensive ingredients if their production is not supervised.

Even though these other ingredients may be safe, you do not want to pay for more water or cereal or nonfat dry milk than is necessary to prepare the product properly.

FEDERAL inspection is required only in processing plants that ship in interstate trade. Not all plants engage in interstate commerce. Thus, only about 65 percent of prepared meat foods are handled under Federal supervision. The percentage is higher for animals inspected at the time of slaughter. About 84 percent of all commercial slaughter is conducted under Federal inspection.

Products prepared for sale only within a State are not subject to Federal inspection.

Some State and local governments require inspection. Some do not. Some States and municipalities have strict requirements for labels; some do not.

About 90 percent of the slaughter and processing of poultry are handled under Federal inspection. Some plants that sell only within a State can qualify for and receive Federal inspection for poultry if they pay the cost.

STORING PERISHABLE FOODS AT HOME

FOOD SPOILS BECAUSE of the action of the enzymes, molds, yeasts, or bacteria in it. Actual spoilage usually is pretty evident—the rancid odor and flavor of fats caused by oxidation, the fermented odor of fruit juices due to yeast growth, the appearance of a moldy slice of bread. These kinds of spoilage are undesirable, but they are not health hazards.

Food spoiled by bacterial action can cause illness, however. Not all bacteria are harmful, but most consumers cannot tell which are harmful and which are harmless. Slime on the surface of meats, off odors in foods, or a sour taste in bland foods are danger signals that indicate bacterial spoilage.

Low temperatures retard spoilage and other changes in the quality of perishable foods. They slow the action of enzymes and the growth of organisms of spoilage.

Foods vary in the degree of cold best suited for maintaining good quality, however. Too-low temperatures may be as detrimental to some foods as too-high temperatures. Some fruits and vegetables decay faster if they are held too long at even moderately low temperatures, Bananas are among them. Some apples and root vegetables keep well in a cool basement or outdoor cellar or storage pit.

Too much moisture on some foods or in the air around them can lead to early spoilage. Wet berries and cherries are susceptible to mold and rot. Molds grow quickly on breads or uncovered cheese in moist air.

On the other hand, water evaporates from the living cells of some foods and causes wilting, drying, and sometimes loss of nutrients. These foods need a high relative humidity to reduce loss of moisture. Control of moisture in the air in storage containers therefore is important, but it may be difficult to obtain such control in most homes. Some control of temperature and relative humidity is possible in cellars or storage pits by opening windows or ventilators at night when the outside temperature is not freezing and the air is not too dry.

A refrigerated food that tends to become unpalatable through drying or shriveling should be kept covered to retard evaporation. Most refrigerators provide at least one covered container for holding fruit and vegetables. The plastic bags in which fruit and vegetables sometimes are packaged retard the evaporation of moisture from food stored in them.

Temperatures in refrigerators vary with the location of the storage compartments. The temperature in most refrigerators is lowest just below the freezing unit at the top of the cabinet. The temperature at the bottom of the cabinet is highest. Air within the cabinet circulates; the cooler air falls and forces warmer air near the bottom upward along the sides. The moving air tends to dry out uncovered and unwrapped food.

One should check the setting of the temperature control by placing a thermometer in different places in the refrigerator. With the control set for normal operation, the temperature in the center storage section usually is between 38° and 42° F. The temperature below the freezing unit is lower—often between 30° and 35°. The bottom of the cabinet is somewhat warmer than the center. An accumulation of thin frost on the freezing unit or frequent openings of the refrigerator door, especially on humid days, raises the temperature inside.

Many refrigerators have a freezer compartment in which frozen foods are kept for short periods. All frozen foods need a storage temperature of 0° or lower to maintain high quality. Frozen foods should be held for only a few days if the temperature in the freezer compartment is above zero.

HOME-GROWN FOODS present few problems as to storage. They need only be placed in the proper place as soon as possible after harvest or slaughter. They may be selected and used at the best stage of ripeness.

Foods bought in retail markets are harder to select at their peak in quality. A purchaser has no way of knowing how much of a food's high-quality life remains when it is bought. It is wise to shop at clean markets and places where foods are properly refrigerated and handled.

FRESH DAIRY PRODUCTS should be kept cold and tightly wrapped or covered so that they do not absorb odors and flavors of other foods. A storage temperature of 40° is most desirable in protecting flavor and food value of milk and cream.

As soon after purchase or delivery as possible, the milk or cream should be refrigerated promptly. Exposure to sunlight is harmful to the flavor and ribo-flavin of milk.

Evaporated and condensed milk may be stored at room temperature until the container is opened. Then it should be refrigerated in the same way as fresh fluid milk.

Dry milks will keep for several months at room temperatures of 75° or lower, or they may be kept in the refrigerator. Nonfat dry milk is some-what more stable than whole dry milk because of its lack of fat. Both should be stored in tightly covered containers to prevent moisture absorption, which causes off-flavors to develop and makes reconstitution difficult.

The flavor of cottage cheese deteriorates rapidly. It (and the other soft cheeses) should be stored—tightly covered—in the coldest part of the refrigerator.

Hard cheeses should be wrapped tightly before refrigerating to protect them from exposure to air. The original wrapping often is satisfactory, or any of the wide variety of wrapping materials available to consumers may be used. Hard cheeses will keep indefinitely at refrigerator temperatures; exclusion of air is the important factor. Any mold that forms on the surface of hard cheese may be trimmed off before using.

Cheese spreads and cheese foods keep well without refrigeration until the container is opened. Refrigeration is advisable for the unused portion in an opened container.

To protect its flavor, butter should be stored tightly wrapped or covered in the coldest part of the refrigerator—preferably at 40° or lower. Exclusion of air will protect the fat from reacting with oxygen to produce a rancid flavor and odor. Only enough butter for immediate use should be held in the butter conditioners featured in some refrigerators. Exposure to warmth or light hastens the development of rancidity, and long periods of exposure should be avoided.

Most other fats and oils need the same protection from air, heat, and light as butter does to prevent rancidity.

Margarine and fat drippings, like butter, tend to become rancid more quickly than other fats and oils because they contain more moisture. They should be covered or wrapped and refrigerated promptly. Lard will keep longer at refrigerator temperature than these fats.

Some cooking and salad oils may become cloudy and solidify at refrigerator temperature, but this is not harmful. If allowed to warm to room temperature before use, they will liquefy and become clear again. The less surface area of these fats exposed to the air, the less chance there is for rancidity to occur. Fats and oils in partly filled containers will keep longer if they are transferred to smaller containers that have little or no air space.

Mayonnaise, other salad dressings, and foods with a high content of fat, such as peanut butter, keep better in the refrigerator after the container is opened.

The oils in some of the firm shortenings have been stabilized by hydrogenation; therefore they can be kept at room temperature without damage to flavor.

SHELL EGGS should be refrigerated promptly. Flavor changes quickly if eggs are held at room temperature but much more slowly at refrigerator temperature. Other quality changes occur if eggs are held too long. The thick white gets thin, and the yolk membrane weakens and may break when the shell is opened. The shell is porous and allows passage of moisture, bacteria, and molds. A covered container is recommended therefore if eggs are kept for several weeks. Eggs are not kept very long in most homes, and they do not require special handling. The carton in which eggs are sold is a good container, or the eggs may be transferred to another covered container.

Dried egg should be kept in the refrigerator. After a package is opened, the unused portion keeps best in an airtight container with a close-fitting lid.

FRAGILE FRUIT needs special handling to protect it from bruising and crushing. The softened tissues of bruised or crushed fruit make them susceptible to faster quality breakdown and the entrance of spoilage organisms.

Fruits should be sorted before storing. Injured fruit should be removed for immediate use or discarded if decay is present. This will protect firm, sound fruit from contamination.

Berries are perishable. The sorted fruit needs to be kept dry and refrigerated until ready for use. Preparation such as washing before refrigerating results in loss of food value and a greater chance of spoilage.

Ripe tomatoes, eating-ripe apples, peaches, apricots, cherries, grapes, pears, plums, and rhubarb all keep better under refrigeration. To minimize wilting and drying, they may be held in a covered container or in perforated plastic bags on the refrigerator shelf.

Even moderately low temperatures can harm some fruits and vegetables, especially if they are kept for a long time.

If grapefruit and lemons are held for several weeks at temperatures lower than 50° to 55°, pitting of the skin and discoloration of the flesh may result. Bananas, both ripe and green, suffer chilling injury at temperatures below 56°. These fruits and melons, avocados, and pineapples are best stored at a cool room temperature. Keeping citrus fruits in the refrigerator for as long as a week or chilling of any of these fruits to a desired serving temperature will not be harmful.

Because temperature is an important factor in ripening, unripe fruit should not be placed in the refrigerator. Slightly underripe fruits that are fresh and sound will ripen in open air at room temperature, but they should not be placed in the sun. Tomatoes, peaches, bananas, avocados, pears, and plums may be ripened. Cantaloups will soften but will not improve in flavor on holding.

Refrigerator temperatures delay the development of rancidity in nuts that have a high content of fat. Nuts should be stored in airtight containers to protect them from contact with oxygen. Unshelled nuts keep better than shelled ones. As salt hastens rancidity, unsalted nuts keep their quality longer than salted nuts.

Opened jars of preserved fruit products such as jellies, jams, and preserves and opened cans of fruits and fruit juices need refrigeration to keep the food from spoiling. Any of them may be stored safely in its original container, glass or tin, but it is advisable to cover the container. Reconstituted frozen juice concentrates should also be covered and refrigerated. Glass or plastic containers are preferred over tin because tin cans may impart a metallic flavor.

Dried fruits should be stored in the refrigerator in humid weather. At other times they keep well in tightly closed containers at room temperature.

Fresh vegetables have better flavor and nutritive value if they are eaten soon after harvest. The aging of foods goes on after harvest. The sweetness of corn, asparagus, beans, and green peas disappears therefore as sugar is changed to starch. The crispness and flavor of green, leafy vegetables deteriorate as water evaporates from vegetable tissues. Because low temperatures delay the aging process, most vegetables keep better in the icebox.

The exceptions—white potatoes, sweetpotatoes, dry onions, hard-shell squash, eggplant, cucumbers—need only cool storage.

White potatoes keep best in a cool, dry, dark place with good ventilation. Light causes greening. High temperatures hasten sprouting. Temperatures of 45° to 50° are best for white potatoes. Lower temperatures may convert some of the starch to sugar, giving the potatoes an undesirable sweet taste. If potatoes have become excessively sweet in too-cold storage, their flavor can be improved by holding them at room temperature for a week or two.

High temperatures and high humidity

GUIDE TO REFRIGERATOR STORAGE

FROZEN FOOD

FREEZER
AT 0° F.

FRESH MEAT, POULTRY, FISH
Loosely wrapped
    Roasts, steaks, chops—
        3 to 5 days
    Ground meats, variety
      meats, poultry, fish—
      1 to 2 days

MILK, CREAM, CHEESE
Tightly covered
    Milk, cream, cottage
      cheese, cream cheese—
      3 to 5 days
    Hard cheese—
      Several weeks

COLDEST
PART OF
REFRIGERATOR

BUTTER, MARGARINE
Tightly covered — 2 weeks

EGGS
Covered — 1 week

MAYONNAISE AND OTHER SALAD DRESSINGS—*Covered*
  Refrigerate after opening

**OPENED CANNED FOODS,
FRESH OR RECONSTITUTED
JUICE**
Tightly covered

NUTS
Tightly covered
PEANUT BUTTER
  Refrigerate after opening

FRESH FRUITS, RIPE—*Uncovered*

Apples—1 week

Berries } 1 to 2 days
Cherries }

Apricots }
Grapes }
Pears } 3 to 5 days
Peaches }
Plums }
Rhubarb }

SOME FRESH VEGETABLES—*Uncovered*

Ripe tomatoes
Corn in husk

Lima beans } In pods
Peas }

OTHER
PARTS OF
REFRIGERATOR

MOST FRESH VEGETABLES

Leafy green vegetables	Beets	Cucumbers
Asparagus	Cabbage	Green onions
Brussels sprouts	Carrots	Peppers
Cauliflower	Broccoli	Radishes
Summer squash	Celery	Snap beans

CRISPER
AND/OR
PLASTIC
BAG

cause sprouting and decay of dry onions.

If onions are purchased in airtight, unperforated bags, it is important to transfer them to a loosely woven bag or container with good circulation of air for home storage.

Others of these vegetables may suffer chilling injury if held at temperatures much below 50° to 55°.

Lettuce, celery, other raw salad vegetables, green onions, and green, leafy vegetables need to be kept cold and moist in the refrigerator after washing and draining. Storing them in plastic bags helps to reduce the evaporation of moisture from them. Asparagus and vegetables of the cabbage family should also be covered or wrapped and refrigerated.

Carrots, beets, and radishes keep best in the refrigerator when the tops and root tips are removed. Sweet corn remains fresher if unhusked. Beans and peas stay better in the pod if they need to be kept a day or two in the refrigerator.

Bruised or soft vegetables should be used immediately or discarded—not stored with sound, firm vegetables.

FRESH MEAT, poultry, and fish and cured and table-ready meat may be held for short periods at temperatures just above freezing. Ground meat and meat that has been mechanically tenderized are more susceptible to spoilage than roasts, steaks, and chops, because a larger surface area of the meat has been exposed to potential contamination from the air, from handlers, and from equipment. Such meat as livers, kidneys, and brains also are especially perishable.

Meat becomes rancid because of the oxidation of unsaturated fats. The oxidation of pigments in meat causes discoloration. Since low temperatures retard these changes and inhibit bacterial growth, meat should always be held in the coldest part of the refrigerator.

Some animal fats, especially those of pork and poultry, are more easily oxidized than others. Shorter holding periods are recommended for them.

Since smoking of meat makes it more resistant to the development of rancidity, smoked pork may be kept slightly longer than fresh meats. There is very little penetration of the smoke to the center of a smoked ham, however; while uncut hams are protected from oxidative changes, ham slices may be unprotected over much of their area.

Some circulation of air is beneficial to fresh meat cuts in a home refrigerator. The transparent film wrappings and cardboard trays used in prepackaging should be removed from fresh meat, poultry, and fish, and the foods should be loosely wrapped before they are put in the refrigerator. The tight packaging, which is convenient and sanitary in handling in markets, keeps fresh meat in a moist atmosphere in a home refrigerator, and the growth of micro-organisms on the surface of the meat is encouraged. Poultry giblets are often packed in a separate bag placed inside of a whole bird or under cut-up pieces. They, too, keep best if removed from the bag and covered loosely before refrigerating.

In packaging cured meats, the exclusion of oxygen and light, which hasten rancidity, is a main consideration. They may be kept in the refrigerator in their original packaging. If only part of the cured meat is used when the package is opened, the unused part should be rewrapped in the original packaging or in any of the various home wrapping materials.

Leftover cooked meat and meat dishes need to be cooled and refrigerated promptly if they are to be held safely. The stuffing should be removed from a turkey or chicken and both cooled separately. After cooked foods have cooled, they may be covered or wrapped loosely to prevent drying in the refrigerator.

DRY FOODS, such as flour, cereals, sugar, and spices, are less demanding in storage requirements than other foods. They keep well at room temperatures in tight containers that keep out dust, moisture, and insects.

In summer, flour and cereals should

be stored only in small amounts and inspected often to detect weevils. Dry mixes may also be held at room temperatures, but they last longer and better in the refrigerator.

Bread that must be kept for several days is better protected from mold in the refrigerator than in the breadbox, especially in hot and humid weather. At refrigerator temperature, however, it will lose the softness many people like. Keeping the breadbox thoroughly clean, well aired, and dry discourages growth of mold. Bread will retain its original freshness for a week or two if frozen in its original waxed-paper wrapping and stored in a freezer.

Honey and sirup in unopened containers keep well at a cool room temperature. When the containers have been opened, they have more protection from mold formation in the refrigerator. If crystals form, the honey and sirup may be warmed by placing the container in a pan of hot water to dissolve the crystals.

TIPS FOR STORING FROZEN FOODS

THE ORIGINAL fresh flavor, color, texture, and nutritive value of frozen foods will reach the table only if they are protected during storage.

Frozen foods need a temperature of 0° F. or lower if they are to keep their top quality longer than a few days or weeks.

At zero, frozen foods change slowly, and fresh qualities are preserved.

Extremely cold temperatures inhibit the growth of spoilage organisms and slow down chemical changes in the food itself and reactions between the food and oxygen in the air around the food.

At higher temperatures, changes speed up; foods may discolor, change texture, lose nutrients, and develop off-flavors.

The length of time a frozen food is stored is just as important as the temperature of storage. There will be even-

tual changes in all foods, even in those held at zero. Some foods may be kept longer than others before any change is noticeable.

Most fruit and vegetables, beef and lamb roasts, and whole chickens and turkeys are relatively stable when good storage practices are followed.

Other foods are more sensitive. Shorter holding periods are recommended for such foods as pork, cut-up poultry, ground meats, and prepared or precooked products.

The relationship between temperature of storage and the length of time foods are held is highly important.

Deterioration in frozen foods accelerates rapidly with a rise in storage temperature. For example, experienced food tasters were able to detect a change in flavor from the original freshness of frozen strawberries after a year's storage at 0°, after 2 months' storage at 10°, and after only 9 days' storage at 30°.

Proper packaging also is important. Moisture-vapor-proof packaging materials that permit no moisture to leave or air to enter the package are best suited to protect the food from drying out and prevent it from contact with air, which may cause oxidized off-flavors to develop. Glass, pottery, aluminum, tin, and rigid plastic are moisture-vapor-proof materials.

Many other materials are resistant enough to maintain satisfactory quality in the food packed in them. Among them are freezer papers coated with wax; laminated freezer paper; various types of plastic bags; and waxed cartons.

Information on the materials and methods for packaging different kinds of food for homefreezing is given in manuals available from the freezer industry, State extension services, and the Department of Agriculture.

Commercially frozen foods already have the packaging they need.

To give frozen foods the best environment possible, two basic rules should be followed.

First, know the capabilities and limitations of your equipment.

Second, tailor your storage and use of frozen foods to these capabilities and limitations.

In American homes, frozen foods are stored in separate freezers, in the freezer compartment of combination refrigerator-freezers, and in the ice-making and iceholding area of conventional refrigerators. This area is usually called the "frozen food compartment."

Sometimes it is difficult to distinguish between a combination refrigerator-freezer and a conventional refrigerator.

You may be sure it is a refrigerator-freezer if each compartment has its own exterior door. The refrigerator-freezer with a single exterior door has a solid piece separating the freezer section from the refrigerator area, and the inner door to the freezer section is insulated.

In the conventional refrigerator, a removable drip tray separates the frozen food compartment from the general storage area, and the door to the compartment is not insulated.

Homefreezers and most combination refrigerator-freezers can maintain a storage temperature of 0° or lower and are well suited for long-term storage of frozen foods. If you have this type of equipment, your first concern is to make sure that the temperature is actually zero in the storage area. The fact that packages are hard frozen to the touch is no assurance they have the storage temperature they need.

If the storage area in your freezer is not equipped with a thermometer, buy one so that you can check the temperature. Then adjust the thermostat or temperature control to attain 0° in the warmest spot in the storage area.

Door storage in some combination refrigerator-freezers is a few degrees warmer than the cold-storage area, and food kept there should not be stored as long as those in the zero area.

Zero storage space gives you latitude in selecting food for the freezer and planning for its use. Consider family preferences and the susceptibility of the food to change during storage.

It is sensible to store quantities of a variety of food especially liked and used often in family meals, but it does not make sense to store such a large amount that the food cannot be used while still in its prime.

A year's supply of favorite fruit frozen in season at the peak of quality and stored at zero will give you good eating throughout the year.

Ice cream, however, can be expected to keep its top quality for only about a month, and storing more than the family will use in that time means poorer eating quality.

Zero storage offers convenience in many ways to all users. Those who grow some of their own food save the most. Those of us who rely solely on market sources for food may save some money by freezing food in season when prices are low, by taking advantage of special sales, or by purchasing foods in quantity. Careful planning and careful pricing are needed to achieve appreciable savings, however.

PREPARATION OF FRUIT for freezing involves cleaning it thoroughly to reduce the bacterial count, removing any material that is inedible, and getting it into the desired form.

Small fruits and berries can be frozen whole. Large fruits are usually halved or sliced. Most fruits and berries also can be frozen crushed or as puree for use as fruit toppings or fillings. Juice pressed from fruit or berries may be sweetened slightly before freezing.

Whether to pack fruit in sugar or sirup or to leave it unsweetened depends partly on how you intend to use the fruit.

Fruit packed in sirup is generally best for dessert use. Fruit in dry sugar or unsweetened is best for cooking, because less liquid is in the pack. Unsweetened packs are useful especially for jams and jellies or in baking, in which you have to know how much sugar the ingredients contain.

Most fruits are satisfactory when packed in either sugar or sirup. The best proportion of sugar to fruit or best sirup concentration varies with the sweetness of the fruit.

Sour cherries and strawberries take three-fourths cup of sugar to a quart of fruit. Apples and apricots take only one-half cup of sugar.

In sugar packs, the sugar is sprinkled over the prepared fruit and mixed in gently before the fruit is packed in the containers. Ascorbic acid (vitamin C) is sprinkled over the fruit just before the sugar is added. Ascorbic acid in crystalline or powdered form can be purchased at drugstores and at some locker plants.

For sirup packs, you put the fruit in the containers and cover it with cold sirup. Fruits that darken easily are best sliced directly into the sirup. Any ascorbic acid or other antidarkening agent is mixed with the sirup.

Blackberries, blueberries, cranberries, currants, figs, gooseberries, grapes, pineapple, plums, raspberries, rhubarb, and strawberries and purees of avocado, dates, and persimmon are satisfactory packed into containers with no sweetening, sealed, and frozen.

Apple slices may be packed unsweetened after they have been steamed to prevent darkening. If apples are not firm and crisp, holding in a calcium chloride solution before steaming will firm them. To make the solution, use 1 teaspoon U.S. Pharmacopoeia grade calcium chloride (available in drugstores) to each quart of water. Hold apple slices in the solution 5 to 20 minutes—the longer time is for the softest apples.

Peaches may be frozen without sweetening but should be packed in water to which ascorbic acid has been added.

Some fully ripe fruits, when used with commercial fruit pectins, gel without cooking to make jams or jellies of fresh flavor and bright, natural color. Mix 3 cups of crushed blackberries, blueberries, raspberries, strawberries, or peaches with 5 cups of sugar; let this stand 20 minutes, stirring occasionally. Dissolve 1 package of powdered pectin in 1 cup of water, heat to boiling and boil for 1 minute. Pour pectin solution into fruit mixture and stir for 2 min-

utes. Put into jelly glasses or freezer containers. Seal. These uncooked products are highly perishable and must be refrigerated or frozen.

VEGETABLES should be thoroughly cleaned, the edible parts cut into pieces (if desired), and then heated to stop or slow down enzyme action. You should do this as soon as possible after the vegetables are picked.

If vegetables are not preheated sufficiently, enough enzyme action will continue during storage to lower the quality of the food. Vegetables usually are preheated in boiling water—a gallon of water to a pound of vegetable. The times required for heating different vegetables in boiling water in a covered kettle are given in the table. When a time range is given, use the shortest time for small vegetables and the longer times for large vegetables. Start counting time as soon as you put the vegetable in the water.

Steaming may be used for some vegetables. Split broccoli and whole mushrooms take 5 minutes; button mushrooms, 3.5 minutes; and sliced mushrooms, 3 minutes. Pieces of pumpkin and winter squash and whole sweetpotatoes may be steamed until soft or they may be heated in a pres-

Vegetable	Minutes
Asparagus stalks	2 to 4.
Beans, lima (or pods)	2 to 4.
Beans, green or wax (1- or 2-inch pieces or frenched).	3.
Beets	25 to 50 (until tender).
Broccoli stalks (split)	3.
Brussels sprouts	3 to 5.
Carrots (small, whole)	5.
Carrots (diced, sliced, or lengthwise strips).	2.
Cauliflower (1-inch flowerets).	3.
Corn on the cob	7 to 11.
Corn (whole-kernel and cream-style—cut corn from the cob after heating and cooling).	4.
Peas, green	1.5.
Spinach	2.
Squash, summer	3.

sure cooker or an oven set at 400° F. until they are soft.

Quick, thorough cooling is necessary to stop the cooking. Vegetables should be plunged in cold water below 60°. The water should be changed often. It is best to use ice water or cold running water.

The cooled vegetables should be tightly packed immediately into suitable containers, leaving ½-inch headspace, except for vegetables like asparagus and broccoli that pack loosely and require no headspace. The containers then are closed and put in the freezer.

MEAT should be of high quality, properly chilled, and frozen in amounts suitable for cooking at one time. All meat should be clean and ready to be cooked before wrapping it for freezing.

Most kinds of raw poultry can be frozen satisfactorily at home. The birds should be well fleshed with well-distributed fat and few, if any, skin blemishes. Freshly killed poultry is best for home freezing. A low scalding temperature should be used when removing the feathers so that the outer layer of skin is left intact. This helps prevent loss of moisture and darkening of the poultry. If you do not know how the bird was scalded, we recommend immediate tight packaging in a material that is moisture resistant.

You should age fryers and broilers in the refrigerator for 12 hours before cooking, either before freezing or during thawing in order to insure tender meat.

Poultry may be frozen whole, in halves, or in pieces in order to provide variety and to make it suitable for different uses.

Turkeys and chickens for roasting are frozen whole, unstuffed.

Poultry for broiling and frying takes less space in a freezer and is more convenient to use if it is cut into serving pieces and then frozen. Poultry should be wrapped tightly to prevent discoloration of the skin by drying. It should be frozen immediately.

When you cook the family meal, plan to prepare a double amount of some food—an extra casserole or a second pie or cake, for instance. Cool the extra food immediately and package and freeze it as soon as possible.

Leftovers often can be frozen satisfactorily if cooled and frozen as soon as the meal is over. Sometimes slight undercooking before freezing will prevent a warmed-over flavor and too soft a texture when you reheat the food for serving.

HOME ECONOMISTS have studied the freezing of baked goods—breads, cakes, pies—a great deal. They have been interested primarily in ingredients and whether to bake the products before or after freezing.

With yeast breads, the question is whether to freeze the dough or bake it before freezing or partly bake it to have brown-and-serve products.

We think yeast breads are better if they are prebaked before freezing. Yeast breads and rolls may be frozen as dough, however, if they are to be stored no longer than 6 weeks. Results are better with unshaped dough than with shaped frozen rolls. Frozen brown-and-serve rolls are another way to hold yeast rolls successfully.

We have not decided whether it is better to freeze cakes before or after baking. Most kinds can be frozen either way fairly satisfactorily if the storage time is no more than 3 or 4 months. Cakes frozen as batter may have less volume and a more compact texture than prebaked cakes because of the loss in carbon dioxide.

Spice cake is better prebaked than baked from frozen batter. Results with frozen batter are best when the batter is thawed before the cake is baked and when the storage period is short.

Most fruit pies may be frozen baked or unbaked, but the quality seems to be better when they are not baked before freezing.

The lower crust of prebaked pies may become soggy during reheating. To counteract this tendency, it may help to roll the crust thinner than usual, brush the crust with melted fat or egg white before adding the filling, or bake the pies in a very hot oven (450°). Or, for a change, you might make a deep-dish fruit pie with only an upper crust.

Fruits that discolor easily in the air need the same treatment in pies as they do when frozen alone.

Single-crust pies should be frozen without meringue, which becomes tough when it is frozen.

Pastry shells can be made in advance and frozen either baked or unbaked. Lard shortenings make more tender pastry than vegetable shortenings, although there may be a problem of rancidity with lard unless antioxidants have been added. Freezing and storage also seem to make pastry more tender.

Many types of cookies can be frozen after baking or as dough. Those baked from dough are usually crisper than prebaked cookies and take less space during storage in the freezer. Macaroon and other meringue-type cookies have poor texture when frozen, regardless of whether they were frozen before or after baking.

Frozen fruit salad with a whipped cream base is best when eaten before it is completely thawed. Because spoilage organisms thrive in it, everything should be fresh and clean.

Fruit or meat-gelatin salads also are satisfactory, particularly if the liquid called for in the recipe is reduced about one-fourth. If too much liquid is used, it separates when the salad is defrosted. Mayonnaise, which separates during freezing, should be used sparingly in frozen salads.

The fillings largely determine the quality of frozen sandwiches. Only freshly made fillings should be used. Sandwiches should be frozen as soon as they are made and eaten soon after they have thawed. These precautions are necessary because bacteria grow easily in many of the ingredients used for fillings, and sandwich making involves much handling of the food and provides chances for contamination.

Suitable for freezing are fillings made of meat and poultry, hard-cooked egg yolk, cheese, peanut butter, pickles, or olives. Anything should be omitted that may soak into the bread, as jelly or salad dressings, cooked egg white, which toughens, and vegetables, which will wilt. There will be less sogginess if the bread is spread to the edges with butter or margarine.

SOME SUGGESTIONS for wise use of your zero storage space follow.

• Store food of original high quality. When you buy food for storage, buy from a reputable dealer.

• Use food quickly; replace food often. Long storage adds nothing to food value or eating quality, but it does add to cost. The more the freezer is used, the lower the cost per package for freezing and storing.

• Keep a record, so that you know at all times what kinds of food and how much of each are in the freezer. Mark each package with the date stored.

• Rotate the food. Place new packages at the bottom or back of the storage area. Keep unfrozen or warmed packages from touching those already in storage. Use the oldest food first.

• For best eating quality, use frozen food before its suggested maximum storage period has expired. The home storage maximums are based on studies with commercially frozen foods but may also be used as a guide in planning length of storage for home-frozen foods. These maximums for well-packaged foods of original high quality held continuously at zero or below are given (in months) on the next page.

The ice-cube compartment of a conventional refrigerator usually cannot hold a temperature of 0° without freezing the perishable foods in the general storage area. This compartment is limited to storage for only a few days if fresh eating qualities and food values are to be preserved.

To use above-zero storage space:

• Keep the temperature control at the setting for just-above-freezing in the general storage area;

Fruit:
  Cherries, peaches, raspberries, straw-
    berries.......................... 12
Fruit juice concentrates:
  Apple, grape, orange.............. 12
Vegetables:
  Asparagus, beans, peas............. 8
  Cauliflower, corn, spinach.......... 8
Meat:
  Beef:
    Roasts, steaks................... 12
    Ground beef..................... 3
  Lamb:
    Roasts......................... 12
    Patties......................... 4
  Pork (fresh):
    Roasts......................... 8
    Sausage........................ 2
  Pork (cured)..................... 2
  Veal:
    Roasts......................... 8
    Chops, cutlets.................. 6
  Cooked meats:
    Meat dinners, meat pies, and swiss
      steak......................... 3
Poultry:
  Chicken:
    Whole......................... 12
    Cut-up........................ 9
    Livers......................... 3
  Turkey:
    Whole......................... 12
    Cut-up........................ 6
  Duck, goose (whole)............. 6
  Cooked chicken and turkey:
    Sliced meat and gravy........... 6
    Pies.......................... 12
    Fried chicken.................. 4
Bakery products:
  White bread, plain rolls............ 3
  Cakes:
    Angel, chiffon.................. 2
    Chocolate layer................ 4
    Pound, yellow.................. 6
    Fruit......................... 12
  Doughnuts...................... 3
  Pies (unbaked):
    Apple, boysenberry, cherry, peach. 8
Ice cream, sherbet.................. 1

   • Buy frozen food just before checking out at the grocery store;
   • Buy only what will be used within a few days;
   • Ask the grocery packer to put frozen
foods in an insulated bag or a double
paper bag and take foods home as
quickly as possible;
   • Place frozen food in contact with
the floor of the ice-cube compartment or the refrigerated ice tray shelf.
   Home storage should not be an en-
durance test for frozen food. Although

cheeses and wines benefit from aging,
frozen food does not. Planning for
their use within the framework of the
capabilities of your home equipment to
hold top quality is good storage
practice.

SAVING FOOD VALUES

THE ATTRACTIVE, flavorful, and nutritious
foods you so carefully select for your
family can lose their color, flavor, and
texture and some of their vitamins and
minerals before they reach the table.
How much depends on how you store,
trim, and cook them.

From harvest to table, some loss of nutrients is inevitable. Some nutrients,
such as carbohydrates (sugars and
starches), are well retained during storage and cooking.

Others, such as some of the vitamins
and minerals, are easily lost from
certain foods, although they are well
retained in others.

Vitamin C and thiamine are among
the least stable. Measures that protect
them from destruction and loss usually
will protect the more stable nutrients
as well.

Methods of storage and preparation
that conserve nutrients usually preserve
the most appetizing color, flavor, and
texture, too.

CAREFUL TRIMMING is necessary to improve the appearance, texture, and
flavor of many foods, but too much
trimming causes unnecessary loss of nutrients.

The dark-green leaves of vegetables
are higher in most nutrients than the
stems and midribs. When you discard
the green outer leaves of cabbage and
lettuce and the leaves of broccoli, you
are throwing away nutritious parts of
the vegetables. On the other hand, removing the stems and midribs from
kale and collard greens involves
smaller losses of nutrients.

Some roots and tubers, such as carrots, potatoes, and turnips, can be
cooked in their skins—a good way to

conserve nutrients, color, and flavor. Beets usually are cooked before peeling to prevent excessive loss of color.

Cut surfaces of such fruit as apples, pears, and peaches darken rapidly when exposed to air. To prevent darkening, peel and cut the fruit just before use or sprinkle it with citrus fruit juice or pineapple juice.

When you peel vegetables, remove only a thin layer.

When trimming or shredding, always use a sharp blade to prevent bruising. Losses of vitamins A and C occur when tissues are bruised.

Wash and stem berries and cherries just before use. They lose vitamin C and spoil quickly if they are washed and stemmed before storage.

It is necessary to wash some foods before you use them. Fruit and vegetables always should be washed thoroughly. Washing rice before cooking is not recommended, however, because it causes loss of nutrients.

If meat needs surface cleaning, it should be wiped with a clean, damp cloth or paper towel. Dipping meat into water or soaking it causes loss of soluble nutrients and flavor.

Raw fruit and vegetables introduce variety in color, flavor, and texture to meals. Cooking changes color, flavor, and texture and causes some loss of nutrients, even when carefully done.

COOKING, however, is necessary to make some foods acceptable. Well-cooked foods look and taste good and retain most of their nutrients.

To help you make sure that the food you serve is both appetizing and nutritious, we give some suggestions.

Cook most foods at low to moderate temperatures. High temperatures cause meat and poultry to shrink excessively, fats to break down and smoke, and eggs and cheese to become rubbery.

At high temperatures, custards are likely to curdle, and milk may acquire a scorched taste. High temperatures also speed the destruction of thiamine (vitamin B_1) and vitamin C.

Use no more water than necessary for cooking vegetables, rice, spaghetti, macaroni, noodles, and other foods cooked in liquid.

When you cook food in a large amount of liquid and then discard the liquid, you are throwing away valuable water-soluble vitamins and minerals. Some of the flavor goes down the drain, too.

Cooking "strong-flavored" vegetables, such as cabbage, in a large amount of water was thought once to make them milder. That wastes nutrients. Even "strong-flavored" vegetables can be cooked in a small amount of water if they are cooked briefly—just long enough to make them tender.

Leafy vegetables often can be cooked in just the water clinging to the leaves after washing.

Rice simmered in approximately twice its volume of water should absorb all of the water by the time cooking is completed. It will retain nutrients better than rice cooked in a large amount of water. Rice should not be rinsed after cooking, because nutrients will be lost.

Use a pan with a tight-fitting lid when you boil, braise, or simmer food. A tight-fitting lid holds in most of the steam and shortens the cooking time. Escaping steam carries with it some of the flavor. Prolonged cooking destroys nutrients.

Even green vegetables cooked in a covered pan retain their natural color fairly well if cooked just until tender. They turn an unattractive olive color only if overcooked.

Do not overcook. Cooking too long makes meat, poultry, and fish dry and tough, eggs and cheese curdled or rubbery, baked products dry and crusty, and vegetables mushy and discolored. It also causes them to lose part of their thiamine and vitamin C, which are easily destroyed by too much heat.

Serve foods as soon as possible after cooking. Holding hot foods at serving temperature is like overcooking them.

Use, do not discard, liquids in which you cook vegetables, meat drippings, and liquids drained from canned foods. Add them to gravies, soups, sauces, and gelatin dishes to enhance nutritive value and flavor.

Refrigerate leftovers as soon as possible and use them within a day or two. Cooked vegetables lose part of their nutritive value and appeal during storage and reheating. Do not count on them to be as nutritious or appetizing as freshly prepared vegetables.

BUY THE BEST DAIRY PRODUCTS

MILK is one of our best and most popular foods. It and food products made from it are so diverse that it is easy to include them in any type of balanced diet—whether high, medium, or low in calories—and in many special diets.

The sanitary quality of our milk supply is guaranteed by a program of protection in which Federal, State, and local agencies, and the dairy industry participate. Most American communities require the pasteurization of fluid milk products.

In pasteurization, the raw milk is heated quickly and promptly cooled to destroy harmful bacteria that may be present and to improve the keeping quality of the milk.

Pasteurization does not change the flavor or the essential nutritive value and goodness of milk.

Most of the fluid milk sold today is homogenized—the fat globules in it are broken up in a special process.

The bottle cap or carton label will give name and grade of the product and tell whether it contains added vitamins, minerals, or nonfat milk solids and whether it is pasteurized, homogenized, or otherwise processed.

THE VARIETY of milk and dairy products is enough to satisfy your nutritional needs, personal tastes, and food budget.

Fluid whole milk contains both the fat and solids-not-fat parts of milk. The content of milk fat usually is standard-ized at 3.5 percent, although minimum requirements of States vary from 3.0 to 3.8 percent. Standards for milk solids-not-fat vary from 8.0 to 8.5 percent.

Homogenized milk has its fat globules broken into minute particles and dispersed throughout the liquid, so that it has a richer flavor and softer curd. A cream layer does not form in homogenized milk.

Skim milk has most of the milk fat removed. In some States, it is milk that has any amount of milk fat less than the amount required for whole milk. Skim milk is a good source of calcium, riboflavin, and protein. It lacks milk fat and vitamin A. Some skim milks are modified or fortified with added vitamins and minerals.

Low-fat, partly skimmed, and 2 percent milk are terms used in some markets to describe a fresh fluid product in which the content of milk fat is lowered and the nonfat milk solids content may or may not be increased. For example, the popular product known as 2 percent–10 percent contains 2 percent milk fat (instead of the usual 3.5 percent) and 10 percent nonfat milk solids (instead of the usual 8.5 percent); "2–10" has the appeal of a heavier consistency and richer taste than skim milk.

Cultured milk products have smooth and mildly acid flavors produced by bacteria cultures, which convert the milk sugar into lactic acid. Cultured buttermilk is made from skim milk or partly skimmed milk.

Sour cream (or cultured sour cream) is usually made from light cream.

Yogurt, a specially cultured product, is made from concentrated whole milk or partly skimmed whole milk and may contain fruit or other flavoring.

These cultured (fermented) products have the same general food values as the products from which they were prepared.

Cream is the milk-fat part of milk. Cream containing about 18–20 percent milk fat is known as light cream, coffee cream, or table cream. It often is homogenized to improve consistency. Whipping cream contains 30–36 percent milk fat and is not homogenized.

Half-and-half is a mixture of milk and cream, usually containing 10–12 percent milk fat. It is used as a creaming agent in coffee and as a dessert topping.

Pressurized whipped cream is a mixture of cream, sugar, stabilizers, flavors, and emulsifiers packed in aerosol cans under pressure. The cream is whipped when the pressure is released through the nozzle.

Butter is churned cream. It contains, by law, not less than 80 percent milk fat. It may or may not contain salt. The butter of highest quality is made from sweet cream or may be made from sweet cream to which a culture, similar to that used in cultured milk products, has been added. Cultured butter has a pleasing, mildly acid flavor.

Most of the butter sold at retail bears a Department of Agriculture shield mark, with a letter grade that indicates the quality of the butter at the time of grading. U.S. AA and A are the grades usually sold at retail.

Whipped butter results when air or an inert gas is incorporated into the butter. This increases volume and makes the butter easier to spread. Most of the whipped butter sold in this country is unsalted.

Cheese is available in many forms, flavors, and textures to suit every taste and occasion.

Cheeses are natural or processed. Natural cheeses usually are made from whole cow's milk in this country, but some are made from skim milk, whey, or mixtures of all three.

Cheeses also are made from sheep's or goat's milk or cream.

Natural cheeses can be divided into four general classifications: Very hard, such as Parmesan; hard, as Cheddar and Swiss; semisoft, as Brick and Blue, and soft, as cream and cottage.

Cheddar cheese is our most popular hard cheese. It is sometimes called by the style in which it is made (Daisy, Longhorn, or Picnic) or by the locality where it is made—Wisconsin, New York, or Oregon. Natural Cheddar cheese is often labeled mild; medium cured or

mellow aged; or cured, aged, or sharp, depending on the length of time the cheese is aged.

Cheddar and other closely related types of cheese are often called American or American-type cheese.

Process cheese is made by blending and pasteurizing fresh and aged natural cheeses with the aid of heat, water, and an emulsifier. Process cheese does not increase in flavor after manufacture. It melts easily when reheated. Pimientoes, fruit, vegetables, or meat sometimes are added to process cheese.

Pasteurized processed American cheese contains at least 50 percent fat in the solids and may contain a maximum of 40 percent moisture.

Cheese food is made in much the same way as process cheese. It contains less cheese, though, and has added nonfat milk solids and moisture.

Cheese spreads are similar to cheese foods but contain less milk fat and more moisture.

Cold pack cheese or *club cheese* is a blend of one or more varieties of natural cheese mixed into a uniform product without heating. The flavor is about the same as the natural cheese used (usually aged or sharp), but the cheese is softer in texture than natural cheese and spreads easily.

Cottage cheese, a widely used unripened soft cheese, is produced by adding lactic-acid-producing bacteria to skim milk. It is sold in dry form or creamed.

Similar to cottage cheese are bakers, farmers, and pot cheeses.

Ice cream is made by freezing while stirring—a pasteurized mixture of milk, cream, sugar, and stabilizer. It is flavored with extracts, fruit, chocolate, or nuts. Eggs are an optional ingredient.

Air is whipped into ice cream during freezing to increase its volume 80 to 100 percent.

Ice cream should have a fresh flavor, the body should be firm (neither fluffy nor soggy), and the texture should be fine grained (neither coarse nor icy).

Ice milk is made like ice cream and with the same ingredients as ice cream, except that it contains less milk fat and more nonfat milk solids. Ice milk may be sold in either soft- or hard-frozen form. It often is sold "soft" in cups and cones from freezers at refreshment stands and frozen on sticks and bars and in packages.

Sherbet is a low-fat, frozen mixture of sugar, milk solids, stabilizer, food acid, and water, with fruit, fruit juices, and extracts used for flavoring.

Evaporated milk is a sterilized, homogenized product that contains about 60 percent less water than whole milk. Most evaporated milk is fortified with vitamin D. It is easily transported and stored. It is cheaper than fresh whole milk and, when mixed with an equal volume of water, has about the same average composition of whole milk.

Sweetened condensed milk is milk from which about half of the water has been removed and about 44 percent sugar has been added as a preservative.

Dry whole milk is whole milk with the water removed. When reliquefied, it has about the same composition as fresh whole milk.

Nonfat dry milk is skim milk with the water removed. Most nonfat dry milk on the consumer market today is "instant"—so named because it dissolves quickly in water. Nonfat dry milk contains the lactose, proteins, minerals, and water-soluble vitamins in the same relative proportions as fresh skim milk.

Goat's milk is similar to cow's milk in composition, but it has smaller fat globules and forms finer curds in the stomach. For these reasons, goat's milk has been used by infants, children, or adults troubled with digestive disturbances. Goat's milk is readily available in some communities. It should be produced and handled from farm to user with the same care as cow's milk.

A GOOD RULE to follow in handling dairy products in the home is to keep them cool, clean, and covered.

Fluid milk products should be refrigerated as soon as possible after purchase. Remove fluid milk products from the refrigerator only as needed, and put the containers back in the refrigerator promptly.

Because milk can absorb odors and flavors from other foods, the containers should be as tightly covered as possible.

Fluid milk products that have been on hand for some time—or have been allowed to stand at room temperature—should not be mixed with fresh milk products. Fluid milk products properly cared for in the home should keep good flavor for at least a week or 10 days after you buy them.

Nonfat dry milk, kept dry and cool, can be stored on the pantry shelf for several months without deterioration. As soon as you reconstitute nonfat dry milk, the liquid product needs refrigeration. Chilling the reconstituted product improves its flavor.

Dry whole milk should be stored in tightly covered, moistureproof containers. Reconstituted dry whole milk needs refrigeration.

Canned evaporated milk keeps well on the pantry shelf until opened. Once the can is opened, evaporated milk needs refrigeration and has about the same storage life as fresh milk.

Natural cheeses should be kept refrigerated.

Soft cheeses, such as cottage and cream cheese, are quite perishable and should be used soon after purchase.

Cured cheeses, such as Cheddar and Swiss, keep well in the refrigerator for up to several months if protected from drying out.

If possible, keep the cheese wrapped with its original wrapper. The cut surface of a cheese may be protected from drying out by covering with wax paper, foil, or plastic wrapping material.

If you wish to store large pieces of hard cheese for several weeks or more, dip the cut surfaces in hot paraffin. Small pieces should be rewrapped.

Any mold that may develop on natural cheeses is not harmful, but it may be scraped or cut off the surface.

Ends or pieces of cheese that have become dry may be grated and kept refrigerated in a clean, tightly covered glass jar. This cheese is excellent for garnishing or accenting other food.

Aromatic cheeses, such as Limburger, should be stored in a tightly covered jar or container. They are fast curing and taste best when used shortly after purchase.

Hard cheeses may be frozen, but freezing may change the characteristic body and texture and cause it to become crumbly and mealy. Many varieties of cheese cut into pieces weighing a pound or less and not over 1 inch thick may be frozen satisfactorily for as long as 6 months if the cheese is frozen quickly at a temperature of o° F. or lower. Before you freeze cut cheese, wrap it carefully with moisture-proof freezer wrap.

You can freeze the following varieties of cheese successfully in small pieces by following the foregoing directions: Brick, Cheddar, Edam, Gouda, Muenster, Swiss, Provolone, Mozzarella, and Camembert. Thaw frozen cheese in the refrigerator and use it as soon as possible.

TIMESAVING TRICKS IN THE KITCHEN

WORKING WIVES, full-time homemakers, single girls, and even bachelors all need at some time or other to prepare a meal quickly.

The most helpful suggestion is: Plan ahead. A little thought can save a lot of steps and time.

Keep on hand a supply of quickly prepared foods for unexpected guests and for days you are late and have to prepare a meal in a hurry. You can prepare quick and good meals with canned and frozen meat, vegetables, and fruit; mixes; and canned and dehydrated soup.

Know well a few tried-and-true quick recipes that you can trust in an emergency.

Plan for leftovers. Buy a roast that will do for two or three meals. The cooked meat can be used in casseroles, salads, sandwiches, and other quickly prepared dishes.

Prepare some foods in advance if you know company is coming and you will not have much time to prepare dinner that evening.

Get ingredients ready to go together —salad greens washed and refrigerated in a plastic bag; onion, green pepper, and other raw vegetables prepared and stored in tightly covered containers; seasonings measured into a small jar.

Some casseroles can be prepared and refrigerated one day and baked the next.

Desserts, such as pie and cake, and gelatin salads can be made a day ahead of time.

FROM SOUP MIXES to chopped nuts, the array of foods that are partly or fully prepared is amazing. They provide an excellent way of speeding things up.

Does your recipe call for a sauce? Try canned sauce, dehydrated sauce mix, or undiluted canned cream soup.

Need a crumb topping for a casserole? Combine herb-seasoned stuffing mix with melted fat.

Want onion, garlic, mushroom, or parsley flavor without peeling or chopping? Use dehydrated onion or parsley flakes, bottled onion juice, instant garlic powder, freeze-dried mushrooms.

Very often one ingredient in your recipe can be substituted for another. On the next page are a few substitutions worth keeping in mind.

THE LABELS on packages of mixes and refrigerated doughs often suggest variations, but your own ideas may be even better.

From biscuit mix or refrigerated dough, for example, you can make sweet rolls, coffeecake, doughnuts, shortcake, cobblers, bread sticks, turnovers, fruit or meat rollups, miniature pizzas, and more.

You can use cake mixes for upside-down cakes, coffeecake, cupcakes, baked Alaska, and Boston cream pie. Or serve the cake warm from the oven with a hot sauce made from a pudding mix.

Homemade mixes for biscuits, pastry, and other quick breads are easy to make.

Pastry mix usually contains flour, salt, and fat; biscuit mix contains those ingredients plus baking powder. Nonfat

For these	You may use these
1 whole egg, for thickening or baking	2 egg yolks. Or 2½ tablespoons sifted dried whole egg plus 2½ tablespoons water.
1 cup butter or margarine for shortening	⅞ cup lard, or rendered fat, with ½ teaspoon salt. Or 1 cup hydrogenated fat (cooking fat sold under brand name) with ½ teaspoon salt.
1 square (ounce) chocolate	3 tablespoons cocoa plus 1 tablespoon fat.
1 teaspoon sulfate-phosphate baking powder	1½ teaspoons phosphate baking powder. Or 2 teaspoons tartrate baking powder.
1 cup buttermilk or sour milk, for baking	1 cup sweet milk mixed with one of the following: 1 tablespoon vinegar. Or 1 tablespoon lemon juice. Or 1¾ teaspoons cream of tartar.
1 cup fluid whole milk	½ cup evaporated milk plus ½ cup water. Or 1 cup reconstituted dry whole milk. Or 1 cup reconstituted nonfat dry milk plus 2½ teaspoons butter or margarine. (To reconstitute dry milk follow directions on the package.)
1 cup fluid skim milk	1 cup reconstituted nonfat dry milk prepared according to directions on the package.
1 tablespoon flour, for thickening	½ tablespoon cornstarch, potato starch, rice starch, or arrowroot starch. Or 2 teaspoons quick cooking tapioca.
1 cup cake flour, for baking	⅞ cup all-purpose flour.
1 cup all-purpose flour, for baking breads	Up to ½ cup bran, whole-wheat flour, or cornmeal plus enough all-purpose flour to fill cup.

dry milk can be included in the biscuit mix if desired.

Use the proportion of ingredients in a basic recipe for pastry or biscuits. Blend the dry ingredients thoroughly; then cut in the fat.

If you make the mixes with hydrogenated vegetable shortening and double-acting baking powder, they will keep several weeks in a tightly closed container at room temperature. When you are ready to bake, just add the liquid ingredients and blend.

Homemade mixes can be varied in

the same way as commercial mixes.

Homemade refrigerated doughs that you can keep on hand include cooky dough and yeast roll dough. Use any recipe for "refrigerator cookies" or "refrigerator rolls."

If it is tightly wrapped, cooky dough will keep up to a week in the refrigerator or 4 to 6 months in a freezer at 0° F. Yeast roll dough will keep 4 to 5 days in the refrigerator.

If you want to freeze yeast roll dough, make a rich dough with twice the usual amount of yeast and freeze it immediately after kneading. Do not allow it to rise first. Yeast dough prepared this way can be stored up to 2 months in a freezer at 0°.

OVEN, pressure cooker, electric mixer, electric blender, electric frypan, freezer —all can make your life easier.

You can prepare a complete meal in your oven (except salad and beverage), if you plan carefully. Select foods that require about the same baking temperature. At 375°, for example, you can bake meat loaf, potatoes (they will require 10 to 20 minutes longer than at 425°), tomatoes, and apples. When the meat loaf comes out of the oven, boost the temperature to 400° and put in a pan of muffins. Make a salad and a beverage, and dinner is ready.

A good broiler meal may include shish kabobs (meat cubes, green pepper pieces, mushrooms, and tiny onions threaded on skewers), broiled tomatoes, and canned whole potatoes brushed with melted fat and broiled.

One-dish meals baked in the oven are timesavers. An example is a casserole that combines meat or poultry, vegetables, and biscuit topping.

A pressure cooker can cut hours from the cooking time for such slow-cooking meats as pot roasts, swiss steak, shortribs, corned beef, and spareribs. Beets, dry beans, and potatoes also can be cooked in much less time than they ordinarily need. Follow the manufacturer's directions exactly. Even a minute or two of overcooking may be too much.

An electric mixer saves time and energy in mixing cakes, cookies, and other batters and doughs and in preparing meringues and whipped toppings. Keep your mixer ready to use in a handy place. You will use it oftener if it is convenient.

An electric blender can quickly puree foods; make soups smooth; whip up drinks, such as milkshakes; chop nuts; blend salad dressings, sauces, and sandwich spreads; and grate cheese, breadcrumbs, and raw vegetables.

An electric frypan is good for frying, panbroiling, braising, and grilling because it produces an even, controlled heat. Perhaps its most timesaving use is to prepare one-dish combinations of meat and vegetables cooked together. A good combination is ham slices with glazed sweetpotatoes and pineapple. Another is pork chops braised with tomatoes and rice.

WHEN YOU HAVE A FREEZER, you can keep on hand a supply of prepared foods that need only to be thawed or heated before serving. You can save time by preparing two or three times the amount you need for one meal and freezing the extra. When you are planning a party, you can avoid some of the last-minute rush by preparing foods in advance and freezing them.

Main dishes that freeze well include cooked meat and poultry, stews, meat or poultry pies, meat loaves, chile con carne, meatballs in sauce, stuffed peppers, various casserole dishes, and creamed meat, poultry, and fish. Cool the food quickly; then package and freeze it at once.

Casserole dishes can be frozen right in the baking dish. If you need the container for another use, line it with foil, add the food, and freeze. Then you can lift out the contents and wrap tightly in foil.

For best quality, plan to use frozen cooked main dishes within a few weeks.

Baked products that freeze well include yeast breads, quick breads, cakes, cookies, and pies (except meringue and custard pies).

Cakes can be frozen either unfrosted

Vegetable	Boiling time (minutes)	Vegetable	Boiling time (minutes)
Asparagus:		Collards	10–20
Whole	10–20	Corn, on cob	5–15
Tips	5–15	Dandelion greens	10–20
Beans:		Kale	10–25
Lima	20–25	Kohlrabi, sliced	20–25
Snap, 1-inch pieces	15–30	Okra	10–15
Beets:		Onions	15–30
Young, whole	30–45	Parsnips:	
Older, whole	45–90	Whole	20–40
Sliced or diced	15–25	Quartered	10–20
Beet greens, young	5–15	Peas	8–20
Broccoli, heavy stalks split	10–15	Potatoes:	
Brussels sprouts	10–20	Whole (medium sized)	25–40
Cabbage:		Quartered	20–25
Shredded	3–10	Diced	10–15
Quartered	10–15	Rutabagas, pared, cut up	20–30
Carrots:		Spinach	3–10
Young, whole	15–25	Squash:	
Older, whole	20–30	Summer, sliced	10–20
Sliced	10–20	Winter, cut up	15–20
Cauliflower:		Sweetpotatoes, whole	25–35
Separated	8–15	Tomatoes, cut up	7–15
Whole	15–20	Turnips:	
Celery, cut up	15–18	Cut up	10–20
Chard	10–20	Whole	20–30
		Turnip greens	10–30

or frosted, but boiled or 7-minute frostings do not freeze well.

You can package and freeze individual portions of cake, cookies, and pies and store them in a plastic bag. They will be handy for packed lunches.

Sandwiches of many kinds freeze well. It saves time to make lunch-box sandwiches weekly instead of daily. Party sandwiches, too, can be made several days ahead of time.

Use soft butter, margarine, cream cheese, or peanut butter as a spread—not mayonnaise or salad dressing, which soak into the bread. And omit egg white (which toughens), raw tomatoes and crisp greens, and very moist fillings.

Well-wrapped sandwiches keep up to

a month in a freezer at 0°; they thaw in 3 to 4 hours at room temperature.

FOR BUSY DAYS when you have to prepare a meal in minutes, here are some suggestions:

The kinds of meat that cook quickly include hamburgers (shape them before storing in refrigerator or freezer), cubed or minute steaks, liver, ham slices, thin pork chops (one-half inch thick), Canadian-type bacon, and frankfurters.

Meat loaf bakes in less than half the time it ordinarily requires if you press it into muffin pans instead of shaping into a large loaf.

Leftover roast meat or poultry (or canned tuna) heated with undiluted canned cream soup and served over biscuits or toast makes another quick main dish.

The guide on the opposite page can be a helpful reference to boiling *fresh* vegetables.

CANNED AND FROZEN vegetables save time because they need not be washed, pared, or shelled.

Solidly packed frozen vegetables, such as spinach and chopped broccoli, cook in less time if they are broken into small chunks before cooking.

You can shorten the cooking time of fresh vegetables by slicing, dicing, or coarsely shredding them.

To speed the slicing or dicing of carrots, celery, potatoes, or onions, line up several on a cutting board and cut across all of them at once with a sharp knife.

Slice small cooked or canned potatoes or beets with an egg slicer.

Potatoes can be baked in half the time it usually takes if they are first boiled for 15 minutes.

Try this for a quick-setting gelatin salad: Empty the contents of a 3-ounce package of fruit-flavored gelatin into a 4-cup measure, add boiling water to the 1-cup mark, and stir to dissolve. Then add ice cubes to the 2-cup mark. Stir often until the mixture begins to thicken. Then stir in fruit, vegetables or cottage cheese. Chill until set. If you use frozen fruit, use cold water instead of ice cubes and add the fruit without thawing; it will chill the mixture enough to hasten setting.

If you have a few minutes early in the day, make an ice cream pie or cake.

For pie: Make a crumb crust by mixing graham cracker or cooky crumbs with melted butter or margarine. Press the mixture into a pie pan. Chill it. Fill the crust with softened ice cream, rippled with sauce or crushed fruit if desired. Freeze until firm.

For cake: Slice a baked, unfrosted cake into three layers and spread softened ice cream between the layers. Top with sifted confectioners' sugar or whipped topping: freeze.

For a last-minute dessert, top sherbet with fruit: Raspberry sherbet topped with raspberries, pineapple sherbet topped with pineapple, lemon sherbet topped with strawberries.

THESE ARE JUST a few suggestions to help you save time. You can think of others. Above all, careful planning and efficient use of modern foods and equipment will help you make the most of your time in the kitchen.

CLOTHING
THE FAMILY

THE MONEY you spend for clothing for the family may be small compared with other spending, but the way you use it bears directly on the well-being of the whole family and the needs of each family member will decide the way it is spent.

Children need many different kinds of clothes, and it is not always easy to meet all those needs.

Generally it is best to buy clothing that fits the child at the time of purchase rather than to buy clothes for the child to grow into. Avoid buying too many clothes lest they are outgrown before they are worn out. Consider sturdy workmanship and ease of cleaning when you buy for young children.

After deciding on individual needs for work, school, play, and social events, take a good look at what you already have on hand.

Decide whether the clothing is wearable as it is; whether it needs some alteration, cleaning, or mending to put it in use; or whether it should be discarded.

When you have made that decision, you can determine more easily which additional items are needed for each family member, what is needed immediately, and which garments can be bought later. Few people buy a completely new wardrobe at one time.

Planning your buying over a period should help you avoid overspending and impulse buying. Too often we need something in a hurry or see something we cannot resist because it is a bargain or lifts our spirits. This type of buying is an ever-present danger to a spending plan. If you plan your purchases, you will be able to take advantage of sales and still buy only the things you need and plan for.

It takes advance planning and some reliable information to shop wisely.

Printed information on the item you plan to buy may not be readily available, but you can get plenty of advice at your local library before you go to buy.

Before you go shopping, decide on a price limit for each item. This helps to keep you from overspending and cuts down on shopping time.

Be alert to what items are available in the stores. Shop in stores that have a reputation for quality and fairness.

Spend some time shopping around comparing quality and price. When you want the longest wear possible from a garment, you need a plan to buy the best quality available at the price you can afford. For certain items, things that will be worn only a few times and not subjected to hard wear, however, price may come first.

Workmanship is how the garment is cut, sewn, and finished. Learn the signs of good workmanship. You are then better able to make selections that give longer wear.

The general signs of good workmanship are:

• Seams are wide enough to allow for letting out and finished to prevent fraying.

• Garment is cut with the grain of the goods.

• Machine stitching should be close and even.

• Hems and facings should be firmly attached but not show on the right side of the garment. Weak points should be reinforced.

• Machine-made buttonholes should be firm and evenly stitched on both sides of the cloth.

• The fabric should be smooth with no puckering at seams.

• The pants crotch should not have small triangles of cloth.

• The fabric lining in pockets

should be firm and closely woven.

- Hems should have a good tape binding.
- The collar and lapel should snap back when rolled up and then released.

Be sure you know what fiber is used in the fabric. You need to know all you can about the material you are buying, regardless of whether it is in ready-to-wear or yard goods for home sewing.

Feel and appearance have been the shopper's guide to quality of fabric, but neither is adequate or dependable today. Your best helps are factual tags or labels. Read them carefully.

A label giving the fiber content is required by the Textile Fiber Products Identification Act and the Wool Products Labeling Act. You thus have reliable information about the fiber content, which is helpful if you prefer one fiber over another or if you need additional information on how to care for the garment.

Some garments carry labels that tell about the workmanship, whether there is a special finish on the fabric (wash-and-wear, preshrunk, crease-resistant, water-repellent) and how to care for the garment (whether it can be laundered and, if so, the proper method to use, or whether it should be drycleaned only).

Some labels contain the manufacturer's name and address. Reliable firms want their name associated with their product.

How the garment is to be cared for is important. The cost of upkeep is greater for clothes that should be drycleaned only.

If fabrics have a finish that requires special handling when they are laundered, you should consider the additional time needed to care for them.

A garment that fits correctly is more comfortable, more attractive, and will give longer wear. Extensive alterations may be expensive and add considerably to the original cost. Making your own alterations is one way of saving money, but be sure to attempt only the alterations that you know you can do easily and well.

SHOP FOR LAUNDERABILITY is an excellent rule to follow. You—the family shopper—make the decisions when it comes to spending clothing and house-furnishing dollars. If you expect to wash an article, it's up to you to look for launderability and to choose the garment and the household textile that will give good service in your household when laundered with your equipment.

Be alert for construction features, minimum-care fabrics, and special finishes that make washing and ironing easier—and save your time and energy. Most textiles on the market today carry a label giving fiber content; some bear statements specifying and guaranteeing maximum shrinkage; and some also have washing directions attached. Read this information carefully—it will help you make up your mind if the garment can be laundered satisfactorily and in which load it belongs.

Save the attached tags and washing instructions, if any, along with the sales slip. Follow directions exactly. If washing results differ from those expected from the information given, see that the store from which you bought the item is informed of your dissatisfaction. You owe it to yourself and to other consumers to do all you can to promote reliability in labels and instructions.

Here are specific features or properties that aid launderability:

- Deep, well finished seams with edges that do not fray easily. Generally, the fewer the seams in wash-and-wear garments, the better.
- Fabric belts backed or lined with materials that wash just as well as the fabric, and are made with buckles that do not rust.
- Colorfastness of all parts of a garment (including buttons, decorative stitching, binding, and trim) to machine washing. Some fabrics are never colorfast to washing. Plastic buttons may fade in the washer or dryer or melt on contact with a hot iron.

• Well-finished buttonholes, hems, trim, and washable linings.

• Closely woven twill or plain weaves are less susceptible to snags and distortions in laundering than loose knits, and satin and damask weaves.

• Fabrics that require little or no ironing—seersucker, terry, plisse or corduroy.

IN TIMES when every young girl was taught to sew and the ready-to-wear market was small and expensive, the homemaker did not have to decide whether she would sew or buy clothing. Now she does. What influences her decisions?

Of the many types of shops available, the homemaker can patronize the specialty shop, department store, chain store, or discount store or order by mail.

Where you choose to shop depends, as you well know, on the availability of goods, the sizes needed, and the time and energy you have for shopping. For example, if you have small children, you may find it easier to select from a catalog and order by mail, rather than take the children on a shopping trip.

Before you decide to make a garment, ask yourself: Do I have the speed and accuracy so that my time is used wisely? Can my time be better spent doing something else for my family? Does the general appearance and fit of the clothing satisfy me and the person for whom it is made? Can I make a garment of better quality at a lower cost than I can afford to buy? Do I enjoy sewing?

Sewing can be a creative and relaxing activity for many women. Knitting and other forms of handiwork and needlework are, too—but that is another story.

Certain things—the simple dresses, housecoats, little girls' dresses, playclothes, for example—are more successfully made at home than more complicated garments.

In deciding whether to buy or sew, consider that clothing costs involve (besides money paid out) an investment of time and energy in shopping or sewing.

The purchase of such accessories as hats, gloves, belts, scarves, neckties, and socks should be planned along with the rest of the wardrobe. The indiscriminate buying of accessories may ruin your clothing budget.

Accessories should complement and not detract from the overall appearance. One accessory, properly chosen, can be used with several outfits or may give the finishing touch to a particular outfit.

RULES FOR TAKING CARE OF YOUR CLOTHES

• Brush your clothes regularly.
• Use wooden hangers that are neither too small nor too big.
• Dry rain-soaked garments in a cool, well-ventilated place before hanging in closet.
• Dry clean regularly—perspiration, grease, and dust rob your garments of their appearance and life.
• Save the hang tags found on garments you buy which give you cleaning and care instructions. It may be a help if you show them to your cleaner.
• Have stained garments cleaned immediately. Exposure to air, heat, and light sets stains, making them impossible to remove.
• Make sure your cleaner knows what the stain is. If he does, removal will be easier.

NINE THINGS YOU SHOULD NOT DO

• Do not press a garment that is stained. The heat will set the stain, making it almost impossible to remove.
• Do not use untested home stain removers. They may aggravate the condition.
• Test the effect of the cleaner on a hidden part of the fabric before using it on a stain.
• Do not use a deodorant without a shield protecting your garment from it.
• Avoid using plastic garment shields

which stiffen when dry cleaned.

- Do not wear a garment you value when using a home permanent. Home permanent solutions cause discoloration. Unless your hair is completely dry after a home permanent treatment, damp hair can also cause discoloration of the garment.
- Do not store clothes at home before cleaning and mothproofing. Be sure that garment storage bags, boxes, or cedar chests are kept dry.
- Do not use nail-polish remover to remove nail-polish stains from fabrics. Nail-polish removers can cause holes in acetate fabric, and they tend to damage many dyes.
- Do not hang knitted garments. Their weight will pull them out of shape. Keep your knitted garments in dresser drawers or purchase some of the hangers for knitted clothing.

CLOTHES THAT FIT

NOTHING GOOD can be said of clothing that fits poorly. It is unattractive and uncomfortable. Strains may develop in seams and fabrics that shorten the life of the garment.

Manufacturers and retailers of garments whose fit does not satisfy the consumer hopefully will suffer through loss of goodwill and the return of merchandise.

Poor fit may mean a garment or pattern is a size too small or too large. Often it means the pattern or garment is not properly proportioned to fit the wearer.

Shrinkage of more than 1 percent will rob you of comfort in fit. If a garment is heavily sized it may shrink as much as 7 percent. Shrinkage of 2 percent to 3 percent is not uncommon, so if you buy a tight-fitting garment because it is eye-catching or fashionable, remember it may become unwearable in a short time.

Getting a good fit was a serious problem a generation ago. Each manufacturer then used his own system of sizing. Those systems had been developed by trial and error from measurements taken on a few individuals according to poorly defined and inaccurate procedures. Garments labeled the same size by different manufacturers differed greatly. Few fit without alterations.

OF COURSE, TODAY you have a good chance of buying clothes that fit with little or no alteration. The woman who sews usually can make well-fitting clothes by using commercial patterns with only minor adjustments—if any.

Educational institutions helped obtain 36 measurements of 147,088 children (age 4 to 17) and 58 measurements of each of 14,698 women. Standards for sizing patterns and apparel were developed through the joint efforts of industry and the Departments of Commerce and Agriculture.

THE STANDARDS are known as commercial standards.

They are of three types: Body measurement standards, which represent the body clothed in underwear or foundation garments; model form standards, which represent special length and girth modifications of body measurement standards for apparel-fitting purposes; and garment-size standards, which give dimensions for specific garments and are also based on the body measurement standards.

Because the body measurement standards are of more general interest, they are discussed here in some detail. A table gives the titles of these standards and the range of sizes covered by them.

BODY MEASUREMENT standard CS 215–58 covers four classifications of women and nine different body types and is the most comprehensive of the standards we have.

The classifications are Misses', Women's, Half-sizes (shorter women), and Juniors'.

The body types are divided into three height groups (tall, regular, and short), with three bust-hip groups for each height group. The bust is the

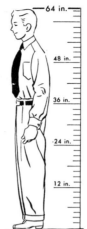
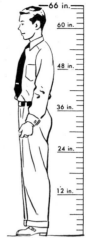

Size 12	Size 14	Size 16	Size 18	Size 20
Height, 58 inches	Height, 61 inches	Height, 64 inches	Height, 66 inches	Height, 68 inches
Weight, 87 pounds	Weight, 100 pounds	Weight, 115 pounds	Weight, 126 pounds	Weight, 138 pounds
Chest, 29½ inches	Chest, 31½ inches	Chest, 33 inches	Chest, 34½ inches	Chest, 36 inches
Waist, 25½ inches	Waist, 26½ inches	Waist, 27½ inches	Waist, 28½ inches	Waist, 29½ inches

same in the three bust-hip groups; the hip types are slender (designated as minus), regular, and full (designated as plus).

The size number is based on the bust measurement but is not numerically equal to it. The number is combined with symbols to give the complete size designation.

Thus, 14R refers to a size 14 bust, regular or average height and hips; 14T— refers to a size 14 bust, tall in height, slender-hip type; and 14S+ refers to a size 14 bust, short in height, full-hip type.

The standard includes tables that give the weight and 47 measurements for each of 111 size designations. These designations include 46 Misses', 28 Women's, 21 Half-sizes, and 16 Juniors'.

The standard explains the various measurements and includes drawings showing how some of the more important ones are taken.

As would be expected, the body measurement standards for the sizing of apparel for infants, babies, toddlers, and children (CS 151–50), for girls (CS 153–48), and for boys CS 155–50) contain fewer measurements for each size designation than the body

measurement standard for women. They differ from the latter in that the size number is based on stature. The standards are limited to the so-called "regulars" in the population; that is, those with the most common body proportions.

Further analysis of the original measurement data has been undertaken to develop standards for the so-called "outsizes" in the population, as slims and huskies for boys and chubbies for girls. Some of these outsize standards have been made available in preliminary form.

It is important to note that the size numbers in any of the standards are not necessarily the same as the ages of the boys or girls whose measurements they give.

Anyone can purchase copies of the body measurement standards. Information on prices and how to order is available from the Office of Engineering Standards, Institute of Applied Technology, National Bureau of Standards, Washington, D.C. 20234.

Issuance as a commercial standard indicates that a standard has been accepted by a substantial segment of the trade. Firms and other organizations who accept a standard before it is is-

COMMERCIAL BODY MEASUREMENT STANDARDS

Number	Title	Size range
CS 151–50.	Body measurements for the sizing of apparel for infants, babies, toddlers, and children.	Up to 6X
CS 153–48.	Body measurements for the sizing of apparel for girls.	7 to 12
CS 155–50.	Body measurements for the sizing of boys' apparel.	2 to 20
CS 215–58.	Body measurements for the sizing of women's patterns and apparel.	

Misses'

8R	to 22R
10T	to 20T
8S	to 18S
10R—	to 22R—
12T—	to 18T—
12S—	to 18S—
8R+	to 16R+
10T+	to 14T+
8S+	to 12S+

Women's

30R	to 42R
32T	to 40T
32R—	to 42R—
28R+	to 38R+
30T+	to 36T+

Half-sizes

10½	to 24½
12½—	to 22½—
8½+	to 20½+

Juniors'

7R	to 19R
9T	to 17T
9S	to 15S

sued as a commercial standard are listed in the printed standard.

All who are concerned with the manufacture and distribution of garments and patterns for women and children are encouraged to use the standards, with or without formal acceptance.

Anyone who accepts one of the standards agrees to use it insofar as practicable in the production, distribution, and purchase of patterns and apparel, but he reserves the right to depart from the standard as he deems advisable.

The Government asks that products that comply with a standard in all respects be regularly identified or labeled as conforming to it. Such labeling is not mandatory. However, the use of labels or advertisements that indicate that a product conforms to a standard makes conformance mandatory. Thus, the absence of a label indicating that the sizing of a garment conforms to the appropriate standard does not necessarily mean that it does not con-

form. On the other hand, presence of such a label is assurance that it does.

In actual practice, labels and advertisements that mention the commercial standards for the sizing of garments and patterns are rare. Industry nevertheless has made extensive use of the information on body proportions contained in the standards in designing and sizing garments and patterns. As a result, women and children have a greater number of sizes to choose from and a much better chance than formerly of finding garments and patterns that give a good fit.

When the standards were developed, it was suggested that the size designations listed in them be used by all manufacturers and distributors for all types of garments. That would greatly simplify the shopper's problem.

For example, if a woman found that her proportions most closely checked those given in CS 215–58 for a size 12R in the Misses' classification, she would buy a size 12 Misses' garment, regardless of what garment she was buy-

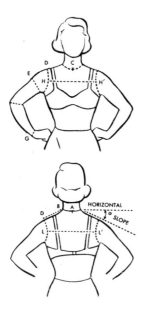

Location of some of the actual body measurements. Front view of woman: Cross-chest width; neck base, armscye, upper arm, elbow, and wrist girths. Back view of woman: Cross-back width; neck base and armscye; girths; shoulder length and slope.

ing or who manufactured it.

As most of us know, this system of designating sizes is not always followed. A shopper will find that she takes a size 12 Misses' dress in most lines. In some, she may find that it is the size 10 that fits her. She will also find that most manufacturers label some garments according to specific body measurements rather than by the size designations listed in the standard. Nevertheless, the chances are that the proportions of the garment are based on those given in the standard.

Several mail-order companies are among the most enthusiastic users of the body measurement standards.

The consumer who shops by mail will find that their catalogs give the more important body measurements for the various sizes and illustrate the proper method for taking the measurements.

The manufacturers of patterns for women who sew at home also include certain key body dimensions in their catalogs and on pattern envelopes as guides to selection of patterns. The values given for these dimensions differ somewhat from those given in the standards. Thus, when you shop for patterns, check your measurements against those in the pattern book. Do not assume that you take the same size in patterns and ready-to-wear.

Whether the consumer shops at clothing stores or by mail, her problem is to select patterns and garments proportioned to fit her figure. Only by doing so can she benefit fully from the improvement in garment sizing.

BASIC FACTS ABOUT SHOES

FEET AND SHOES travel many miles. An average, healthy 7-year-old boy may take 30 thousand steps every day. That adds up to about 10 miles a day and more than 300 miles a month. His mother, on a busy shopping day, may walk 10 miles. A policeman walks about 15 miles on his beat.

Feet carry the weight of your body and provide means to propel you when you walk, climb, and jump. As you step off, your body's weight travels down through the heel, along the outside of the foot to the ball, across the heads of the long bones to the first metatarsal, and to the big toe. The big toe launches the walking motion. Each foot in turn bears the total weight of your body.

SHOEMAKING is a complex process.

All shoes are made over lasts—wooden forms—which give the shoe its shape, size, and style.

Shoemakers in 1887 approved a chart of standard measurements for lasts. Successive changes in styling and mass production have introduced variations in the original measurements. Two lasts, marked 13C, for example, may differ considerably in their shape and dimensions.

More than 50 kinds of materials and more than 85 hand and machine operations are used in making a shoe.

Shoes consist of outsole (bottom), insole (if used), upper, and heel.

The insole, of leather or other materials, forms the foundation of the shoe. The front part of the upper is the vamp. The back part is the quarter.

Good shoes have lining of kid or finer portions of cowhide. Lining should be neat and fit smoothly. Best for patent leathers are enameled colt or horsehide. Insoles should be made of lightweight, even-grained leather. Stitches should be small and even, properly caught in the leather. In good shoes there should be 2 to 3 rows of stitching.

A hidden counter—stiffened material between quarter and lining—keeps the back in shape. The insole is fastened to the last. The finished upper is drawn over the last and securely joined to the insole. The outsole is permanently attached to the insole-upper components. Heels are attached. Finally the shoes are given several finishing touches.

Sewed, cemented, and nailed are names of three major shoemaking processes.

In welt construction, sole and upper are joined by being mutually stitched to a leather strip or welt. This type wears best and repairs most easily.

Welt shoes made without stitching inside are sturdy and flexible. The Goodyear welt process produces high-quality men's, women's, and children's oxfords.

In the stitchdown process, uppers are turned out and stitched directly to the outsole. This provides a smooth inner surface and resembles the Goodyear welt.

Advantages of cemented shoes are their lighter weight, greater flexibility, and greater variety in styling.

Many grades of shoes can be made with the same method of construction. Many grades of materials are used.

Almost all rubber-canvas footwear is made by the vulcanizing process. By applying heat and pressure to an unvulcanized rubber mixture, a complete sole and heel are formed and permanently attached to the upper.

The newest method, similar to vulcanizing, is the injection-molded process. A vinyl (liquid plastic) is poured into a mold shaped like the finished product. Sole and heel are quickly attached to the finished upper.

Shoes have been made from almost everything—paper, raffia, felt, fur-skins, bark, and fabric.

Leather, the tanned skin or hide of an animal, is the traditional material. It is a favorite because of its toughness, durability, flexibility, shape retention,

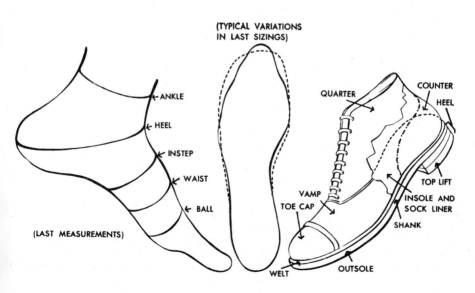

(TYPICAL VARIATIONS IN LAST SIZINGS)

ANKLE
HEEL
INSTEP
WAIST
BALL
(LAST MEASUREMENTS)

QUARTER
COUNTER
HEEL
VAMP
TOE CAP
TOP LIFT
INSOLE AND SOCK LINER
SHANK
WELT
OUTSOLE

insulation, ability to absorb and pass off moisture from the foot, permeability to air, and attractive looks.

COMMON SHOE LEATHERS

Calf skin: Very durable and waterproof. It should be close-grained.

Alligator: Scales can almost be lifted.

Suede: (Calf with nap): This consists of the flesh side of the calf and is buffed to provide a soft nap.

Kid and Goat: Both are very soft and pliable.

Reptile: These are very sturdy and usually require little care.

Sheep skin: A leather that is suitable only for the lining.

A new tanning process using glutaraldehyde, a chemical, makes leathers more resistant to breakdown by water, sweat, acids, and alkalies. Such leathers make better work shoes for farmwear. Use of other chemicals provides scuff resistance, improved wear, and water resistance.

Cotton and linen fabrics, nylon, straws, and plastics also are used for uppers.

Industry in 1964 announced many new manmade materials for shoe uppers, designated by coined or trade names. In general, the classes of new materials are poromeric, expanded vinyls, and nonexpanded vinyls.

Poromeric refers to a porous, permeable, leatherlike sheet material made up of a group of chemical compounds. An example is Corfam, a product of du Pont.

Expanded vinyl is a plastic sheet with tiny air cells evenly spaced in it to allow passage of air. One example is Pervel.

The nonexpanded is described as a flat sheet coated with vinyl to resemble patent leather.

The new materials resist scuffing, are easy to care for, need no polishing, hold their shape, keep out moisture, show no water spots, are light in weight, and have clear colors that will not rub off. Some shoes of the new materials have leather linings.

Even newer are vinyl and fabric uppers bonded to cowhide splits—hides horizontally cut into layers. These uppers combine long wear with easy care.

SOLES of children's shoes should preferably be slip resistant, lightweight, and flexible, but firm. Avoid boardlike soles.

Solings may be of leather, natural rubber, or manmade materials.

Synthetic rubber applies to any vulcanizable synthetic polymer having rubberlike properties. Solings of styrene-butadiene (synthetic) rubber are termed nuclear. Neolite is an example. Cellular designates a nuclear sole filled with blown air cells. Synthetic crepe soles are in this group.

The Children's Bureau recommends that for children up to age 6, shoe heels be one-fourth to one-half inch. After age 6, heel height may gradually be increased to 1 inch. Rubber heels or top-lifts help prevent jarring when a child walks.

ONE COBBLER, Wilbur Gardner, of Medford, Oreg., became exasperated some years ago over the growing number of shoddy shoes people brought to his repair shop. He started a campaign for the labeling of materials in shoes. Through the support of Oregon's representatives in the Congress and interested organizations, his efforts gathered force and resulted in the Federal Trade Commission's Guides for Shoe Content Labeling and Advertising, adopted in October 1962.

Its main purpose is to insure that the consumer is not deceived. Shoe materials must be precisely identified.

Manufacturers and retailers cannot claim that a shoe is made of leather if part of it is some other material.

All labeling must be in the form of stamps, tags, or labels embedded in or attached to the product itself. The guides do not offer opinions or information as to the relative merits of various materials.

THE SIZE of a shoe is its length for a standard width. The width is expressed in letters and the length in numbers.

Stock widths range from triple A, the narrowest, to triple E, the widest. Whole sizes increase in length by one-third of an inch. The American size-system runs from 0 to 13⅓ in the first series and continues from 1 on in the second series. In the first series, size 0 is 4 inches long and size 13½ is 8½ inches long. In the second series, size 1 is 8¾ inches long and size 12 is 12⅓ inches long.

Other classifications of size are: Children, 8½ to 11; Misses and Youths, 11 to 2; Growing Girls and Boys, 2½ to 5 or 6.

Do not ask for shoes by size. Always ask the clerk to measure both feet. Stand with your weight evenly divided between the feet and gauge the comfort. The foot will alter slightly in length and width when it takes the body's weight, so make sure your new shoes fit comfortably. Test them for comfort by walking on a rug and also on a hard surface before you buy the shoes. New shoes, if they fit correctly, will be comfortable from the start. They will not need "breaking in."

Examine the edge trim of the shoes. Shoes of good quality have smooth, clean sole edges.

Examine the "break" of the leather uppers at the ball of the shoe. Break refers to the tiny wrinkles formed on the grain (outer) surface when you bend the leather. Many fine wrinkles per inch indicate high-quality leather. A few large wrinkles indicate a poorer quality.

THINK ABOUT shoe needs before you shop. Infants sometimes need foot coverings for warmth. Their shoes should be soft and loose. Bootees are mostly for appearance sake; babies quickly kick them off.

Most children do not need shoes until they begin to walk. Ask your doctor to recommend the type of first walking shoes.

Check the length, width, and height of instep to see that nothing restricts or cramps the toes and foot.

Enough toe height at the tip of the shoes is most important.

Buy shoes to fit the present foot size. Do not buy shoes too small or too large.

Sloppy fit may harm feet as much as tight shoes.

Check your child's shoes for fit about once a month.

Children need and want shoes for school, play, and dress. Up to about 6 years, children (especially little girls) tend to outgrow shoes before wearing them out.

After about 6 years, most children wear out even the best shoes before they outgrow them.

At school, a child sits a great deal. Laced oxfords make good school shoes.

Between school and bedtime, his active feet need good shoes. Have his sneakers or other play shoes fitted as carefully as his school shoes.

Let children go barefoot only in clean sand or grass. Protect their feet by sandals or shoes in places where there is apt to be broken glass, splinters, insects, hard floorings, or pavements.

If your 7-year-old boy weighs 55 pounds, he puts more than 800 tons of weight on his shoes every day (55 pounds times 30 thousand steps), or about 24 thousand tons a month. But a boy does more than walk. He jumps, kicks, and wades through puddles. His shoes lead a rough life. Estimates of the active life of shoes range from 20 days to 7 or 9 months, and average about 10 weeks.

No single component or characteristic determines the life of a shoe. Fit is most important. Only the wearer can tell if a shoe fits. Price does not guarantee good fit. Comfort, materials used, flexibility, weight of shoe, ability to hold its original shape and appearance influence shoe life. Length of service depends also on the wearer, where he wears his shoes, and his activities.

Wornout shoes may harm the feet. Ripped seams or soles with holes should be repaired promptly and worn top-lifts replaced.

Half soles or resoling may change the size or shape of shoes and result in a poor fit.

Costs of repairs have risen. Sometimes it is better money management to buy new shoes to fit rapidly growing feet.

Lack of proper care, willful misuse, and perspiration can cause breakdown of shoes. Thousands of small sweat glands are located in the skin of the feet. The soles perspire a great deal to regulate foot temperature. When you walk briskly, each foot pours out about a tablespoon of sweat an hour. Accumulated sweat is hard on leather uppers, insoles, and linings.

Tight fitting, closed, sweaty shoes are ideal places for growth of micro-organisms. Micro-organisms contribute to bad foot odors and irritated skin and to breakdown of shoes.

You should have two or more pairs of shoes and wear one pair every other day to allow the shoes to dry out.

An occasional sprinkling of about one-fourth teaspoon of salt in your shoes will absorb moisture and keep your feet drier. Paint spots on leather shoes can be removed if you moisten the head of a kitchen match and rub over the spots.

KNITTED FABRICS

A KNITTED FABRIC, a structure of rows of loops hanging on other rows of loops, is made by pulling loops through loops.

Each vertical or lengthwise row of loops is called a wale. Each crosswise row of loops is called a course.

If the loops are stretched in any direction, they tend to return to their normal or relaxed shape. Knit goods therefore are elastic and have an advantage over woven goods.

Knitting is a craft that dates from antiquity. Master knitters made exquisite carpets, berets, shirts, afghans, shawls, and hosiery, some of which now, centuries later, are on exhibit in museums. The beginning of the machine age in the 19th century brought the decline of hand knitting as an industry.

Knitting continued in the home, however. More and more women (and men, too) knit now.

They consider knitting a rewarding, creative, relaxing, and inexpensive hobby and a productive undertaking for the odd moments at the hairdresser, say, or during longer periods.

Knitting is easy. One needs only two needles and some yarn. Pattern books and books on knitting give enough information for you to get started, but it is best to have some instruction at first. The needlework sections of department stores often give free lessons. In many communities you can get professional help in classes or schools.

The two classes of knitted fabrics are the filling knit and the warp knit.

Filling knit fabrics are quickly identified. They can be raveled readily, and they easily develop runs, or ladders, when a yarn is broken. In a flat piece, the yarn is raveled back and forth; in a circular fabric, around and around, as in a hand-knitted sock.

In filling knitting, the two basic stitches are the plain (jersey or stockinette) and the purl. The rib is made by alternating the plain and purl stitches. The way the loops are meshed determines the kind of stitch.

In the plain stitch, all the loops are drawn through others to the same side of the fabric. The face of the fabric is characterized by the wales running lengthwise; the back, by crosswise ridges.

In the purl stitch, also called the links-and-links stitch, the loops of alternate courses are drawn to opposite sides of the fabric. Both sides of the fabric look the same; the ridges run widthwise.

In rib knitting, the loops of the same course are drawn to both sides of the fabric. A rib fabric is the same on both sides. If the loops alternate, one on one side and one on the other, it is called 1 x 1 rib. A 2 x 2 rib is called a Swiss rib.

Hand- and machine-filling knit fabrics may be circular or flat knitted. The circular knit comes off the knitting needles in a tubular form; the yarns run continuously in one direction across the fabric. The flat knit is a flat form in which the yarns run alternately back and forth.

Filling knit comprises a large part of the knit goods manufactured by machine and is organized around four major knitting systems: Plain, rib, purl, and interlock.

Of these, the plain knit comprises the largest yardage and is used in hosiery, underwear, and outerwear. It can be knit of the finest of yarns with as many as 50 wales per inch or with coarse yarns with as few as 3 loops per inch. Plain knit has considerable elasticity in both directions.

Rib knitting has much more elasticity in the width than the plain because loops in certain wales are meshed in

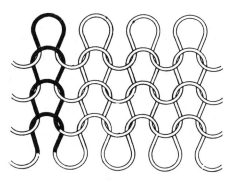

WALE

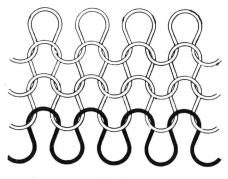

COURSE

Knitted structure showing wale and course.

opposite directions to those in remaining wales.

Rib fabrics are used for slim-fit lingerie, half hose, and welts for pullovers. Rib fabrics are used in an unstretched

form for many garments in which double thickness is desired.

Purl knitting is used largely in the manufacture of infants' and children's garments, as it more closely resembles hand knitting and produces the desired characteristics of softness and loftiness.

Interlock is a circular filling knitted material. This type of construction may be thought of as a double cloth made of two separate 1 x 1 rib fabrics so that the wales of one fabric lie between those of the other on both the face and back. The yarn forms loops on both sides of the fabric. Both sides have the appearance of a plain knit fabric.

Interlock is ideal for garments such as T-shirts, sport shirts, pajamas, children's play clothes, and gloves.

Many double-knit fabrics that are variations of the plain interlock constructions are manufactured. Many are fabrics used by the garment trade for women's high-fashion dresses and suits. The double knits most commonly used for outerwear are the French and Swiss double piqués. In each, alternate yarns form loops on the back and not on the face of the cloth. These fabrics do not stretch so much and hold their shape better than the plain interlock.

Unlimited variations in designs in filling knit fabrics are produced by using stitches other than plain, purl, and rib. Three of the commonest are the tuck, lace, and float stitches.

WARP KNITTING is one of the major knitting systems. Fabrics made by this system can be identified by determining the direction of the yarns that run lengthwise instead of crosswise. These fabrics do not readily develop runs when a yarn is broken and cannot be easily raveled. Most must be raveled on three or more yarns.

Warp-knit fabrics range in design from tight constructions to open structures similar to laces. The cloth is finished in widths from 80 inches or less up to 160 inches and is sold as piece goods, which is cut and made into garments.

Warp-knit fabrics are not so elastic and cannot compete with the production of circular filling knit fabrics, but designs of greater variety can be made.

Warp-knit fabrics must have at least one yarn for each wale of the fabric. Filling knit fabrics need but one yarn to form all the wales. A thousand or more yarns from a beam are fed into the knitting machine at the same time and are laid on needles. By the knitting action of the needle, each warp yarn is formed into loops, which are interlocked with adjacent loops made by warp yarns on either side.

The primary stitches in warp knitting are ordinary, chain, inlay, and float. In one of the drawings, the ordinary stitch is shown with the open loop, *a*, and the closed loop, *b*. The

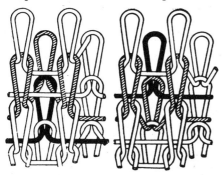

FRENCH PIQUE   SWISS PIQUE

Double-knit fabrics.

loop may mesh with a loop in an adjacent wale or with a loop in another wale. This stitch when used alone forms the simplest of warp fabrics.

The chain stitch may have open loop, *a* and *b*, or closed loop, *c*. The loops of one yarn mesh in only one wale. Therefore, unlike the ordinary stitch, it cannot form a fabric when it is used alone, but it imparts a great deal of stability to the structure when it is combined with other stitches.

The inlay and float stitches do not form loops. They impart bulk and stability to the fabric. The float extends lengthwise of the fabric without changing direction, while the inlay extends over one or more wales.

By far the greater portion of warp-knit materials is made on the tricot machine. The most popular fabric knit

on this machine is made of two sets of warp yarns and is commonly called a two-bar tricot. The face of the tricot fabric shows vertical rows of loops and has the same appearance as the face of a plain knit fabric. The back shows horizontal rows of laps or floats. The fabric may be made in stripes, mesh, and elaborate designs. Examples of this fabric are the rayon and nylon jerseys used for women's dresses, blouses, and lingerie.

THE INHERENT characteristics of knitted fabrics make them desirable for many purposes. They will stretch under tension and recover their dimensions to a considerable extent when tensions are released.

Knitted garments conform to the shape of the body and are comfortable to wear. Knitted fabrics are more absorbent and warmer than woven fabrics of comparable weight. It is not always necessary to iron them after they are laundered. These materials are especially desirable for underwear and for sport and travel outerwear.

The most distinctive characteristic of a knitted fabric is its ability to take

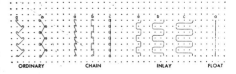

ORDINARY   CHAIN   INLAY   FLOAT

Primary stitches used in warp knitting.

up the shape of the wearer and to recover its original shape—elasticity—after being worn.

Knitted fabrics are elastic because of their loop construction. Each loop behaves like a tiny spring, which tends to return to its normal or relaxed shape if stretched in any direction. Fabrics vary in their elasticity because of the fiber of which the yarn is spun and of the way the yarn is knit.

A wool fiber is more elastic than a cotton fiber. A fabric knit of wool therefore will hold its shape better than a fabric knit of cotton in the same construction. If cotton yarn is firmly knit, however, the fabric will hold its shape.

Some knitted garments shrink in length and stretch in width in laundering. The cause of the excessive change in dimensions is the distortion of the shape of the knitted loop, which has been elongated in the finishing opera-

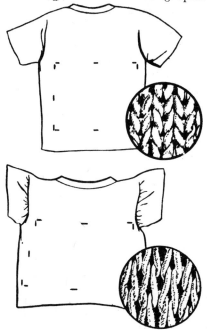

T-shirts after 20 washes with tumble drying. Inserts show closeup of knit fabric before laundering; ink marks on shirts originally marked a 10-inch square.

tions. In laundering, the loop is relaxed and returns to its natural round shape.

Because of distortion in finishing, many knit garments are unsatisfactory in size and in appearance after laundering.

For example, the plain knit cotton T-shirt in one of the drawings made of the fabric with elongated loops shrank in length and stretched in width and has ruffled sleeve seams and a stretched neckband. The T-shirt made of the fabric with round loops held its shape in laundering and maintained its attractive appearance.

HOW CAN ONE select knit garments that will not shrink or stretch?

Choose those with the round loops. This is not always easy, especially in a finely knit fabric. A sure way is to count the number of loops in a 1-inch distance both lengthwise and widthwise of the fabric. In case of a plain knit, the number of loops lengthwise should be approximately 1.1 times the number widthwise. For example, plain knit that has 30 wales per inch should have about 33 courses per inch.

Much of the knit piece goods in retail stores is not properly finished and hence will shrink and stretch in laundering. These materials may be relaxed in the home before they are made into garments.

Knit fabrics of wool may be lightly steamed, pressed, and allowed to lie flat before cutting.

Piece goods knit of cotton as well as other fibers may be relaxed by wetting out thoroughly, extracting or drying in a towel, and tumbler dried. If you do not tumble dry it, lay the fabric flat without distorting it for drying.

STRETCH FABRICS

STRETCH FABRICS are the sort of thing that leads one to ask, "Why didn't somebody think of it before?"

They provide better fit for many items, from baby clothes to upholstery. They come in many weights, fibers, colors, and finishes. Some have little stretch; others, much. Some give ease of movement or a smooth fit; others, forceful control.

We can classify their stretch in two ways.

One is the power stretch, of the kind built into foundation garments, swimsuits, men's tummy-restraining shorts and briefs, and so on.

The other is comfort, or action, stretch. It is used in children's garments, sport and casual clothes, men's shirts, and other items in which movement is involved and a smooth fit is desired.

Many people know about power stretch. Comfort stretch is a newer idea, and it is the one discussed here.

You cannot tell by looking at cloth whether or not it is a stretch fabric. It probably looks just like a similar fabric—gabardine, batiste, taffeta, or print cloth—which has only a normal stretch.

The amount of stretch in the finished fabric depends somewhat on the fiber and the method of producing the stretch.

THREE BASIC METHODS are used in making stretch materials.

Spandex—a fiber with rubberlike elasticity—is made from polyurethane. Spandex lasts longer than rubber and requires no special care.

Spandex is seldom used alone, but forms the core around which other fibers are spun. The amount of stretch is determined by the amount of elongation used during the spinning process. The treatment of the fabric is determined by the other fibers used.

Many of the power stretch fabrics are made from spandex. It also is used for comfort stretch, sometimes alone and sometimes as the core for spun yarn.

The second method is thermoplastic, or the heat setting of yarns. Any method for producing texturized or crimped yarns may be used. A common procedure for manmade fibers is to twist the yarn to the desired amount; heat-set it; then twist it in the opposite direction.

This process gives a tight curl that uncurls and returns to a less tense position when forces are removed.

Cotton may be processed by this method, if resin is applied before the heat treatment. Again, the amount of stretch is predetermined by the manufacturer.

When stretch yarns are woven or knitted into fabrics, some of the stretch may be lost in the manufacturing.

The type of fibers, the original amount of stretch in the yarn, the tensions of the yarn during fabric construction, the temperatures and chemicals used in making, dyeing, and finishing, all affect the amount of

stretch in the finished fabric, the amount of shrinkage to be expected, and the care required.

Slack mercerization, the third method, is a treatment applied to fabric. Cotton fabric is treated with sodium hydroxide while there is no tension in the direction that is to stretch. The fabric is then washed and finished to the chosen stretch, which may be 20 percent or less. Stretch may be lengthwise, widthwise, or both.

In general, the trade has agreed that stretch in the widthwise direction (also called east-west, horizontal, or filling stretch) should be about 20 percent; in the lengthwise direction (called north-south, vertical, or warp stretch), 50 percent or more.

Sometimes a fabric stretches in both directions (but usually only in one), and garments are cut lengthwise or crosswise, depending on the type of garment.

Pants and slacks usually are cut with the stretch lengthwise; other garments, with the stretch widthwise.

ALTHOUGH this section has discussed stretch only, fully as important to you is whether or not the material returns to its original size and shape after the forces are removed. If not, the material is said to "grow."

Growth is the percentage of increase in length after the fabric has been stretched and released. If the fabric grows, a garment made of it may become wrinkled and baggy.

The ideal fabric would have zero-percent growth. Some fabrics have a large amount of growth—20 percent or more. But the aim of reliable manufacturers is 2 inches per yard (about 5 percent) or less for children's and sports wear and less than 1 inch per yard (2 percent) for dressier wear.

Of course, the farther you stretch the fabric, the more it will grow. You therefore should select a fabric which has much more stretch than you actually need.

Since there are no labels to tell you how much a fabric stretches or grows, it will be necessary to check both to see if they are sufficient for your purpose. A test at the store does not guarantee that the material will wear well or that growth will not increase with wear. All that you are doing is assuring yourself that adequate stretch and minimum growth are in the fabric at the time you buy it.

As you can see, there are many places where mistakes can occur in making or selecting the right fabric for the purpose. It is more important than usual, therefore, that you consider before buying what you want and what you expect it to do.

The manufacturer of garments makes them so that the same garment will fit more different shapes of the same general size more comfortably and more attractively than a nonstretch fabric can. His judgment may vary from yours.

So, first consider carefully what the advantages to you will be if you choose a stretch fabric. You may not need stretch at all. A sleeveless blouse or a full skirt of stretch would be a waste of money. Why pay extra for stretch you will not use?

On the other hand, slacks or a blouse with sleeves may be much more comfortable in a stretch material. Certainly, a stretch slipcover would be much easier to fit around the corners of a chair than would a nonstretch fabric.

Having decided what you need, you next examine the cloth. Does it stretch any more than the same type of fabric not labeled stretch? Does it stretch enough to give a smooth, comfortable feeling in the use you plan for it? Does it stretch less than 20 percent? Perhaps a good knit which may be less expensive would serve as well for your purpose.

How much is 20-percent stretch? If you grasp the cloth at two points 5 inches apart, you should be able to stretch it 1 inch, or one-fifth of the original length.

If you are planning a garment to stretch widthwise, 20 percent is enough. If it is lengthwise stretch you want, better look for 50-percent elongation or more.

Does the fabric spring back to its original length after you have pulled it out the desired amount? Is there a bulge or a stripe of puckered threads? Only a slight ripple should appear.

If the answers are satisfactory, the cloth should be suitable.

Another thing to check in garments is whether lining, interlining, and lace (if any) stretch, too. If not, why use stretch for the part of the garment to which they are attached? It will neither wear nor clean satisfactorily. On the other hand, are shoulder seams, buttonholes, front opening, and other parts of the garment which should not stretch, properly reinforced?

Stretch will not prevent shrinkage. Read the label. Unless the manufacturer guarantees a shrinkage of less than 2 percent, you should probably buy a larger size in order to assure a good fit after the garment is laundered. Or, in the case of cloth, you should shrink it before you make it up. Drycleaning does not cause as much shrinkage as washing, but there may be some dimensional change, and you should plan accordingly.

Stretch may take care of some of the fitting problems, but it will not be an advantage if you force something into a space that is too small, so that there will be no chance for expanding and contracting. Just as well buy a nonstretch—it is cheaper.

BEFORE YOU PURCHASE stretch fabric, be sure that you know how to handle it. Stretch fabrics require special sewing techniques.

The fabric should be laid flat at least overnight so that folds and bumps can relax, and the material will be smooth before cutting.

No special patterns are needed, but each piece should be placed so that the stretch will be in the chosen direction.

Make test stitchings before sewing on the garment.

In general, fine needles and fine stitches are required. Fine zigzagging may make the seam more elastic. Seams may need machine overcasting to prevent fraying.

As mentioned in connection with

purchase of readymade items, linings, interlinings, trimmings, laces, and such should be as elastic as the outer fabric to which they attach or the purpose of the stretch will be lost. Tape stays, however, should be applied at shoulder, waist, and other places where no stretch is desired. Buttonholes need reinforcement.

Press the seams lightly with a cool iron and a press cloth.

As styles or manufacturing methods change, fabrics may change too, and the sewing instructions also may change. More detailed up-to-date instructions for sewing with stretch fabrics may be obtained from the thread or pattern companies.

As FOR THE CARE of stretch materials: As a rule, follow the same procedure for washing or drycleaning that you would use for any other fabric made from the same kind of fibers.

Read the labels, mark them for identification, and save them, if there are special instructions about care.

Most stretch fabrics can be washed, but the kind of fiber, weave (or knit), colors, and finishes may affect the method and temperature of cleaning.

Washing may bring back to shape a fabric that has stretched too much. If the garment is too small, however, the time will come when it will be poorly shaped, no matter what the treatment.

The best method for drying stretch fabrics is tumbler drying, with the dryer set at the correct temperature for the fiber. If you cannot use a dryer, the garment should be laid flat and blocked, if necessary, to insure the correct size in the dry garment.

Under no circumstances should an article with lengthwise stretch be hung up for drying—it will stretch.

Whatever method you use, be sure that the fabric is thoroughly dry before you use the article. Otherwise, it may lose its shape.

Usually no ironing is required, but if pressing is necessary, use a press cloth, a cool iron, and a light touch. Slack-mercerized fabrics are especially sensitive to a hot iron and pressure; overpressing may destroy the stretch or make the garment too large.

Stretch fabrics, wet or dry, should not be hung for long periods of time. Store the cloth flat in a drawer or on a shelf. Hanging in the closet is especially undesirable for lengthwise stretch, because the weight of the garment will cause it to lengthen an inch or more.

SINCE LABELS do not list stretch properties, you will probably always have to check the amount of stretch and growth in any fabric you buy to be sure that it is suitable for the use you plan. You will need to check garments and household articles to be sure that they stretch enough and that the manufacturer has not decided to use a less elastic fabric in order to cut costs. A cheaper product that does not perform properly is not an economic buy—why pay for stretch you do not get?

In short, a careful examination of each item you buy will be the best way to obtain the performance you expect. If the material does not live up to its guarantee, it should be returned for adjustment. Stretch is a "magic" word today, but be sure you receive the magic you pay for.

NEW COTTON TEXTILES

COTTON ALWAYS has been a good material for clothing. Now it is even better. It is modified chemically to make textiles with such chemical and physical properties as wash-wear, stretch, and resistance to water, stains, mildew, shrinking, flame, glow, and heat.

Wash-wear fabrics and garments dry smooth after laundering and resist wrinkling during use. Improvements in the first wash-wear methods have led to the domestic use of more than 2 billion yards of fabric a year.

The smooth-drying and wrinkle-resistant properties are put into cotton by imparting memory to fabric, so that once the fabric is set flat and smooth, it will return to the original condition despite external influences, much as curls put in by a permanent wave return after the hair is washed.

White fabric treated with some of the earlier wash-wear finishes sometimes became yellow or the fibers became weak when it was bleached with common hypochlorite solution. Some of the fabrics tended to soil easily.

The finishes now used on white fabrics are not affected adversely by hypochlorite bleach, and the newer special additives—polyethylene, for example—do not appreciably attract soil. Many of the fabrics do not have to be ironed, but if ironing is considered desirable, the job is quick and easy.

Wash-wear finishes also produce other durable dividends: Very little shrinkage during use, quick drying, and resistance to many micro-organisms.

You can dryclean wash-wear goods and launder them at home with detergents, but repeated severe laundering can destroy the wash-wear characteristics of many fabrics. The acid rinse used in commercial laundering does most of the damage.

Some of the better finishes, such as those used on men's white shirts, can withstand commercial laundering. Wash-wear cotton fabrics can be tumble dried with generally fewer wrinkles than drying them on a line.

Since wash-wear garments tumble dry in about half the time needed for untreated cotton garments, it is more efficient to dry them in a separate load. You therefore should remove the clothes from the dryer as soon as they are dry and hang them so that any wrinkles can straighten out.

Tumbling hot garments after they are dry causes excessive linting and much more abrasion than when wet goods are tumbled.

Durable creases and pleats can be put into wash-wear clothing. Manufacturers have several methods of producing such garments, but they are not suitable for use by the home seamstress. In each method, creases, shape-holding, and wash-wear properties are imparted to the cotton by cross-linking cellulose molecules. The creases are put in after the garments are made.

STRETCH COTTON garments have become popular because of their comfort, ease of fitting, and neat appearance.

Commercial methods for producing stretch goods include slack mercerization of fabric; mechanical compaction of fabric, followed by resin finishing; elastic core yarns of spandex fiber; a blend of spandex fiber with cotton; and torque-crimp thermoplastic yarn with cotton yarn.

The slack (or tensionless) mercerization method of producing stretch cotton goods is inexpensive and effective. It is used for many types of outer garments, slipcovers, other household items, and industrial commodities.

Woven stretch fabrics are suitable for some household and industrial uses without additional chemical treatment. For use in apparel, however, a wash-wear finish is applied to produce better recovery from stretch as well as smooth drying and wrinkle resistance.

Stretch knit goods, especially cotton socks, have all the desired qualities of cotton and also have good stretch and recovery properties.

Stretch fabrics produced by mechanical compaction followed by a resin treatment have the stretch in the warp (length) in contrast to those produced by slack mercerization, which generally have the stretch in the filling (width), although they can have both warp and filling stretch.

Fabrics produced with about equal amounts of torque-crimp thermoplastic yarns and cotton yarns may have either warp or filling stretch. Fabrics made of yarns containing a spandex fiber core with a cotton sheath or of yarns containing a blend of cotton and spandex can have warp and filling stretch.

These fabrics generally contain at least 90 percent cotton, but their content of elastic spandex fiber requires that they be carefully laundered. Water for washing should be about 100° F. Chlorine bleaches must not be used, because they turn the spandex yellow or brown and degrade the fiber.

COTTON exposed to conditions of high humidity and warmth is readily attacked and destroyed by certain micro-organisms (fungi and bacteria) unless they are protected by chemicals.

Mildew is a common term for the fungi responsible for most cotton degradation.

Bacteria can flourish and rot cotton only when it is nearly soaking wet.

Cotton is subject to degradation by micro-organisms in end uses that include tents, tarpaulins, shoe linings, sandbags, boat covers, ditch liners for irrigation, and fishing equipment. The degradation can be retarded or prevented by treatment with additive finishes, such as copper-quinolinolate, copper naphthenate, and phenyl mercury esters.

Other useful additives are pentachlorophenol and quaternary ammonium compounds. The most effective and durable treatments for cotton include acetylation, cyanoethylation, and deposition of polymers of melamine or of acrylonitrile. These agents give excellent rot resistance in sandbags, ditch liners, and other products in which the fabric touches soil.

WATER- and stain-repellent fabrics are used widely.

A fabric is termed water-repellent if it resists wetting and penetration. Water-repellent fabrics are needed for raincoats, sport coats, jackets, umbrellas, and other items.

Stain repellency is desired in some of these items but is especially needed for tablecloths, upholstery, and party dresses.

Water and stain repellency are imparted to cotton by chemicals that interact with the surface of the individual fibers and lower the surface energy of the fabric.

Three general classes of water repellents are those based on metallic salts and oxides, those based on polymers deposited on or in the fibers, and those based on some chemical in which there is union between the repellent and the cotton.

A water-repellent fabric is different from a waterproof fabric in that its interstices are not closed, so that it is permeable to air and water vapor.

In waterproof fabrics, the interstices are filled and function like plastic films in that they do not allow free passage of water vapor and air. Waterproof fabrics and plastic films thus are less comfortable than water-repellent fabrics in garments.

An easy test for water repellency is to place a drop of water on a flat surface of the fabric. If it takes on a spherical shape, it has not wet the surface. If it flattens out, it has wet the surface, and the fabric is not water repellent.

Most water-repellent fabrics are also repellent to waterborne stains and spots, such as those caused by coffee, tea, fruit juices, and soft drinks. The repellents containing silicones or fluorocarbons are most effective against waterborne stains.

Fabrics containing fluorocarbons may also be resistant to greasy stains. A test is to place a drop of cooking oil on the surface of the fabric. If it takes on a spherical shape, the fabric has repellency to grease.

OILY OR GREASY PRODUCTS should be removed from a garment by blotting with an absorbent cloth. Rubbing causes greater penetration and makes removal difficult.

Water- and stain-repellent finishes applied to fabrics used in garments are durable to at least three to seven mild launderings or drycleanings.

Sometimes silicone-finished garments appear to have lost their water repellency during laundering, but generally it can be revived by a more thorough rinsing to remove all the detergent. Ironing also helps revive the repellency. The water and stain repellents generally used on upholstery fabrics are not durable to repeated laundering, however.

HEAT-RESISTANT cotton fabrics resist scorching when heated at temperatures that normally scorch cotton fabrics, but they are not flame resistant. Moist heat causes more degradation than dry heat, but a completely wet fabric is degraded least of all.

Heat-resistant fabrics are needed for ironing board covers, for hot-head presses, and for other industrial uses. One way of making cotton resistant to heat is by chemically blocking some of the hydroxyl groups in the cellulose.

Moderate heat resistance is exhibited by most easy-care or wash-wear cottons and by fabric treated with various additive-type chemicals, such as dicyandiamide. They are generally less expensive than the acetylated cotton but wear out sooner.

WARM GARMENTS that weigh less are welcomed by almost everyone. This advantage is one of several provided by foamback fabrics.

Textile goods composed of a rubbery foam, usually polyurethane, bonded to a fabric or between two fabrics are called foamback fabrics. Because of the construction, they are sometimes called two-faced fabrics, sandwich laminates, and bonded foam fabrics.

The polyurethane foam can vary in density, flexibility, and thickness. It is resilient and elastic. It is dimensionally stable.

Cotton, cotton blends, and almost any other textile fiber may be bonded to polyurethane foam. The fabrics may be knit or woven goods. They are bonded to the foam by an adhesive or by the foam itself after it is softened by heating.

Foamback fabrics have great possibilities, particularly for winter garments. They generally have wrinkle resistance, dimensional stability, shape retention, and insulating properties and can provide additional body without much increase in weight.

Some of the sandwich-type structures have a knit fabric on one side and a woven fabric on the other, with the foam in between. One side may even be a fleece fabric. Bonding stretch fabrics to the elastic foam produces particularly attractive apparel.

Polyurethane foams have been used as backing for carpets and rugs. Newer uses for foambacks include tablecloths, mats, and slipcovers for furniture.

YOU MAY have noticed the new and brighter colors of apparel. They are produced by new classes of dyes that can react with cellulose to form primary valence bonds. Older coloring substances are held in the cotton by various other means, such as by hydrogen bonds, by deposition of insoluble particles, and by resin bonding of pigments.

The new colors are used extensively. They are less resistant to fading by light than some of the older and duller colors are, but they have adequate resistance for the life of most garments.

Fluorescent brightening agents, which are chemicals closely related to dyes, are used on cotton fabrics to make white fabric whiter and colored clothes brighter. These brightening agents are added to most laundry detergents. They reduce the amount of bleach needed in the laundering of white goods.

STRETCH COTTON LACE can be made by slack mercerization, which converts inexpensive lace into goods having much more three-dimensional character as well as good stretch and recovery. This is a timely development for cotton, because lace is again becoming fashionable.

Laboratory methods have been developed for the production of stretch yarn that can be woven or knit into items such as sweaters.

Fabrics that soil less and are more easily cleaned are being developed to make household chores easier. For example, the factor most conducive to reduced soiling and easier soil removal is the attachment of anionic groups to cellulose.

Also of value to most consumers is cotton with more luster. Progress has been made: New laboratory products exhibit a desirable degree of luster, but more basic research and developmental work must be completed before we can expect to see this development in wide use.

Fabrics with bactericidal properties are becoming available, especially for apparel and bed linens used in hospitals. This property is imparted by treating fabrics with bactericides that are slowly released during use.

Research has begun to develop bulky, warm cotton fabrics for fall and winter use. The bulk would be obtained by modifying yarn and fabric structures rather than by bonding the fabric to a polyurethane foam.

WOOL

CLOTH AND CLOTHING made of wool are good looking, soft, comfortable, relatively soil resistant, easy to clean and tailor, and flame resistant.

Nevertheless, manmade—synthetic—fibers have become popular because they are easy to care for, resistant to shrinkage and moths, more resistant to wear, and quick to dry.

However, research and new methods of treating wool have been developed that build superior and durable properties into wool with relatively little treatment and little sacrifice of its natural qualities.

One development is the Wurlan treatment, which was designed primarily to reduce the amount of shrinkage in machine laundering. The treated fabrics also are more resistant to pilling and abrasive wear. They are stronger and more dye-fast than wools treated by earlier shrink-proofing treatments.

The first part of the word "Wurlan" are the initials of the Western Utilization Research and Development Division of the Department of Agriculture, where the process was discovered.

Wurlan-treated woven fabrics have come into large-scale commercial use as machine launderable yard goods, men's sport shirts, and women's and children's wear. The name "Wurlan" does not appear on any wool product on the market, because manufacturers prefer to use their own labels.

Like chemically modified cottons, Wurlan-treated fabrics are slightly altered in the feel to the hand. The change is described as "slightly more crisp." The amount of change depends on the level of treatment given, and that depends on the weave of the fabric.

The Wurlan treatment employs the same chemicals used to make nylon fibers. The basic principle used is called interfacial polymerization.

The chemicals react to form ultrathin resin films, surrounding and chemically grafted to each wool fiber so that they withstand washing and drycleaning.

Even though the total weight added to the wool by the film is generally 1 percent or less, the resistance to felting shrinkage on laundering of the treated wools is comparable to that of blends containing at least 50 percent of manmade fibers.

Obviously, the small amount of chemicals in the modified wools is an advantage for wool. Since the films anchored to the wool are so thin, there is relatively little change in the desirable properties of wool. For example, the moisture uptake of treated wools is essentially the same as that of normal wool.

Garments made from treated goods go through many machine washings and drycleanings satisfactorily. Socks, for example, have been machine washed for as long as 5 hours without shrinkage, and the hand has remained good.

The procedure in machine washing garments made of Wurlan-treated fabrics may depend on the particular fabric and garment. In that case, the manufacturer recommends a method. For example, for Wurlan-treated men's sport shirts, the advice of one manufacturer is: "Wash at warm setting and spin dry; before pressing, hang to dry; do not tumble dry; press with a steam iron on the reverse side."

The rates of drying of the treated fabrics are the same as those of the untreated materials. The treated fabrics soil slightly less than untreated controls. They show no change in flammability. They may be steam pressed or dry pressed at 250° F.

Durable pleats and creases can be set as desired into the treated goods. In this case, the Wurlan fabrics may be treated as ordinary wools with chemical setting agents—such as sodium bisulfite, ammonium thioglycollate, or ethanolamine, or ethanolamine sulfite. These treatments are not recommended for home use.

The wrinkling properties of Wurlan-treated wools are altered only slightly. The treated goods recover from wrinkling under wet conditions somewhat faster than do untreated wools and hence dry smoother. Under dry conditions, the wrinkle recovery and the draping properties of the treated materials are essentially unchanged.

Manufacturers have had no special problem in sewing the cloth. They use shrink-resistant thread and linings.

The Wurlan treatment can be applied to wool before it is spun into the yarns from which knit goods are made. Knit goods are harder to treat chemically than woven materials because they are distorted more easily in handling.

Wurlan-treated knit garments and treated woven goods are sold in stores across the country.

The interfacial polymerization principle employed for the Wurlan treatment can be used to apply a variety of chemically different resin films to wool. The research indicates potentialities for adding further desirable and durable properties to wool.

SCIENTISTS have undertaken investigations to develop treated wools with even greater resistance to wear, with more durable resistance to moths and mildew, resistance to yellowing, higher luster, and greater resistance to wrinkling.

They seek quicker drying fabrics; durable resistance to soiling, acid, and alkali, and bacteria; and fabrics with greater pilling resistance and less scratchiness.

As the result of growing knowledge of wool and its modification, you can buy all-wool fabrics that are repellent to oil and water-carried soils.

Research promises to make these treatments permanent.

Also available are new types of wool fabrics—for example, foam-backed wool fabrics in which an undercoating foam plastic is bonded to the fabric to give firmness and wrinkle resistance; and stretch all-wool fabrics, in which the component yarns and fibers are chemically set into a highly crimped condition, which gives extra elasticity to the treated fabrics.

The day is at hand when scientifically designed, superior man-modified wools provide the answer to the threat to wool by the manmade fibers.

BLENDS OF FIBERS

THE VEGETABLE FIBERS (cotton and linen), animal fibers (wool, silk, mohair, and cashmere), furs, and pelts once provided most of the raw material for fabrics for clothing and household furnishings. Now, a variety of new fibers from the chemist's laboratory make up at least 35 percent of the total of textile fibers used in the United States.

Thus the textile industry has many fibers from which to create many fabrics—so many and so different that the consumer may not know which to buy for apparel, drapery, and other uses.

The labels and hang tags on garments contain not only general names for the manmade fibers, such as acetate, nylon, and polyester, but also the names of the companies that produce them, such as Celanese Fibers Co., Chemstrand Co., E. I. du Pont de Nemours & Co.

Further, registered trade names, such as Arnel, Avril, Dacron, Estron, Fortrel, Kodel, and Orlon, also appear on hang tags or labels, and handling instructions and claims may be printed on the hang tags.

These tags and labels are our most important guides to proper handling and claims as to performance.

The first table in this section gives a partial list of the major manmade fibers produced and distributed in the United

States, with their generic name, trade name, the producer of the fiber, the chemical class of the giant molecules that make up the fiber, and the major uses for each group.

The fibers are used alone or in combinations or blends with each other or with the vegetable and animal fibers.

Although we are primarily concerned here with fabrics made from blends or mixtures, we must remember that all-cotton fabrics are still a major source of textile fabrics. Slightly more than 4 billion pounds of cotton and about 500 million pounds of wool were used in 1965 by the American textile industry.

A TEXTILE FIBER may be a short, thin structure about an inch long, like cotton; 3 to 6 inches long, like wool; several hundred yards long, like silk; or several miles long on a single package, like a continuous filament acetate or nylon.

Very short fibers are called staple fibers. They are combed or carded and twisted by modern machinery to accomplish what our grandmothers did on their spinning wheels in order to produce a spun yarn.

All manmade fibers may be produced as staple fibers or as very long strands or bundles of fibers, which are referred to as continuous filament yarns.

Yarns spun from staple fibers usually are woven into fabrics that have subdued luster and a fuzzy surface. Continuous filament yarns are woven into a smooth, lustrous fabrics.

Two or more staple fibers mixed together before they are spun into yarn form a blend of fibers. Some of the more important blends, which are discussed later, are the polyester blend with cotton and the acrylic blend with wool.

When 100 percent of a given fiber is spun into yarns, and these yarns, made up of different fibers, are arranged as stripes or checks in the fabric, it is called a combination fabric. A fabric woven with a 100-percent cotton warp and a 100-percent triacetate continuous filament filling is one.

Knitting acetate and nylon continuous filament yarns together produces a combination tricot fabric for use in lingerie and dress goods.

Upholstery fabrics may have four or more fiber combinations of cotton, rayon, acetate, nylon, or other fibers to achieve various properties and color effects.

MANY FACTORS contribute to the consumer's satisfaction in using a garment, drapery, or upholstery material.

The Textile Fiber Products Identification Act was approved and made a part of the Federal Trade Commission's rules in July 1960. Its purpose is to protect producers and consumers against misbranding and false advertising of the fiber content of textile fiber products. The fiber name and the generic or family name of all fibers present in amounts above 5 percent and the content of each as percentage by weight must be listed in the order of predominance.

Thus a label may read 100 percent combed cotton, 100 percent virgin wool, 100 percent Du Pont nylon, or 100 percent Celanese acetate. The label on blends or combination fabrics may read 65 percent Dacron polyester-35 percent cotton, or 50 percent Fortrel polyester-50 percent Avril rayon, or 50 percent Arnel triacetate-50 percent cotton.

This labeling program, however, gives no assurance that the garment will perform to your satisfaction in the specific end use, such as washable shirting; drycleanable printed dress; hand washable,

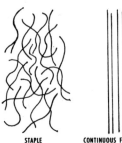

STAPLE
Short fibers
(1-8 inches)

CONTINUOUS FILAMENT
Silk 200-1,000 yards
Acetate and nylon miles
in length

SPUN YARN
Staple fibers
twisted into
long strands

MAJOR MANMADE FIBERS

Generic name	Manufacturer's trade name	Manufacturer	Fiber type	Major end uses
Acetate	Celanese* Estron* Avisco* Acele*	Celanese Fibers Co. Eastman Chemical Products, Inc. American Viscose Div. (FMC). E. I. du Pont de Nemours & Co.	Secondary cellulose acetate, filament and staple.	Lingerie, dress goods, drapery, sports and casual wear. Fiberfil.
Triacetate	Arnel*	Celanese Fibers Co.	Cellulose triacetate, filament and staple.	Tricot lingerie and outerwear dress goods, sports and casual wear.
Acrylic	Orlon* Acrilan* Creslan*	E. I. du Pont de Nemours & Co. Chemstrand Co. American Cyanamid Co.	Polyacrylonitrile (primarily staple).	Sweaters, knit goods, men's and women's slacks, carpets, blankets.
Nylon 66	Du Pont* Chemstrand* Celanese Beaunit	E. I. du Pont de Nemours & Co. Chemstrand Co. Celanese Fibers Co. Beaunit Fibers.	Polyamide (primarily continuous filament).	Hosiery and socks, lingerie, dress goods; blouses, upholstery, carpets, knit sports goods, uniforms and work clothing, and industrial yarns.
Nylon 6	Caprolan* Enka* Beaunit Firestone*	Allied Chemical Corp. American Enka Corp. Beaunit Fibers. Firestone Synthetic Fibers Co.	Same as for Nylon 66.	Same as for Nylon 66.
Polyester	Dacron* Fortrel* Kodel* Vycron*	E. I. du Pont de Nemours & Co. Fiber Industries, Inc. Eastman Chemical Products, Inc. Beaunit Fibers.	Polyester (primarily staple, filament for special applications.	Blends with cotton for shirting, sports clothing, dress goods, slacks. Blends with wool for suitings. Knit goods for shirting and sports wear. Fiberfil.
Rayon	Avril* Zantrel* Cuprammonium Fibro*	American Viscose Div. (FMC). American Enka Corp. Beaunit Fibers. Courtaulds North America, Inc.	Regenerated cellulose filament and staple.	Men's and women's slacks and suitings. Women's wear. Linings and drapery. Blankets, carpets, industrial yarns.
Glass	Fiberglas* Beta Fiberglas. PPG* Garon* Vitron*	Owens-Corning Fiberglas Corp. Owens-Corning Fiberglas Corp. Pittsburgh Plate Glass Co. Johns-Manville Fiber Glass, Inc. Johns-Manville Fiber Glass, Inc.	Silicon dioxide (sand) plus fluxes to lower melting point.	Nonflammable drapes, curtains, bedspreads, industrial fabrics.

*Registered trademark.

A FEW OF THE IMPORTANT BLENDS AND THEIR APPLICATIONS

End use	Fiber blends	Fabric construction	Important properties
Dress shirts	65/35 polyester/cotton.	Batiste. Broadcloth. Oxford.	Ease of care, fast drying, wrinkle resistant, durability.
Blouse	65/35 polyester/cotton.	Broadcloth. Crepe Combinations. Taffetas. Failles.	Ease of care, lightweight, appearance retention, fast drying, durability.
Dress goods. Printed and plain. Dyed.	65/35 polyester/cotton. 50/50 polyester/cotton. 50/50 polyester/rayon. 50/50 triacetate/cotton.	Broadcloth. Challis. Checks. Crepes. Twills. Linens.	Washability, ease of care, color styling, shape retention.
Sportswear. Shirting. Circular knit goods. Slacks.	65/35 polyester/cotton. 50/50 polyester/cotton. 55/45 acrylic/wool. 50/50 acrylic/rayon.	Sharkskin. Serge. Twills. Linens. Poplins. Sateens. Oxfords. Flannels.	Ease of care, durability, appearance retention, color styling, pleatability.
Slacks. Casual. Dress.	65/35 polyester/cotton. 50/50 polyester/cotton. 55/45 polyester/wool. 55/45 acrylic/wool. 70/30 polyester/acrylic. 50/50 triacetate/rayon. 50/50 acetate/rayon.	Gabardine. Twills. Tropicals. Denims. Sharkskin.	Appearance retention, washable or drycleanable (wool), ease of care.
Lightweight	55/45 polyester/wool. 50/50 acrylic/wool.	Gabardine. Tropical worsted. Twills. Flannels. Serge.	Durability, shape retention, ease of care.

IMPORTANT NATURAL FIBERS AND THEIR PROPERTIES AND END USES

Fiber	Fiber characteristics	Important end-use properties	Major end uses
Cotton	Very short lengths—⅞" to 1.5". Strong, low elongation. High moisture absorbing.	Excellent washability and comfort. Can be made "ease-of-care" by chemical finishing but loses strength and abrasion resistance. Slow drying.	Sheets and pillowcases, toweling, dress goods, work clothing, shirting. Blended with polyester fibers.
Wool	Short length, 1" to 8". Coarsest of the natural fibers. High moisture absorbency. Low strength.	High moisture absorbency. Comfort at high relative humidity. Fabric can be felted and fulled. Excellent wrinkle performance and crush resistance dry. Drycleanable. Careful washing and ironing.	Suitings, coating, blankets, carpets, sweaters and knit goods. Women's suiting, slacks, dress goods. Blended with polyester or acrylic fibers.
Silk	Long filamentous fibers 300–1,000 yards. Very fine, strong, and elastic.	Semilustrous and crisp feel. High strength makes possible sheer fabrics. Careful washing and ironing, drycleaning preferred.	Dresses, scarfs, hosiery, blouses. Combined with acetate, nylon, etc.
Linen	6–18 inches. Very coarse, strong, stiff fiber.	Silky luster, very strong and durable, poor wrinkling properties.	Tablecloths. Satin damask, dress goods, lace (blended with polyester fibers).

lace-trimmed lingerie; machine washable-"no-iron" slacks, and so on.

HOME ECONOMISTS, RETAIL store buyers, and consumers realize that the fiber composition of a fabric or garment is only one factor involved in producing a satisfactory product. Among the requirements are esthetic appeal, ease of handling, form stability, physiological aspects, special functional needs, retention of esthetic appeal, resistance to chemical degradation, resistance to mechanical fatigue and wear, and ultimate strength and resistance to wear and tear.

Even when the best possible fibers are spun into proper yarns, woven and knit into well-designed fabrics, dyed to mode shades, finished to the desired feel and drape, and cut and sewn into fashionable styles, the product still can be displeasing to the consumer because the seams may pucker on washing, or the color may fade on exposure to excessive sunlight, or the cuffs, collars, or pockets may fray or wear out, or the crisp, firm feel may become soft and mushy after the first wash or drycleaning.

TEN OR SO major natural and manmade fibers account for more than 95 percent of textile fibers consumed in the United States in the mid-1960s.

Each has properties that make it suitable for one or several specific uses, but no one fiber is satisfactory for all of the dozens of garments and homefurnishings for which textiles are used.

All-cotton or all-rayon fabrics absorb moisture well, but manufacturers blend cotton and rayon with polyester fiber to achieve resistance to wrinkling and greater durability. All-cotton fabrics lose about 40 percent in strength and abrasion resistance when they are chemically treated for wash-and-wear performance.

A major development in blends has been the mixing of 65 percent polyester staple with 35 percent cotton fibers in lightweight batiste, broadcloth, and print fabrics for shirt and women's wear. Half-and-half blends of polyester and cotton are used in mediumweight fabrics of poplin, twill, gabardine, and sharkskin cloth for sportswear, rainwear, slacks, and sports jackets.

The cotton fiber contributes moisture absorption, comfort, a familiar touch or feel, antistatic properties, economical processing, and low fiber cost. The polyester fiber, because of its strength and resistance to abrasion, permits the construction of serviceable lighter weight fabrics.

For wash-and-wear garments, all-cotton fabrics are chemically treated to improve resistance to wrinkling. The treatment reduces the strength and abrasion resistance of the cotton fiber, but the addition of polyester fiber to the cotton increases the durability of collars and cuffs.

Because the polyester fiber absorbs little water, the polyester/cotton-blended fabrics dry faster than all-cotton fabrics of equal weight and build.

Fabrics woven or knitted of 100 percent wool fiber have become standard in men's and women's suiting, dress and casual slacks and trousers, and sweaters and other knit outerwear. Although great improvements have been made in the washability, shrinkage resistance, and the mothproofing of wool, this wonderful natural fiber still has to be handled with care in service and cleaning.

Blends of 55 percent wool and 45 percent of the polyester or acrylic fibers have improved the washability and "ease-of-care" properties. The polyester fiber, in particular, increases the resistance of the fabric to creasing.

Because the polyester fiber is so strong, blends with wool may show a tendency to pill. Firm, densely woven fabrics will pill much less than loosely woven or flannel fabrics.

Acetate and rayon fibers, the first manmade fibers, became available in the twenties. Nylon became available in the forties. Fifty percent blends of acetate and rayon are used extensively in women's suitings and dresses, men's and women's slacks, and in outerwear that can be drycleaned. The garments drape well, have an excellent feel, and are comfortable and inexpensive.

Nylon, which is highly resistant to abrasion, often is blended in 10 to 25 percent amounts with cotton or wool to improve the durability of the garments. Cotton work clothing containing 15 percent nylon staple will have two to three times the wear resistance around the pockets and cuffs.

Some fabrics are made up of arrangements of yarns, each of which is of only one fiber. These combination fabrics may use spun yarns of two different fibers or arrangements of spun and continuous filament yarns.

A variety of check and stripe fabrics is woven with six yarns of 100 percent cotton followed by six yarns of 100 percent continuous filament triacetate. When the fabrics are dyed with selected dyes for the cotton only, the resultant fabrics will have colored stripes or checks of cotton surrounded by white undyed triacetate stripes.

Because cotton shrinks and triacetate does not, puckered or seersucker fabrics can be produced. By stabilization of the two fibers by chemical and thermal treatments, washable, flat fabrics can be prepared.

Tens of millions of pounds of continuous filament acetate, triacetate, and nylon are warp knit into tricot fabrics for use in lingerie, bedwear, shirting, and dress goods. Frequently, fine yarns of nylon are warp knit together with continuous filament acetate or triacetate. The nylon contributes considerable strength and reinforces the acetate or triacetate yarn, which contributes drape, cover, and comfort to the fabric.

For stretch garments, particularly ski pants, specially textured nylon and polyester filament yarns have been used in combination with cotton or wool yarns. The textured strong yarns behave like springs, and permit a stretch of 25 to 35 percent in sports clothing.

WHAT TO KNOW ABOUT SOAPS

You can buy soap and synthetic detergents in liquid, powder, premeasured packet, and tablet forms, with or without pigments and with and without bleach. Some produce many suds. Some make few suds.

We can simplify the selection somewhat if we separate the products according to their general characteristics and intended purpose.

Soaps and synthetic detergents act as cleansing agents by aiding in removing soil from fabrics and by holding it in the water until the washing is finished.

Soap, the oldest and most familiar laundering product, is formed from animal fat and caustic soda (lye).

Synthetic detergents (sometimes shortened to "syndets") are made by processes in which petroleum products or animal and vegetable fats and oils are converted by chemical reactions into many complex products suited for a variety of cleaning tasks.

WE LAUNDER things to remove inert or insoluble material, such as sand, dirt particles, and oily soil (either by itself or in combination with other insoluble soil).

Soap and syndets remove the soils by wetting the fabrics and the soil; promoting emulsification (surrounding the insoluble oily substances with a film of detergent solution and thus separating it from the article); dispersing, or breaking, the soil into small particles that are more easily removed from the fibers; and holding the finely divided soil in suspension until the wash is completed, so that the soil is carried away with the wash water and does not become redeposited on the fabric.

Soap is most effective when it is used in a slightly alkaline solution. It undergoes decomposition in acid solutions, which may occur in large wash loads of heavily soiled articles. Manufacturers therefore add mildly alkaline substances to some soaps and to some syndets to increase their cleaning power.

Such soaps and syndets are referred to as "all-purpose," "heavy-duty," or "built" products, as contrasted to the "light-duty" or "unbuilt" products that are intended for lightly soiled articles and for special items, such as hose,

lingerie, and other articles of delicate construction.

Light-duty soap and syndets are suited especially for use in laundering by hand, where mildness to the skin is important.

Labels indicate whether the products are for all-purpose or special use.

Most soap and syndets also contain small amounts of optical whiteners—colorless fluorescent dyes that increase the reflectance of light and so make the laundered articles look whiter and brighter.

The whiteners vary in their effectiveness on different fibers and in their ability to withstand different laundering and drying procedures.

Various pigments are added to some syndets, mostly to make them look more attractive. Pigments have no effect on cleaning effectiveness.

SEVERAL POINTS should be considered when you choose a soap or syndet.
• Heavily soiled articles require a heavy-duty or all-purpose product.
• You get good results when you launder lightly soiled fabrics with a light-duty or unbuilt product.
• Use a mild or neutral soap or an unbuilt synthetic detergent for fabrics containing silk or wool, which are damaged by alkaline soaps and built syndets.
• White or colorfast cottons, linens, and manmade fibers can be laundered safely with either soaps or synthetic detergents. If the fabric is not colorfast, an unbuilt soap or synthetic detergent generally causes less fading than a built soap or syndet.
• Sometimes, as when you launder a heavily soiled article of delicate construction or poor colorfastness, you must choose between maximum cleanliness with a heavy-duty product and safeguarding the fabric with an unbuilt soap or syndet.

A DISADVANTAGE of soap is that it forms insoluble curds when it is used with hard water containing salts of calcium or magnesium. Until the soap precipitates all the calcium or magnesium or both from solution in the water, no suds will form and no soap will be available for cleaning.

Also, fabric grayness and stiffness result when the insoluble soap curd combines with particles of soil from the wash load and settles into the clothes being laundered.

Since the lime soap curd will not dissolve in water, the grayness will not be removed by subsequent launderings.

Results are good, however, when you use soap in naturally soft water (water that contains few mineral impurities) or when the water has been softened.

If the water is of only moderate hardness, you can choose to use a synthetic detergent or to soften the water and use soap.

Unless the water is extremely hard, you should have no great difficulties when you use synthetic detergents. Some ingredients of the syndets do react with calcium and magnesium salts, but the resulting compounds remain in solution and do not interfere seriously with cleaning ability of the product.

Slightly more syndet is required for comparable cleaning tasks in hard water than in soft or softened water. If the water is extremely hard, you may have to increase the amount of syndet or combine the use of synthetic detergents with the use of water softeners.

Water may be softened at home in two ways. A water-softening system that softens all the water coming into the house from the supply line is convenient, but you may decide to soften only the water you need for special tasks, such as laundering. Then you add water-softening chemicals to the wash water.

The chemicals are of two types, precipitating and nonprecipitating.

The precipitating water softeners settle out the minerals in the water, making the water cloudy or turbid as the minerals are removed from solution.

Nonprecipitating products combine with the minerals in such a way that they remain dissolved and do not react with soap to form insoluble soap curds.

Nonprecipitating softeners also can be used to dissolve soap curd from fabrics.

How MUCH soap or syndet should you use?

Soap provides its own guide as to the amount needed. When a good suds is formed and maintained throughout the washing period, enough soap is present to overcome any hardness in the water and to be effective in removing and suspending soil. A drop in the suds level indicates that the soap has picked up all the soil it can hold and that you should add more soap to complete the removal of soil and to prevent redeposition of the soil held in the wash water.

Because synthetic detergents differ in amount of suds, it is not quite so easy to judge the correct amount to use.

You should be able to determine the amount of syndet needed for good cleaning if you use the manufacturer's directions on the container as a guide and take into consideration the size of the wash load, the degree of soiling, and the volume and hardness of the water.

The concentration of detergent, not the amount of suds, is the major factor in laundering when you use synthetic detergents, because the presence of suds is not an indication of cleaning power. Some syndets have been formulated with ingredients to increase and stabilize foaming. Others contain suds suppressors and form few suds.

Too much or too little soap or syndet can give poor results. If too little, the fabric is not thoroughly cleaned, and the chances for soil redeposition are greater. Redeposited soil is harder to remove than the original soil, because the fibers hold the smaller redeposited particles more firmly. The clothes become gray.

If too much is used, there is the chance of suds overflow, consequent difficulty with the machine, less free agitation of the fabrics, and the problem of rinsing clothes free of suds. High-sudsing syndets cause more difficulty of this sort than low-sudsing products or soap. Low-sudsing products therefore have become popular for use in automatic washers, especially front-loading machines.

BY THE EARLY SIXTIES, considerable publicity was being given to a major disadvantage of the syndets then available to consumers. These products were degraded so slowly by the bacteria in sewer systems that they got into streams and water supplies.

Detergents were by no means the only contributors to water pollution, but the fact that they produced foam made their presence more noticeable.

To overcome this difficulty, manufacturers developed new formulations, known as "soft" or "bio-degradable" detergents, which can be broken down more easily in sewer systems. As of this year, the changeover to these biodegradable detergents is in progress. Most manufacturers are expected to continue use of their present brand names, and indications are that there will be no change in laundering performance.

RECOMMENDATIONS FOR LAUNDRY HYGIENE

BACTERIA can remain alive on fabrics a long time. *Staphylococcus* ("staph") can live on wool blankets for 18 weeks and on muslin sheets for 12 weeks.

Contaminated clothing and household textiles thus can become carriers of disease-producing micro-organisms.

Micro-organisms — microbes — include bacteria (examples: *Staphylococcus, Pseudomonas*); viruses (examples: influenza, poliomyelitis); fungi (examples: those causing mildew and ringworm); protozoa (examples: those causing amebic dysentery and malaria).

Used clothing and textiles often contain large numbers of microbes. As many as 5 million bacteria per square inch have been isolated from the underarm parts of a T-shirt, and 53 million bacteria and 900 thousand fungi per square inch from a washcloth.

Even at the end of the spin-dry cycle of home laundering, the fabric may contain 25 thousand bacteria per square inch.

Many of these microbes are harmless, but some are harmful: *Staphylococcus aureus*, for example, can cause skin lesions (boils), pneumonia, or kidney infections. *Pseudomonas* also can cause skin infections (green pus producer), infections of the middle ear, and kidney infections. Paracolon bacteria can cause intestinal infections.

Whenever beds are made, towels are used, clothing is put on or taken off, and dirty clothes are sorted in the laundry, the fabrics are shaken enough to release microbes from them into the air. The microbes may then settle on other surfaces or may enter the body through the nose or through breaks in the skin.

Bacteria from one article may be transferred to another article during laundering. Harmful types that are present on the clothing or bedding of one person may be deposited on the clothing or bedding of another person.

Many bacteria can remain alive on the inner surface of the washing machine for at least 24 hours.

These are not, of course, the only ways in which microbes are spread. They do form one link in a chain of ways. If this one link can be broken, the whole chain is weaker.

IF WE HAVE ever thought about the problem of microbes in fabrics, most of us have probably assumed that laundering would solve the problem.

In former days it probably did, because many people used very hot wash water, and heat is one of the best ways to destroy micro-organisms. They sometimes even boiled the clothes, especially if there was sickness in the family.

But most people now use wash water at much lower temperatures. The average in home-type laundering in the United States is now 125° to 130° F. That is lower than the 160° to 180° used by commercial and institutional laundries and very much lower than boiling (212°).

A factor often overlooked in home laundering is the drop in temperature between the hot water tank and the washing machines and after several wash loads.

Most machines also have a warm-water setting, which delivers water at approximately body temperature and is used oftenest when the wash includes manmade fibers or certain dyed fabrics.

Furthermore, cold-water laundering has been introduced, in which special detergents are used. Water is used as it comes from the cold-water tap; the temperature could be 35° to 85°.

Why do people use these lower temperatures for wash water? Probably there are many reasons. Some are lower fuel costs, possible danger to children of very hot water, the use of new fibers and finishes, and lack of facilities for boiling clothes.

At any rate, whatever the reasons and however valid they may be, the use of lower laundering temperatures is an established practice in home management. In a program of household hygiene we cannot depend therefore on heat to control the problem of microbes in home-type laundering.

Another change is the greater use of coin-operated washing machines. Or, to put it another way, many of us use each other's laundry facilities. Since some microbes remain alive on the inside of the machines and since we do not use water that is hot enough to kill them, they can be transferred from the laundry of one family to the laundry of another family.

You cannot depend on the dryer to kill all bacteria that are still alive in the clothing. Some things are removed before they are really dry—to avoid wrinkling, perhaps, or because the timer on the dryer has stopped the machine, and all articles are removed, even though some are not dry. Dryers do, however, reduce the numbers of bacteria.

During drying, many bacteria are released from the fabrics, and the air movements force them out of the machine. Dryers therefore should be vented to the outside to prevent this atomizing of the bacteria back into the room.

What about the effectiveness of outdoor line drying? Ultraviolet light has germicidal activity, but the amounts of it in the atmosphere vary in different parts of the country and may be reduced by clouds, smog, and smoke.

There is a considerable interest in making fabrics "self-sanitizing" or "resistant to microbes." This is also called "residual" disinfection, because if fabrics are soaked in solutions containing certain disinfectants, some of the disinfectant clings to the fibers even after drying and is therefore a residue.

When the fabrics are wet again, some of the disinfectant washes off and kills some of the microbes with which it comes in contact.

Such products often are used in the final rinse of diaper laundering to aid in the control of diaper rash. They have been used also on bedding and clothing of bedridden patients to aid in the prevention of bedsores.

Cloth that is to be made into tents, awnings, sails, and such often is treated with disinfectants to prevent rotting by fungi.

Considerable moisture is present under the special in-use conditions mentioned (urine, perspiration, rain). Blankets and certain articles of clothing that have been treated with disinfectants can be bought.

Final judgment as to the usefulness of such treated articles under the relatively dry conditions of normal use must await further research and improved test procedures.

It should be emphasized, however, that treated fabrics are not the solution to the problem of laundry hygiene. When disinfectants were added in the rinse cycle during in-use experiments on home laundering, a residue was left on the fabrics. When the clothes were used and laundered again, there was no discernible reduction in the number of bacteria found on them.

Research, carried out under in-use conditions, has demonstrated that the most effective solution to the problem is to add a sufficient amount of a suitable disinfectant directly to the wash

DISINFECTANTS FOR USE DURING LAUNDERING

Type	Examples of available products	To be used in—	Amount to be used	Active ingredients
Chlorine (hypochlorite)	Clorox. Fyne-Tex Liquid Bleach. King Liquid Bleach. Purex Liquid Bleach.	Wash cycle.	As directed on label for bleaching. Usually: Front loading machines—4 oz. Top loading machines—8 oz.	Should contain 5.25% sodium hypochlorite. (Cannot be used on silk, wool, spandex, and certain dyed fabrics.)
Phenolic..........	Al-Pine. Pine-Sol.	Either wash or rinse cycle.	Front loading machines—5 oz. Top loading machines—8 oz.	3% orthobenzyl para chlorophenol or 3% chloro-o-phenylphenol.
Pine oil..........	Fyne-Tex. King Pine. Pine-O-Pine. White Cap.	Either wash or rinse cycle.	Front loading machines—4 oz. Top loading machines—6 oz.	Product must contain at least 80 percent pine oil.
Quaternary.........	Co-op Sanitizer. Roccal.	Rinse cycle.	Front loading machines—3 oz. Top loading machines—4 oz.	10% solution of alkyldimethylbenzyl ammonium chloride.

water or the rinse water.

To be suitable for use in home laundering, a disinfectant must not discolor or injure the fabrics; it must not leave a residue on the fabrics that is toxic to the user or wearer; it must not leave a disagreeable odor on the fabrics; it must kill many kinds of microbes; it must be available on the consumer market; and the cost must not be prohibitive.

These four types of disinfectants have been found to be effective: Chlorine (hypochlorite), phenolic, pine oil, and quaternary.

It is important to read the label on the bottles in order to be sure of the name and amount of disinfectant in any product. To insure effectiveness, it is also important to measure the amount to be used.

Future research may, of course, demonstrate the effectiveness of still other types of disinfectants.

When used as directed during home laundering, the four types of disinfectants listed will reduce the numbers of bacteria to a safe level.

It is also helpful to sanitize the washing machine occasionally. This will kill the bacteria that live on the interior surface. Pour a disinfectant into the empty machine; then complete a 15-minute cycle at the hottest water setting.

Sort dirty clothes and clean clothes at different times. Do not shake dirty clothes near clean laundry or near surfaces that will later be used for sorting laundry. Shaking dirty clothes releases bacteria which then settle on nearby surfaces.

If possible, sort dirty clothes on a table or in one area. Sort and fold clean clothes on a second surface in another area. If this is not possible, cover the table or work area with clean paper, plastic sheeting, or any other clean material before working with clean clothes. This will prevent bacteria from being redeposited on fresh, newly washed clothes. For the same reason, cover canvas-bottomed carts with clean paper or plastic before loading them with clean laundry. Such precautions are especially important at coin-operated laundries.

REMOVING STAINS

USUALLY it is easier to remove fresh stains than old ones. Identify the stain, if possible, or determine whether it is a greasy stain, a nongreasy stain, or a combination of the two.

The kind of stain remover you select should not harm the fabric on which you use it. Test the stain remover on a sample of the material or on a seam allowance, hem, the inside of a pocket, or the tail of a blouse or shirt.

Absorbent powders, such as corn-starch, cornmeal, talc, and powdered chalk, are used to remove some fresh stains, such as spattered grease. Spread the powder over the stain before it dries. Then remove it, as it absorbs the stain, by shaking or brushing.

Other absorbent materials, such as absorbent cotton, sponges, white or fast-colored paper towels, facial tissues, and soft cloths, are used to soak up staining liquids before they soak into a fabric and to absorb stains as they are rinsed out of the fabric. This will work only on fabrics that absorb the staining liquid slowly.

Soap and synthetic detergents are used to remove many nongreasy and some greasy stains. Either can be rubbed into the stained place and rinsed out with water.

Solvents for nongreasy stains: Water alone or water and a detergent will remove many nongreasy stains. Rubbing alcohol can be used on some stains, such as those caused by medicine dissolved in alcohol, shellac, alcoholic beverages, and duplicating carbon paper, if it does not cause the dye on the fabric to bleed.

Acetone and amyl acetate (amyl acetate for fabrics of acetate, and Dynel and Verel modacrylic fibers) are used to remove such stains as fingernail polish and ballpoint-pen ink. Turpentine is used on oil-based paint stains.

Another way to remove ball-point ink spots is by a quick rinse with clear water and washing in soapsuds. If it's a permanent ink, rinse, treat with lemon juice, and rinse again. Lipstick stains can be removed by first rubbing the spots with petroleum jelly and then washing them with warm suds.

SOLVENTS for greasy stains are known as grease solvents, drycleaning fluids, and spot removers. Some are flammable. Some are nonflammable.

All are poisonous and should always be used in a well-ventilated area.

Arrange your working space so that the fumes are blown away from you by a fan or breeze from an open door or window. Use small amounts at a time. Keep the solvent bottle stoppered when you are not using it. Do not pour solvent into an open bowl unless you are working outdoors.

Never use your washing machine as a drycleaning machine. Flammable solvents can cause fires. With non-flammable solvents, the large amount needed to provide adequate coverage of a garment in the washing machine could produce enough poisonous fumes to be fatal.

The same hazards are present when drying articles damp from cleaning solvents in the clothes dryer.

Many of the stain removers sold in grocery and drug stores are mixtures of solvents. It is best to read the label on the bottle or can to see which solvents are used in the mixture, and then follow the manufacturer's directions for safe usage.

To remove greasy and nongreasy stains, place the stained place on a pad of soft cloth or other absorbent material with the stained side down, if possible. Dampen a piece of cotton or soft cloth with the solvent and sponge the back of the stain. Use small amounts of solvent repeatedly rather than large amounts fewer times. Work from the center of the stain toward the outer edge. Use light brushing or tamping motions. Change the pad or cloth as soon as it is soiled so the fabric will not reabsorb the stain. Sponge the stain irregularly around the edge so that no definite line will be present when the fabric dries.

CHEMICAL STAIN REMOVERS include bleaches, acetic acid, ammonia, iodine, oxalic acid, and sodium thiosulfate.

Three kinds of bleachers are recommended for home use—chlorine bleaches, peroxygen bleaches, and color removers. Test dyed fabrics for colorfastness when you use either type of bleach.

Chlorine and peroxygen bleaches remove the same types of stains.

The two cannot always be used interchangeably because of damage to some fabrics and some colors.

Do not use chlorine bleaches on fabrics containing silk, wool, or spandex fibers, on polyurethane foams, and on fabrics with special finishes (wash-wear, wrinkle resistant, et cetera) unless the label on the fabric or textile article clearly states that chlorine bleach is safe.

The peroxygen bleaches act quickly when used in hot water. Fabrics that contain wool, silk, or Dynel modacrylic fiber are sensitive to hot water and must be treated at lower temperatures; it therefore takes a longer time for the bleach to act.

Color removers generally are used for stains on which chlorine and peroxygen bleaches are not effective, such as dye stains, yellow stains caused by the use of chlorine bleaches on fabrics with some types of resin finishes, and a few types of ink. They are safe for all fibers but will fade or remove many dyes.

Acetic acid (or vinegar) is used for neutralizing alkalies and restoring colors changed by action of alkalies.

Ammonia is used for neutralizing acids and restoring colors changed by the action of acids.

Iodine is used only for silver nitrate stains.

Oxalic acid is used for rust and other metallic stains.

Sodium thiosulfate is used for removing iodine and chlorine stains.

Ammonia, iodine, and oxalic acid are poisonous.

To APPLY CHEMICAL STAIN removers, dampen the stain with cool water and stretch the stained place over a bowl or place on an absorbent pad.

Try a mild treatment first; then strengthen the treatment if the stain is not removed.

Apply liquid removers with a medicine dropper. If you use dry removers, sprinkle them over the dampened spot. If the article is washable, the stained area or the whole article can be soaked in a solution of the remover. Do not let the remover dry on the fabric. Keep the stain wet with cotton dampened with the remover (or with water if a dry remover is used) until the stain is removed.

Remover may be rinsed from washable articles either by sponging the area repeatedly with water, rinsing the area, or rinsing the whole article in clear water.

Nonwashable articles may be rinsed by sponging the area repeatedly with water or placing the treated area over a bowl or sponge and forcing water through the spot with a syringe.

Some greasy stains in washable articles can be removed from clothing and linens by usual laundering procedures, by hand or machine. Others can be removed by rubbing detergent into the stain, then rinsing with hot water.

It often is necessary to use a grease solvent. This is effective even after an article has been washed. Sponge the stain thoroughly with grease solvent and dry. Repeat as often as necessary. Fabrics with a special finish often require extra time to remove greasy stains.

Greasy stains in nonwashable articles can be removed with the use of a grease solvent. Sponge the stain with a grease solvent and dry. Repeat as often as necessary.

Some nongreasy stains are removed from washable articles by regular laundering procedures. Other stains are set by them. For example, protein types, such as egg, blood, meat juices, and fish slime are set by hot water. Sponge the stain with cool water or soak it in cool water for 30 minutes or more.

Certain stains that have become set through aging may require soaking overnight. If the stain remains after soaking or sponging, work a detergent into it; then rinse. If a stain remains after the detergent treatment, use a chlorine or peroxygen bleach after you have tested them to see which bleach is safe for the fabric.

Nongreasy stains from nonwashable articles can be sponged with cool water, or cool water can be forced through the stain with a small syringe. A sponge under the stain absorbs the water. If the stain remains after this treatment, rub some detergent onto the stain and work it into the fabric; then rinse with clear water. After the final rinse, a sponging with alcohol helps to remove the detergent and dry the fabric more quickly. The alcohol should be tested on the fabric, in a hidden spot, to make sure it does not cause the dye to bleed. Alcohol should be diluted before use on acetate. Any stain remaining after the detergent treatment can be treated with a chlorine or peroxygen bleach after tests show which bleach is safe for the fabric.

Combination stains are caused by materials that contain both greasy and nongreasy substances.

Combination stains in washable articles can be sponged with cool water. Or they can be soaked in cool water for 30 minutes or longer. If the stain remains, work a detergent into the stain and then rise thoroughly and allow the article to dry.

If a greasy stain remains, sponge it with a grease solvent. Allow it to dry and then repeat if necessary. If a colored stain remains after the fabric dries, then use a chlorine or peroxygen bleach.

If the combination stain occurs on nonwashable articles, the directions for cleaning are the same as for washable articles except that you should not soak the article in cool water. Rather, you can force cool water through the stain with a small syringe using a sponge under the stain to absorb the water from the syringe.

AVOIDING DAMAGE FROM CHEMICALS

You can see what ordinary wear and tear does to clothing. Sometimes you cannot account for holes in fabrics or changes in color of dyes that appear suddenly.

Certain chemicals used in homes can make holes in fabrics or change the color.

Among them are strong alkalies, such as those in products sold for cleaning drains and ovens; strong acids, such as those in storage batteries, brick and mortar cleaners, and some toilet bowl cleaners; and oxidizing and reducing agents, such as those in fabric, hair, and wood bleaches and in home permanent-wave solutions.

The damage may appear instantly, so you have no doubt as to the cause, but often it does not appear until later—perhaps during washing or dry-cleaning—when you have forgotten the culprit.

If damage does not appear immediately, quickly rinse out the spilled substance. Otherwise the chemical reaction may continue until a hole or color change appears.

Fibers themselves are chemical compounds, and different types of fibers react in different ways.

The speed with which they react with other chemicals (and thus the danger of fabric damage) usually increases at higher temperatures and when more of the chemical touches the fiber.

Wool and silk are damaged more easily than cotton is by oxidizing bleaches and alkalies, but are less readily damaged by acids.

Rayon reacts in much the same way as cotton does to acids, alkalies, and bleaches, but is somewhat more easily damaged.

The manmade fibers generally are less reactive chemically than the natural fibers and therefore less likely to be damaged by chemicals used in the home. Among the exceptions are nylon, which is damaged easily by acids, and most spandex fibers, which may be damaged by chlorine bleaches. Some fabrics with wash-wear finishes turn yellow when a chlorine bleach is used on them. Others do not turn yellow immediately, but may be discolored or destroyed when ironed.

Not all finishes are affected by chlorine bleaches. Fabrics with chlorine-retentive finishes should have a warning, *"Do not use a chlorine bleach,"* on the label.

A hot lye solution can make a hole in wool or silk quickly. A cold solution of the same strength, if rinsed out promptly, may do little damage.

A concentrated acid solution that instantly makes a hole in nylon, acetate, rayon, or cotton produces no immediate effect if it is used in a more dilute solution. Concentrated solutions of bleaches are more likely to harm fabrics than dilute solutions.

Combinations of some chemicals, such as chlorine bleaches and acids, can do more damage than either used separately. A mixture of a strong acid with a chlorine bleach, in fact, can produce highly poisonous fumes as well as damage fabrics.

A dilute solution of a chemical, which causes little damage, becomes concentrated if it is allowed to dry on a fabric, and may cause damage—another reason for promptly washing out spilled chemicals.

A TRICKY KIND of acid damage occurs when the acid is formed from some other substance.

For example, aluminum chloride, sometimes used in deodorants, can react with water (this can come from perspiration) to form hydrochloric acid, which damages the underarm area of garments.

Nylon hose may disintegrate on your legs when soot particles contaminated with sulfuric acid settle on the hose. The acid can be formed by oxidation of sulfur compounds, formed when coal is burned and water vapor is present. Similar damage sometimes occurs in clothes dried outdoors in industrial areas or in winter in places where homes are heated with coal.

Neoprene synthetic rubber, some-times used in shoulder pads or bonded wool interlinings, unless carefully compounded, can break down in time to form hydrochloric acid.

Celluloid articles, such as collar stays, combs, and knitting needles, also may decompose and give off acid fumes when they are left in a closed space for a long time. Fabrics in contact with these materials can be damaged.

There have been reports of similar damage in laundry establishments in which washers, dryers, and drycleaning machines are in one room. If perchloroethylene fumes from the drycleaning machines are not properly vented and get into a dryer, hydrochloric acid can be formed by the combination of heat, moisture, and perchloroethylene vapor.

BROWN SPOTS or holes may appear suddenly in a garment that is being ironed, usually a dampened, starched dress with a zipper.

They are caused by the formation of a simple electrochemical cell—a battery, so to speak—in the garment. Two different metals in the zipper—usually aluminum in the teeth and copper or nickel-plated copper in the slide—act as the two electrodes. The salt used in many liquid starches acts as the carrier of the electric current in the wet garment. The small amount of acid formed in such a cell causes no apparent damage until it is concentrated by the heat of the iron.

Metals from other sources also can cause similar damage—impurities in a metal can act as the second electrode, as when dampened, starched clothes are stored in aluminum containers before they are ironed. Salt from liquid starches may act as the carrier of the current; but in some sections the water contains enough minerals to cause this type of damage.

The number of instances of electrolytic damage has been decreasing, no doubt because wash-wear fabrics seldom are dampened before ironing. Nylon zippers are also replacing the bimetallic zippers.

SUNLIGHT, that age-old bleaching agent, can weaken fibers and cause colors to fade.

The resistance of fibers and dyes to sunlight varies with the kind of fiber and dye. Only glass fibers are completely unaffected.

Other conditions, such as the amount of ultraviolet radiation in the light and the amount of moisture in the atmosphere, influence the reaction.

Some dyes, particularly yellow and orange vat dyes, make fabrics especially sensitive to photochemical damage. Yellow or orange figures in curtains may disintegrate, while other parts are still strong.

Drycleaners often are blamed wrongly for this damage, because the weakened spots may not show any visible change before drycleaning.

Most of us recognize that many dyes fade on exposure to sunlight and select "light-fast" dyes for draperies.

Some other color changes in dyes are more difficult to predict or explain. It is not uncommon, for example, for a blue acetate dress to change to a reddish shade while hanging in a dark closet.

This kind of color change is called "fume fading" and has been traced to a reaction between certain dyes and oxides of nitrogen in the atmosphere. Minute amounts of these oxides (less than 1 part per million in the air) can cause fume fading.

Dyed acetate and triacetate fabrics are more likely to be affected, but fume fading also occurs in cotton, rayon, nylon and wool.

Oxides of nitrogen in the atmosphere come from natural sources, such as electrical storms, but the main source of this type of pollution is from burning fuels, such as gasoline, natural gas, and oil. Automobile exhausts are a major source of such pollution.

Inside the home, oxides of nitrogen can come from unvented gas heaters and from gas-fired appliances, such as stoves and clothes dryers. Fabrics colored with dyes sensitive to oxides of nitrogen sometimes change color after being dried only a few times in a gas

dryer. Some yellowing of used and laundered white cotton articles has also been traced to reactions with oxides of nitrogen in dryers.

HUMIDITY is a factor in the reaction between dyed fabrics and atmospheric pollutants. Color changes in acetate and triacetate are not dependent on humidity, but high humidity usually increases color changes in fabrics made of other fibers.

A different kind of damage is this:

A homemaker hung the family's winter clothes on plastic hangers in closed garment bags with paradichlorobenzene (a moth preventive) in a hot attic. When she removed the clothing in the clothing in the fall she discovered that the hangers had apparently melted into the fabric and then hardened. The temperature was not high enough to melt the plastic, however.

The trouble was traced to the combination of paradichlorobenzene vapor and the plastic. Plastics in some buttons, storage boxes, and in coatings on wires in electric blankets may also be affected by this vapor.

The perchloroethylene used in coin-operated drycleaning machines can also cause plastic hangers to soften and stick to clothes. Be sure that all solvent has evaporated from drycleaned garments before placing them on plastic hangers.

DRYING ARTICLES containing foam rubber in tumble dryers has been known to cause fires. Foam rubber oxidizes when it is heated, and this reaction produces considerable heat. The heat continues to build up and, together with the heat from the dryer, sometimes causes the rubber to burst into flame. A fire can also start outside the dryer if an article containing foam rubber happens to be on the bottom of a pile of hot clothes taken out of a dryer.

Heat can also damage fabrics even if they do not burn. All fabrics can be scorched by too hot an iron, but some of the manmade fiber fabrics have a very low sticking point. Blends of cotton and manmade fibers are especially vulnerable, because they look like cotton and are more likely to be ironed at the temperature used for cotton.

Sparks from burning cigarettes and fireplaces will quickly melt a hole in heat-sensitive fibers. Hot ashes from a fireplace, for example, may melt a hole in a nylon rug, although a wool rug would not be damaged.

HOW TO COMBAT INSECT DAMAGE

CLOTHES MOTHS are well recognized as fabric pests. Housewives throughout country are on guard against them. The fact that they cause widespread damages is due more to weakness in control measures than to lack of awareness of the need for control.

THE LARVA, or worm, stage of two species of clothes moths and four species of carpet beetles cause most of the insect damage to clothing, furs, blankets, pillows, carpets, rugs, upholstery, and furniture padding that contain animal fibers or feathers.

Those items can be a complete diet for the entire life of any of the fabric insects, but the damage they do can be prevented by using protective fabric treatments, proper storage procedures, good housekeeping practices, and effective insect-control measures.

THE TWO COMMON species of clothes moths found in the home are the webbing clothes moth and the casemaking clothes moth. They look much alike.

The adult moths are yellowish or buff colored and have a wingspread of about one-half inch. They usually stay in dark, secluded places but may come out and fly aimlessly about. The small eggs are white or cream colored and are laid directly on fabrics suitable as food for the hatched larvae.

The larvae of both species remain on the material they feed on throughout their lifespan of 30 to 45 days.

THE FOUR COMMON species of carpet beetles found in homes are the common carpet beetle, the furniture carpet beetle, the varied carpet beetle, and the black carpet beetle.

The first three look much alike. The adults are small, round beetles, usually less than one-eighth inch long. They fly freely and, since they are attracted to light, may be found on window sills. They are mottled with white, yellow, brown, and black.

Each female lays about 100 tiny eggs directly on material the larvae feed on. The eggs hatch in 8 to 15 days.

The larvae are the feeding stage. Their oval bodies are covered with brownish or black bristles that give them a fuzzy appearance, from which they get their common name, "buffalo moths." As the carpet beetle larvae grow, they shed their skins several times. In 45 to 60 days they are full grown and about one-fourth inch long.

The black carpet beetle is easily distinguished from the other three species. The adults are black. The larvae are golden to dark brown and reach a length of about one-half inch. They are slender and tapered, with a characteristic tuft of long, brown hairs at the end of the body. They live considerably longer as larvae (9 to 12 months) than do the other carpet beetles.

THE EASIEST and most effective way to protect wool clothing, rugs, blankets, and other susceptible items against fabric insects is to have them treated with a moth-resistant compound.

The simplest way of getting this built-in protection is to purchase items treated for moth resistance. Select items already treated by the manufacturer with a permanent-type, moth-resistant compound.

Some treatments resist aging, dry-cleaning, and several washings and are usually guaranteed by the manufacturer for the life of the item. Others provide only temporary protection which may disappear soon after you purchase the item. Read the label carefully.

You undoubtedly have many susceptible articles that have not been treated

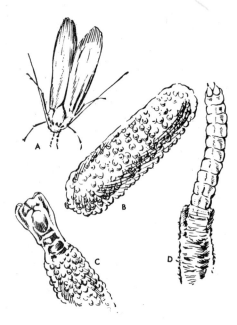

WEBBING CLOTHES MOTH
A, Adult; B, Cocoon; C, Cocoon with cast
pupal skin protruding;
D, Larva and silken feeding tube

to withstand moths. You can have a moth-resistance treatment applied to wool clothing, blankets, and sweaters when you have them drycleaned and to your rugs and carpets when they are shampooed.

Such treatments are temporary and must be repeated each time the articles are cleaned.

You can treat some items yourself. There are a number of approved moth-proofing solutions you can buy and apply yourself to clothing, rugs, and other items. Mothproofers are sold as liquid sprays or aerosols.

Regardless of which one you select, apply it as directed on the label.

Some labels specify that the treated garment should be drycleaned before wearing. If you have no intention of doing so, or if there is a possibility that you may overlook having the treated suit, sweater, or blanket cleaned before it is used, then do not select such a mothproofing compound. Pick one that will permit you to wear the treated garment either with or without dry-

cleaning. Some of the mothproofers in this category are DDT, methoxychlor, Strobane, and Perthane.

PROPER STORAGE can be used effectively to protect woolens and other susceptible items. It is important to store only clean items and in insect-tight containers.

Soiled clothing attracts fabric insects more than clean clothing, and clothes that have been hanging around for some time may be infested. Therefore, before storing your materials, have them drycleaned or laundered. Or, hang them outdoors, brush very thoroughly, especially the seams, folds, and pockets, and let them hang in the direct sun for several hours. Thorough brushing and exposure to sunlight are effective methods of ridding woolen articles of insects.

Well-constructed chests and closets and airtight garment bags make good storage containers. Before using any of them, however, make sure they are insect tight when closed. Seal all cracks or openings with masking tape.

Cedar chests and cedar-lined closets provide little or no protection against insects unless they are made with red cedar heartwood three-fourths inch thick, are tightly constructed, and are less than 3 or 4 years old. To be safe, use them as any other container or closet.

For added protection, place paradichlorobenzene crystals or naphthalene flakes or balls in the storage containers before sealing the lid or door.

In a trunk-size container, use 1 pound of these chemicals. In a closet, use 1 pound for each 100 cubic feet of space. Place them high in the storage container, because the vapors are heavier than air.

Large, bulky items can be wrapped in heavy kraft paper. Sprinkle naphthalene or paradichlorobenzene around around the article as it is being wrapped. Then seal all edges of the wrapping paper with masking tape to make the package insect tight.

GOOD HOUSEKEEPING practices are important in preventing insect damage and in controlling insects in the home.

One of the most important practices is to get rid of old wool clothing, furs, feather pillows, and other susceptible items. Do not stick them in the attic or in the basement.

Old wool clothing and soiled wool rugs are the commonest haven of fabric insects in the home. If you must save some old garment for sentimental or other reasons, have it cleaned, and then treat it with one of the recommended protective sprays before you put it away.

The insects also live in the lint and hair that accumulate in corners; in cracks in the floor, baseboards, and molding; behind radiators; in heating or ventilator ducts and wells; and in other such places.

Thorough and frequent vacuum cleaning of all these places is recommended. Cleaning removes the food on which fabric pests feed and picks up insect eggs and larvae that happen to be there. In this way you stop an infestation before it becomes serious.

Wool rugs and carpets become infested under heavy pieces of furniture, along the walls, and in places where there is little or no traffic. Pay particular attention to vacuum cleaning these places thoroughly and frequently.

After each vacuum cleaning, dispose of the sweepings carefully. They may contain insect eggs and larvae. Sweepings that stay in your cleaner for any length of time may spread the infestation throughout the house.

Inspect your rugs periodically. If you see any bare spots or if the nap of the rug seems to have been clipped down to the base, you may have the beginning of an infestation of clothes moths or carpet beetles.

Look for clothes moth webbing, for live carpet beetle larvae, or for cast skins. If you find signs of insect or insect damage, spray the rug with one of the recommended protective sprays or have it done by a commercial carpet cleaner or pest-control operator.

IF YOU FIND damage or actually see fabric insects in your home, it is best to take steps to control the infestation as soon as possible.

Do not panic and run to the nearest drugstore or hardware store to buy the first bottle or can of insecticide you see on the shelf, rush home, and cover everything in the house with it. The spraying should come last.

First, inspect the susceptible items in your house, especially in the room or part of the house where you have found

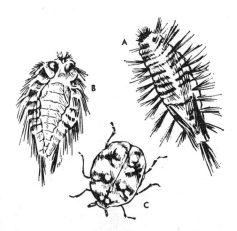

FURNITURE CARPET BEETLE
A, Larva; B, Pupa; C, Adult

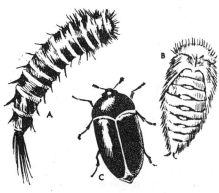

BLACK CARPET BEETLE
A, Larva; B, Pupa; C, Adult

insects or damage. Find out how extensive the damage or infestation is, where it is, and, if possible, the source of the infestation. Do not forget the attic and the basement.

Discard old clothing, rugs, stuffed furniture, feather pillows, and other articles that may be sources for the infestation. For your good clothes, rugs, and other susceptible items, follow the suggestions for protective treatments.

Give your house a good cleaning.

Then you are ready to spray to control the insects.

Select an insecticide that is effective in killing fabric insects and is safe to use in the home.

Some of the insecticides that have been approved for this purpose are 3 to 6 percent DDT, 2 percent chlordane, 3 to 5 percent of premium-grade malathion, and one-half percent of lindane. These insecticides can be purchased as oil solutions, water emulsion concentrates, or as pressurized sprays. Aerosols are not recommended for this purpose.

Apply liquid sprays with a sprayer that produces a continuous coarse mist. If only a small area is to be covered, the insecticide can be applied with a paintbrush about 2 inches wide.

Do not apply the insecticide indiscriminately.

It should be applied only on the surfaces where the insects may be or are likely to crawl—along the edges of wall-to-wall carpets; in closets; behind radiators, baseboards, and moldings; and in corners, cracks, and other hard-to-clean places.

Before treating the closets, take the clothing out, vacuum-clean floors and shelves, then apply the insecticide to corners, to cracks in the floors and walls, along baseboards, around shelves, and at ends of clothes rods.

Remember that most insecticides are poisonous to people and to animals. Keep them where children and pets cannot reach them. Oil-base insecticides are flammable and may discolor certain floor coverings, such as asphalt tile.

Before you use an insecticide, read and follow the precautions and directions that are printed on the container label.

If the infestation persists, repeat the procedure every 3 months until it is cleared up. If the infestation is heavy and widespread, a professional pest-control operator may be needed.

DRYCLEANING

THERE ARE several reasons why an article should be drycleaned by a professional drycleaner.

Many types of soil are not removed from fabrics by water. Drycleaning solvents remove oily and greasy soil more readily than water.

The removal of spots and stains requires a knowledge of fabrics, dyes, and finishes in relation to the spotting reagent used, and the methods and techniques required to effect removal.

Specialized finishing equipment used by drycleaners is designed to accommodate the intricate garment details that cannot be pressed by hand iron on the home ironing board.

Cleaning a garment in a drycleaning solvent rather than water has the advantage of minimizing shrinkage, preserving tailoring details, and preserving many of the colors and finishes applied to modern fabrics.

When garments and household items are received for drycleaning, they are marked for identification and inspected. Notation is made of any rips, tears, unusual stains, and fabrics or construction that require special handling in drycleaning. Breakable articles such as buckles, buttons, and ornaments are removed and sent to the sewing department, where they are replaced on the cleaned and finished garment.

The items or articles are then sorted according to types. The woolen and worsted garments are separated from the silks and synthetics. Then they are classified further according to white, light, and dark colors. Items that require special handling are separated from those cleaned by regular procedures.

Pockets, cuffs, and seams are brushed

to remove loose soil and lint to eliminate the possibility of shine or seam impressions.

Any soil, spots, or stains that have water as an integral part must be removed by a prespotting or prebrushing treatment or by spotting after cleaning. Some stains are set more tenaciously if they are not removed before they are drycleaned. Grass stains, gutter splash, and paint stains, for example, are removed before drycleaning.

The sequence and method of processing depend on the many classifications of items to be cleaned. The fundamental process for all items involves the immersion and agitation of the garment in solvents, which are of two general classifications: Petroleum (Stoddard, 140 F.) and synthetic (perchlorethylene, trichloro-trifluoro-ethane).

To remove soil and dirt from fabrics, there must be a certain amount of action, as in the washing cylinder of a drycleaning machine or, in some types of equipment, through reverse action of the washing cylinder. The cylinder may have a number of holes to allow the proper amount of solvent to flow through it. Ribs may be built inside the cylinder to aid in picking the garments up and then dropping them down gently to provide the action necessary for removal of soil.

Soaps and detergents used to get the dirt and soil from fabrics are different from those used at home, but they perform the same function when used with drycleaning solvents—they help to emulsify all loose soil and dissolve all oily and greasy soil.

When you wash a fabric that has oil or grease on it, you usually cannot remove the grease unless you have treated the stained area, because water and oil do not mix. But the reverse is true in drycleaning fabrics, and soil or stains that have water as an integral part of them are not removed by drycleaning solvents. Research has now made it possible to use methods that facilitate the removal of many of the water-soluble soils during the drycleaning operation proper.

Dirty solvent is drawn from washers continuously and replaced with clean solvent in order to prevent loose soil from redepositing on the cleaned items. The solvent is pumped out of the washer, through a filter, and then back into the washer again. Depending on the size of the filter, solvent may be circulated at the rate of 2 thousand to 10 thousand gallons an hour. Various filtering aids, such as diatomaceous earths, clays, and absorbent powders, are used to keep it in condition.

After cleaning and rinsing, excessive solvent is removed from the garments by extraction. The last traces of solvent are removed in a special type of equipment called a tumbler. Here a carefully controlled current of warm, fresh air is circulated through the garments.

Some items, because of their construction, bulk, or size, are more effectively dried in a cabinet than in a tumbler. Here warm, fresh air is circulated through the fabric to remove any traces of solvent odor.

Up to this point, if a garment or household textile is not a specialty item, it has been processed together with a number of other articles. From now on it is handled individually. It goes to the spotting department where it is examined for spots and stains that require skill to effect removal.

A spotter has the responsibility of selecting the proper solvent, whether it be dry, wet, or semiwet; the proper lubricant; and the correct chemical for the particular fabric and stain involved.

The main problem in spot and stain removal is not that of finding the chemical reagent that will remove the stain, but, rather, the selection of a reagent that will remove the stain without resulting in damage to the fabric or dye-stuff. You may get the identical stain on two different garments made of two different fabrics. In one case the spotter may be able to remove the stain; in the other, he may not be able to do so without damaging the fabric.

When garments or household items are thoroughly clean and free from spots and stains, they are sent to the proper finishing department. The term "finishing" is used rather than "pressing," because often no mechanical pressure is used. Only steam and air are applied. Pressure is not applied in the same manner as it is applied in home pressing. Pressers have been built to accommodate every type of fabric. For example, men's and women's coats and suits are finished in the wool finishing department, and women's dresses and blouses are finished in the silk finishing department.

The modern drycleaning plant uses a variety of equipment to accommodate every size and shape of garment and every size and shape of household item.

Some items lend themselves readily to steam-air finishing so that an entire garment or household item may be finished on a form that is inflated with air. On this form, the fabric is softened with steam to remove the wrinkles. Then it is cooled to its original shape. Some parts of the article may require touching up by hand pressing, as the lining of a coat.

Puff irons are perforated metal forms of various sizes and shapes that are padded and covered. They make it possible to finish the narrow frills, shirring, tucks, gathers, and darts of the most complicated bodice or waist of a garment.

The employees are trained to recognize what must be finished on the wool press in the wool finishing department and what must be finished on the type of presses found in the silk finishing department. Decisions are made on the basis of fabric and construction.

WHEN GARMENTS or household textiles get so badly soiled that drycleaning does not remove all the soil, general grime, and dirt, they must be further cleaned by a process known as wetcleaning. Items that may need bleaching and articles that are so stained that they may require the digestive action of enzymes can be cleaned by wet processing. Some items are drycleaned first to remove all solvent-soluble soil.

Sometimes measurements are recorded before wetcleaning. Dyes are tested to determine if the item can be wetcleaned successfully, as some dyes

bleed and run when wet with water.

Wetcleaning is not washing—rather, it is a hand-brushing operation. Quick drying is essential in wetcleaning. To accomplish this, a special piece of equipment, called a "windwhip," is heated to hasten quick drying and thus helps to eliminate the possibility of bleeding and streaking of the dye.

THE SELECTION and care of modern fabrics has become quite complicated.

Many properties combine to make a fabric or garment or household item perform satisfactorily in wear and in cleaning, whether laundering, wetcleaning, or drycleaning.

Among them are fiber content (an all-silk fabric does not have the same qualities as one made of 20 percent silk and 80 percent wool); yarn construction; fabric construction, whether simple or complex; dyeing or printing (dye chemistry and the proper application of dyes to fabrics are important); finish (of the many physical and chemical finishes applied to fabrics, a particular finish may cause limitations in use and care); decorative designs applied to a fabric surface or woven into the basic weave construction; they may give satisfactory performance in wear and in cleaning, but also may limit the wear of the fabric; and garment findings and trim (if the stitching thread shrinks or bleeds or the bias or stay tape and ribbon or embroidery trim do not perform satisfactorily in cleaning, the value of the entire garment is lost).

SELF-SERVICE coin machines, of course, provide only the cleaning part of drycleaning. Necessary pressing, shaping, ironing, or pleating is done at home.

Before using this service, you should check and follow cleaning instructions on garment labels and fabric tags; clean light-colored fabrics separately from dark, and fragile from heavy clothing; brush out the lint-catching areas, such as trouser cuffs and inside pockets; remove trimmings, fancy buttons, and belts, which are not suitable for cleaning; check the pockets for lipstick, fountain pens, and all loose articles; refer difficult stains to a professional cleaner; make necessary repairs; and follow the instructions for using the machine. It should not be overloaded.

Remove articles immediately after the cleaning and drying cycles. Hang on hangers to prevent wrinkling.

If there is a cleaning solvent odor in the articles, hang them in the open air or a well-ventilated room until they are thoroughly dry.

In coin-machine cleaning, the machines are automatically set so that all articles are cleaned the same length of time and with the same process.

In professional cleaning, sorting and classifying articles are part of the service. They are not cleaned the same way, for the same length of time, or in the same cleaning machine.

Some garments, depending on the type, fabric, and extent of soil, need little or no touching up after drycleaning. However, most apparel requires pressing and shaping if the finished work is to look well.

Hard-wear wrinkles will not come out in any cleaning-only operation. Soft wrinkles ordinarily fall out during hanging. Hard wrinkles can be removed only through careful pressing.

Generally speaking, water removes only the stains that water has caused. Drycleaning solvents will remove some stains but have no effect on others.

Stubborn stains must be removed individually by the drycleaner with special treatments, called spotting.

repair may be more important than durability.

Some repairs that are both durable and inconspicuous are possible on many fabrics, however.

WHEN YOU REPLACE buttons and the fabric under the button has become weakened, reinforce it by sewing a patch under the place where the button is to go.

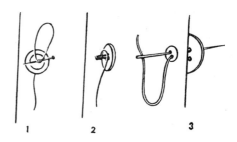

1   2   3

Replacing buttons.

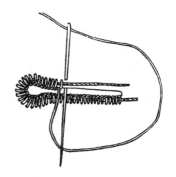

Worn buttonholes.

SOME POINTERS ON MENDING

YOU CAN MAKE many garments last longer if you repair breaks and tears in them and strengthen weak spots when you first notice them.

Choose the method of mending on the basis of the results you want. A durable repair, for example, is essential on garments that get hard wear or strain. On some garments, an inconspicuous

Sew buttons on with a shank so as not to be tight on the fabric. The shank should vary in length with the thickness of fabric.

To make a skank: Place a pin, toothpick, or match stem (depending on the desired length) across the button and between the eyes. Sew over this object as you sew the button on. Pull out the object, pull the button away from the cloth, wind the thread around the shank, and fasten off.

In some types of garments (such as

topcoats and sports jackets, in which there is much strain on the button closing), it is wise to sew a tiny stay button directly under the top button on the inside of the garment. Sew through both buttons at the same time.

Some drycleaners sew on missing buttons on men's and boys' topcoats and suits as a special service. If they cannot match the button, they even may replace the entire set.

To repair worn buttonholes on lightweight garments where strain is great on the buttonhole, you should reinforce the place that receives strain by sewing a patch on the underside of the hole. Rework the buttonhole by hand.

On coats and suit coats, use buttonhole twist thread or double regular thread. If the entire buttonhole is to be done over, reinforce with gimp or several strains of thread twisted together and waxed.

When you replace zippers, avoid stretching the fabric when you remove the old zipper. Steam-press the place from which the zipper was removed. Place the new zipper in place. Use a needle or pin to work the zipper ends under the facing or band at the top. Baste the zipper in place. Sew on the old line of stitching.

Snaps and hooks and eyes should be put in their original places. Use a buttonhole stitch for more lasting results.

THERE ARE SEVERAL ways to make patches.

The set-in patch is a good one to use on lightweight outer garments. On printed fabrics it can be inconspicuous and durable. Take the cloth for it from a pocket or hem or leftover scraps. If the garment has faded, the scrap should be shrunk and hung in the sun and faded to match the garment.

Prepare for the set-in patch by cutting a square or rectangle around the hole. Follow the weave of the fabric. Clip one-fourth inch diagonally in corners so that the raw edge can be turned under. Turn the seam under and crease. Place the patch under the hole and match the design. Baste the patch in place. The patch should extend at least one-half inch beyond the hole on every side. With small thread (up to 100 for very fine fabrics) and a fine needle, make the smallest possible overhand stitch or blind stitch. Press the seams open on the wrong side and tack down as you see fit.

A darned-in patch is good for heavy and bulky fabrics. Trim the hole with the weave of the fabric, making it square or oblong. For woolens, place a lightweight fabric (lawn or organdie) on the underside of the hole and baste in place. For corduroy and some other napped fabrics, use fine net, since the darning stitch will be done from the underside and by hand. Cut the patch so that it fits exactly into the hole, matching the grain, the nap, and the pattern. Baste the patch to the reinforcing material. Hand-darn if the patch is to be as inconspicuous as possible. On some fabrics, the zigzag machine stitch may be satisfactory.

You can buy various kinds of press-on mending fabrics and patches. They will withstand drycleaning and careful laundering if they are applied with a hot iron as instructed on the package.

These patches may be used to reinforce thin places and to hold together a cut place in a garment or as a substitute for stitching in the darned-in patch.

You can make almost invisible patches by using press-on plain percale mending fabric on the underside. To do this, shape the hole so the corners are square and the cut is with the weave of the cloth. Cut a piece of fabric matching in design and size and nap from a seam, pocket flap, or facing. Fit this piece into the squared hole in the garment. With press-on mending tape on the wrong side, press the patch in place on the patch side with a warm (not hot) iron to insure perfect matching. Then carefully turn the garment over and press against the mending tape, as instructed on the package. Such patches may be reinforced by machine stitching along the plaid or stripe in matching thread.

The knees and elbows of sports clothes and children's play clothes may have decorative patches to extend their life. You can buy such patches (with adhesive backing) at notion counters, or you can make them from old hats, leather gloves, or leather purses. They may be applied by hand; a blanket stitch or a long machine stitch may be used.

Another type of patch, a rewoven one, is suitable only for material that is fairly coarsely woven. To do it, mark a square or rectangle around the hole to be covered. Clip and pull out one yarn on each side, thereby outlining the patch you want to make.

Cut a matched patch piece about one-half to 1 inch larger all around than the space to be covered. Fray the edges of the patch equally on all sides until it matches in size and design the outline you have made. Lay the matched patch on top of the hole on the right side of the material. Tack it in place.

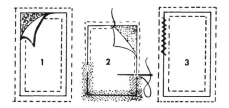

Darned-in patch.

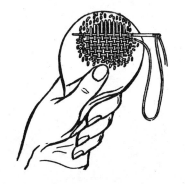

How to darn socks.

With a very small crochet hook draw the frayed yarns through the spaces left by the pulled-out yarns that formed the outline of the patch. If the patch is perfectly matched, there will be one frayed yarn on the patch to pull through each space created by the pulled-out yarn.

When all the ends are pulled firmly to the underside, take little stitches, by hand, to hold the patch in place.

HOLES IN SWEATERS can be mended with a knit stitch.

Match the yarn as nearly as possible. To make the knit stitch, cut the knitting lengthwise to a point a little above and below the center of the hole. Then make two horizontal slits, one above and one below the hole.

Ravel out the lengthwise knitting within the cut area. Thread each loose crosswise end of the yarn and run it back into the underside of the knitting.

Place a piece of cardboard under the hole. With the matching yarn, zigzag lengthwise back and forth across the hole. Run the beginning and ending thread far enough into the corner of the knitting to prevent pulling out. These threads catch the loops of knitting at the top and bottom of the hole.

The knit stitch is made in horizontal rows, beginning from inside the loop at the lower right-hand corner of the cut hole. The knitting stitch is done over the lengthwise yarns. Keep the loops in line with the rows of knitting below and above the hole until the side of the hole is reached. Reverse, and continue back and forth until the hole is filled. Weave the end of the thread into the backside of the knitting to hold it in place.

To DARN lightweight socks, snip away ragged edges; leave the hole in the round shape it took as it developed. Insert a darner or firm cardboard to keep the soft knitted fabric in shape for working. Match the darning yarn to the weight of the stocking. (Hard-twist yarns may cause discomfort in wearing.)

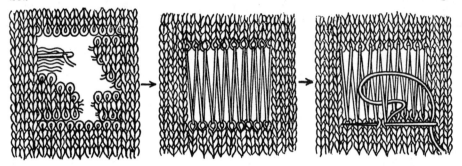

Mending sweaters.

Stitch in one direction, then the other, weaving in and out to make a plain weave. Do not try to bring the edges of the hole together when some of the fabric has been lost. That, too, will cause discomfort.

Press-on patches may be used to reinforce weak places before a hole appears. Turn the sock and put the patch on the inside.

To darn heavy knit socks, see the instructions for mending sweaters.

To TURN A COLLAR on a man's shirt, first find the center of the collar and neckband by bringing together the ends of the collar and neckband. Mark the center of both.

Remove the collar from the neckband by ripping the stitches carefully, so as not to tear or stretch the fabric.

Steam-press the collar and neckband carefully. Keep the seam edges turned in on the neckband.

Turn the collar over so the underside will be on top. Match the center markings. Insert the collar between the folded edges of the neckband as it had been. Pin and baste.

Be sure the old stitching lines are matched on both sides so that both edges of the neckband are caught in one stitching. Working from the neck side, machine stitch on the old stitching line.

To REPAIR FRAYED CUFFS: Carefully rip out all stitching on the lower edge of the cuff and into the curved ends. Steam-press the ripped seams. Turn the worn edges in on both sides of the cuff deeper than the old seam and worn edges. Pin and baste the edges together carefully. Stitch along edge from right side of sleeve.

To turn a folded cuff: Carefully rip the cuff from the sleeve. Steam-press the seam edges of the cuff. Turn the cuff over and replace it on sleeve as it was originally. This brings the worn edge to the inside fold of the cuff. Pin, baste, and stitch it in place to look like the original stitching.

ONE EASY WAY to take care of frayed sleeve edges on women's coats and jackets is to shorten the sleeve—various sleeve lengths are popular in women's wear.

On garments of soft fabrics, such as cashmere, where the nap has merely worn away, the sleeve edge may be

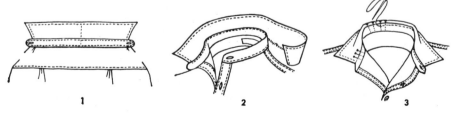

1   2   3

Turning a shirt collar.

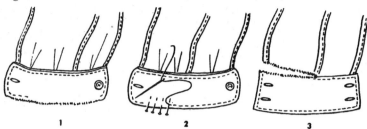

Repairing cuffs on shirts.

rolled under about one-fourth inch, pressed, and tacked in the new position.

Worn cuffs may be removed and the sleeve edge refinished without them. Understitch the seam to the facing side.

To mend frayed places on sleeves of men's jackets, remove the sleeve buttons and detach the lining at the cuff.

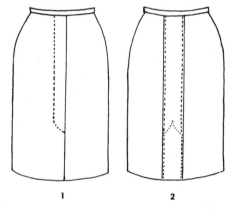

Ripped skirt pleats—knife pleat and box pleat.

Press the crease out. Fold the facing to outside of the sleeve and press the crease on wrong side. Seam out the frayed part along this new crease. Trim to one-eighth inch seam. Understitch the seam to the facing side. Turn the facing back in the sleeve, press, and rejoin the lining and replace the buttons.

FOR RIPPED skirt pleats, if the fabric has been damaged, darn or apply press-on mending tape. Shorten the line of stitching (making the pleat longer) or lengthen the line of stitching (making the pleat shorter). End the line of stitching with a curve toward the fold of the pleat.

In box pleats, a curve toward each fold of the pleat is made, one at a time, after the pleat has been pressed open. The curved seam prevents undue strain on only a few threads, and it will not tear again.

YOU CAN MAKE DO with children's clothing in several ways.

Take advantage first of built-in expansion features, such as tucks for increasing sleeve and dress lengths, long straps, and extra lap for buttons. When you have exhausted those possibilities, consider these:

If the neck is too small, set the buttons over or cut out the neck opening and refinish with binding or facing.

If an armhole is too small, remove the sleeve or finish, enlarge the opening, and refinish by applying bias binding or a narrow bias facing. If a facing was used originally, you can make the armhole larger by turning and facing it to the outside, stitching around the armhole, and trimming the new seam, turning the facing back to the inside.

If the waist is too short, make a set-in belt with matching fabric or appropriate contrasting material.

Or, separate the blouse from the skirt at the waistline with matching fabric or contrasting material set in a band or belt.

If the skirt is too short, face it with matching or contrasting fabric; make the contrasting insertions a part of the design.

WAYS TO SAVE ENERGY

MOST HOMEMAKERS want to know how to save—or to make better use of—the time and energy they need to care for their families and homes.

Organizing their work and improving their skills can help, but the arrangement of work areas, the design of the house, and the selection of tools also are important in reducing the time and the energy required for homemaking.

The homemaker (like everybody else) expends energy when she works. Even when she rests or sleeps, her body is performing work to keep the heart beating and other organs functioning to maintain life.

Much work is done by the muscles in maintaining their own tension, for there is tension in every muscle even when it is completely relaxed. The total energy the homemaker expends varies with the amount of internal and external work the body does.

How then can the design, arrangement, and equipment of a home help minimize fatigue and save energy?

WHEN WORK SURFACES, such as counters, sinks, baby bathtubs, and ironing boards are too low for the worker, proper posture cannot be maintained.

Good posture helps to assure the proper use of the muscles. When posture is correct, the bony framework supports the weight of the body without strain on the muscles and ligaments.

In correct standing, the body should be aligned so that the center of the hips, of the trunk at the shoulders, and of the head are in a direct line over the center of the arches, the weight-bearing parts of the feet.

In sitting, where the base of support is the chair rather than the floor, the head and trunk should also be aligned with no flex or bend at the waistline.

Fatigue can result from poor posture or continued stooping over an improperly adjusted work surface level.

What, then, is the most convenient and comfortable height for work surfaces for homemakers?

In performing certain hand-arm motions associated with food preparation and cleaning, housewives 5 feet 2 inches to 5 feet 5 inches tall expend least energy when working at counters placed 32 to 40 inches from the floor.

For ironing while standing, least energy is expended when the board is adjusted to a height of 36 inches.

For loading and unloading a mechanical clothes dryer, these same housewives expend least energy when the center of the opening of the dryer is installed at 38 inches from the floor and the clothes are transferred to or from a basket on a table 29 inches high.

Heights for built-in ovens also have been determined according to the energy expended by women using them.

For certain tasks performed over short periods of a few minutes, the homemaker expends less energy to work while standing than sitting.

For longer tasks performed while seated, the work area should be designed for comfortable sitting with the feet supported and with ample room for the knees. The work surface and chair should be arranged so that it is possible to work with elbows near waist level.

In the kitchen, the design should allow for free space under the counter or a pullout lapboard deep enough to give the necessary knee space.

For tasks performed while sitting on a chair, the height of the work surface should be 24 to 30 inches. For sitting to work at higher surfaces, such as a counter or sink 36 inches high, a stool with a seat and footrest that can be adjusted for comfort is recommended.

Important in lowering the expenditure of energy and minimizing fatigue is a design of facilities that allows for change of body position. Changes from sitting work to standing work and changes of tempo and type of work, together with interspersed rest pauses, help to improve working efficiency.

USING THE CORRECT TOOL can also help to maintain good posture and efficient methods of work.

Long-handled equipment can be chosen to avoid bending one's back. Some house-cleaning tools have the controls high on the handles so that the homemaker does not have to stoop to start and stop the equipment.

Human dimensions help to determine the form and size of equipment, the location of controls, and the space requirements in a work center.

Tools should be as simple as possible and of proper size and have handles that meet the normal grasp limitations of the human hand.

Control levers of equipment should be placed conveniently between elbow and shoulder height.

Efficient design in storage facilities can reduce the amount of reaching and bending. It takes about 19 times as much energy to get something 3 inches from the floor as to get it at elbow level.

The limits of comfortable reach have been established for wall cabinets hung over work counters that are 36 inches high and 25 inches deep.

The top shelf in a wall cabinet should not be higher than 52 inches from the floor for the woman 5 feet 2 inches to 5 feet 5 inches tall, if the item to be stored requires two hands to place it on the shelf.

For lightweight items that can be placed or removed with one hand, the top shelf should not be more than 68 inches from the floor.

In base cabinets, the space below 28 inches—about fingertip height—should be reserved for storing pots and pans that are seldom used.

If seated work is planned at the mix counter, the top shelf of the wall cabinet should be only 64 inches from the floor.

The space between the counter and the bottom of the wall cabinet is the space easiest to reach, but also the one frequently neglected for storage in the conventionally designed kitchen.

This space can be used to hang utensils used often. It takes less energy to hang a pan on a wall than it does to store it in base cabinets that require opening and closing of cabinet doors.

Space often overlooked on wall and door surfaces can be utilized in food preparation, sewing, and laundry areas for easy-to-reach storage.

A housewife can determine how convenient work and storage facilities are for her if she stands about a foot away from the wall and moves her arm freely from the shoulder so that the hand makes a large circle. Another person can record the high and the low points of the circle.

A smaller imaginary circle made by moving the arm only from the elbow should define the work and storage areas for things used most often.

Storing articles within these imaginary circles can help the homemaker to eliminate bending in laundry, sewing, and kitchen work centers.

Walking, like bending, takes considerable energy. Walking requires two to three times as much energy as standing quietly.

Many extra steps are taken in a year by walking through the living room in order to get from the kitchen to a bedroom or a poorly located bathroom.

If an American woman weighing 125 pounds walks 7.5 miles a day or takes roughly 19 thousand steps, her feet take a daily load of more than 2 million pounds. Some women may walk as much as 500 feet in preparing a simple meal. Good design of work centers can considerably cut down on the energy expended in needless walking.

The relationship of rooms and the arrangement of work and storage facilities should be considered if walking is to be reduced.

Storing things near the place they are used should eliminate many steps. For example, bath linen should be stored near the bathroom; bed linen, near the bedrooms; sewing supplies, wherever sewing or mending is done; dishes, near the dining table and sink or dishwasher; all mixing supplies and utensils, at the mix center; and other foods and utensils, where they are first used.

Walking upstairs requires three to five times as much energy as walking on the level. Getting work done in a house in which the work and living centers are on different floors requires more energy than does similar work in rooms on one floor.

PREPLANNING of work should help to eliminate unnecessary stair climbing.

An analysis of ways of working—including body movements in relation to design of the house and its facilities —should also be helpful: Can the effort put into washing dishes, cleaning, sewing, ironing, and caring for the children be reduced?

Are work centers planned to allow free body movement, which for greatest ease should be rhythmical and, if possible, circular? It saves effort to learn literally "to swing" the job.

Are counters free of clutter and big enough to allow you to work with both hands?

Are storage and work surfaces designed so that tools and materials can be stored in readiness for use? ("A place for everything, and everything in its place.")

Are tasks planned to minimize controlled movements and are working-space designs adequate to allow the use of the pull of gravity whenever it can aid the operation?

Is there counter space enough to allow the left hand to carry its share of the workload or alternate with the right hand? Time spent by the homemaker in the critical appraisal of the arrangement and equipment of the work facilities of the house—the one

being planned, the one already occupied, or the one considered for purchase—will be time well spent.

The returns will be in energy and time saved and less fatigue in the years ahead.

WHAT TO LOOK FOR IN HOUSEHOLD EQUIPMENT

HERE ARE some general guidelines that may help you when you buy household appliances.

An appliance bought chiefly because it is on sale at so many dollars less than the "regular price" may be satisfactory, but you are more likely to select equipment appropriate for you if you evaluate your needs and all the facts you can get about it.

• Do you need the appliance?

• Will it make your homemaking tasks easier?

• Will it contribute to more effective performance of homemaking tasks?

• Will it make your home safer? More livable? More enjoyable?

• Will it make extra space in your home by replacing items that take more space?

• Will it save energy for members of the household and permit more creative activities than they now undertake?

Consider possible negative factors.

• Will the appliance add excessive heat or noise in your home?

• Is it better to save the money or use it for another purpose?

• Will the appliance occupy space that you prefer not to give up?

• Will it complicate your way of doing things? For example, if your laundry has been done out of the home, what changes are likely to take place in your work habits if you acquire laundry equipment? If you buy a separate freezer or a large refrigerator-freezer, will you feel you should do home-freezing that you do not now do?

Only if the positive considerations outweight the negative ones are you concerned with selection. If they do not, you do not need to make a choice now.

NEW HOUSES sometimes have equipment that the contractors supply. Many contractors are willing that the home buyer specify the models. In some instances, you will pay more than you would if you accepted the contractor's choices—but that means you are making a selection according to your estimate of your needs rather than on price alone.

Consider the kitchen sink, for example. How wide it should be and whether it should have one, two, or three wells depend on the layout of the kitchen and on plans for a built-in dishwasher next to the sink.

You know your work habits better than the contractor does, and you know whether you want more counter and storage space or a sink with two wells rather than one.

Also, you may want a sink of better quality than the contractor plans to supply. You will be wise, then, to consult retailers of plumbing supplies, visit the showrooms of a large manufacturer, or compare prices and details given in mail-order catalogs.

Stainless steels vary in composition. Two sinks of the same type of steel may have different thicknesses. Different types of fittings are available at different costs.

Somewhat similar considerations apply to a waste disposer to be installed in one well of a kitchen sink. If you inform yourself about what is available, you may want a more expensive model than the contractor has planned. If the model you choose is cheaper, you may expect a cash allowance for some other part of the kitchen or house. An informed consumer will ask that the disposer have its own trap to insure better operation. That means two traps for a double-well sink.

YOU GET and evaluate information in this way: Check printed sources—books on household equipment, bulletins, advertisements, articles in magazines, catalogs of mail-order firms.

Check recent issues of Consumer Bulletin and Consumer Reports for articles on the type of appliance in which you are interested. Current issues may not have the information you want, but for many appliances, issues that are 2 or more years old may supply useful tips on construction and operating characteristics. For example, in purchase of a gas water heater, the recovery rate (gallons of water that will be heated through a 100° temperature rise in an hour) is as important as the size or gallon capacity of the water heater. A Consumer Bulletin or a Consumer Reports article that alerted you to recovery rate would do you a service regardless of whether the article was new or old.

Chat with friends who own the type of appliance you are interested in to learn what they like and do not like about a particular model. Find out why. A woman may say she does not like a dishwasher because it does not get dishes clean. You may learn in chatting with her that she uses water that is not hot enough, or the water is excessively hard, or she expects too much —for example, she puts unscraped, heavily soiled breakfast dishes into the appliance and operates it after the evening meal.

When you visit stores that sell the appliance, have in mind the main points in which you are interested. Look at the appliances on display. Try to visualize different ones in your home. Request a sales presentation on features and ask for printed specifications and the user's folder or booklet. If a manufacturer's representative is in the store, chat with him.

Ask questions: When a salesperson speaks of automatic defrosting in a refrigerator-freezer, is only the refrigerator section automatically defrosted or are both sections automatically defrosted?

Ask the salesman about local codes. He may be able to tell you, for example, whether the type of chimney you have is suitable according to local codes for venting a gas incinerator.

He may say a particular clothes dryer will receive a washer load—meaning a load from a washer that is the companion model to the dryer. But will it handle the load of the washer you already have?—or will you have to divide the load?

Ask particularly about features that are new to you. Some new features may be useful; some you may not care for.

Ask about safety seals; warranties (which parts are covered and who pays for labor); arrangements for servicing; trade-in values and installation cost; the approximate operating cost per month, day, cycle of operation.

Servicing arrangements may include the purchase of a service policy. Most household appliances are not designed for servicing by the user, and do-it-yourself work within a warranty period invalidates the warranty.

CONSIDER costs. The most deluxe models of small electrical appliances—mixers, coffeemakers, saucepans, frypans—are not inexpensive. Indeed, the total cost of three or four most deluxe (top-of-the-line) models may equal or exceed the cost of a stripped-model range.

Consider also where you will store such appliances. You may not often use a stand mixer if you have to keep it in a cabinet near the ceiling. Perhaps you can store a smaller one in the storage space in the mix area or on a countertop.

A point to remember is the size of an appliance in relation to the way in which you are most likely to use it.

If, for example, you usually make only 2 cups of coffee at a time, a 10-cup model that is to be used for 2 cups regularly and 10 cups once in a while is a poor choice.

IT IS UNREALISTIC to buy an attractive and expensive frypan that can be used at the dining table if, like most persons, you do not take an electric pan to the table. On the other hand, if you plan to use a waffle iron for informal entertainment, a large size may be best, for you can serve several persons at one time.

Some knowledge of the automatic features helps. A light that indicates an appliance is on is different from a control that turns the appliance on and off

automatically. It is not reasonable to expect complete accuracy in the thermostats of some small electric appliances.

Some knowledge of materials also is helpful. A nonporous material like stainless steel, ceramic, or glass for the inside of a coffeemaker is easy to keep clean, as is Teflon in pots and pans.

FINALLY, these points should be checked:
• The warranty or seal of a recognized agency—Underwriters' Laboratories, Inc., for electric devices and nonelectric household wares such as pressure saucepans and American Gas Association seal for gas appliances.
• Effectiveness of the appliance for the primary purpose you have in mind.
• Ease of use.
• The space it takes in your kitchen.
• Ease of cleaning and maintaining. (It may be easy to clean the surfaces of a nonvented range hood; is it easy also to clean or replace the filter or filters and to oil the motor?)
• The design of the appliance.
• Durability.
• Availability of servicing.
• The reputations of the manufacturer and dealer for standing behind the articles they sell.
• Price.

RANGES AND ELECTRIC APPLIANCES

WHEN YOU LOOK for a kitchen range today, the three basics you should consider first are the space you have, how much your budget will allow, and how at ease you feel with the controls and gadgets of the model you select.

Ranges for homes are of four types; Freestanding, built-in, drop-in, and slide-in. They are 19 to 42 inches in front dimension and may have one or two ovens. Ovens may be at eye level, below the range surface, or both.

Most electric and gas (LP, natural, or manufactured) ranges have four surface units. Usually one unit (or two) is larger and has greater heat output than the others and so can heat larger containers of food more quickly.

Electric surface units may have five or seven switch positions. Some have graduated cooking positions over the entire dial. Some have pushbuttons for 4-, 6-, or 8-inch heating coils to suit the size of pan.

Many gas ranges are equipped with burners with four click positions and may be used at any number of positions. The gas and electric ranges may be equipped with thermostatically controlled surface units. The unit operates on full heat until the food reaches a selected temperature. Then the heat lowers or cuts off automatically and continues to cut on and off to maintain the temperature.

Some ovens have a clock mechanism that turns the oven on and off at a time set in advance. The clock also may control an outlet, to which a small appliance, such as a coffeemaker, may be connected.

The heat controls on some ovens have a range of 140° to 550° F. Low settings may be used for thawing frozen food, warming plates, or keeping food at serving temperatures.

The controls on some gas ovens automatically change from one oven temperature to another, usually from a cooking to a keep-warm temperature.

An automatic meat thermometer eliminates the worry about undercooking beef or a turkey. When the meat reaches the preset internal temperature, the heat is reduced, and the oven keeps the meat serving hot without further cooking.

You may like to have a rotisserie in the oven or on the top of the range if you enjoy barbecued foods. Thermometers built into the spit assure properly done fowl or heavier cuts of meat.

Ceramic burners, higher wattage units, and reflectors provide concentrated heat for broiling. Multiheat broilers eliminate raising and lowering the grill. Grills on some constant-heat types can be raised or lowered from the range

control panel. Vertical broilers that cook both sides at once are also available. To keep down spattering on the oven walls, some ranges have a high-walled pan, which is cooled by a water pan below.

Thermostatically controlled griddles are built into the surface of some models of gas and electric ranges. In one gas range, the griddle may be substituted for a large grate and converted to a fifth surface burner.

In one electric range, the oven can be cleaned automatically by setting the proper controls. A high temperature in a closed oven burns off the soil.

A plastic or Teflon coating, easily cleaned with a damp cloth, on slideout oven sides is a feature of other ranges.

On other models, oven doors that lift off, an oven lining that rolls out, and sides and backs of ovens that are covered with replaceable aluminum foil contribute to easier cleaning.

Knobs, burners, trim rings, surface units, and drip pans are easy to remove for washing in many ranges. Several ranges have built-in ventilating or exhaust systems.

No one model has all the convenience features outlined here. As models increase from the low end of the line to the top of the line, convenience features generally increase, with corresponding increases in price.

WHEN YOU SELECT a range, check for sturdy construction and a well-insulated oven.

• Look for well-spaced surface units.

• Check the clearance between the surface units and the oven on high-oven ranges.

• Check for easy-to-read controls so placed that you do not have to reach over steaming pans to make adjustments, shelf stops that prevent oven and broiler racks from being pulled out accidentally, and parts that are easy to clean.

• Pass up features that duplicate the jobs of small cooking appliances you already own. Choose the features that will make cooking easier and more pleasurable.

• Look for the approval seal of the American Gas Association on gas ranges and the Underwriters' Laboratories seal on electric ranges.

• Check the availability of adequate and prompt service.

THE PROPER SELECTION and use of utensils for the top of the range and for the oven are important.

The material used in top-of-the-range utensils should be a good conductor of heat so that the bottom of the utensil will heat quickly and evenly, with no hot spots on which food can stick and burn.

The bottoms of utensils should be flat and remain flat after heating to make good contact with the heating unit. The sides should be straight to conserve heat.

Covers should fit closely to hold steam within the pan and reduce cooking time. Covers, knobs, and handle grips should be of heatproof material and be easy to grasp without burning the fingers.

The handle should be firmly attached so that it cannot come loose and turn in the hand.

Pans are easier to clean if they have a pronounced curvature between the sides and bottom and no ledges or rivets on the inside where food can collect.

THE SIZE OF THE PAN should be matched to the size of the burner. Thermostatically controlled surface units are calibrated to operate with medium-weight aluminum utensils. If skillets of other materials are used, you will have to modify the temperature settings.

Utensils to be used in the oven should be selected to produce the product desired.

For double-crust pies, glass, Pyroceram, anodized aluminum, or porcelain enamel will give crisper crusts.

For cakes, pans with dull, rough bottoms and shiny sides will give the largest volume and tenderest crumb.

For cookies, use a moderately shiny

sheet of a size that allows 2 inches of free space in the oven on all sides for circulation of heat.

Casseroles of glass, Pyroceram, and porcelain enamel are good selections.

When you use several pans in the oven at the same time, you should stagger them to allow for proper circulation of heat and place them so they do not touch each other or the sides of the oven.

IN ELECTRONIC RANGES, cooking times are one-third to one-tenth those of conventional ranges.

High-frequency microwaves penetrate the food to a depth of about 2.5 inches from all sides. The air in the oven is not heated.

Glass, china, and paper transmit microwaves, but metals reflect them. Cooking in a microwave oven, therefore, must be done in glass, china, or paper containers.

Because food does not brown in an electronic oven, some electronic ranges have incorporated a high-speed conventional broiler in the top of the oven for browning. Ovens available are about the size of a separate built-in oven and operate on a standard 240-volt range outlet.

MANY PORTABLE ELECTRIC cooking appliances supplement or substitute for the kitchen range. Most of them provide fast, controlled heat. Most have relatively high wattages. To use them efficiently, the home wiring system must be adequate to carry the wattages that are indicated on the nameplate of the appliance.

Some portable appliances have permanently attached heat controls. Others have detachable controls.

Those with detached controls have a water-sealed heat unit, so that you can immerse them completely when you wash them. The same heat control is interchangeable among appliances of one manufacturer but not with other brands.

Select portable cooking appliances that have easy-to-grip handles and heat-

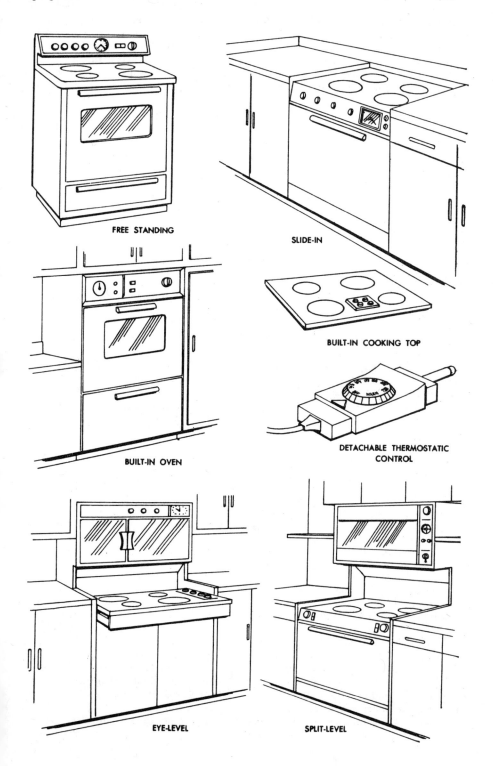

FREE STANDING

SLIDE-IN

BUILT-IN COOKING TOP

BUILT-IN OVEN

DETACHABLE THERMOSTATIC CONTROL

EYE-LEVEL

SPLIT-LEVEL

resistant, nonmar feet, with adequate airspace beneath the appliance to prevent damage to tabletops.

Frypans are of several sizes and may be round or square. Covers are sometimes sold separately. A domed cover will make the pan usable for pot roasts, fowl, and stews.

Some lids are vented to allow steam to escape and permit browning. Some skillet covers have broiling units that make the skillet a broiler as well. Large skillets are easier to handle if they have an auxiliary handle opposite the long handle, or have two side handles, as on a casserole.

An electric griddle should be large enough to eliminate frequent refills but not so large that it is awkward to handle or heats unevenly at the corners and around the outer edge. A grease-drip container that holds 6 ounces and is large enough at the top to insert a spoon for basting, and with provision for emptying hot fat from the container is desirable.

On a rotisserie, foods are cooked as they turn on a motor-driven spit. A rotisserie may also be used for broiling. Some, which have a second heating unit in the bottom and a means of closing the spit opening, may also be used for baking. Some of the models have a thermometer on the end of the spit to indicate the interior temperature of the meat, a timer, and a switch that turns off the motor when the rotisserie is being used for other cooking. Some are large enough to handle a large fowl or roast.

Portable ovens and broilers come in a variety of sizes and wattages. Many are equipped with thermostats. Some have a unit for baking and one for broiling. One has a single unit that serves for baking and broiling; the oven itself is turned upside down to broil. Most controlled-temperature ovens are satisfactory for baking a single pie, a cake, or casserole, biscuits, and potatoes and so may make unnecessary a second oven in a range.

Electric coffeemakers are of the percolator or vacuum types. Most switch to a keep-warm temperature after brewing. Some have signal lights, flavor selectors, and reheat settings.

Coffeemakers make the best brew when they are used to capacity. The size you buy, therefore, should provide the number of servings you need frequently. Most deliver fewer servings than the rating indicates and disregard the ratio of coffee to water for top-quality brew.

To determine the number of servings a coffeemaker delivers, measure the number of ounces of cold water required to reach the full mark, divide by 6 to determine the number of servings, then use two tablespoons of coffee for each serving.

Points to check on percolators: Securely fitting lids, glass perk top, and tight-fitting basket tube; a basket large enough to hold the required amount of coffee when the grounds are wet; and a tight-fitting spreader plate to prevent the grounds from floating off into the brew.

Vacuum types should have filters that are easy to clean.

POINTERS ON REFRIGERATION

REFRIGERATORS are cooled by the absorption of heat required to change a solid to a liquid (as in a refrigerator that uses ice) or a liquid to a gas (as in the mechanical refrigerator). The heat is disposed of outside the refrigerator.

The mechanical refrigerator uses electricity, gas, or kerosene as its source of energy.

The electric type has moving parts, which become worn and may be slightly noisy in operation.

Gas or kerosene refrigerators have additional flame heat to dispose of.

THE COST OF ENERGY and the cost of the refrigerator itself are factors to consider. The initial cost of the electric refrigerator is less than that of the other mechanical types.

The types of mechanical refrigerators

are all-refrigerator, conventional, and combination refrigerator-freezer.

In the all-refrigerator, most of the interior space is above freezing.

The conventional type usually has a single outside door and an inner door enclosing a freezing section at the top.

In the combination, the refrigerator and freezer spaces are two separate compartments, each with a separate door. The freezer may be above or below or at the side of the refrigerator space.

THE SIZE you should buy depends on your shopping habits; the size, age, and health of your family; and the amount of entertaining you do.

A family of two should have a refrigerator of at least 6 (preferably 8) cubic feet. Add an extra cubic foot for each additional family member, plus 2 cubic feet if you have guests often.

If a separate freezer is not available, the freezer space in the refrigerator should contain 2 cubic feet per family member.

Next, you should consider where the refrigerator is to be placed, because the wall space available determines its height, width, and depth.

The three sizes of refrigerators—compact, standard, and combination—vary in total capacity from 0.37 to 27.5 cubic feet. The freezer spaces are 0.2 to 16.11 cubic feet, depending on total size and style. If the freezer space is given in pounds, divide by 35 to determine the relative size in cubic feet.

These refrigerators come in free-standing and built-in styles. The standard size is a smaller, less expensive conventional type and has fewer features than the combination one.

Dimensions do not necessarily determine food-storage capacity. Thin-wall refrigerators with storage to the floor give more interior space without increasing the exterior dimensions.

Most refrigerators have right-hinged doors, but left-hinged ones usually are available at additional cost. Choose a refrigerator whose door opens on the side nearest the counter workspace. Door hinges are usually flush, and the door opens within the dimensions of the cabinet.

MOISTURE from warm air within the refrigerator condenses when it comes in contact with the evaporator coils and freezes.

The frost acts as unwanted insulation and increases the operating cost if it becomes more than one-fourth inch thick.

Defrosting, to remove this crystalline ice, is done in one of three ways—manual, semiautomatic, and automatic.

In the manually defrosted refrigerator, you set the control to "defrost" and reset to normal temperature after defrosting.

The semiautomatic defrost cycle is started by pushing a button, which causes the refrigerator to defrost, but it rests itself automatically.

In the automatic, the refrigerator defrosts at predetermined times. A clock timer, a compressor cycling, or a door counter are the control devices.

Freezer and refrigerator spaces may be defrosted in the same way or by a combination of ways. A few less expensive refrigerators do not provide a mechanical or electrical means of defrosting.

The defrosting period is reduced by having an electric heater come on during defrost cycle, or a hot gas flows through the evaporator coils or a separate set of coils.

In the frost-free combination, the evaporator coils are located outside the refrigerated spaces. A fan is used to blow cold air into these spaces. Forced-air circulation makes it important to protect foods from moisture evaporation. Frost on the evaporator coils melts during the automatic defrost cycle, and the moisture flows into a pan located at the base of the refrigerator. Here heat from the condenser evaporates it.

The frost-free refrigerator maintains a more uniform interior coldness and a lower door-shelf temperature, but

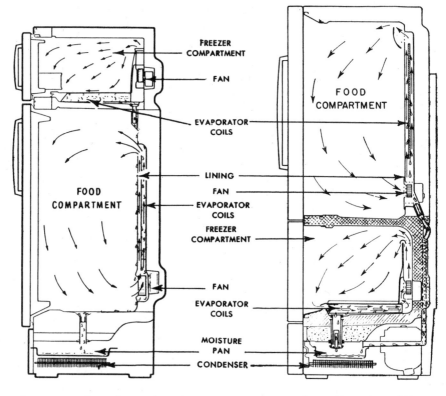

Airflow and Water Disposal Diagram—
Top Freezer Models

Airflow and Water Disposal Diagram—
Bottom Freezer Models

Schematic drawing showing the operation of a frost-free refrigerator-freezer.

it may take longer to freeze ice cubes than a conventional model.

The initial cost of the frost-free refrigerator is higher than the conventional type. Operating cost may be 40 to 100 percent more because of the fan used for circulating air and the heater used in defrosting.

The freezer temperature of the conventional refrigerator is above 0°. That of the combination is 0° or below. If you wish to maintain frozen food at top quality for more than a few days or at most 2 weeks, the freezer space must maintain 0°.

Most refrigerators have a single temperature control for the refrigerator and freezer compartment. Avoid setting this temperature too low, because foods may freeze in the refrigerator space. The operating instructions give the normal setting, which should maintain a refrigerator temperature of 37° to 40° and a freezer temperature of 0°.

THE EXTERIOR FINISH usually is a bonderized steel with an acrylic or a baked-on enamel in white or color. A few are of porcelain-enameled steel. Porcelain is more expensive and more durable than baked enamel. Vinyl-coated steel is another durable finish. Brushed chrome and chromium are used as trim.

The interior may be acid-resistant porcelain, baked-on enamel, aluminum, plastic, or combinations of them. The door liner and its shelves are made of high-impact plastic. The gasket of the door is of plastic or rubber—which grease causes to soften.

The construction should be sturdy and without cracks and crevices. Since you cannot see all construction features, you should buy from a reliable manufacturer. Door construction may be checked by putting weight on it to see if it sags.

Features built into refrigerators include slide-out shelves with stop lock and stop rail at the back; revolving or swing-out shelves; half or divided shelves; adjustable shelves; full- or half-width crispers; meatkeeper; removable egg and cheese containers; butter compartment; removable shelf front on the door; interior lights; a separate drawer for vegetables; a foot pedal for opening the door; a can dispenser on the freezer door; ice-tray ejector; automatic icemaker, which needs a water connection; pull- or swing-out baskets or trays in the freezer space; and levelers.

Each, of course, raises the cost of the refrigerator, and may or may not be of value to you.

You can reduce the operating cost by keeping the evaporator coils defrosted; cleaning the condenser; providing air circulation to remove heat given off by the condenser; placing the refrigerator in a cool, dry area; and cooling foods to room temperature before storing them.

A home freezer is a convenience, but it saves money only if turnover is rapid and you use it at full capacity.

In the following example, you can see what a year's cost for home freezing (exclusive of food cost) might be. The example is based on use of $250, 16-cubic-foot freezer (480-pound capacity) with three conditions—no turnover of frozen food and with turnovers of 50 percent and 150 percent. Since all costs except those for packaging and freezing food, remain the same regardless of the quantity of food in the freezer, the higher the rate of turnover, the lower the cost per pound of frozen food, as shown:

Expenditure item:	480 lb. of food	720 lb. of food	1200 lb. of food
Net depreciation (15 years' expected life)	$16.67	$16.67	$16.67
Repairs (2% of purchase price)	5.00	5.00	5.00
Electricity for—			
Freezing food (0.1 kw.-hr. per lb. at 2½ cents per kw.-hr.)	1.20	1.80	3.00
Maintaining 0° F. (0.22 kw.-hr. per cu. ft. per 24 hr. at 2½ cents per kw.-hr.)	32.12	32.12	32.12
Packaging (2½ cents per lb.)	12.00	18.00	30.00
Total annual cost	$66.99	$73.59	$86.79
Cost per pound of food	.14	.10	.07

If all the food is to be stored is purchased packaged and frozen, the charge for packaging and for electricity for three quantities of food considered in the table, the cost per pound will then be 11, 8, and 5 cents, respectively.

Locker-plant costs, for comparison with home-freezer costs, can easily be computed from the plant's rates for locker rental and charges for the services provided.

The details of selecting a freezer are similar to those mentioned for refrigerators.

Its size is most important because it is a 15-year investment. Freezer sizes range from 3.2 to 30.1 cubic feet. Selections tend to be 13 cubic feet or more.

The freezer space you need depends on how much freezing you do at home at one time; how much and what kind of frozen food you plan to store; how long the growing season is; how much frozen food is available in your market; how large your family is; and how much space is available for the freezer.

Two medium-sized freezers may be better than one large one, for you can disconnect one when you have little food in it, store only the food from one during mechanical failure, or use one as a freezing space and the other one for storage, thereby reducing fluctuations in temperature.

Types of freezers are the upright (vertical or front opening) and the chest (horizontal or top opening).

The upright occupies less floorspace and usually provides more convenient storage, but it costs more than the chest type.

The vertical type is no more expensive to operate than the horizontal one.

The flat top of the chest freezer can be used for workspace. It does not need to be defrosted so often, but defrosting is more difficult than in the upright model. A freezer scoop or plastic dustpan helps you remove ice before it melts.

The upright freezer may be frost free the same as the combination refrigerator. In a no-frost freezer, storage space is not reduced because of frost, packages of food are easily separated, and labels are not frosted over. This type is more expensive to buy and to operate than a comparable conventional type. The operating cost is about twice as much.

Freezers need to have better insulation than refrigerators.

The cost of buying a freezer will vary with its size, finish, and construction. The cost per cubic foot drops as the size increases.

The best place for a freezer is one that is convenient, cool (usually not below 40°), dry, and well ventilated. The floor should be strong enough to carry the weight.

Before you decide on the freezer and its location, be sure that it will fit the space and go through the passageways.

The upright freezer may have drawers or dropdown door shelves, which increase accessibility but add to the cost of manufacturing.

The chest freezer may have baskets or space dividers to make food more accessible. They reduce storage space and are harder to lift when filled.

Freezer features include locks; warning devices to indicate that the temperature has risen or the electricity is off; built-in defrost drain; interior lights; a thermometer; toe space; and rollers for moving the freezer.

The wisest recommendation is that you buy a freezer made by a well-established company and from a reliable dealer who will install and service it.

To learn the manufacturer's responsi-bility, read the warranty carefully. With the warranty there usually is a card that you must fill out and return to the manufacturer to make the warranty valid.

A gas refrigerator should carry a star of approval from the American Gas Association (AGA), which means it meets requirements for good construction and performance.

All refrigerators and freezers should carry the seal of approval of underwriters' Laboratories, Inc. (UL), which indicates that the refrigerating system and electrical connections are safe.

WHAT TO LOOK FOR IN DISHWASHERS

TWO MAIN TYPES of dishwashers are available.

Portable models can be moved around—even to another house, if you move. Others are permanently installed. The convertible is a combination of the two types.

The portable costs little to install but is not always convenient to use. It must be rolled to the sink, where it blocks easy access. Connections are made to the sink faucet. Some models are so made that you cannot use water for other purposes while the portable dishwasher is operating. It needs a parking space in or near the kitchen.

Permanently installed dishwashers come in freestanding, countertop, and undercounter models. All require plumbing and electrical connections.

The undercounter models, generally bought without tops or sides, must be built in. Installation therefore requires a carpenter, a plumber, and an electrician.

Installed dishwashers do not interfere with use of the sink, but usually they are a permanent part of a house and cannot be moved to another.

The convertible is a freestanding dishwasher on wheels. It can be used first as a portable and later converted to an undercounter model by removing the wheels and top and connecting it to the plumbing lines.

Portable and installed dishwashers are available in top- or front-loading models. In some top-loading dishwashers, the lid lifts up. In others, the tub pulls out—drawer style. In front-loading machines, the door drops down and the racks pull forward.

The choice between the two types of loading is mostly a matter of individual preference and perhaps the user's ability to reach into a deep tub.

Models with dropdown doors and pullout drawers require 42 inches of floorspace in front of the dishwasher to allow for opening and loading.

An important detail is the cycle for washing a regular load—the complete sequence of an operation from start to finish.

Only one cycle is provided on some machines. It may be minimum—a wash and two rinses, followed by drying. It may be a more complex sequence on some washers—a rinse, a wash, a second wash, two rinses, and drying.

Some deluxe models have several different cycles, such as "regular wash," "china and crystal," "pots and pans," and "rinse and hold."

The way a dishwasher is to be used will determine whether the extra cycles are worth the extra cost.

The cost of a dishwasher usually is not related to the basic cycle, for the more complex sequences are available on a number of low-priced models. If you plan to scrape and rinse dishes before putting them in the dishwasher, one with a minimum cycle probably will be satisfactory.

If dishes are to be washed without rinsing and with only enough scraping to remove bones and other large pieces of food, a cycle providing two separate washes and at least three rinses is vitally important.

The detergent holder generally indicates the kind of cycle. A dishwasher with two containers for detergent, both covered, gives a prerinse with clear water and two separate washes with detergent.

In a machine with a double holder but with only one covered container, the washing compound in the open holder is dispersed in the first fill.

Later in the cycle, there will be a second wash.

Machines with a single holder, with a cover, give only one wash unless the user puts detergent on the tub floor to be dissolved in the first fill.

Other dishwashers have only a single uncovered holder—or none at all. With these, the first fill provides the only wash.

Water temperature boosters and rinse injectors are special features on some models. Many washers have heaters that operate during the cycle, but they help to maintain—not increase—the temperature of the water. A booster provides water at a specified temperature in the wash or in the final rinse, or in both.

A gas burner in some dishwashers heats water before it is circulated. In others, the cycle is delayed until the electrical unit in the bottom of the tub heats the circulating solution to a specified temperature. A booster may increase the time required to complete the cycle.

The rinse injector automatically adds a solution in the final rinse to help the water slide off the dishes and keep them from spotting. This may be important in places where the water is hard.

Some racks are designed for random loading. Some are arranged in such a way that certain kinds of dishes go in certain places.

Personal preference should be the basis for choice, because either kind is satisfactory if it is loaded so that the dirty side of each article faces the washing mechanism and if dishes in one rack do not block the cleaning solution from the other rack of dishes.

WASHING MECHANISMS are of two major types, each of which has adaptations.

The hydraulic mechanism employs a perforated hollow tube, which turns on a shaft as the recirculating water is pumped through it.

Some dishwashers bring in cleaning

solution from more than one area; for instance, from hydraulic mechanisms under both racks or on both sides of the dishwasher.

The impeller mechanism is a type of rotor. It is in the lowest part of the tub, and so is in the water when the tub has filled. The turning rotor throws the water with considerable force over the dishes.

Both types of washing action give good results, but the trend has been toward the use of more hydraulic systems and fewer impellers.

Drying methods vary. Some dishwashers use only natural evaporation from hot dishes, but most use an electrical heating element in the bottom of the tub to heat the air.

Some designs employ a heating element and fan outside the tub to blow hot air into the tub and over the dishes.

Another utilizes a gas burner to heat the final rinse water to 180° F. before circulating it. Then the door pops open and water evaporates from the hot dishes.

The drying method may not be so important as the rack design, or the way dishes are loaded, or the shape of the cups, glasses, or other objects to be dried. Some water will remain in a deeply indented surface flat on a rack, regardless of the drying method. The same dish properly tilted on the same rack, or on a rack designed so the dish must be tilted, probably will dry.

THE DISHWASHER can do a good job if it is properly used.

If the cycle provides two separate washes and several rinses, it generally is not necessary to scrape and rinse dishes, glasses, and flatware before putting them into a machine.

If a dishwasher has only a minimum cycle, a wash and two or three rinses, dishes should be scraped and rinsed.

This extra handwork can be eliminated, however, if (after the wash and first rinse) you stop the machine, add a second measure of detergent, and reset the control for the complete cycle.

Whether pots and pans can be satis-factorily washed depends on your willingness to accept discoloration in aluminum and copper and to pretreat utensils in order to loosen cooked-on food.

Good management can make the difference between delight and disgust with a dishwasher. It makes good sense for the small family to accumulate dishes from several meals before operating the dishwasher. Time, energy, water, and cleaning compound are saved.

If used dishes are put in the dishwasher for later washing, they should be rinsed by hand, by using the rinse-and-hold cycle, or in a single-cycle machine by manually supplying one of the rinses and then turning the machine off.

If platters and other large dishes and the tableware from a meal will fill the dishwasher, you can wash the utensils you used in preparing the meal while you are eating. Then they will be ready to put away when the dishes go in.

At company time, one particularly likes to be with guests, and a dishwasher frees one for that. Therefore, if your company dishes must be washed by hand because their decorations may be damaged by the washing compound and the high temperature in the machine, good management suggests consideration of the purchase of new dishes guaranteed to be washable in the dishwasher.

Sometimes a simple rearrangement may provide a convenient place closer to the sink for a portable and thus encourage more frequent use than if it must be stored in a back hall or other out-of-the-way location.

To get the maximum satisfaction from a dishwasher and to operate it effectively, you should:

• Read the instruction booklet carefully and get acquainted with the various visible parts of the dishwasher and with the directions for use, care, and cleaning.

• See that the machine is properly grounded. If a dishwasher is installed, the electrician should connect the ground. With portables, this responsibility rests with the user. Most portables are equipped with three-pronged plugs, including a ground connection, while outlets are generally designed for the older, two-pronged plugs. The safe way to ground these dishwashers is to have a proper outlet installed. Manufacturers generally supply adapters, but unless the outlet itself is grounded, the adapter is useless. If one must be used, see that the outlet is grounded and always be sure that the grounding wire is connected to the center screw on the cover plate. Never leave it hanging loose.

• Try several of the special dishwashing compounds for mechanical dishwashers to find the one best suited to local water. Never use a detergent formulated for hand dishwashing or laundering; the heavy sudsing may cause flooding.

• Store the dishwashing compound in a tightly closed container, once the box is opened. The ingredients are especially susceptible to moisture and will deteriorate rapidly if the container is not airtight.

• Load the dishwasher so that the cleaning solution can reach all pieces in a load.

• Be sure the water temperature is at least 140° at the source. If the water heater tank is small, operate the dishwasher at a time when demand for hot water is light.

Whether care by the user is related to length of service is a question difficult to answer. Most of the internal mechanisms—the pumps, motors, and hoses—are not accessible to the user and probably do not require much special care. But precautions should be taken that such things as small bones that may damage a pump do not get into the drain.

Special care should be taken that children do not tamper with the controls and that the washing mechanism and heater are not damaged by carelessly loaded articles. Gaskets should be replaced if there is leakage.

In general, a dishwasher is more likely to be replaced because newer models are superior than because it is worn out.

GARBAGE DISPOSALS

Two TYPES of appliances are available for disposing of food wastes—the grinder and the incinerator.

The electrically operated grinder, which utilizes water to carry food wastes down the sink drain, is probably the most familiar type.

The grinder, in the sink, is essentially a small metal cylinder, or hopper, and a motor that operates some type of pulverizing mechanism in the cylinder bottom. It cuts food wastes into tiny bits and flushes them into the drain as water flows through the hopper.

In a batch-feed disposer (which is one of two types), you put the wastes into the hopper (capacity 1 to 2 quarts) and then lock the cover in place. Water and the electric switch are turned on, and the food is ground up.

Some grinders have a double switch arrangement. One is turned on by locking the lid in position. The other is turned on automatically as the water reaches an adequate flow. Neither starts the mechanism without the other. Thus the ground food usually cannot go into the drain without enough water to wash it away. In a double-bowl sink, however, the grinder will operate when the water is running into the wrong sink.

The continuous-feed disposer can be fed as it operates. It disposes of large amounts of waste more conveniently than does the batch feed because it is not necessary to load and lock the hopper before grinding.

Since one can operate the continuous disposer without the cover, households with small, adventuresome youngsters may feel it safer to use the other type. The possibility that a piece of bone will be ejected or a stray spoon will slip into the hopper is less if the cover is placed loosely over the opening of the continuous disposer.

A grinder is less expensive to purchase, install, and operate than an incinerator. It is small and out of sight, and so are food wastes that accumulate during the preparation of meals.

A grinder will not dispose of non-grindable but burnable waste, metal, glass, and ceramic materials; these must still be handled by other means.

Materials such as soft dough, liquid fat, and fibrous vegetable wastes may require special handling for proper disposal.

In other words, everything cannot be dumped into a grinder and made to disappear like magic. There are limitations on size of waste. For instance, watermelon rinds must be cut into small pieces.

The sink drain may become clogged if something is put in that should not be, if a particular kind of waste is loaded improperly, or if too little water is used. In that case, the advantage of location at the sink becomes a disadvantage, because the sink is unusable.

If a dishwasher drains through the disposer, manufacturers generally recommend that the grinder be emptied first so that the dishwasher can drain properly.

Grinders are relatively noisy, and in some installations may cause nearby items to vibrate.

Wastes from a grinder will increase the load on a septic tank by as much as one-third. Therefore, the size of the septic tank must be adequate, or it will have to be cleaned oftener. Ordinances in some localities prohibit grinders.

In some places where water is limited, too much may be needed (even though it may be only a few gallons each day) to permit the use of the grinder type.

To USE a disposer efficiently, you should:
• Read the instruction booklet and be familiar with types of wastes that the grinder will handle. Many give suggestions for special ways to handle fibrous or doughy wastes.
• Locate the overload switch and find out how to reset it. Learn how to use the wrench (if one is provided) or to follow directions for unjamming the grinder. Knowledge of the minor problems and how to deal with them may save service calls.
• Be sure that there is always a good flow of water when the grinder is operating. It is the water that carries away the wastes.
• Use cold water in flushing away wastes. This is especially important with fats. When hot water is used, melted fat is flushed into the drain-pipes, where it cools and can coat and clog the pipes.
• Be sure the split rubber disk at the opening to the hopper on continuous-feed disposers is in good condition. The disk helps to protect the user from bits of bone or fruit pits that otherwise might be forcibly ejected.
• Never use drain-cleaning chemicals in the grinder. They may corrode the shredding mechanism.

THE GAS-FIRED INCINERATOR, while now not nearly as common as the sink-disposal type, is becoming more popular in suburban areas. Incinerators which burn garbage are fired by a number of fuels, but since gas-fired appliances are more widely known, our discussion is limited to that type. It consists of a heavy metal container with a grate, a gas burner, and an ash drawer built into the bottom.

Wherever it is placed, it requires a connection to the fuel and to a chimney with a tiled flue of proper capacity.

The gas-fired incinerator is available with a low-input or high-input burner. The latter consumes wastes much faster. Some models provide special settings for extra-wet or for dry loads. Capacities range from 1.5 to 2 bushels.

Models that carry the American Gas Association Seal for Smokeless and Odorless Operation have a special afterburner that consumes smoke, fly ash, and odors. This is a desirable feature, especially if the burning of wastes may be annoying.

City ordinances in some places prohibit incinerators.

The incinerator will dispose of anything that will burn, including wet food wastes, old shoes, and newspapers. It will not handle metals, glass, or ceramic materials. It is relatively quiet and will take large pieces of waste. Its purchase price and cost of installation and operation may be considerably higher than for the grinder.

The location of the incinerator, even in the kitchen or nearby utility room, is probably less convenient than the grinder in the sink.

Heat generated by the burning may or may not be a disadvantage, depending on where the incinerator is placed and the season of the year.

Although the accumulation is small, ashes must be emptied every few weeks.

The user of an incinerator should:

• Read the instruction booklet and be familiar with the types of wastes it will handle. Follow the directions for use. Load the incinerator properly.

• Learn how to relight the pilot. If the unit fails to operate properly, check with the local gas company to be sure that the burner is adjusted correctly.

• Remove ashes as often as necessary. The pilot may be extinguished and the burner may not operate properly if ashes build up.

• Remove nonburnable material from the grate to prevent clogging.

• Consider the convenience of a grinder or an incinerator installed in a home. Is it worth the investment? Spilled-over garbage cans and smoky trash burners may provide an affirmative answer. In communities where garbage is disposed of by the householder, they are almost necessities.

The ideal situation may be to have both types—the grinder-disposer in the sink and the incinerator-disposer in the utility room.

SUCCESSFUL HOME LAUNDERING

POWER AND AUTOMATION have eliminated much of the drudgery and toil from home laundering, but the family wash still presents problems.

The complexity of mechanized equipment, the multiplicity of laundry additives, the diversity of fibers and finishes in fabrics all call for new information and new skills and, possibly, a change in your laundering methods.

Planning and know-how are necessary wherever and however you do the family wash. Coin-operated washers and dryers are usually "home" size, too. Although most commercial laundry facilities do not offer the choices that home equipment does, the principles here apply to their use.

AN EFFICIENT laundry center makes the entire laundering process easier. Arrange your laundry equipment to save steps and to suit your work habits. Allow sufficient workspace around each piece of equipment for freedom of movement.

If space permits, provide counters at a comfortable height for sorting, folding, and sprinkling clothes. A storage cabinet for supplies and a deep sink or laundry tub for hand washing or pretreating clothes are added conveniences.

A minimum space of 3 feet is required in front of an automatic washer or dryer for normal use; 4 feet is desirable, and is necessary if laundry equipment is located in a passageway.

Allow a space 6 feet 6 inches by 8 feet for a wringer washer, two free-standing tubs, and a laundry basket. Stationary tubs are more convenient if open at both ends than if closed in with other equipment or cabinets.

A counter height of 22 inches is comfortable for sorting laundry from a basket, but is too low for pretreating or sprinkling. A counter 36 inches wide, 24 inches deep, and 32 to 37 inches high is convenient for pretreating, folding, and sprinkling, but leaves little room for the article before and after handling. The tops of your washer and dryer often provide additional workspace.

If your ironing equipment is portable, it can be set up in free space anywhere in the house. Allow a space 7 feet square for ironing board, clothes-basket, garment hanger, and a small table for folded articles. With a built-in board, you will want to allow space for these ironing aids near the stationary board.

INDIVIDUAL ELECTRIC circuit should be provided for an automatic washer and for an electric tumbler dryer whether they operate on 115 or 230 volts. A hand iron or ironer needs another 115-volt circuit if used at the same time as the automatic washer or dryer.

Make certain that the automatic washer is connected in such a way that both hot and cold water can be shut off after washing is finished. This relieves pressure on the hose and valves of the washer. Locate your washer as close as possible to the hot water source to avoid drop in temperature in a long pipe. A gas dryer should be installed with its own gas cutoff valve for emergency or repair.

Venting the exhaust of a clothes dryer to the outdoors eliminates this source of warm, moist air in the room where it operates.

Adequate lighting is essential for good sorting, pretreating, and ironing, and makes any laundry task more pleasant. If your laundry area does not have sufficient natural light, make sure that the work area has good artificial light. A well-designed lamp that can be fastened to the wall may supplement other light adequately.

BEING ABLE TO WASH at home anytime and to care for emergency needs are conveniences. But washers and dryers are almost certain to need repair sometime during the 10 years and 14 years, respectively, that they are estimated to last when they are bought new and have only one owner.

On the other hand, you may prefer—or, at times of breakdown, be forced to—take your washing to a coin-operated laundry, which supplies hot and cold water and has enough machines so that you can wash several loads at one time. But for the purposes of this article, let's assume you have, or will purchase, your own washer.

WHEN YOU BUY A WASHER, you can choose between nonautomatic and automatic types—the automatic being the most common and popular type today.

In a nonautomatic washer, an electric motor provides for agitation and runs the mechanism for extraction of water. The user controls the filling of the tub, temperature of the water, washing time, water extraction, and emptying of the tub.

Several small nonautomatic washers are available. From some of them the clothes must be wrung by hand. They are suitable for washing personal laundry or small loads of family laundry, but generally are neither large enough nor sturdy enough to be the only washer for a household.

An automatic washer fills itself with water of a preselected temperature, washes, rinses, extracts water, and stops —all at one setting of the controls and without further attention from the user.

Unless an automatic has a suds-saver attachment (the wash water is drained into a stoppered tub, then pumped back later for reuse), it will fill with fresh water for each of its processing steps and automatically empty used water down the drain.

Automatics range from the simplest (with a single speed and cycle) to the multiple-speed washer that has automatic dispensers for cleaning agents and programed cycles activated by push-buttons to suit almost any combination of laundering needs.

Cycles may include such variations as a soak; choice of washing time, water temperature, and washing and spinning speeds; and choice of rinsing without spinning. But even the simpler automatic models are versatile and with ingenuity can be made to achieve some actions that are automatic on higher-priced models. For instance, for wash-and-wear articles, the user can shorten the washing cycle, cool the rinse, and interrupt the spin to minimize wrinkling.

Agitator automatics and those with adaptations of the agitation principle open at the top. For most users, they are more convenient to load and unload than the tumbler type, which opens at the front and requires stooping and bending.

There are also washers that dry the clothes. Combination washer-dryers are all front-opening tumblers. They automatically complete both washing and drying or do either job separately. Electric and gas models are available.

The washer-dryer needs less floorspace than two separate appliances, and the clothes need no handling between washing and drying. Since one mechanism does both jobs, it may need repair or replacement earlier than a separate washer and dryer would. The washer-dryer and other tumbler automatics generally use less water for each load than top-loading washers.

For safety, the equipment should be so designed that all operation ceases when the lid or door of a washer or dryer is opened.

POINTS TO CHECK ON ALL WASHERS

Water Needed

If water is scarce or expensive, or if heating water is inconvenient or expensive, the amount of water the machine uses will be important. Ask your dealer how much water a washer uses in its complete cycle.

The amount of water required for one filling of the tub in different washing machines ranges roughly from 5 to 26 gallons. Laboratory tests show no definite relationship between effectiveness of washing and the amount of water the washers use.

Capacity

Most family-size washers are rated by the manufacturers as having a capacity of 8, 9, 10, 12, or 14 pounds of dry clothes. Laboratory studies of washers of 8-, 9-, and 10-pound capacity showed that most machines of this size gave better washing results with a lighter load than when the maximum rate load was washed. For better soil removal, load at least 3 or 4 pounds short of capacity.

General Workmanship

A well-built washer, whatever the type, is made from sturdy materials that are well-braced and welded. It is free from sharp edges and rough screw and rivet heads that might tear clothes. Parts that come in contact with clothes are rustproof. Gears are enclosed so that nothing can get caught in them. Tub and motor are mounted on rubber or hung on springs to lessen vibration and noise.

Placement of Controls

All controls on a washer should be easy to reach and operate—and the purpose of each one should be clearly indicated.

Tub Materials

For the tub that holds the clothes, porcelain enameled steel is the most commonly used material. It is easy to clean, moderate in cost, attractive, and fairly durable. It is usually white, although some automatic washers have tubs of other colors. White or pastel enamel has no special advantage over dark blue or black other than appearance. Porcelain enamel is glass fused on a metal base; it may crack or chip from sharp blows. Such damage cannot be repaired satisfactorily.

Aluminum and stainless steel are sometimes used for the tub. These materials are long-wearing, sturdy, and more expensive than porcelain enameled steel. Aluminum, if not processed by the manufacturer to resist discoloring, may gradually become dark from soapy water. This will not affect washing results in any way. Stainless steel is easy to clean and keeps its luster even with long use.

Outside Finishes

The outside of most washers is a special housing or cabinet that encloses the washing tub or tubs. This housing usually is synthetic enamel on sheet metal. The enamel scratches and nicks rather easily, but it can be touched up at home to keep a satisfactory appearance and protect the base metal from rusting. Some cabinets are made of porcelain-enameled steel.

Motors

The motor in most electric household washers is ½-horsepower; in a few it is ¼-horsepower. The motor is placed where it is shielded from water, grounded, and insulated from the metal of the machine. A sealed-in lubricant that permanently oils the machine is especially desirable.

The Warranty

Buy the product of a reliable manufacturer. Most manufacturers furnish with the washer a warranty of the materials and workmanship in the machine for a specified time—usually for 1 year from purchase and only to the original purchaser. Certain machine parts may have a longer coverage. Also, some manufacturers have a kind of insurance on some washer parts, for which the buyer pays a fee and receives certain repair and replacement services within a set time without further cost.

Read carefully and understand the warranty on the machine you buy, so that you know what to expect in the way of repairs or replacement at the manufacturer's expense. Since servicing is usually supplied by a local dealer it is wise to buy from a dealer with a dependable service department that can take care of repairs promptly.

Underwriters' Approval

Look for the seal of the Underwriters' Laboratories on any washer you buy. This assures you that the washer has fulfilled the Laboratories' specifications for electrical safety. It means the washer is made of suitable materials assembled with satisfactory workmanship. If the washer has a wringer, the seal also assures you that the wringer is provided with safety features that reduce the likelihood of accidents.

BEFORE YOU WASH any garment or household textile—
• Repair rips, tears, and seam pull-outs that may get worse in laundering.
• Shake out any loose dirt.
• Turn down cuffs and brush out lint.
• Close side fasteners and take belts out of carriers.
• Remove any ornament, trim, or shoulder pads that you know or suspect will not wash well.
• Empty pockets; many a service call is caused by extraneous articles in the washer or dryer. An overlooked lipstick or crayon tumbling in the dryer can stain a whole load of clothes; cleansing tissues can spread troublesome lint; and a hard object— a small tool, nail, or coin—can cause drainage problems, or may damage a dryer.
• Gather up belts, aprons or any item with long ties, handkerchiefs, children's socks, and other small or fragile articles that belong in the same laundry load. Put them in a mesh bag for washing.
• Remove any stains that may be present before washing clothing or household textiles. Once a fabric is wet, you may not be able to see the stain. Some stains may be set by washing in hot water or by the heat of the dryer or iron.

THE SOLUTION to many laundering problems is proper sorting into loads of the right size and composition. Washers, particularly automatics, are frequently blamed for poor washing when the fault lies in washing very dirty clothes with those slightly soiled, mixing colors with whites, and making the loads too heavy or bulky.

Generally the first sorting of the family wash is by *color*. White or light-colored fabrics should be separated from darker colors. Light fabrics may lint onto dark; dark colors may discolor or make light colors dingy. White nylon is easily discolored by washing with colored fabrics.

Light and dark colors may then be further separated according to—

• Amount of soil. Lightly soiled, moderately soiled, and heavily soiled laundry go into separate loads.

• Weight and construction of fabric. Delicate lingerie and summer sheers should not be washed with, or for the same time period as, sturdy denims or sheets. Bulky bedspreads, slipcovers, and the like fill the washer and should be washed alone.

• Water temperature safe for fiber and finish. White cottons go into the hottest water available; silk and wool into warm or cool water; and fabrics from manmade fibers (acrylic, modacrylic, polyester, nylon, etc.) in warm-to-cool water to minimize wrinkling.

• Similar use. Tablecloths, place mats, napkins, and dish towels may be numerous enough to make up a separate wash load. Bedding and bath towels combine well; pajamas and underwear may make up a load.

• Capacity of the washer. Generally, the capacity given by the manufacturer is the maximum load that should ever be used in the washer. When making up loads remember that they must have room to move about in the water; avoid overloading the machine.

Sample Washer Loads

1

Cottons and Linens

Fabrics must be of fast color and sturdy construction. Wash in very hot water, with all-purpose detergent, for full washer cycle. Results are better if white fabrics are washed by themselves. Two large sheets or tablecloths and a variety of smaller articles wash more effectively than a load made up of all large articles.

Load may include:

Aprons	Shirts
Dresses	Slips
Nightwear	Table linen
Pillowcases	T-shirts
Sheets	Towels

White or pastel gloves, handkerchiefs, socks (in a mesh bag).

Load size: To get good washability, load washer about 3 pounds light of manufacturer's rating (6 pounds in a 9-pound washer).

2

Lightweight or Sheer Cottons and Rayons

Wash in water as hot as color can stand, with an all-purpose detergent, and a shortened washing cycle.

Load may include:

Blouses	Petticoats
Dresses	Slips
Negligees and robes	

Load size: Similar to load 1 or smaller (lighter).

3

Similarly Soiled Articles of Manmade Fibers

Use warm or cool water, an all-purpose detergent, and shortened cycle. Include white nylons only in an all-white load; they easily pick up color from other fabrics. If badly soiled, these fabrics may need a hot water wash.

Load size: A 3- or 4-pound load of easy-care fabrics washes and dries with fewer wrinkles than a capacity load.

4

Heavy Work Clothes and Other Badly Soiled Laundry

Divide into loads according to color. Use water as hot as colors will stand, plenty of all-purpose detergent. Pre-

treat, soak, and use full washer cycle.
Load may include:
    Children's sturdy play clothes
    Coveralls, overalls, work pants
    Shop or laboratory coats
    Heavy socks
    Shirts, skirts, slacks, shorts
Load size: Light. Allow plenty of
room for washer action.

5

Articles Not of Fast Color

Some dark-colored cottons, denims,
socks, and blue jeans may be washed
together if you do not mind some mixing of colors. Otherwise, sort out the
fabrics that are likely to bleed color
and wash them separately. Use wash water at temperature of 100° or 120° F.,
full washer cycle, or shorter, if lightly
soiled. An unbuilt synthetic detergent
protects the colors, but may not remove
soil effectively if articles are very dirty.
For heavy soil, a short wash in hot water with built detergent may be a better
choice.

6

Miscellaneous Items
That Do Not Fit into Loads

These usually include:
    Bulky pieces, blankets, bedspreads,
throw rugs, that need to be washed separately because they fill the washer;
        or
    Woolens, electric blankets, sweat-
ers, and other items that require special
handling.

GENERALLY it pays to soak—
    • Heavily soiled work and play clothes.
    • Dusty curtains and draperies.
    • Heavily soiled slipcovers.
    • Certain stained articles to help loos-
en stains.
    The most satisfactory way of soaking
clothes is to agitate them in the washer
a few minutes in warm water with detergent. The addition of detergent
helps hold the dirt suspended in the
water. Use about half the amount of de-

tergent needed for washing. Extract water, and follow with complete washing
cycle.
    If you have only a few things to soak,
use a small container rather than the
washer. Submerge clothes in warm detergent solution, let soak for 15 minutes. Soaking to remove stains may take
longer. Then swish the clothes around a
bit, extract water, and add them to a
normally soiled load of similar fabrics
for the complete washing cycle. If
soaked clothes are extremely dirty, wash
them by themselves.
    White or light-colored fabrics of man-
made fibers or combinations with natural fibers may be soaked for a short
period in water softened with a nonprecipitating water conditioner to
help loosen soil and avoid tattletale
gray. Do not soak colored fabrics together that are not fast to washing.

THE FOUR CLASSIFICATIONS shown on the
thermometer in the accompanying water-temperature guide are those commonly used in home laundering. You
can check the water temperature for
different laundry operations in your
washer with a reliable utility thermometer.
    Although you want piping hot water
for washing, it is not advisable to set
the thermostat of the water heater much
above 140° F. for a long period of time.
Prolonged high heating may shorten
the life of the water heater and pipes.
Moreover, running water that is much
above 140° is a safety hazard.
    Some persons set the thermostat of
the heater higher for washing and then
turn it back after laundering is finished.
If washing is done every day this is not
a practical solution.
    If you have ample water, you may
want to partly fill the washer with hot
water and empty it to warm the washer
and get the water as hot as possible for
loads that require very hot water.
    Medium hot water (approximately
120° F.) is a good temperature for
washing some bright or dark colors that
do not actually run in the wash, but
may fade in time from washing in hot

Your Guide to Wash Water Temperatures

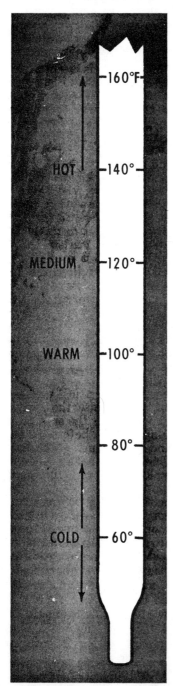

Very hot; water fills only from "hot" line of water heater, with temperature control set for "hot". Provides most soil removal and sanitizing; ideal for white cottons and linens, heavily soiled articles of washfast colors. Wrinkles manmade fabrics; may cause some colors to run.

Hot, mixed with some cold water. Fills automatically on "medium" water control. Lightly soiled loads usually wash clean. Provides no sanitizing; somewhat superior to warm water in soil removal.

Temperature of "warm" setting in automatics. Suitable for silk and washable woolens, comfortable for hand washing. Provides no sanitizing; protects colors. Wrinkles manmade fabrics less than hot water.

Temperature of unheated water supply. For lightly soiled or thoroughly pretreated laundry. Use plenty of liquid detergent, a cold-water detergent, or a granular detergent dissolved in hot water before adding. Gives least cleaning, no sanitizing, minimum wrinkling of manmade fabrics, may not remove wear wrinkles.

water. This temperature also works well for washing lingerie that you do not want to put in very hot water.

The "warm" setting of an automatic washer usually controls temperature at about 100° F. Most automatic washers rinse with water at this temperature. In some cycles, and at the "cold" setting, cold water may be used.

Cold water (80° F. or less) is recommended only for lightly soiled items and fabrics and fibers that lose color, wrinkle, or shrink in hotter water.

For more information on the right temperature for various washing jobs, consult the water-temperature guide.

A WASHING PERIOD of 10 minutes is generally sufficient. It is certainly long enough if clothes have been soaked or pretreated. If a laundry load is not clean after this treatment, it probably needs a second washing in clean water and detergent. Many washer loads may not need a full 10-minute agitation. For lightly soiled wash-and-wear, and sheer, delicate fabrics, a 4-minute agitation may be adequate.

THOROUGH RINSING is essential for a bright, clean wash. Plenty of warm or cool rinse water and good agitation are are necessary to remove the detergent and soiled water left from washing.

Soft water insures good rinsing. If washing with soap in hard water, add a nonprecipitating water softener to the first rinse. By the end of the rinsing process rinse water should be fairly clear and have no feeling of slipperiness to the hand.

Many automatic washers completely fill the tub just once for the rinse and usually follow the fill with a continuous flow of fresh water. The fresh water mixes with and dilutes the soiled water remaining from washing, overflows the tub, and carries away loosened soil, detergent, and other washing agents that are drained away with the water via the pump.

In some automatic washers, sprays of water rinse the clothes several times during the spin from the washing process, before the tub refills, and again during the final spin. These sprays flush away suds and other loose material clinging to the fabric.

Automatic rinsing is generally satisfactory if the washer is in good working order and properly used. If you are not getting good rinsing in your automatic washer, you may be overloading your washer or adding too much detergent, or the extraction of the wash water may not be as effective as it should be. See that the spinning mechanism of the washer is in perfect working order.

FABRIC SOFTENERS are designed to do just what their name implies—make textiles soft and fluffy. They also reduce the static electricity that builds up on some fabrics when they rub against each other, and tend to minimize wrinkles and deep creases.

Softener is added to the final rinse water in proportion to the weight of clothes rather than the amount of rinse water. For best results, check the directions on the softener you buy and use accordingly.

Use softener each time you want fabrics softened because the effect is removed in the next washing. An overdose of softener may decrease the absorbency of fabrics.

ADVICE ON DRYING AND IRONING

ELECTRIC DRYERS are available for use on the regular 110/115-volt service of the home or for 220/230-volt service. The low-voltage dryer is considerably slower than the high-voltage dryer, but uses about the same amount of electrical energy. Either dryer should be on a separate circuit.

Gas dryers may be purchased with appropriate burners for use with natural, manufactured, mixed, or liquefied petroleum gas. They are generally more expensive to buy than similar electric models.

Gas and electric tumbler dryers are much alike in appearance and operation. Many manufacturers make models alike in shape, size, and controls—the only difference is in the fuel supplying the heat.

IF YOU ARE CONSIDERING whether to buy a gas or an electric dryer, the cost of operation may be the deciding factor. Fuel rates vary greatly across the country; the national average is used here only as an example of the calculation that provides a basis of comparison.

To dry an 8-pound load of clothes in an electric dryer requires approximately 4.4 kilowatt-hours of electricity. At $4.05 per 100 killowatt-hours, this current would cost 18 cents. A gas dryer would use about 13.6 cubic feet of gas to dry the same load of clothes. Natural gas at $7.21 per 100 therms would cost about 1 cent per load. The electric motor of the gas dryer uses approximately 0.3 kilowatt-hour of current per hour of operation to revolve the tumbler, which adds slightly to the cost. Use your local rates with the above consumption figures to calculate costs for your vicinity.

For a condenser-type dryer, in which cold water flows to dispose of moisture and lint, the cost of the water used in the moisture-condensing system has to be added to the cost of electricity. The condenser-type dryer is impractical in areas where the water supply is expensive or limited.

A TUMBLER DRYER saves the time and energy of transporting and hanging clothes, and completes the laundering process in a minimum of time—at any hour—in any weather. It also saves ironing time because many modern fabrics need little or no ironing after tumble drying.

Families with fast-growing children get more use of clothing before it is outgrown when a dryer is used because garments can be washed and dried and reworn more frequently within a given period of time.

During the seasons when pollen is abundant, laundry dried in a tumbler dryer indoors contains considerably less pollen than laundry dried outdoors. This is a definite advantage for persons allergic to pollen.

Most tumbler dryers can be used without heat to fluff pillows, table pads, and ironing pads and to freshen textile articles that have been in storage. Damp, but not dirty, stuffed toys, snowsuits, and mittens may be dried with heat in the dryer. If the load is very small, you can add a couple of bath towels to help the tumbling action.

Tumble drying, especially overdrying, makes most fabrics soft. Softness is an asset in bath towels, T-shirts, and diapers, but is not necessarily desirable in sheets, pillowcases, and table linen. For this reason, careful sorting may be necessary for drying, too. Articles that dry in about the same length of time can be combined in a load and the time regulated to give the desired result. Some modern dryers have moisture-sensing mechanisms that terminate drying when the desired moisture content is reached.

Although a good deal of lint is shed during drying and is collected where you can see it as you clean the lint trap after each dryer use, tumbling in a clothes dryer causes no greater loss of fabric strength than other drying methods.

There may be as much lint with other methods, but it is not apparent because it disappears in the air or clings to fabrics and comes off during subsequent handling and use.

Some fabrics shrink more in tumbling than in other drying methods. Loosely woven fabrics without shrinkage control are particularly susceptible. Knits may need to be purchased in larger sizes to allow for shrinkage in the dryer.

WITH A LITTLE PRACTICE and experimentation, you soon become familiar with the operation and performance of your dryer, and can load it and adapt settings to give the degree of dryness you want.

By careful sorting and timing you can make up a load of clothes and dry them until just enough moisture is left for ironing and thus save the work of dampening the clothes again. Some loads can be made up that do not need ironing, or that can be pressed without dampening.

The time required to tumble dry depends on—

• Heat and air circulation in the dryer.

• Moisture left in clothes after washing.

• Size of the load.

• Type of fabric. Minimum-care fabrics dry quickly, may need to be dried by themselves.

New colored articles may shed bits of colored lint on other fabrics in the first few dryings. For this reason, it may be a good idea to dry them with similar colors by themselves until the loose fibers are dislodged.

THE CONVENTIONAL METHOD of line drying outdoors in good weather costs little except the work involved and leaves the clothes with a fresh though fleeting odor.

Clothes hung outdoors should be brought inside as soon as they are dry because continued exposure, especially in sunlight, can cause fabric deterioration. The sun causes fading of some colors, and some fade even when hung in the shade.

Line drying indoors is slower than other methods but can be speeded up by increasing air circulation with an electric fan, by raising room temperature, and by installing a dehumidifier.

Drip drying minimizes the need for pressing articles and garments made of certain fabrics. For example, dripping may be the only way to handle a so-called permanently pleated skirt.

If drip-dried articles are a regular part of your laundering, a convenient, drained, well-ventilated area for drying is almost a necessity.

If you find that such articles require overall pressing, some other washing-drying combination is advised that is less trouble and that makes use of mechanical equipment. Complete machine washing and tumble drying is the easiest solution.

IRONING—the least-liked task of many homemakers—has been greatly simplified by modern equipment, laundry aids, and fabrics.

Temperature control is more important in ironing today than ever before. Some manmade fibers fuse onto a too-hot iron and leave a hole in the fabric and a messy iron soleplate. Dynel and Verel modacrylic fibers can be ironed only at a very low setting. Some irons do not operate at low enough temperature to iron these fabrics.

TO GIVE SATISFACTION, a hand dry iron should have—

• A rating of at least 1,000 watts.

• A smooth, scratch-resistant soleplate shaped to slip easily between buttons and into gathers.

• An easily grasped handle that is comfortable to hold.

• An insulated cord approved by Underwriters' Laboratories, Inc.

• A well-marked and easily adjusted thermostatic control.

• A weight of approximately 3 pounds for ease of handling.

Steam irons are of two types—the boiler type, in which all the water is heated to boiling before steam is available; and the flash type, in which steam is produced quickly as water drips from the iron's reservoir onto the hot interior surface. The steam-spray iron sprays a mist of moisture ahead of the iron when a control is pushed, in addition to the steam from the soleplate.

A steam iron should have all of the features specified for the dry iron, plus a reservoir that holds enough water (at least 1 cup) for a reasonable period of steam ironing and a water opening that is easily filled and is safe to empty when hot.

One iron that can be used either dry or with steam is more convenient than two separate irons, one for dry, and one for steam use. A combination dry-steam iron should be easily converted from dry to steam and vice versa.

If you have a variety of fabrics to be ironed, start with those that can be ironed at the lowest temperature and progress toward those that require the highest temperature.

The following order has been found satisfactory for ironing articles made of manmade and natural fibers without special finishes: Modacrylic; acrylic, Dacron polyester; triacetate; acetate; nylon, wool; Kodel polyester, rayon, silk; cotton; linen. How much you can adjust the thermostat upward from these settings depends partly on dampness of the fabric and speed of ironing.

A portable ironing table that can be adjusted to several heights is a good investment. You can move it to any part of the house—into a room where you can be company for a sick child or can view your favorite television program. On a hot day you can iron in the coolest room in the house.

The adjustable height feature is a convenience for persons of different statures who stand to iron. Some tables also adjust to comfortable height for sit-down ironing.

If you sit to do all or part of your ironing, a good posture chair will give you comfort and support.

FOR DAMPENING, a bottle that is easy to hold and is corked with a sprinkler top usually dispenses moisture more evenly then hand sprinkling. Atomizer sprinkling devices are also available.

Some dryers are equipped to dampen clothes. A measured amount of water, suited to the number and type of clothes to be sprinkled, is poured into a container provided for that purpose. The water is automatically dribbled over the dry clothes as they tumble in the dryer, usually without heat.

If some of the articles to be ironed are too damp or unevenly dry and some are too dry, roll them together and put them in a plastic bag or wrap them in a sheet of plastic for a few hours to equalize the moisture.

Dampened fabrics enclosed in a fairly tight wrapping to keep the moisture right for ironing may mildew if held too long. If dampened articles are to be held for ironing later, put them in the refrigerator or freezer or some other cold place. Low temperatures prevent germination of the mold spores that cause mildew. If no cold storage place is available, dry the articles and dampen them again the day you iron.

A rack on which ironed flat pieces can be hung to dry thoroughly before storage is a convenience. A hanging bracket that fits over the top of the nearest door or a rack for garments on hangers keeps clothes in good shape until they are folded or hung in closets. A small table or tray, placed nearby to hold small ironed pieces until you put them away, saves steps.

Other ironing aids may include—

• A sponge and small bowl of water for dampening too-dry spots.

• A bottle of distilled water or tap water (whichever your iron uses) and a funnel or cup with a pouring lip for filling and refilling the steam iron.

• A basket or container to hold unironed clothes within a comfortable reach.

• A vaporproof bag or a sheet of durable, pliable plastic sheeting (available by the yard in variety stores). Use the sheeting to protect the surface on which dampening is done and to fold tightly around the dampened articles to keep them damp until ironed.

Usually, table linens and untreated cottons and rayons require more moisture than a steam iron provides.

Ironing without added moisture is satisfactory for numerous manmade fabrics, some resin-finished fabrics, and some of the blends. It is relatively quick, saves sprinkling and waiting for added moisture to equalize through the clothes. No extra ironing is needed to dry out seams or multiple layers of fabric. For a good many items, a quick dry pressing is all that is needed to make them flat for storage.

BUYING YOUR SEWING MACHINE

THE PURCHASE of a sewing machine for home use is a lifetime investment. Machines of reputable manufacture are built to last for many years, with only minor replacement of inexpensive parts. The cleaning, oiling, and adjusting of machines are within the ability of any homemaker and are the major maintenance necessary for continued good service.

Today's choice of machines gives a wide range to fit the purchaser's needs and purse. It is often a bit confusing to make a decision. Your present needs may change as the family grows or the children leave to establish their own homes. No one machine is likely to have all the features you consider desirable, so a compromise is in order in selecting the machine that you consider best suited to your present and possible future needs.

PART OF YOUR DECISION should be made at home before looking at different makes of machines.

The first point to settle is the kind of sewing for which you are buying the machine. Many homemakers use their machines only for occasional plain sewing, for patching, mending, or darning, or for the making of simple garments. For this work a straight-sewing machine is satisfactory. This type may be preferred by the woman whose chief interest is fine dressmaking and tailoring and who has little use for machine-made decorative effects.

The more versatile swing-needle or zigzag-type machines are designed to handle a wider range in stitch styles and such speciality sewing as decorative stitching and embroidery; the making of place mats and napkins, decorative blouses and children's clothes; and seam finishing and buttonholes. These machines, in part, do the jobs intended for the attachments that can be bought for the straight-sewing machines— and which are so seldom used. Your decision here is whether the specialty job will be done often enough to warrant the added cost.

ANOTHER CHOICE is between cabinet and portable machines. A cabinet with well-supported leaves and sturdy legs gives good sewing support and is ready for instant use. There are many cabinets to choose from for any one machine head. Since its main purpose is to house the machine, choose the cabinet for com-

fort, sturdiness, and convenience. A machine in a permanent cabinet or table is more convenient and time-saving for anyone who does much sewing. The extra cost of a fancy cabinet may better be invested in useful furniture. However, choices in cabinets allow a selection that will fit in with any type of home furnishing.

The portable is the usual choice where space is limited, as in small homes and apartments, or where a machine must often be moved from place to place. Some portables are fitted with an extension table for greater work surface; all can be set into a sturdy worktable flush with the top to give the same stability and work area as cabinet machines. Some portables are merely the regular, heavy sewing head sometimes inadequately wired and set into a cheap, heavy, and unwieldy carrying case; but portables can be purchased with lightweight construction and with base and carrying case designed for the machine—sturdy and well finished. The choice between lightweight and regular-head portables depends partly on how much bulky sewing or mending of heavy fabrics will be done. Does the space between the bed and the arm of the machine allow space to handle bulky articles? If you need to move a portable machine often, can you lift it comfortably from the floor to the table?

A PERSONAL INSPECTION of a variety of machines will help you decide on the one best suited to your purpose. Visit your friends and neighbors, and the dealers, and check the features of one machine against another. You want to choose a machine that is easy to handle and operate, is readily adjusted to your varying sewing needs, and is easy to care for and keep in perfect running order.

You may have a choice between the long-shuttle machines and the round-bobbin types. The long-shuttle mechanism is simple and direct, usually easier and quicker to clean and oil, but noisier and not designed for as high-speed operation as the round-bobbin class. Unless especially balanced, these machines are not well adapted to electric motors. The round-bobbin machines are either oscillating or rotary. They are usually smoother in operation and better balanced for higher speed.

The following points are offered as a guide in making your comparison.
Look for easy-to-use features.

• Is the upper tension setting shown by markings that are easy to see?

• Is the upper thread tension released when the presser foot is raised?

• Does the lamp throw light where you need it?

• Is the lamp placed so that it will not burn you during the normal use of the machine, for instance, when raising the presser foot?

• Is the stitch-length control scale easy to read?

• Are there adjustable lock positions for the forward and reverse stitching control?

• Will the machine stitch backwards?

• Is there a quick release mechanism for darning and embroidery?

• Is there a footrest on the electric foot control?

Try out the machines for good operation.

• Is the machine quiet and free from objectionable noise and vibration?

• Does the machine run smoothly at all speeds?

• Is the knee or foot control comfortable for you to use?

• Does the motor start smoothly, providing easy starting as well as slow running?

• Is the machine easy for you to thread?

• Is the bobbin easy to take out and put back?

• Is the bobbin easy for you to thread?

• Try the machine on some of your own materials, both straight and curved seems. Is it easy to guide when stitching curved seams?

• Notice whether the material has a tendency to drift to right or left, whether one layer of material tends to creep over the other during sewing. Does the machine satisfy you in these respects?

• Is the bobbin winder easy to use and does it fill the bobbin evenly?

Check on adjustments.

• Is the bottom tension conveniently located and easy to adjust?

• Are the tension adjustments clearly explained in the instruction book?

• Is the stitch-length control easy to set?

• Can the feed dog be dropped?

• Is the control easy to get to?

• If the feed dog cannot be dropped, does the machine have a special cover plate for darning and embroidery?

SEWING MACHINE LIGHTS help when threading and using a machine. They do not provide enough illumination for regular sewing and should be supplemented by a good local light such as a floor lamp. Often the kind of sewing machine lamp, its position, and the type of paint finish on the machine, combine to reflect sufficient light to produce an objectionable glare. Frosted lamp bulbs, diffusing covers for the lamp, or a choice of paint finish, can help reduce this glare.

MACHINES FINISHED with a smooth, glossy surface are easiest to keep clean, but light reflections may prove annoying. Some manufacturers recognize the effect of color on eyestrain and finish their machines in green, brown, or tan. Others use a crackle surface to prevent glare, but this may reflect many points of light as disturbing as the glare from a gloss finish.

CONSIDERATIONS GIVEN to buying a new machine also apply to secondhand or rebuilt machines. Knowing the dealer is reputable is even more important, however, because the machine is not new. Many of the secondhand machines of the foot-treadle type can be motorized at a small cost. It is best not to motorize a machine if it vibrates when foot-treadled at high speeds.

MOST STRAIGHT-SEWING MACHINES can be fitted with attachments such as the one for buttonholes that shifts the cloth from side to side, creating a zigzag stitch. The zigzag sewing machine swings the needle bar from side to side,

Blank circles have been used to show the appropriate location of some of the important parts, because the design of the machines and the parts vary so greatly.

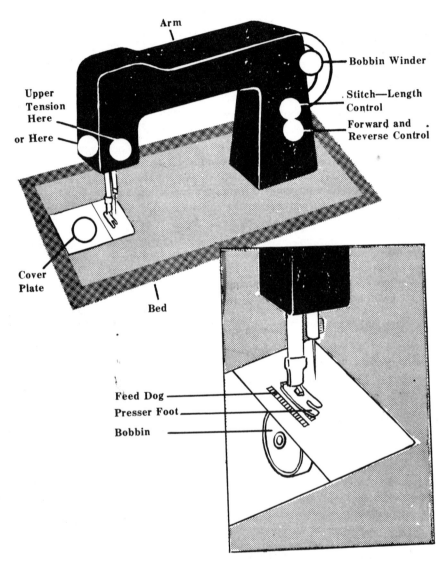

producing a stitch that can be used for a wide variety of effects. Most of these machines swing the needle to both sides of the center sewing line, while a few move only to the right or to the left. A greater variety of decorative stitches is possible when the needle swings to both right and left. Skill in operation is required to develop a uniform pattern or design with the controls operated by hand. Many machines are built to use templates which automatically produce distinctive patterns. Although these machines are considered automatic, it requires a complete knowledge of the machine to utilize its varied operations. When purchasing a zigzag machine, test it for a good straight stitch and the ease of switching from straight to zigzag stitching.

Swing needle machines vary greatly in their versatility. Be sure that the machine you select can produce the designs you want.

THERE ARE TWO TYPES of motor controls used with sewing machines—the step control and the carbon control. The step control changes the speed in a series of steps or jumps, usually 5 to 8, from slow speed to fast speed. With some machines the first step of this type of control does not provide the slow speed required at times in sewing operations. The carbon control increases the speed from slow to fast smoothly and uniformly, resulting in easier control of speed, especially when starting and at very slow speeds.

KNOW YOUR DEALER. Has he a reputation for giving good service? Most dealers who sell sewing machines offer some form of guarantee and free service agreement. The guarantee protects the buyer against the possibility of inferior or defective parts, or concealed damage, for varying periods of time after purchase. The free service period also places the responsibility on the seller to correct any defect in adjustment or parts other than normal wear at no charge.

These agreements *should be in writing and signed by an agent who has satisfactory credentials.* Verbal agreements are unsatisfactory because they may be impossible to prove or because the exact sense of such agreements depends upon memory.

HANDY TOOLS

THE JOBS you plan to do, the money you wish to spend, and storage space are matters to consider when you buy tools.

Buy tools of good quality. Premium-quality tools are not necessary, but very cheap tools, especially edge tools, such as saws and chisels, often are unsatisfactory.

Usually it is wise to rent costly tools that you use only occasionally.

Keep your tools in good condition. The teeth of a crosscut saw should be nearly as sharp as a needle. Keep chisel and plane irons nearly razor sharp. If you lack the ability or equipment to sharpen tools, have a skilled craftsman do it for you.

Keep your tools clean. Dry metal tools to prevent rust. Put a light coat of oil on sharp-edged tools, such as saws and planes, before storing—especially if they are kept in a place that may be damp.

Tools and equipment should be stored as close as possible to the site of frequent use. The crate opener, jar and can openers, scissors, ruler or yardstick, screwdriver, and pliers, for example, may be kept in a drawer or closet in the kitchen, workroom, or utility room.

A carrier for cleaning supplies may be used to carry cleaning supplies or tools needed for jobs of household maintenance. When not in use, it may be stored with the other cleaning supplies, polishes, waxes, or tools.

Store other larger and less frequently used tools in one common area. Duplicate items of the more frequently used tools, such as screwdrivers and pliers, also are stored there. Storage in one specific place makes it easier to find the desired tool.

Well-planned storage also provides protection for the sharp edges of cutting tools and protects the user from accidentally cutting himself on one tool while reaching for the other.

Cutting edges of saws, auger bits, planes, chisels, and rasps should be protected so they will not bump or come in contact with other metal. They should be stored so that other tools will not fall on them and they will not fall on anything else.

The storage area may be simple or elaborate, as determined by space, in-

TOOLS FOR HANDYMAN AND HANDYWOMAN
FOR HOUSEHOLD OPERATION, MAINTENANCE, AND REPAIR

If you plan to do—	Minimum equipment	Desirable equipment	Supplementary equipment
Household or kitchen activities:			
open crates and boxes..........	crate opener or pry bar or 8″ screwdriver.	12 or 13 oz. claw hammer.	
open jars, can, etc............	jar and can openers.	combination opener.	
cut cardboard............	scissors and paring knife.	utility knife.	
lubricate appliances, locks, hinges, etc.	high-grade oil suitable for small appliances.	powdered graphite. graphite in oil.	
measure and space items.......	ruler or yardstick or good-quality measuring tape.	6′–10′ steel tape or folding rule.	25′ or 50′ tape.
attach items to walls..........	paste-on tabs for light items. hangers with nails or screws for heavier items:	Hollow-wall screw anchors and toggle bolts:	For masonry or concrete: screw anchors and screws.
	12 or 13 oz. curved claw hammer.	hand or electric drill and twist drills ¼″ and up.	proper size star drill or electric drill and tungsten carbide masonry drill.
	hand drill and bits. screwdrivers.	stud locator.	
level items.................	pan of water to level appliances. string with attached weight.	level as part of combination square.	9″–12″ level.
Small repair jobs:			
tighten or loosen screws.......	4″ and 6″ screwdrivers. Nos. 1 and 2 Phillips screwdrivers.	hex wrenches. special screwdrivers and wrenches.	ratchet screwdriver.
tighten nuts or hold small items.	6″–7″ slip joint pliers. adjustable wrench.	locking-type wrench pliers. needle-nose pliers.	open-end and box-end wrenches.
drive or pull nails, etc........	12 or 13 oz. curved claw hammer. 6″ screwdriver.	hand stapler. pry bar.	staple gun. tack puller.
repair plastic items..........	plastic mending tape.	liquid mender for type of plastic.	plastic repair kit with strips and adhesive.
seal openings and joints........	special sealants and tapes.	calking gun.	
replace ordinary faucet washers.	adjustable wrench. screwdrivers.	tape or cloth to place between wrench and polished fitting.	
open drains and pipes.........	force cup.	small wire. putty knife.	flexible drain auger. glass cutter.
other minor jobs............	packaging material and string. polishes and waxes. cleaning supplies and equipment. step stool.	vacuum cleaner. stepladder.	fabric mending and fastening kits.
Small jobs with wood:			
measure and mark..........	sharp pointed No. 2½ or 3 common pencil.	8″ by 12″ utility, steel combination, or try square.	dividers, rafter or framing square.

(NOTE.—Operations are listed in their usual sequence.)

cut wood	ruler or yardstick. tablet back or drawing triangle may serve as a square. pencil compass. coping saw. friction vise or bench hook to hold wood.	6' to 10' steel tape or folding rule. 20″–22″, 10–11 point hand saw. two 4″ C-clamps.	hand ripsaw. miter box. electric hand and sabre saws. jack or smoothing plane. electric sander.
smoothen wood (may be repeated after assembly)	fine, medium, and coarse sandpaper. sandpaper block.	block plane, or multiblade wood smoothing tool. rasps and scraper.	
assemble pieces into unit	assorted sizes of wire nails and brads. 12 to 13 oz. curved claw hammer. 7/16″ nail set. 6d nails. white glue (not moisture resistant).	wood screws. countersink. 4″ and 6″ screwdrivers. hand drill with drills and bit brace with bits or light duty electric drill with bits. nails with heads cut off may be used as small drills. urea or plastic resin glue (moisture resistant).	gluing clamps. 8″ or stub screwdriver. assorted sizes of common, finish, and special nails. set of combination drill and counter-sink bits for use with screws. resorcinol glue (waterproof).
fill holes in wood:			
nail holes	colored putty.		
larger holes	wood dough, plastic wood, or surfacing putty.	spackling compound for surfaces to be painted.	
finish wood	see other chapters.		
Work with metals:			
measure and mark	see measure and mark wood.	see measure and mark wood.	metal scribe.
cut	utility saw or keyhole-type hack-saw.	tin snips. 3/8″ cold chisel. vise. hacksaw with set of blades.	power grinder and safety goggles.
drill holes	hand drill with twist drills.	light-duty electric drill with a set of twist drills.	high-speed drill bits desirable for frequent heavy use.
smoothen or sharpen	8″ mill file. sharpening stone.	8″ half round file. 8″ round file.	emery cloth. grinder and safety goggles.
assemble	4″ and 6″ screwdrivers. Nos. 1 and 2 Phillips screwdrivers. 6″–7″ slip-joint pliers.	locking-type wrench pliers. adjustable wrench.	small sets of open-end and box-end wrenches.
polishing		emery and crocus cloths.	
repairing	epoxy resin.	epoxy resin and fiber glass.	soldering equipment.

terest, and finances.

Providing ample storage space should be the first step. Pegboard or shelves installed in an existing area or closet may be the simplest arrangement. A specially built tool cabinet could very well be an improvement.

A workbench is a practical means to provide both a work area and storage facilities. Hip height is a comfortable and practical height for the workbench top unless you plan to do a great deal of hand planing. In that event, it may be well to build it a little lower.

Light the workbench with fluorescent fixtures placed over the front of the bench and 48 inches above the work, or use an incandescent 150-watt silvered-bowl bulb in a 12- to 14-inch-diameter metal reflector.

Keep all instruction books and warranties with your important household records and papers. However, some people may wish to keep some instruction books in the workshop. In that event, protect them from damage.

BASIC POINTS
OF LANDSCAPING

WE KEEP several basic details in mind when we undertake landscaping—the overall plan, balance, orientation, scale, soils, ecology, plant material, texture, three dimensions, restraint, and repetition. Patience, too.

Ideally, the overall plan should be drawn when the building is being designed, so the building and grounds may be planned as a single, interrelated unit by a qualified landscape architect and an architect.

We say this over and over, but still many owners are left with a building on bare ground. They still have the task of forming a happy relationship between ground and architecture.

In Japan one can observe a more desirable method of planning. The Japanese design and build the structure and garden at one time, because they consider the garden as important as the structure. The result is a complete harmony.

Balance is essential in landscape designing. Balance may be symmetrical (or formal) or asymmetrical (or informal).

Formal—symmetrical—balance is the easier for most Americans, because we have lived more with it than with informal balance. Many of the European gardens with which we are familiar typify formal balance. The garden of Versailles is an outstanding example. Some of the American gardens in Williamsburg are noteworthy.

In this type of balance, an axis extends down the center. Whatever is placed on one side is duplicated exactly on the other. Frequently plants are clipped, lines are straight, and edges are clearly defined. Sometimes there are retaining walls and different levels.

Informal—asymmetrical—balance is a little more difficult for most persons of European ancestry and experience to express. Many Japanese gardens exemplify this subtle form, but it is more easily observed in Ikebana—flower arranging.

Although both sides of an imaginary axis are in balance with each other, informal balance is accomplished by deliberately leaving some elements unequal in form, color, size, or position.

The natural look of the unclipped plants, curved lines, obscure and merging edges, and natural contours identify asymmetry in the garden.

Some pleasing effects are achieved in modern gardens by the combination of formal and informal balance.

ORIENTATION also is highly important.

If you have a voice in the placing of your house, you probably will consider the orientation of the planting as well.

The placing of the structure depends on the site, the neighborhood, the existing zoning laws, the climate, and the need for privacy.

Planting is determined more by climate and a desire for privacy.

If you build in a section where the afternoon sun is intense in summer, you must think of some shade for the western exposure by choosing sun-loving plants. Some plants thrive in a sunny southern exposure. Others prefer shade. Since most plants like at least a little sun each day, however, a place north of the structure will not do for a colorful, varied garden.

Keep in mind that the plants you select ought to be in character and in scale with the building and with each other for interest.

The ultimate use of the area is decisive in the selection of plants. Is the area to be used by babies, or teenagers, or young adults, or elderly persons? If, for example, babies and old people will visit the area, you would hesitate to use plants with thorns, but such plants may be useful for restricting or confining purposes in another situation.

SCALE of the plant does not necessarily mean its size at the time of purchase, but the ultimate height and spread it will attain in the future.

In the small garden, plants as a rule should be kept to a minimum number. Their leaf texture should be medium to fine. Their growth habits should be compact.

Let me illustrate the use of scale by assuming that you live in a small, one-story house. The most natural solution would be for you to plant a medium-sized tree that grows to about 30 feet as the main accent to the house. That would be in scale.

If you were to choose a tree that grows to about 15 feet, your house would appear much larger than it really is. If you chose a tall shade tree, one that grows to about 120 feet, your house would look like a dollhouse.

By your choice of scale you can create various illusions or effects. You must decide which one you wish to achieve, for, especially if it is distorted, the effect should be planned and not the result of a mistake.

YOU SHOULD CONSIDER the type of soil with which you must work before you choose your plants.

The soil may be acid, sweet (alkaline), sandy (well drained), clay (poorly drained), or swampy. A bit of reading in garden books will tell you that most plants have preferences for a certain type of soil and show inclinations to grow with wet or dry feet. Usually, however, you need not reproduce exactly the original conditions under which they grew.

Ecology is concerned with plants as neighbors in Nature. You can see their relationship when you drive in the country. If you keep this natural association in mind and try to combine plants that originated under the same conditions of light, shade, mois-

ture, soil, and so on, you will achieve unity more easily and your garden will be more successful. This does not mean, however, that the observance of ecology is mandatory for success.

Although the type of soil (or the ecology) sometimes limits the use of certain plants, there are some plants for almost every kind of situation. Choose them carefully.

DECIDUOUS PLANTS, which lose their leaves in winter, offer much beauty in the way of flowers, fruit, and color, which change with the seasons. They are lovely and interesting not only when they are in leaf, but, if you choose carefully for their structure, they can contribute beauty of shape and outline in winter.

The conifers, the needled evergreens, usually are dark green, but at times their shade of green is more on the blue or yellow side. Perhaps because of their silhouette or because the needles absorb rather than reflect light, they strongly accent the garden, and should be selected wisely. For a more dramatic effect, they usually should be used with deciduous material and broad-leaved evergreens.

The broad-leaved evergreens appear to be lighter green than the conifers, perhaps because they reflect light and often have shiny leaves. Rhododendrons, azaleas, and hollies are examples.

Again, for best results, try to combine the three types of woody plants—deciduous plants, conifers, and broad-leaved evergreens.

REMEMBER texture also.

Texture may be fine, medium, or coarse, with gradations in each. The texture of a plant may vary at different times of year.

For example, in winter, when you see only its structure of thick and heavy branches and twigs, a deciduous plant may appear coarse. It may appear medium in summer, when it is covered with medium-sized leaves, and fine when it is in bloom if its blossoms are small.

You get the best results when you combine different textures of leaves and branches. Otherwise, you achieve only monotony.

ANOTHER WAY to avoid monotony is to work in three dimensions. Consider the plant material from the top of the tallest shade tree down to the ground material. Sound selections insure an interesting, attractive, and natural-looking planting.

First, decide on the large tree to complement your building. Suppose you choose a tulip tree, *Liriodendron tulipifera;* a sweetgum, *Liquidambar styraciflua;* or a plane tree, *Platanus occidentalis,* which would tend to join your garden and the sky sympathetically.

Next you will want to plant an understory tree or large shrub, one that has horizontal, rather than upright or drooping, branching habits, and grows naturally under other trees. It may be the flowering dogwood, *Cornus florida;* doublefile viburnum, *Viburnum tomentosum;* or western dogwood, *Cornus nuttali.*

Near and under the understory tree, you can plant evergreen or broad-leaved evergreen shrubs, perhaps rhododendrons, azaleas, or leucothoe.

Finally a layer of ground cover, such as ivy, *Hedera helix,* or myrtle, *Vinca minor,* will give the finishing touch to your garden and also tie it to the ground.

According to this system, you will have at least four different levels to attract the eye.

If you build in a locality where you must forgo the tall shade tree and the understory tree, by all means consider constructing an overhead arbor or trellis as a substitute. It also will achieve the desired three-dimensional effect.

RESTRAINT is a good principle. If you plan to construct supplementary buildings, the materials you choose for them should be well coordinated with your original building. Use as few different types of materials as possible.

The same principle applies to the use of plant materials. One reason for restraint is that you are dealing with living, growing, ever-changing materials, all of which must have room to develop.

It is better to use too few materials than too many, and it is wise to repeat some of the same plants, the same texture, the same color, or various tones of the same color in different parts of the garden.

Restraint will help unify your garden by making it rhythmic and harmonious. Your application of restraint, like the use of repetition, however, should never be carried so far as to make all your plants a uniform size, texture, and color. Try to vary the height of the plants. Try to use at least three of the textures and either two complementary or two contrasting colors and their tones.

Do not forget that living things require food, water, and maintenance (some more than others). Plants have their likes and dislikes, just as they have their own characteristics and life-span. It takes time to make a garden. The finest gardens have taken years to develop. The most fundamental precept of all, therefore, is patience.

FACTS ABOUT FENCES

THE GOLDEN RULE applies to fences, too, and you will do well to talk over your plans for them with your neighbors. They will see and like or dislike the fences you build, as you do theirs.

Neighborly consultation will help you have a fence that is functional and attractive (the main points in selecting its style and appearance) and suited to the neighborhood and your landscaping.

Fences of straight, prim, formal lines go with formal landscaping or must be softened with shrubs or shadow lines in the design to make them blend better into an informal setting.

Wood, masonry, and steel fences may be used informally in many ways to increase the attractiveness of the landscape.

You can be imaginative as well as practical when you fence your residential lot.

Solid fences for screening usually are 5 feet 6 inches to 6 feet 6 inches high. Because the lengths are short, cost is not a major factor. An attractive fence that hides trash, provides privacy for outdoor living, or adds living space to your property may add to the value of your house.

If a wall needs to be ventilated so as not to shut off breezes, yet must be screened solidly, wood in basketweave, alternate side covered or of a louvered design, serves its purpose and is attractive. Masonry can be designed for this purpose by alternating airholes 2 to 4 inches wide.

Enameled-steel strips woven into steel chain link fences produce decorative patterns and give solid visual screening.

Fences with straight lines may be too formal to suit the landscaping around houses set in a natural landscape—woods, rock gardens, and ungraded sites. Screening fences to fit such sites may be built of rustic timber, cobblestone, or rubble masonry.

Open fences for boundary lines usually are 2 feet 6 inches to 3 feet 6 inches high. Materials of construction and design should fit into the landscape plan. Cost is also a factor in the lengths required for large lots.

Many people like the old rail-type fences. Few city lots are big enough to let land use be taken up by a zigzag rail fence, but mortise and tenoned split-rail fences may give a pleasing antique look.

If fence boards are to be painted, they should be treated with pentachlorophenol or an equivalent preservative that will not bleed through the paint. Apply two liberal brush coats of pentachlorophenol to the ends of all boards and to all parts where wood touches wood and may leave a crack that may retain moisture.

Posts and wood in contact with the ground should be impregnated with a preservative like creosote or pentachlorophenol applied at the rate of 6 pounds per cubic foot of wood. Forcing the preservative into the wood under pressure is the usual way to get this level of impregnation. When purchasing the wood for your fence, check with the dealer to see that the preservative has been applied.

Ordinary mild steel corrodes quickly in the open air. Steel fences therefore must be treated to resist corrosion.

They may be made of corrosion-resisting alloys, but the best of the alloys, stainless steel, is too high priced for consideration as fencing. Manufacturers therefore coat the wire with a corrosion-resistant material—zinc, aluminum, or plastic resins. The durability of zinc or aluminum coating is greater for greater thickness of coating.

A steel wire coated with 2.7 ounces of zinc per square foot of surface may be expected to be uncorroded after 16 years in an industrial atmosphere. Comparable life for a wire with 0.4 ounce or no coating of zinc would be 9 years and 5 years.

A steel wire with 0.24 ounce per square foot of aluminum on the surface of the wire has a life of 35 years under the same conditions.

Vinyl resin jacketing of 6 to 10 mils thickness produces a colorful chain link fence. The mechanical wear resistance of the coating has not yet been fully evaluated. Vinyl resins melt at temperatures above 180°F.

Permanent fencing on productive farmland often is made with a combination of woven wire and barbed wire. Woven wire is packaged in 20-rod (330 feet) rolls. The size of woven wire is designated by two numbers—the number of horizontal wires (line wires) and the height of the fence in inches. For example, fence 939 has 9 line wires and is 39 inches high. The vertical wires (stay wires) may be 12 or 6 inches apart.

Bracing of corners, ends, and long runs of fences is important. Suspension-type fences should be braced every 80 rods (one-fourth mile) by placing posts 8 feet apart with a horizontal compression strut between them and an X-bracing of 9-gage galvanized wire twisted to tension the brace assembly.

Double-corner braces are serviceable when they are properly aligned and set firmly. Firmly tamped corner posts set with the bottom 3 feet below the ground surface will be rigid enough in most soils.

BACKYARD— OR GARDEN?

THE AMERICAN BACKYARD usually is just that and no more.

In new housing developments it may be a bit of lawn next to another bit of lawn: Montony.

In older neighborhoods, there may be a few trees, a flowerbed, a vegetable patch, play equipment, a bench: Hodge-podge.

We Americans do not appreciate the true meaning and importance of *garden*. A garden to most of us is a patch of worked earth, a gesture of petunias in front, and a rose or two in back.

But *garden* is a larger, more important concept. A garden, said Garrett Eckbo, an American landscape architect, is outdoor space around private homes, enclosed for the use and pleasure of the family. A garden is an extension of indoor living space into the out-of-doors.

We create a garden in the full sense if we apply some of the principles of organizing indoor living space to organizing outdoor space. We also make use of otherwise wasted or misused space.

Backyards need only to be planned to become gardens.

Gardens need some sort of walls, just as houses do.

Indoors, walls are solid and have openings for doors and windows. Draperies, paintings, bookshelves, light brackets, tapestries, and decorative panels are hung on them for variation. Even when wall is treated as wall, it usually is painted, papered, paneled, or otherwise altered to create background for objects.

To create an outdoor living space—a garden—we use shrub borders (a single line of one kind of shrub is better than a conglomeration of different kinds), hedges, fences, and building walls to create an enclosure for garden space and provide some privacy. Unlike indoor walls, however, the outdoor walls need not be continuous, nor need they be completely limiting.

If you wish to create an outdoor living space in a corner lot, for example, it is necessary to use a fairly solid fence or hedge to cut out the view of passers-by on the side street. It becomes a restricting wall.

But if you live at the edge of an open meadow or field or by the edge of a woodland or park, the view would contribute so much to your enjoyment that you would not want to block it off. If there is no public intrusion, there would be no reason to do so. The pleasant view in itself, then, becomes a part of your garden wall, unrestricting and indefinite though it may be.

Just as indoor walls serve as background for paintings and furniture, so the outdoor walls can serve as background for a handsome shrub, bright flowers, a specimen evergreen.

NEW HOMEOWNERS often start landscaping with flowers, but they do not succeed because most flowers, beautiful as they are, are so fragile as an element in design that they need background structure.

To clarify the point: Try to visualize the difference between a handsome desk or chest standing in the middle of the living room (as when you are in the process of moving into a house) and how much more effective it is against a wall that complements its color and shape. The wall provides the strong structural background the chest needs.

If you keep that vision in mind when you plant roses, tulips, or zinnias, you will find that organizing a garden is not so difficult, either.

Indoor floors may be wood, stone, carpeting, or composition of some sort. Garden floors are made of many materials, some of which we walk on and some of which we do not. Paving stones, concrete, brick, wooden decks, gravel, smoothly mowed lawn are practical and durable garden floors comparable to the ones indoors.

On the other hand, in gardens we also have flooring materials that provide only variation in texture, color, and pattern and are not meant to be walked on.

Evergreen ground cover and beds of low-growing plants provide rich texture or color and are used much as a brightly colored small rug is used indoors to focus attention in a certain place and provide additional interest. With these special carpets outdoors, however, seasonal change enters the picture and adds much to the challenge of planning outdoor space for year-round enjoyment.

Garden ceilings are even less confining than garden walls, but they exist. The sky itself, the most important ceiling, is the source of sunlight, which plants need, as do we for psychological and physical health.

But because we also need protection from sunshine at times, we plant trees, whose overhanging limbs become a garden ceiling, too.

Arbors, trellises, awnings, and other overhead enclosures are other ceilings.

A porch is a part of garden space (it is more outdoor living space than indoor), so its solid roof becomes a part of the garden ceiling, too.

Once the relationship of floor, walls, and ceiling in outdoor space is understood, organizing your property for the use, pleasure, and comfort of your family becomes relatively easy.

FIRST, get a plan or a map of your property down on paper.

No matter how poorly you draw or how limited your understanding of mechanics, you ought to be able to make an understandable plan of your property as it exists now.

A fairly accurate plan of the house floor plan is important, because in planning your outdoor living room you windows from various rooms, too.

Perhaps your plan shows the location of the kitchen sink under the window. If your sink has a window over it, why not plan something lovely to look at when you stand there? The hours spent at the kitchen sink will be easier if a flowering tree (maybe one that has bright leaves in autumn and a bird feeder in winter) or a handsome evergreen with a birdhouse and a spring family of wrens is seen through the window—these things add pleasure to everyday activities.

The second step is the analysis of the property on the plan you have already drawn. If you use a red pencil for the undesirable features and a green for the desirable ones (which you will want to keep), it will be easier to separate each when you come to the planning stage.

Once you start analyzing your lot, you will find several features that you will wonder how you have put up with, but you will also find some that are really on the plus side of your landscaping ledger and that maybe you have not even noticed before. This is an eye-opening experience.

In your analysis, use symbols to denote features or problems or make notes. You are the only one who needs to understand the final plan; use whatever notation comes to mind.

Once you have proceeded this far, it is simply a matter of doing something about the problem spots and making the best use of the good features.

How TO ACHIEVE the most pleasurable results from a small space?

In one word: *Planning*.

Planned backyards become gardens.

Well-planned gardens add to the richness of your environment, extend indoor living space outside, use what often is wasted space, and give you a place for dining, reading, entertaining, and taking a Sunday afternoon nap.

PLANNING FOR A PATIO

ONCE UPON A TIME, a terrace was what you called a sloping lawn. Even if your lawn didn't slope, you didn't sit on it (that was what front porches were for). Nor did you sit in the backyard. That's where the kids played, except on wash days. Eating outside took place when you carted baskets to a more or less remote picnic spot. And, if any cooking was part of these occasions, it consisted of hot dogs and marshmallows stuck on sticks and roasted over a small fire.

The *good* old days? Hardly, when you compare the fun we discovered as we played outdoors and put our own property to enjoyable use. Everyone loves it because warm weather chores become blissfully easier with an outdoor living room for entertaining and for family meals, too.

A GOOD IDEA is to plan your outdoor living spaces as though they were roofless rooms.

Plan them so members of your family can use them now and later, when they will need space for new activities. Undeveloped space in the beginning will be useful in the future.

Use is the key. People plan rooms for use, not just as backgrounds for furnishings. By the same token, it is a mistake to place too much emphasis on landscaping an outdoor room and not enough on its present and future use. The consequence is that more time is spent maintaining the outdoor areas than enjoying them.

Another error is to use too many plants and too many of the kind that spread into space intended for people. Tall, dense plants are good sound barriers; they belong in the background.

Neither a room nor a patio, furthermore, should be so cluttered or indefinite in purpose and function that getting it ready for use becomes a discouraging chore.

Your climate determines more or less what you do outdoors and how often you use your outdoor areas. Let me suggest some uses, based on the relation between indoor and outdoor "rooms."

IF YOU LIVE in a contemporary house without an entry hall, an entrance patio will shield your front door from the street.

It is smaller and less elaborate than the front patios of the Spanish-style houses. A masonry wall, structural panels or vertical louvers to head height, and paving are essential.

Potted plants are attractive during the growing season. Evergreens do well in the shade and give this patio an all-season look.

THE LIVING PATIO, a quiet place for relaxation, extends the living room for informal hospitality.

It may be one to three times the size of a living room. An irregular shape can be interesting and useful. Small patios, 300 to 400 square feet, generally are more useful if the surface is paved.

If the living patio is twice the size of a living room, or larger, it may have a plot of grass, but a generous amount of paving is desirable. Paving makes it usable when the ground is damp. In larger patios, a shelter with screening for privacy and a windbreak is pleasant and useful.

Select plants that mature to an appropriate size for the space that is allotted to them. Specimen plants add interest because of their form, foliage, or color. Evergreens and nonplant materials, such as rocks, give an all-season appearance. Annuals and potted plants add color. Outdoor furniture and built-in seats are ready to use. Additional chairs should be stored nearby. If there is a tree, put a square or circular seat around its trunk.

For a swimming pool in a living patio, allow at least 800 square feet. Concrete decking, in a color that reduces glare, adds to the appearance of the patio. Grass in front of the pool and evergreen shrubbery or trees back of it make a good setting. Short walls that form sheltered corners on the patio side are useful and attractive.

If you include a pool, design the living patio so that it is not accessible to uninvited persons. Remember that a pool may entail legal responsibilities and liabilities, about which you should find out.

A living patio convenient to the kitchen may be used for dining. If it is on the opposite side of the house, you may want to reserve a terrace near the kitchen and equip it for outdoor cooking and eating.

Portable charcoal braziers provide amply for most patio cooking and are more popular than outdoor fireplaces in many new homes. Food that is prepared in the kitchen may be served from a buffet table indoors.

THE MULTIPURPOSE PATIO may change its name during the family cycles. It may begin as an unassigned plot on the back of your lot. It should be accessible to an alley or side driveway. A double carport size is minimum space.

Without grass, it is a good place for children to play. If so, enclose it with a high wall or permanent fence that cannot be climbed and a drive-through gate.

Later, this patio is a safe place for children to pitch a tent and cook out. It meets the requirements of a puppy yard, rabbit hutches, or a pigeon loft. When an interest in animals has passed, it can be a place to remodel an old car or drydock the family boat. Sometime it may become a garden. Vines on the fence will provide some privacy. Put a bench in the shade for adults.

A UTILITY PATIO is a workshop.

It is a good place for a shelter for garden tools and supplies, a portable brazier, fireplace wood, the stepladder, outdoor furniture, and sports and camping equipment. It should be convenient to the kitchen entrance, the carport, and, if possible, to the outdoor living area. An area 20 feet by 24 feet is ample for it.

The craftsman in the family has a place here for a workbench and lumber. The gardener may like a potting bench.

An 8-foot extension of the carport roof gives protection. Vertical board or plastic siding on the ends keeps out the sun and rain. It costs less to protect an area with the long side open than it costs to build storage cabinets. A concrete slab raised a few inches above ground level is desirable under the roof.

The open area is a good place for a drying line.

If a homesite is selected because there is a wooded area, distant hills, or a stream, the view should be featured in the development of a terrace. It is especially nice when patios are active and noisy. Trees and shrubbery can hide an unattractive foreground. Such a terrace may be a few steps higher or lower than other patios.

LIKE THE ROOMS in a house, patios should be connected with passageways that are direct and avoid crossing conversational, work, or recreational areas.

If walkways are used frequently, paving is desirable. When they are used infrequently, steppingstones are adequate and attractive.

If your family's interest in gardening exceeds the space in the patios, make the passageways wide enough for planting along the walks.

You need dividers to define the different patios, reduce noise, give privacy, and provide background. You can avoid the "rat in a maze" feeling by planning short dividers. Structures or plants may be used.

When dividers serve as windbreaks, solid masonry blocks, wood louvers, and slender evergreens should be considered. Vary the kind of dividers, but do not use so many kinds that your patio will look like a display room.

Finish two different materials in the same color to avoid the impression of too many materials.

Seldom is a housesite so level that grading is not necessary. One or more steps may be required between patios.

Keep the utility and living patios near the floor level of the house for

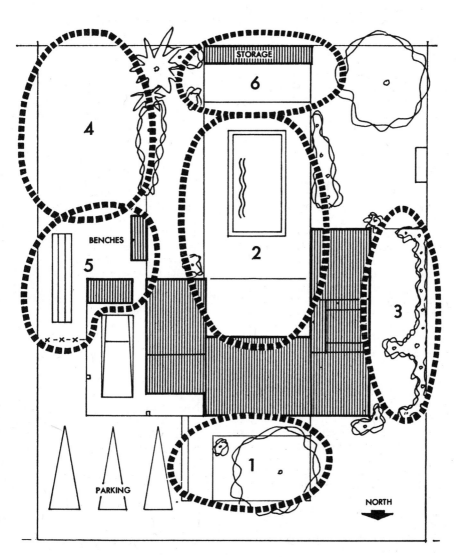

ALLEY

STORAGE

6

4

2

BENCHES

5

3

PARKING

1

NORTH

STREET

1. ENTRANCE PATIO   4. MULTI-PURPOSE PATIO
2. LIVING PATIO   5. UTILITY PATIO
3. BEDROOM PATIO   6. VIEW TERRACE—ROOFED

Layouts for different kinds of patios.

convenience but low enough to prevent water from flowing into the house or through covered areas. Establish grade levels beyond the living and utility patios.

When grading requires one or more steps between patios, plan wide treads and low risers. They look better and they are easier to climb. Make the steps wider than the openings that connect the patios for safety.

A sunny day is a good time to plan a patio, but a poor time to remember that good drainage is needed. It is difficult to change a natural drainage feature and seldom advisable. Make ditches a part of your plan and use bridges where they are needed.

Lighting may be functional or decorative. Steps in the dark are a hazard, but low lights can make them safe. Decorative lights are nicer than a strong floodlight in conversational centers.

Swimming pools and work areas especially need adequate light. Floodlights, controlled within the house, are a protection and convenience.

Eating areas should be lighted if you plan to eat outdoors in the evening.

Electrical outlets for power tools, work lights, and kitchen appliances should be placed in appropriate places.

Investigate the tax rates (and building codes) on the various kinds of structures, paving, and fencing before you build. The rates may vary according to the kinds and heights of walls and the kinds of paving and fencing.

In some localities, everything is taxable except noncommercial trees and shrubbery. The taxes may influence your choices, but the higher taxes you may pay on some materials and structures may be offset by maintenance and replacement costs on less durable materials.

Decide if the use of a patio will justify the cost and labor.

Avoid conflicting uses in the same patio.

Do not overplan. Plan before you build or plant.

If you plan to do some of the building yourself and it includes brickwork, you will be wise to consult local brick-

layers for most projects. But there may be a certain amount of brick work you will enjoy doing yourself—such as paving your own terrace or patio. With that in mind, here are two methods of how to pave your terrace.

Method One— (Without Mortar)

1. Outline terrace with stakes and string.
2. Remove all grass and roots in the area you are paving. Excavate to a depth of 1/2 to 1 inch deeper than the brick you are using.
3. Slope slightly away from house or retaining wall so that terrace will not hold water.
4. Dig a small trench around the sides. The border brick can be placed either horizontally or vertically. If you place the brick horizontally, make the trench 2 inches deeper than the rest of the terrace excavation. If you frame the edge with brick set on end, the trench should be correspondingly deeper.
5. To start, frame two adjoining edges. Line up brick inside string and tap in place firmly with hammer handle or block of wood.
6. Fill in terrace area with sufficient sand (generally 1/2 to 1 inch) so that when the terrace brick is laid flat, the top will be even with the edge brick. Smooth sand as much as possible.
7. Now, place a layer of tar paper over the sand. This will aid in keeping the sand level, provide a smooth bed for the brick, and discourage the growing of grass.
8. Starting at the corner, lay the brick flat and tight, one against the other, in the pattern that you have selected.
9. When you have finished laying the brick to the desired length and width, frame the other two sides of the terrace with brick set like the first two sides.
10. When you have finished placing the brick, fill in the slight crevices between them by sweeping in fine sand.

Method Two— (With Dry Mortar)

1. Follow the first seven steps of the mortarless method.
2. Then lay the brick with open joints (1/2 inch space between brick in the desired pattern). You can jockey the brick into position by using a small piece of board as a spacer.
3. After bricks are in place, mix two parts of sand to one of cement and throw this dry mixture on with a shovel, sweeping it into the open joints. Tap it firmly with the edge of a thin board and sweep into joints so that all are evenly full.
4. Now, use the spray nozzle of your garden hose and regulate the flow so that it barely trickles with a weak stream. Play this on each brick, washing it clean and settling the joint at the same time. Spray a very fine mist of water over the complete job at frequent intervals for a few days in insure penetration and aid curing.

HOW TO
GROW PLANTS

CITY AND SUBURBAN householders who are beginners in gardening should first size up the gardening possibilities of their own places and find out how to grow the plants that can be grown in those places.

Gardening is an art.

To be successful in it, the gardener must learn what conditions different kinds of plants require.

Then he can choose plants that will grow well under his conditions as he finds them. Or he can try to change conditions so he can grow other plants that he wants to grow. Most gardeners do both.

NO ONE KIND of plant grows well everywhere, even within one locality. Climate and soil largely determine what can grow where. Other factors also enter.

Most common garden plants can grow reasonably well on many kinds of soil, ranging from sands to clays.

Sandy and clay soils are generally less desirable than sandy loam, loam, and clay loam or silt loam soils.

Sandy soils are poor in plant nutrients and dry out quickly. On the other hand, they are easy to work and can be improved with peat, sawdust, manures, composts, and fertilizers.

Clay and other "heavy" soils are hard to work, may form troublesome clods, and generally take up water very slowly.

It is difficult for small seedlings to emerge through heavy soils, and these soils become badly compacted when repeatedly walked upon. It is possible, however, to improve gradually the physical properties of these heavy soils by repeatedly working manures, composts, and other organic matter into them.

Peat and sawdust improve the physical properties of both very light (sandy) and very heavy soils. The use of sawdust, however, creates a problem of nitrogen fertilization.

Many soils in humid sections are so acid that they must be limed before one tries to grow acid-sensitive plants on them. In the arid and less humid regions, many soils are salty or so alkaline that they must be treated before salt- or alkali-sensitive plants can be grown.

Soil must be well drained naturally or drained by effective tiling or ditching. Garden plants will not tolerate waterlogged soil.

Irrigated soils also must be well drained, although there may never be too much water in them—they must be drained so that excess salts from irrigation water and fertilizers can be leached from the root zone.

Agricultural agencies in most states operate soil-testing services and make specific recommendations for fertilizing or otherwise treating the soils tested. Take advantage of this service if you need it. Your county agent can give you instructions and addresses.

Growing one kind of plant year after year in the same spot favors the buildup of disease agents and insects that affect that plant and persist in the soil. When it is feasible, change the location of planting each season, so that one kind of plant is grown in any one spot only once in 3 or 4 years.

During late winter or in early spring, before the garden plot is spaded or plowed, all coarse plant remains that would interfere with plowing or spading should be removed. If there are no remains of badly diseased vegetables in this trash it may be placed on the compost pile, but any badly diseased plants from a previous crop should be burned. Crop residues or weeds that can be worked into the soil should be spaded under. Any stones or other debris large enough to interfere with working the soil should be thoroughly removed and hauled away or so placed that no inconvenience or unsightliness will result.

Most town and city gardeners will not be able to hire the plowing of their gardens, so the job will have to be done by hand with a spade or spading fork. In fact, most urban gardens are either so small that hand spading is the only feasible method of breaking the soil. Before proceeding with plowing or spading, one should remember not to work soils when they are wet. There is a great temptation to plow or spade the garden while it is still too wet, in order to make an early start. This error, however, may so "puddle" the soil, packing the particles closely together, that it will be hard and cloddy for weeks or months afterward.

To determine if the soil is dry enough to work, squeeze a handful tightly into a ball and then break it apart with the fingers. If the mass crumbles it is safe to work the soil, but if the soil clings together and cannot be readily broken up it is too wet. Sandy soils dry out more quickly than silty and clay soils. Furthermore, sandy soils are damaged less by working when somewhat wet than are heavy silty or claylike soils.

Areas in sod or that have not been in cultivation for many years should be spaded or plowed in the fall, and such manure or other organic matter as is feasible should be turned under. A cover crop adapted to the locality should

be sown if there is time for it to make enough growth to protect the soil before cold weather. If the soil is spaded too late for a cover crop, the surface should be left rough, and generous amounts of straw, strawy manure, leaves, or other coarse organic matter should be chopped into the surface. This may appear a little unslightly, but it will increase absorption of rain and help prevent blowing and washing of the soil. The coarse material that might interfere with working the ground can be raked off in the spring and put on the compost pile.

Almost all lawns and gardens need some irrigation water, even in the so-called humid parts of this country. No section is always free of dry spells.

Supplemental water may be needed for valuable perennial specimens as well as annual plants. Shallow-rooted shrubs, such as azaleas, may be lost in a short time for lack of water.

A relatively small amount of water may be of great value in establishing a stand on seedlings, or transplants and (applied at the proper time) keeping them in good growth.

One or two moderate irrigations later may spell the difference between success and failure with an important part of the lawn and garden.

Sprinkling is generally the easiest way for the householder to apply water, but it is not always the best. Frequent wetting may increase damage from leaf diseases of many garden plants or impair the quality of flowers or edible products.

Running the water through furrows near the plants is preferable when the contours and properties of the soil permit.

Perforated or porous hose helps to place water precisely where it is desired on small plots without waste and without wetting the aboveground parts of the plants.

It is better to water plants thoroughly and wet the soil down to a depth of several inches, at intervals of about a week, than to sprinkle or dribble a little water on the soil every day.

Mulching the soil with straw, leaves, peat, wood chips, or similar materials helps to conserve moisture and to control some weeds. Black polyethylene film is also used as a "mulch." Such mulches also prevent crusting of the soil and reduce the bad effects of walking on it when it is wet.

Do not work the soil when it is wet. Do not walk on it when it is wet unless you must do so.

Too LITTLE LIGHT causes trouble in home gardening oftener than you may suppose.

For most vegetables and many flowers, it is necessary that unobstructed sunshine reach them more than half of each day. Such plants may not develop as desired when grown close to the east, north, or west sides of buildings or trees although the sky above them is unobstructed. Leafy salad vegetables and greens will tolerate some shade, but tomatoes, for example, are highly intolerant.

When you grow seedlings in the house for transplanting, set the container of young plants close to the glass of a window that receives unobstructed sunshine. You should turn the plant container every day to keep the plants from growing crooked.

A spot near a window that receives 25 to 30 foot-candles of light may appear bright enough. One can read and work well in such light. But it takes 50 to 75 times that much light for most of the popular garden plants to develop normally. So-called house plants require much less.

If your prospective garden spot is at all shady any part of the day, choose carefully the plants you want to grow. Shade seriously reduces the fruitfulness of tomatoes, peppers, cucumbers, and other fruit-bearing vegetables.

EACH KIND OF PLANT has its characteristic temperature requirements and tolerances to heat and cold.

Do not expect all plants to grow equally well at any one temperature or season of the year—plants differ greatly in this respect.

In sections where the temperature changes markedly from season to season, one must learn when to plant and when not to plant each species. The aim is to plant each at such times that its temperature requirements will be met by the naturally occurring temperatures of the season.

YOU NEED only a few simple tools for home gardening—but the tools should be good ones. Cheap, light materials and shoddy construction will be unsatisfactory and expensive in the long run.

Minimum needs, even for small and simple garden activities, are:

A spade or a long-handled, round-pointed shovel; a steel bow rake; a common steel hoe of the socket type; garden hose of large enough bore to deliver ample water; a sprinkler, mainly for the lawn, and porous or perforated hose; a trowel; a sturdy, all-purpose bucket; a jackknife; a strong cord for marking rows; a small sprayer; hand shears for trimming shrubs; hand shears for trimming grass edges; and, of course, a hand or power lawnmower. The hand-pushed reel type is adequate for small- to medium-sized lawns.

Those items, including 100 feet of good rubber hose but not the lawnmower, cost about 70 to 90 dollars.

For larger operations, the list of tools can grow almost endlessly. Gardeners are fascinated by gadgets as well as by plants, but even for fairsized and varied operations you need relatively few additional tools.

The most important are heavy, long-handled shears for pruning cuts too heavy for hand shears; a pruning saw for cuts too heavy for shears; hedge shears for hedges and related pruning; a hand sickle; a mattock for heavy digging or grubbing roots; a wheel hoe for working between rows of plants; and a good wheelbarrow. These added items cost about 50 to 60 dollars.

Try to have an obscure or hidden spot for composting leaves, grass clippings, and all manner of plant residues. If space is limited, a simple pen or crib of wire or stakes will contain these materials neatly.

A WIDE RANGE of vegetable and ornamental plants for transplanting can be bought at garden-supply and other retail stores and by mail.

If you need only a few plants, you may prefer to buy them rather than produce them.

Often, however, varieties you want may not be available at convenient commercial sources, and you will have to start them at home.

Few residences have enough indoor light, a suitable temperature range, and convenient space for growing good seedlings ready for transplanting to the garden. The job can be rather messy unless you take care to protect against spillage of soil (or another planting medium) and leakage of moisture from the containers. The plant-growing containers should all be set in a larger shallow pan or tray that is leakproof.

If you grow more than a few plants, you need a small hotbed or coldframe on the sunny side of the house in which to start them and later acclimate them gradually to outdoor conditions before planting them in the garden.

IT IS BETTER to plant seeds in a moist soil than to plant in a dry soil and sprinkle it to get the seedlings up.

Seeds should be pressed into contact with the moist soil and covered immediately with moist soil. The soil over the seeds should then be pressed down firmly but not packed. If the seed is not in intimate contact with the soil, it may be unable to absorb moisture rapidly enough for prompt and vigorous germination. Light pressure can be applied to the uncovered seeds with the straight edge of a board, or a light, narrow wheel can be run over the seeds. After covering, the flat side of a hoe or a conventional pressure wheel of a planter can be used.

An accompanying table shows planting distance and planting depths for seeds of vegetables. The depths given are for a moist sandy loam soil. In heavy soils, plant less deeply. On sandy

soils, plant more deeply to reach more moisture.

In general, plant seeds only deeply enough to insure they are in moist soil and that they will not be splashed out by an ordinary rain.

FOR MOST SOILS in good workable condition, a general garden fertilizer containing 5 percent nitrogen, 10 percent phosphoric acid, and 5 percent potash (5–10–5) will be useful. Amounts to use depend on the original fertility of the soil and its past treatment. If it is rich enough to produce a rapid and rank growth of weeds, it may need little, if any.

New ground, especially ground that is disturbed by construction work, generally will need up to 4 to 5 pounds per 100 square feet (about a ton per acre) of 5–10–5 fertilizer. It should be mixed thoroughly into the surface 6 to 8 inches.

If the plot has been heavily manured, superphosphate alone may be all that is needed, at about 2 to 3 pounds per 100 square feet.

Keep the weeds down by cultivating, hoeing, or mulching. Kill them when they are small.

After planting, work the soil no more than necessary to control weeds. Avoid trampling the soil, especially if it is wet.

Watch for evidence of insects and diseases, and apply control measures promptly.

Examine the soil and the plants to see if they lack water. Do not let the plants wilt. Dig into the soil a few inches to see if it is losing its moist appearance. If so, water thoroughly about once a week unless a rain has moistened the soil well down into the root zone.

Harvest products at prime quality.

Remove spent annual plants promptly when they are no longer useful for harvest or beauty. Trample them into the compost pile or work them into the soil.

Then plant another crop in the vacated space if there is time for it to develop before frost. If there is not time for that, cultivate or mulch the space

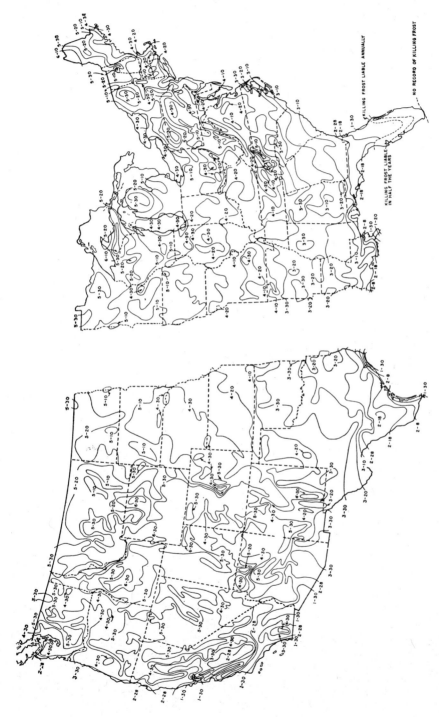

Map showing average dates of last killing spring frosts in the Western and Eastern United States.

Map showing average dates of first killing fall frosts in the Western and Eastern United States.

SEEDS AND SPACE REQUIRED FOR VEGETABLES WHEN GROWN INTENSIVELY FOR HAND CULTURE

	Approximate distance between—			Seeds or plants required for—		
Crop	Rows	Plants or hills in rows	Depth to cover seeds or roots	1 foot of row or per hill	100 feet of row	1 acre
	In.	In.	In.	No.		Lbs.
Asparagus [1]	30	18	8	......	70 plants....	3
Beans, lima (bush)	28	4	1½	4	¾ pound....	100
Beans, lima (pole) [2]	36	24	1½	2 4	½ pound....	60
Beans, snap (bush)	28	3	1½	5	¾ pound....	100
Beans, snap (pole) [2]	36	24	1½	2 4	¼ pound....	40
Beets	16	3	¾	6	1 ounce...:.	12
Broccoli, sprouting [3]	30	18	½	3	1 packet.....	¼
Brussells sprouts [3]	30	18	½	3	1 packet.....	¼
Cabbage [1]	30	18	......	......	70 plants....	¼
Carrots	16	1½	½	20	¼ ounce.....	4
Cauliflower [1]	30	18	......	......	70 plants....	¼
Celery and celeriac [1]	24	6	......	2	200 plants...	¼
Chard	24	6	¾	4	1 ounce.....	12
Chives	16	2	½	15	......	.....
Chicory, witloof	20	4	½	10	1 packet.....	2
Collards [3]	30	18	½	3	1 packet.....	¼
Corn, sweet	36	12	1½	2	¼ pound....	15
Cress, upland	16	3	¼	20	1 packet.....	2
Cucumbers [2]	72	72	1	2 12	½ ounce.....	2
Eggplant [1]	36	30	......	......	40 plants....	¼
Endive	20	10	½	10	1 packet.....	2
Garlic [1]	16	3	1½	4	1 pound.....	325
Horseradish [1]	30	18	2	......	70 roots.....	.....
Kale [3]	24	10	½	4	1 packet.....	4
Kohlrabi	16	4	½	10	¼ ounce.....	4
Leeks	16	3	½	20	¼ ounce.....	4
Lettuce, head [1]	16	12	......	......	100 plants...	¼
Lettuce, leaf	16	6	½	10	1 packet.....	2
Mustard	16	6	½	10	1 packet.....	2
Okra	36	18	1	3	1 ounce.....	8
Onions, seed	16	3	½	20	¼ ounce.....	4
Onions [1]	16	3	......	4	{ 1 qt. sets....	600
					400 plants...	3
Parsley	16	4	¼	20	¼ ounce.....	2
Parsnips	16	3	½	15	½ ounce.....	3
Peas, garden (dwarf)	18	1	1½	12	1 pound.....	120
Peas, garden (tall)	24	1	1½	12	1 pound.....	120
Peas, black-eye	28	3	1½	5	½ pound....	60
Peppers [1]	30	18	......	......	70 plants....	¼
Potatoes	30	12	4	1	7 pounds....	1,200
Radishes, spring	12	1	¼	15	1 ounce.....	12
Radishes, summer or winter	20	3	½	10	½ ounce.....	6
Rhubarb [1]	42	42	4	......	30 roots.....	....
Rutabagas	20	4	¼	20	¼ ounce.....	2
Salsify	20	2	½	15	1 ounce.....	12
Spinach	12	4	½	12	½ ounce.....	10
Spinach, New Zealand	30	12	1	3	1 ounce.....	4
Squash, bush [2]	48	48	1	10	½ ounce.....	3
Squash, trailing [2]	96	48	1	10	½ ounce.....	2
Sweetpotatoes [1]	36	12	......	......	100 plants...	....
Tomatoes, [1] not staked	48	48	......	......	26 plants....	⅛
Tomatoes, [1] staked	36	24	......	......	51 plants....	¼
Turnips	16	3	½	20	¼ ounce.....	2

[1] Plants or sets.   [2] Hills of about 4 plants each.   [3] 4 or 5 seeds planted in 1 spot where plants are to stand; later thinned to 1 plant.

to control weeds.

Protect the garden spots against winter erosion by mulching with plant residues or compost.

It requires years of study and experience to become an expert gardener, but a reasonable amount of study and careful attention to simple instructions will enable a beginner to avoid disastrous or humorous errors and to obtain some gratifying results. To help the inexperienced gardener keep out of some of the commonest troubles, here are a few important "don't's".

• Don't spade, plow, or cultivate soil that is too wet.

• Don't apply too much lime.

• Don't run the rows up and down a slope.

• Don't sow seeds too thickly, and don't fail to thin out plants to the proper distance.

• Don't guess at the amounts of fertilizer or strong manure to apply per unit area of land.

• Don't cultivate deeply enough to injure the shallow roots of the vegetables.

• Don't let the weeds get big before you try to destroy them.

• Don't apply water in numerous light sprinklings, but water thoroughly about once a week if rainfall is deficient.

• Don't forget to obtain the necessary dusting or spraying equipment and materials early in the spring—before you need them.

• Don't let the vegetables become too old before harvesting them, thereby losing high quality.

• Don't let any vegetables go to waste.

• Don't leave any land idle during the growing season.

• Don't leave the soil in such condition that it will wash or blow away during the winter.

• Don't try to grow vegetables on a lot that is—

Too poor to make a good growth of weeds or grass.

Made up mostly of rubble or unweathered subsoil "fill."

Contaminated with coal-, chemical-, or oil-product wastes.

So wet that it grows weeds common to marshy or poorly drained spots.

Likely to be flooded often by stream overflow.

Located so that it receives much storm drainage or surface water from above.

Shaded by large trees more than a few hours a day.

ADD LIFE TO SOIL

The wonderful stuff we call organic material is rotting leaves, stems, and other parts of plants. It is a soil amendment; it adds life to soil.

With it and some planning and effort and lime and chemical fertilizer, which also are called soil amendments, you can modify almost any soil to meet the needs of a wide range of vegetables, flowers, shrubs, and trees.

Decomposing organic matter mellows stiff, compacted clay soils and adds body to loose sands.

On the surface of the soil, where it serves as a mulch, it provides protection from beating rains, prevents soil crusting, reduces runoff and erosion, conserves moisture in the soil, helps to control dust, and reduces weeds.

The improved soil condition that results increases plant growth and root development. Each plant, therefore, has a larger volume of soil from which to obtain water and nutrients.

Organic matter also increases the ability of soils to release nutrients gradually to plants during the growing season.

It is not a substitute for commercial fertilizers, but it increases the efficiency of fertilizer applied.

Leaves are the most common and available form of organic material.

Organic materials differ in nitrogen content and in rate of decomposition.

Certain types release nitrogen to the soil during decomposition.

Other types require additional nitrogen during decomposition, and nitrogen fertilizer must be added. Materials that decompose readily if enough nitrogen is supplied for them to rot include leaves, sawdust and bark from some trees, small woodchips, straw, cornstalks, ground corncobs, cotton burrs, cane bagasse, and peanut hulls.

When you mix them with the soil, you should add nitrogen fertilizer. Otherwise, the material, as it breaks down, will take up nitrogen from the soil, and plants will grow poorly because the available nitrogen is tied up.

Ammonium nitrate applied at the rate of 4 or 5 pounds per 100 pounds of dry organic matter of 12 to 15 pounds of lawn fertilizer, such as 10–6–4, will correct this deficiency.

Materials that contain enough nitrogen to decompose include grass clippings, legume hay, well-rotted manure, sewage sludge, tobacco stems and stalks, spent hops, and coffee grounds.

Materials that decompose so slowly that very little tie-up of nitrogen takes place include peat, buckwheat hulls, and sawdust and bark from redwood and cypress trees.

Cottonseed, soybean, and cocoa meals, castor pomace, activated sewage sludge, dried blood, meat and fish meals, process tankage, hoof and horn meal, guanos, and manipulated sheep, cattle, and poultry manures contain enough nitrogen for use as fertilizers.

Some people advocate that only organic fertilizers be used. The fact is, though, that the nutrients in organic fertilizers are available for plant growth only as the organic matter decomposes and the nutrients are changed to the same forms present in chemical fertilizers. Fertilizer elements are far more concentrated in chemical fertilizer than in organic matter. They therefore are cheaper and less bulky.

Organic fertilizers do have the advantage of releasing nutrients more slowly over a longer period, and an overdose of organic fertilizer is far less likely to burn the plant than an overdose of chemical fertilizers.

COMPOSTING is a biological process that encourages the activity of micro-organisms, which break down organic materials.

An adequate and balanced supply of nutrients, air, and water and warmth are needed.

Smaller particles decompose faster than large ones, although particles that are too small may pack together and shut out air.

Soft organic materials, such as grass clippings, compost better if they are mixed with coarse material, such as leaves and straw.

The compost pile should be moist but not excessively wet. It should be large enough to maintain favorable

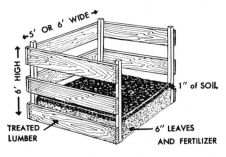

Compost pile.

temperatures. The best size is 6 feet high and 5 to 6 feet wide. It may be of any length.

A compost pile has alternate layers of organic materials and soil. Make each organic layer about 6 inches thick and put a few shovelfuls of soil between each layer. Add plant nutrients to each layer of organic material.

For the nutrients, as a general guide, it is recommended that you add a cup of ammonium sulfate, one-half cup of superphosphate, and a level tablespoon of epsom salt to each packed bushel of leaves or organic material. If you do not plan to use the compost for acid-loving shrubs, add two-thirds cup of ground limestone or wood ashes.

Other recipes for compost piles may be just as good—for example, one and one-half cups of 5–10–5 lawn fertilizer or two and one-half cups of a 5–10–5 garden fertilizer to each packed bushel of leaves or organic material. Two-thirds cup of ground limestone or wood ashes are added when the compost is for general use rather than for acid-loving plants.

It is advantageous to build the pile with a flat top that slants toward the center to catch rainfall or hold water when watered with a hose.

If you use dry materials in building the pile, composting can be speeded by adding water as the pile is built.

Composting will not kill all disease-carrying organisms, insect eggs and larva, and weed seeds. Therefore, you should avoid using obviously infested materials.

ORGANIC MATTER is particularly good for flowerbeds, which need a loose, friable soil that is easily cultivated and planted. Organic materials are added to develop such a soil.

Compost, peat, sawdust, shredded leaves, and ground corncobs are suited for flowerbeds. If the soil is extremely hard and cloddy, you should spread a layer of organic matter 2 or 3 inches deep over the bed and work it into the soil to a depth of 6 or 8 inches. Remember to add ammonium nitrate or a lawn fertilizer to balance organic materials, such as sawdust, shredded leaves, and ground corncobs.

Lime, if needed, and phosphorous fertilizer should be worked into the soil at the same time. If the soil below 8 inches is extremely compact, pile the top layer of soil to one side, loosen the subsoil, and replace the topsoil. Mix a little organic matter with the subsoil. Do all this when the soil is moist but not wet.

After spading in the organic material, spread a complete fertilizer, such as 5–10–5, on the surface at the rate of 50 pounds per 1,000 square feet. Rake to mix in the fertilizer and level the bed. Break up any large clods.

If the soil has a tendency to crust after a heavy rain, spread a thin layer of organic material on the surface. You may have to buy some topsoil. Allow time for rain to settle the soil or add water to firm it before planting.

Additional organic matter should be incorporated each year or as needed to keep the soil in good condition. A mulch will further protect the soil and aid in the control of weeds. Mulches are particularly desirable for perennials.

In preparing the flowerbed, provide for drainage. Once in a while, tile drainage may be needed, but usually all that is needed is to build the bed up a little so that surface water drains away.

BECAUSE SHRUBS are a long-term investment, a little extra time in preparing the soil for them will be rewarded.

Work organic matter, lime, and phosphorous fertilizer into the soil as we recommended for flowerbeds.

Remember, though, that lime should not be applied if azaleas, rhododendrons, or other acid-loving plants are to be grown. Peat is especially recommended as a source of organic matter for azaleas and rhododendrons. Pine needles are effective as a mulch. They do not dry out and blow away in winter. In places where acid-loving plants are to be grown, remove any building debris containing liming materials, such as plaster and cement.

Allow time for rain to settle the soil or add water to firm it before you set out the shrubs.

When you transplant in beds the shrubs you bought bare rooted, dig a hole large enough so you can spread the roots as they were before they were dug at the nursery. Place the plants in the hole with the original ground line of the plant at ground level. Arrange the roots and half fill the hole with the granulated soil-organic mixture carefully placed around the roots. Add water to settle the soil around the roots. Then finish filling the hole.

Balled-and-burlapped or container-grown plants are planted in holes larger than the packaged roots, so that the soil-organic mixture can be filled in around the package. If the container is a clay pot or metal pot it must be removed. Peat pots or pots of other decomposable materials are not removed before setting out the plant.

Set the ball of roots in the hole with the top of the ball at ground level. Add enough soil to half fill the hole.

Then add water to saturate the soil. This aids in eliminating air pockets between the ball of roots and the side of the hole. After the water soaks into the soil, fill the hole with soil. Then mulch and water the entire bed.

Except in special situations, the mulch should be maintained at all times, particularly for evergreens, which must have water available to the roots throughout the year.

INDIVIDUAL SITES are prepared for planting trees and isolated shrubs. If the subsurface drainage is not good, water will collect in the hole, and the roots will rot.

Trees and large shrubs usually are moved with their roots in a ball of soil, which has been wrapped in burlap.

Sites for them are dug one and one-half to twice the diameter of the ball and about one-third deeper, especially if the subsoil is hard or poorly drained. An equal volume of organic matter (such as peat, compost, and sewage sludge) is mixed thoroughly with the soil that is removed from the hole. While mixing, add a quarter of a cup of a mixed fertilizer, such as a 5–10–5, to each bushel of the soil-organic matter mix to be returned to the hole. Put enough of this mix in the hole so the ground line of the ball will be 1 to 2 inches above the ground line of the soil. This allows for some settling.

Hold the tree erect and fill the hole halfway up with the soil-organic mixture. Thoroughly wet the hole to settle the mixture and fill any air pockets before filling the hole.

When the planting is complete, build a ridge around the root area to hold water. Keep the site mulched until the tree is well established.

Watering the trees during dry weather is especially important the first year.

GROUND COVERS

THERE ARE MANY areas in yards and gardens that can be brought to full beauty by adding a "carpet." These are the spots where something has to cover the ground to avoid a barren, lifeless look. Landscape architects have coined the phrase "ground cover" for these plants. They include grass and low mat-like plants that creep along the soil.

GRASS is the best of all the ground covers. It can be walked on, played on, and trampled on frequently, yet it remains an excellent cover for the ground if it is fertilized, watered, cut regularly, and weeded occasionally.

Some other plants withstand a certain amount of pedestrian traffic, but grass still is the most serviceable of all.

Many gardeners look for other ground-covering plants that require little or no care. Trees and shrubs that grow with branches touching the ground do well in certain situations. Annual and perennial flowering plants will suffice in other places.

If you want other plants in order to make a planting more interesting or to avoid the care that grass needs, you should consider certain factors before you choose a specific plant:

• Is the site in the sun or the shade?
• Is the soil poor and dry or medium to good?
• Do you want evergreen plants?
• How high is the ground cover to be—a few inches or a foot or more?
• Need the ground cover be serviceable all year, or can it be an herbaceous one, which dies to the ground in the late fall, leaving the ground bare and ostensibly lacking in plant material during the winter?

Those questions are important. Once you have made your decisions respecting them, it is much easier to select the proper plant as a ground cover for the area.

Careful preparations should be taken in the planting. The ground should contain organic matter, such as well-rotted manure, compost, or peat moss. Work it in well before you plant.

Water should be available in order to get the plants off to a good start and to prevent them from suffering during dry periods.

The planting can be done in the

spring or the fall, according to the general practice in your area. Fall planting often is satisfactory if it is done early enough to allow the young plants to become established thoroughly before the ground freezes. Spring planting may be better in many sections.

To space the individual plants properly at planting time, you should know the growth rate of the plants you select and decide whether you want a complete ground cover the first season or whether you can wait a few years until the plants eventually grow together.

For instance, the honeysuckles and the memorial rose grow rapidly, and individual plants may be expected to cover several square feet during the first year.

Other plants, like the European wildginger, grow slowly, and it may be several years before plants spaced a foot apart will grow together.

Evergreens, such as some of the creeping junipers, are expensive compared to small herbaceous plants, yet an individual evergreen may cover 4 square feet when you buy it.

Large clumps of herbaceous plants may be bought and pulled apart at the time of planting to cover as much space as possible. With certain exceptions, it is well to allow about 2 square feet of space for each of the herbaceous plants generally used as ground covers.

One of the purposes of ground-cover plants is to help prevent soil erosion. All plants prevent erosion to some extent, but fast-growing vines and shrubs that root readily along the branches that touch the soil are better to use in such situations than are herbaceous perennials, which die to the ground in winter and give little protection to the soil in early spring, when melting snows cause the worst erosion.

Give careful thought to ways to prevent erosion at planting time. One method is to terrace the bank and planting slightly in such a way that the runners of the vines go at right angles to the slope. Also, you can sink boards at right angles to the slope; let them protrude a few inches above the soil, and keep them in place for the first

year or two until the plants become established.

Mulching with hay or straw helps prevent runoff for the first year or two. Placing large wire hairpins over the stems of the plants to keep them in place on the soil surface may encourage rapid rooting, especially if you put a shovelful of soil over the stem to keep the branch moist.

In any event, select healthy, vigorous-growing woody plants for this type of planting.

Among such plants are the dwarf bush honeysuckle (*Diervilla lonicera*), Arnold Dwarf Forsythia, English ivy (*Hedera helix*), varieties of creeping juniper (*Juniperus horizontalis*), Henry honeysuckle (*Lonicera henryi*), Hall's honeysuckle (*Lonicera japonica halliana*), dwarf Japanese fleeceflower (*Polygonum cuspidatum* 'Compactum'), fragrant sumac (*Rhus aromatica*), and memorial rose (*Rosa wichuraiana*).

Some of these rapid-growing ground covers, like the Hall's honeysuckle and the dwarf Japanese fleeceflower, can become pests in good soil, unless they are rigidly restrained.

Before any ground covers are planted, the soil should be prepared well by adding generous quantities of humus. A general formula fertilizer should also be worked into the ground.

If you select the right plant for the situation, maintenance will be reduced to a minimum. It is always well, when possible, to add mulch just after the plants have been set in the ground. The mulch keeps the soil moist about the young plants and aids in their rooting. It helps control weeds.

An application of fertilizer can help after the plants are started, but of the two things, the mulching is the more important.

Peat moss, wood chips, pine needles, ground sugarcane stalks, ground bark of almost any kind, ground corncobs—any such material aids in conserving the moisture in the soil and reducing weed growth, but none of them should be applied more than 2 inches deep.

In northern regions, one must watch for the heaving of small plants in the early spring. Heaving is brought about during the late winter and early spring by warm, sunny weather alternating with freezing temperatures. Covering a young planting with evergreen boughs, burlap, or hay the first winter helps to prevent the heaving of small plants. Replanting of heaved plants should be done immediately.

Pruning a planting of ground cover sometimes is necessary to aid the plants in becoming bushy and dense. Sometimes a shrub may grow too vigorously and need to be reduced to conform with the rest of the planting.

Certain plants, like the yarrow, can even be mowed if necessary with a reel-type or rotary-blade mower. You could also use a brush scythe on some of the woody ground covers if its use will improve the general appearance of the planting.

A few bulbs here and there in a low ground cover create a color contrast during the early spring.

To SELECT the best possible plant as a ground cover for a specific situation, one must consider the extremes of winter and summer temperatures, the amount of rainfall, and the vagaries of the site itself.

On sunny slopes there are many forms of *cotoneaster* that thrive easily. Rockspray (*cotoneaster horizontalis*) is the most commonly found form. Other handsome ones include bearberry cotoneaster (*cotoneaster dammeri*) and cranberry cotoneaster (*cotoneaster apiculata*). Juniper, both Sargent and the creeping forms, are also recommended for sunny slopes.

You can plant several forms of sedum on gradual slopes where the soil is moist and sandy. But remember to confine them with border strips or they will quickly grow outside the area.

There are many excellent ground covers for shaded areas under trees which cut down maintenance. Pachysandra, myrtle, and ivy are the most common ones.

A few suggestions of some of the better ground covers for specific situations are noted in the following lists. An asterisk in front of the name indicates hardiness in the colder parts of northern New England and the northern Great Plains states. Specific notes on hardiness of the other plants should be noted in standard reference books, but all are grown as ground covers in gardens throughout the United States.

Ground Covers That Increase Rapidly

Aegopodium podograria (goutweed), *Ajuga reptans* (bugleweed), *Convallaria majalis* (lily-of-the-valley), *Forsythia* 'Arnold Dwarf,' *Lonicera japonica halliana* (Hall's honeysuckle), *Phalaris arundinacea picta* (ribbongrass), *Polygonum cuspidatum* 'Compactum' (dwarf Japanese fleeceflower), *Rosa wichuraiana* (memorial rose), *Sasa* species (hardy bamboos), *Vinca minor* (periwinkle).

Evergreen Ground Covers

Arctostaphylos uva-ursi (bearberry), *Euonymus fortunei* varieties (wintercreeper), *Galax aphylla* (galax), *Gaylussacia brachycera* (box huckleberry), *Hedera helix* (English ivy), *Juniperus* species (junipers), *Mahonia* species (hollygrape), *Packysandra terminalis* (Japanese pachysandra), *Thymus serpyllum* (mother-of-thyme), *Vinca minor* (periwinkle).

Flowering Ground Covers

Ajuga reptans (bugleweed), *Calluna vulgaris* (Scotch heather), *Cytisus* species (brooms), *Erica* species (spring heaths), *Helianthemum nummularium* (sunrose), *Hosta* species (plantain-lilies), *Hypericum* species (St. Johnsworts), *Lonicera* species (honeysuckles), *Phlox* species (phlox), *Rosa* species (roses).

Ground Covers for Shade

Ajuga reptans (bugleweed), *Aegopodium podograria* (goutweed), *Asarum* species (wildgingers), *Epimedium* species (epimediums), *Hedera helix* (English ivy), *Hosta* species (plantain-lilies), *Pachysandra terminalis* (Japanese pachysandra), *Sasa* species (hardy bamboos), *Tiarella cordifolia* (Alleghany foamflower), *Vinca minor* (periwinkle).

Ground Covers for Dry Soils

Aegopodium podograria (goutweed), *Coronilla varia* (crownvetch), *Genista pilosa* (silky-leaf woadwaxen), *Hosta* species (plantain-lilies), *Hypericum calycinum* (Aarons-beard St. Johnswort), *Juniperus* species (junipers), *Phalaris arundinacea picta* (ribbongrass), *Polygonum* species (fleece-flowers), *Rhus aromatica* (fragrant sumac), *Vaccinium angustifolium laevifolium* (lowbush blueberry).

Ground Covers for Wet Soil

Asarum caudatum (British Columbia wildginger) *Asperula odorata* (sweet woodruff), *Galax aphylla* (galax), *Geranium sanguineum prostratum* (dwarf blood red geranium), *Hosta* species (plantain-lilies), *Lysimachia nummularia* (moneywort), *Myosotis scorpioides* (true forget-me-not), *Phlox divaricata* (wild sweet-william), *Veronica repens* (creeping speedwell), *Xanthorhiza simplicissima* (yellowroot).

Ground Covers for Seashore

Arctostaphylos uva-ursi (bearberry), *Artemesia stelleriana* (beach wormwood), *Calluna vulgaris* (Scotch heather), *Campanula* species (bellflowers), *Cerastium tomentosum* (snow-in-summer), *Comptonia peregrina* (sweetfern), *Cytisus* species (brooms), *Juniperus conferta* (shore juniper), *Rosa wichuraiana* (memorial rose), *Vaccinium vitis-idaea minus* (mountain cranberry).

Ground Covers That May Be Cut With a Lawnmower

Aegopodium podograria (goutweed), *Hypericum repens* (creeping St. Johnswort), *Lysimachia nummularia* (moneywort), *Mazus reptans* (mazus), *Nepeta hederacea* (ground-ivy), *Potentilla tridentata* (wineleaf cinque-

foil), *Prunella vulgaris* (selfheal). *Thymus* species (thyme), *Veronica* species (speedwells), *Viola* species (violets).

Ground Covers for Warm Areas of Gulf Coast and Pacific Coast

Gazania species (South African daisy), *Hypericum calycinum* (Aaronsbeard St. Johnswort), *Mesembryanthemum* species (ice plants), *Lippia canescens repens* (creeping lippia), *Ophiopogon japonicum* (mondograss), *Pelargonium peltatum* (ivy-vine pelargonium), *Santolina chamaecyparissus* (cypress lavender-cotton), *Saxifraga sarmentosum* (strawberry saxifrage), *Sedum* species (sedums), *Verbena peruviana* varieties (Peruvian verbena).

SIMPLE WAYS TO BETTER LAWNS

YOU DO NOT have to be an expert to make and maintain a good lawn. Follow a few general principles. Avoid hit-or-miss methods.

Some common causes of poor lawns are: The use of grasses not suited to the locality, too little or too much fertilizer, improper mowing and watering, too much shade, too much traffic, and poorly drained or droughty soils.

Choose a grass that is adapted to your locality and to the maintenance program you plan to follow. For example, bentgrass lawns require frequent mowing, watering, fertilizing, and treatment with chemicals to kill fungi. If you do not want to expend labor and money for this kind of lawn, you should choose a grass that requires less care.

Three broad groups of lawn grasses are:

Cool-season grasses for cool, humid areas (Kentucky bluegrass, red fescue, tall fescue, and bentgrasses); warm-season grasses for warm, humid areas (carpet, zoysia, centipede St. Augustine, and bermudagrasses); and grasses for the dryland area of the Great Plains (crested wheat, blue grama, and buffalo-grasses).

Temperature and moisture largely determine the adaptation of grass.

In general, the best time to seed or plant cool-season grasses is in the fall or early spring.

Warm-season grasses are planted in the spring or early summer.

A POORLY COLORED, thin, or weedy lawn is a hungry lawn.

Nutrients that grass plants need in large amounts are nitrogen, phosphorus, and potassium. They are listed as as N, P, and K on all fertilizer bags, in that order, with the percentage of each.

Many kinds and ratios of fertilizers are suitable for lawns. Choose one whose first—nitrogen (N)—number is as large or larger than the amounts of P and K. For example, a 10–6–4 fertilizer contains 10 percent nitrogen, 6 percent phosphorus, and 4 percent potassium.

The amount of fertilizer to apply to lawns we calculate on the percentage of nitrogen in the fertilizer. It is generally recommended that not more than 1 pound of actual nitrogen per 1 thousand square feet be applied at any one time. That would amount to 10 pounds of 10–6–4, 5 pounds of 20–10–5, 20 pounds of 5–10–5, and so on per thousand square feet of lawn.

Grasses vary in their need for nitrogen. A rough guide to the annual requirements is given in the table.

Too much fertilizer applied at any one time may burn the grass and will overstimulate top growth and weaken the plant. You can reduce the danger of burning by applying fertilizer when there is no moisture on the leaves and by watering immediately after you apply the fertilizer.

Organic types of fertilizer may be used in greater amounts than chemical types without burning the grass.

Lawn grasses grow poorly in acid soils. Test your soil and apply ground limestone if the tests show a need for it.

Soils in the Eastern States generally require lime.

If you do not make a test and if you have not used lime in the past 4 to 6 years, apply 50 to 80 pounds of ground limestone per 1 thousand square feet of lawn area.

Lime may be put on at any time of the year, but fall is the best time. Rain and snow will wash it into the soil.

Climatic regions, in which the following grasses are suitable for lawns:

1. *Kentucky bluegrass, red fescue, and Colonial bentgrass. Tall fescue, bermuda and zoysia grasses in the southern part.*

2. *Bermuda and zoysia grasses. Centipede, carpet, and St. Augustine grasses in the southern part; tall fescue and Kentucky bluegrass in some northern areas.*

3. *St. Augustine, bermuda, zoysia, carpet, and bahia grasses.*

4. *Nonirrigated areas: Crested wheat, buffalo, and blue grama grasses. Irrigated areas: Kentucky bluegrass and red fescue.*

5. *Nonirrigated areas: Crested wheat grass. Irrigated areas: Kentucky bluegrass and red fescue.*

6. *Colonial bent and Kentucky bluegrass.*

How HIGH you should move the grass depends on the kind of grass that predominates in your lawn.

Upright-growing grasses (Kentucky bluegrass, bahia, tall fescue, and red fescue) are mowed at 1½ to 2½ inches.

Grasses that spread by runners (zoysia, bermuda, centipede, and bentgrasses) will withstand close mowing, one-half to 1 inch.

The lawn should be mowed with a sharp mower often enough so as not to remove more than one-half of the top growth at any one time.

In the spring, mow the lawn as soon as growth reaches cutting height. Continue throughout the season until the growth stops in the fall. Excess growth remaining over the winter may smother and kill the grass.

MOST GRASSES show remarkable tolerance to drought. Grasses may become brown and dormant if not watered, but generally they recover when the fall rains come.

Established lawns should not be watered until they show signs of wilting or going offcolor.

Footprinting and the appearance of a bluish cast in parts of the lawn indicate that the lawn needs water. Then water the soil to a depth of 6 inches or more. Frequent, light watering encourages shallow rooting and increases the chance of plant diseases.

Sandy soils, because of their low moisture-holding capacity, require more frequent watering.

Clay soils require less frequent watering, but more water should be applied at any one time.

STEPS IN MAKING a new lawn:

Shape the soil to provide the desired contours and landscape features. The most satisfactory grade generally is one that slopes gently away from buildings in all directions.

Dark-colored loam soils are ideal surface soils for lawns. Organic matter is an important part of the surface soil.

It can be supplied by mixing sawdust, peat, muck, sewage sludge, or green plant material into the soil. Organic matter may be omitted if 4 to 6 inches of good-quality top soil is present, but it should be added to heavy clay and sandy soils.

If you did not have the soil tested and if you live east of the Mississippi River, apply 50 to 80 pounds of lime per 1 thousand square feet. The addition of 30 to 40 pounds of superphosphate per 1 thousand square feet is desirable in many sections. After liming, you should spread a complete fertilizer uniformly at the rate of 20 pounds of 10–6–4, 10–10–10, or similar analysis per 1 thousand square feet.

Work the organic matter, ground limestone, and superphosphate (0–20–0) thoroughly into the soil to a depth of several inches. If 4 to 6 inches of good-grade top soil has been added, omit the organic matter.

Prepare a fine, firm seedbed by raking several times. Loose, fluffy seedbeds should be rolled in order to firm the soil. Before final raking, apply the recommended amount of fertilizer.

Seed, sprig, or sod with adapted lawn grasses. Most southern grasses are established from sprigs (individual plants and runners) or pieces of sod. The sprigs or sod may be planted in the soil

LAWN GRASSES: PLANTING TIME, PROPAGATION, FERTILIZATION, AND MOWING HEIGHT

		Method of propagation			
Grass	Best planting time	Seed (lbs. per 1,000 sq. ft.)	Sod (sq. ft.) [2]	Fertilizer (lbs. per 1,000 sq. ft.)	Height of mowing (in.)
Bahia...................	Spring......	2–3	....	4	2
Bentgrass, Colonial.......	Fall........	1–2	....	4–6	½–1
Bermuda (hulled).........	Spring......	1–1½	5–10	5–10	¾–1
Blue grama..............	....do......	1–1½	....	(1)	1–2
Buffalo (treated).........	....do......	½–1½	25–30	(1)	1–2
Carpet..................	....do......	3–4	8–10	2–3	2–2½
Centipede...............	....do......	2–3	8–10	2–3	1–1½
Crested wheat............	Fall........	1–2	....	0–1	2
Ky. bluegrass...,........	....do......	1½–2	....	3–6	1½–2
Red fescue...............	....do......	3–4	....	2–3	1½–2
St. Augustine............	Spring......	None	8–10	4–5	2–2½
Tall fescue...............	Fall........	5–6	....	3–5	2
Zoysia..................	Spring......	None	8–10	4–6	¾–1½

[1] Seldom required on most soils.   [2] Needed to sprig 1,000 sq. ft.

at intervals of 1 foot or more. The closer the sprigs or sod pieces are planted, the more rapidly will your lawn become established.

An even distribution of seed may be had by adding a quantity of dry soil or fertilizer to the seed for bulk. Sow one-half of the seed in one direction and the remainder of the seed at right angles.

Rake the soil lightly to cover the seed to a depth of one-fourth inch or less.

After planting a new lawn, you can reduce erosion and seed washing by a light application of straw, pine needles, bark, or other mulch material. Approximately 50 percent of the soil surface should be visible after applying a mulch. Mulch also creates a more favorable medium for germination of seeds.

Water the seeded area lightly two or three times daily until the seedlings become established.

Mulching materials need not be removed if you use them in moderate amounts and distribute them well.

Mow the lawn as soon as the grass reaches the recommended mowing height.

OFTEN it is more economical to improve an old lawn than to make a new one. If 40 to 50 percent of perennial grasses remain, it is possible to improve the lawn a great deal.

Steps to renovate a lawn are:
• Apply herbicides according to manufacturers' directions to eradicate the weeds. Weed control should precede seeding by 2 or 3 weeks. Mow closely.
• Rake up the clippings and other debris.
• Apply 50 to 75 pounds per 1 thousand square feet of ground agricultural limestone if none was applied in the past 4 to 6 years.
• Apply fertilizer of 10–6–4, 10–10–10, or similar analysis at the rate of 10 to 15 pounds per 1 thousand square feet.
• Rake the bare areas to loosen the soil.
• Seed, sprig, or sod perennial grasses in bare areas.

• Water the seeded or sprigged areas lightly. Keep the soil moist until the grass is well established.

Continue mowing the lawn.

CONTROLLING LAWN DISEASES

MOST OF THE GRASSES in lawns grow under artificial conditions and are more subject to attack by disease organisms than they would be in a natural environment. Healthy, vigorously growing, adapted lawn grasses that are properly managed can best survive disease attacks.

The homeowner's best defense against lawn diseases is to follow these basic principles of lawn establishment and maintenance:
• Select grasses adapted to the soil, climatic, and light conditions under which they will be grown.
• Spend the necessary time, effort, and money on caring for the lawn. In addition to disease control, lawn care includes proper fertilizing, watering, mowing, and insect and weed control.

Proper care does not completely prevent or cure diseases, but it helps to curb them so that chemical controls can be more effective if they become necessary.

Knowing how to diagnose the most common causes of dead or injured grass and knowing the recommended treatments for various unhealthy conditions will help the homeowner to prevent serious lawn damage. Poor turf may be due to disease or to any one or a combination of other causes—undesirable or unadapted species, insect damage, fertilizer and chemical burning, dog urine, improper mowing, improper watering, localized dry spots, and compacted soil.

Fungi cause most of the serious and widespread diseases of lawn grasses.

THE RELATED GROUP of fungi responsible for Helminthosporium leaf and crown disease attack most grasses except St. Augustine and centipede. Kentucky bluegrass may be severely damaged.

Symptoms of the disease are most conspicuous on leaves, but the pathogen, the disease-inciting organism, also attacks the sheath and crown and kills the plant. Leaf and stem spots usually are tan to reddish-brown or purplish-black and often have a brown to light-tan center.

Affected areas containing dead grass may be several inches to several feet in diameter and resemble drought injury.

Merion Kentucky bluegrass, Pennlawn red fescue, and the Tifton bermudagrass hybrids are moderately resistant to Helminthosporium diseases.

Mow upright-growing grasses to a height of 1½ to 2½ inches. Apply enough fertilizer to keep the grass thriving. avoid overstimulation with nitrogen, especially in the spring. Remove clippings if growth is excessive.

Fungicide treatments help control Helminthosporium diseases. Do not use phenyl mercury formulations on Merion Kentucky bluegrass, because it is injured by the fungicide.

BROWN PATCH is prevalent in warm, humid regions. Practically all grasses are attacked by the causal fungus. The disease occurs during periods of warm, humid weather and is most damaging on heavily fertilized, succulent turf.

Brown patch develops in roughly circular areas, a few inches to several feet in diameter. The fungus threads (mycelium) frequently are observed as filmy, white tufts, while grass is wet with dew. As the leaves dry, the mycelium shrivels and becomes less conspicuous.

The fungus attacks so rapidly that grass leaves become infected and severely damaged almost overnight. Affected areas first appear darker gray-green; then they turn brown. If weather favorable for the development of brown patch lasts only a few days, just the leaves are infected, and the turf recovers in 2 or 3 weeks.

If the disease is severe and weather conditions remain favorable for disease development, the fungus attacks the crown and kills the plant. Dead grass blades generally remain erect and do not lie flat, as does grass killed by Pythium fungi.

To combat the disease, avoid excessive applications of nitrogen fertilizers. When watering is needed, water the turf early in the day to give grass leaves time to dry before evening. Remove excess clippings.

Apply recommended fungicides when symptoms of disease are first observed. Fungicides containing mercury should not be applied at rates higher than recommended, because the turf may be injured. Apply fungicides during the coolest parts of the day.

THE DOLLAR SPOT fungus attacks most lawn grasses in the United States. It is particularly severe and conspicuous on bent, Kentucky blue, bermuda, and zoysia grasses.

Dollar spot is most prevalent and damaging in lawns of low fertility and during droughts.

The disease occurs as small, brown spots a few inches in diameter. The spots bleach to a light straw color and often merge to form large, irregular damaging areas. The affected grass dies, and the turf becomes pitted. Whitish lesions develop on individual grass blades at the margins of diseased areas.

Dollar spot can be controlled by treatment with fungicides and by applications of additional nitrogen.

OF THE LAWN GRASSES commonly grown, only ryegrass, bermuda, and Merion Kentucky blue are damaged seriously by attacks of rust fungi.

Symptoms are presence of yellow-orange or reddish-brown powdery pustules on leaf blades. When a white handkerchief is brushed across diseased leaves, the spores adhere and leave a yellow or orange stain.

Pure stands of susceptible grasses are especially prone to attack by rust fungi. Damage is reduced if mixtures of grass are seeded.

Merion Kentucky bluegrass should be seeded with common Kentucky bluegrass or with red fescue. Rust-resistant varieties of turf bermudas and annual ryegrass are available in the South. Common annual ryegrass used for winter lawns in the South is usually heavily infected and damaged by rust.

Maintain an adequate fertility level so that new leaf growth can be mowed often to remove developing rust pustules.

Treatment with fungicides reduces the incidence of rust but does not prevent infection on new leaf growth.

PYTHIUM DISEASES (grease spot, cottony blight) occur during periods of wet weather, especially on poorly drained areas, when temperatures exceed 70° F.

Young grass seedlings are most susceptible to attack by Pythium fungi, but older grass stands can be killed or damaged severely.

Affected areas may be a few inches to several feet in diameter. Damage sometimes occurs in streaks as though the fungus has spread from mowing or from waterflow following heavy rain. Diseased leaves appear water soaked, tend to mat together, and feel slimy. Cottony tufts of fungus mycelium develop on leaves if humidity is high.

The darkly discolored grass blades wither and rapidly turn reddish brown as they dry. Diseased grass usually dies within 24 to 48 hours. It lies flat on the ground rather than remaining upright.

Provide adequate drainage for low-lying places. Avoid excessive watering during hot weather. Avoid keeping the foliage and ground wet for long periods. Delay seeding until the weather is cooler and dryer.

Treatment with fungicides at the earliest sign of disease is helpful.

SNOW MOLD, or winter scald, is caused by several different fungi. It is most severe in places where snow accumulates and covers grass for long periods. Grass that is growing actively when covered by lasting snow is especially susceptible to injury. Diseased grass is particularly noticeable at the thawing edge of a snowbank.

Snow mold also occurs in the absence of snow if the turf is excessively wet and the temperature is above freezing.

Patches of diseased grass, usually 1 to 12 inches or more in diameter, are a discolored dirty white, gray, or slightly pink. Diseased leaves bleach grayish tan and mat together.

One of the fungi that cause snow mold forms tiny, hard, brown to black fruiting bodies (sclerotia), which are embedded in diseased leaves and crowns.

Do not apply high nitrogen fertilizers late in the fall. Keep grass cut to prevent it from matting. Apply fungicides before lasting snow covers the grass.

MUSHROOMS that grow individually or in clumps in lawns usually develop from buried organic matter, such as pieces of construction lumber, logs, or tree stumps. Such mushrooms are harmless to grass. They usually develop following long periods of wet weather.

Most mushroom fruiting bodies disappear when the soil dries or after the grass has been mowed several times. Mushrooms that grow from buried lumber, logs, or stumps can be eliminated by digging up the buried wood. If this is impractical, drench the soil with a fungicide or treat the affected area as we recommend for the control of fairy rings.

FAIRY RINGS are distinct circles or arcs of stimulated grass surrounding areas of unthrifty or dead grass. The bands or arcs may be 1 or 2 feet to more than 100 feet in diameter.

The fungi that cause fairy rings grow outward from 5 to 24 inches annually, depending on growing conditions. During wet periods, usually in spring and fall, mushroomlike fruiting bodies of the causal fungi outline the circle or arc.

Fairy rings seldom occur in lawns that are adequately fertilized and treated with fungicides to control other diseases.

The simplest control measure is to punch holes 6 inches apart and about

FUNGUS DISEASES, CAUSAL ORGANISMS, AND SOME EFFECTIVE FUNGICIDES

DISEASE	CAUSAL ORGANISMS	FUNGICIDE
Helminthosporium leafspot (blight, going-out, or melting-out).	*Helminthosporium* spp.......	Acti-dione-thiram, captan, Dyrene, Ortho Lawn and Turf Fungicide, PMA.
Fading-out...........	*Helminthosporium* spp. and *Curvularia* spp.	Do.
Brown patch..........	*Rhizoctonia solani*..........	Mercury-containing fungicides, Dyrene, Ortho Lawn and Turf Fungicide, Tersan OM.
Rust.................	*Puccinia* spp...............	Acti-dione-thiram, zineb.
Grease spot, cottony blight.	*Pythium* spp...............	Dexon, zineb.
Dollar spot...........	*Sclerotinia homeocarpa*......	Cadmium-containing fungicides, Dyrene, Ortho Lawn and Turf Fungicide, Tersan OM.
Snow mold and fusarium patch.	*Fusarium* spp. and *Typhula* spp.	Dyrene, mercury-containing fungicides, Ortho Lawn and Turf Fungicide.
Mushrooms and fairy rings.	*Marasmius* spp., *Psalliota campestris*, and *Lepiota* spp.	Do.
Slime molds...........	*Physarum cinereum* and *Mucilago spongiosa*.	Any good garden or turf fungicide.

12 inches deep in the ground within the affected area and about 2 feet beyond the visible outer edge. Fill each hole with a double-strength fungicide solution to which some detergent has been added.

FUNGI known as slime molds often cover grass blades with a dusty, bluish-gray, or yellow mass.

Slime molds do not parasitize the grass. They discolor grass blades and are unsightly when they occur in spots several feet in diameter.

Slime molds occur during wet weather. They disappear rapidly as soon as it becomes dry.

The slime mold masses can be destroyed by sweeping them with a broom or by spraying them with a strong stream of water.

Masses that persist can be eliminated by treating the affected areas with any good garden or turf fungicide.

NEMATODES are microscopic eelworms that feed on roots of lawn grass and other plants.

Most nematode injury occurs in the southern half of the United States. It is a serious problem.

The affected turf is generally unthrifty and has the appearance of suffering from drought or fertilizer deficiency. Plants are frequently offcolor, and the turf thins out.

Affected turf may respond temporarily to increased applications of water or fertilizer, but the symptoms soon return.

The only effective control is treatment with a nematocide.

HOW TO GET RID OF LAWN INSECTS

ALL OF THE LAWN GRASSES grown in the United States are susceptible to attack and damage by one or more of some 50 species of insects that we regard as important lawn pests.

Some of the insects live in the soil and feed on the roots. Some feed on the leaves or stems. Some suck juices from the plants.

Damage by most of these pests is not consistent enough to justify annual preventive treatment. It is important therefore to obtain early identification of any pest causing injury so that you can apply the proper insecticide before injury becomes extensive.

The most destructive soil-inhabiting insects that attack lawn grasses are the grubs that are the larvae of several species of beetles.

The grubs of different species generally look much alike. They are soft bodied, whitish, or grayish. They have brownish heads and brownish or blackish hind parts and usually lie in a curled position.

The grubs hatch from eggs deposited in the ground by the female beetles. Most of them spend about 10 months in the ground, although a few species may stay in the soil for 2 or 3 years. They feed on the roots about 1 inch below the surface of the soil.

Moles, birds, and skunks feed on grubs and often damage a lawn as they search for them.

Larvae of May beetles (or June beetles) are known as white grubs, of which there are more than 200 species in the United States.

The blackish or brownish adult beetles are common from May to mid-July. They feed on the foliage of plants and trees.

Grubs of the Japanese beetle cause extensive turf damage from North Carolina to New England. The adult is about one-half inch long. It has a shiny, metallic-green body with coppery-brown wings and six small patches of white hairs along each side and back of the body just under the edges of the wings.

Other important grubs that infest lawns are the larvae of the Asiatic garden beetle, the oriental beetle, and the European and masked chafers.

Several species of ants damage lawns mostly as a result of their nesting habits. Some ants form hills around the openings of their nests. Others, like the fire ants, build large mounds, which smother the grass. When ants build their nests near grass roots, they often destroy them.

Some species, such as fire ants and harvester ants, attack people. Their bite is painful.

Several other soil-infesting insects damage lawns. Mole crickets feed on the grass roots and may uproot seedlings. They are about 1.5 inches long and velvety brown. They have large, shovellike front legs.

Wireworms, certain bees and wasps, desert termites, and the larvae of billbugs frequently damage lawns.

THE WORST chewing insects that feed on leaves and stems of grass are the sod webworms, armyworms, and cut-worms.

Sod webworms are the larvae of small, whitish or grayish moths or mil-lers. Often they are called lawn moths. The moths fold their wings closely about their bodies when at rest. They fly over the grass in the evening and the females scatter their eggs over the lawns.

The larvae, on hatching, feed on the grass leaves. As they become larger they build silk-lined tunnels close to the soil surface, cut off blades of grass, and drag them into the tunnels for food. The larvae attack many kinds of grasses, and damage is apt to be especially se-vere in new lawns.

Larvae of armyworms and fall army-worms are about 1.5 inches long when full grown. Their color is greenish to nearly black. The adults are brownish-gray moths that measure about 1.5 inches across the wings.

Cutworms are occasional pests that feed on the grass, cutting it off near the soil surface. They may damage new seedlings severely.

INSECTS THAT SUCK the juices from lawn grasses include chinch bugs, scale in-sects, and leafhoppers.

Two species of chinch bug are major lawn pests. The adults are similar and are about one-sixth inch long and black with white markings. Newly hatched nymphs are bright red and have a white band across the back. They become darker as they mature.

The hairy chinch bug, *Blissus hirtus,* is important in the East from Virginia into New England. Another species, *B. insularis,* is destructive in the South from Florida west to Texas, where it se-verely damages St. Augustine grass, oc-casionally injures centipedegrass, and rarely attacks bermudagrass and pasture grasses.

Plants infested by chinch bugs turn brown. The damage is usually seen in patches. In severe infestations, the grass is killed.

The rhodesgrass scale occurs in Texas, the Gulf States, and in Arizona, New Mexico, California, and Hawaii.

These white, cottony-covered scale in-sects, about one-eighth inch long, attack the plant crowns and cause the plants to turn brown and die. This scale attacks bermudagrass and St. Augustine grass.

Other scales that may cause damage to lawns are the bermudagrass scale and ground pearls. Both cause irregular brown or dead spots and are especial-ly important pests on lawn grasses in the South.

Leafhoppers of several species are sometimes numerous on lawns. They suck the sap from the grass leaves and stems and produce whitish-looking patches. New lawns may be so exten-sively damaged that reseeding is some-times necessary.

MOST LAWN INSECT PESTS can be con-trolled with insecticides.

An accompanying tabulation gives current recommendations for some of the important lawn pests. There are at present no satisfactory control methods for scale insects in lawns.

Insecticides are available in different formulations that contain varying amounts of the insecticide. The recom-mendations given here specify the amount of actual insecticide needed for control.

Most pesticides are poisonous. Be sure that pesticides are clearly labeled. Keep them away from children and pets.

Follow the directions on the con-tainer label and heed all precautions. Wear clean, dry clothing when you ap-ply them. Avoid inhalation and skin contact. Keep pesticides away from the eyes, nose, and mouth. Wash thoroughly with soap and water immediately af-ter you apply the pesticides.

Insecticides are sold under various trade names by garden supply houses, and hardware, seed, and drug stores.

Dusts and granules are ready-made formulations that are used dry. You can apply them directly from the container, but it is usually better to mix the amount recommended for 1,000 square feet with 10 to 15 pounds of dry sand or fertilizer. Apply them with a hand or power duster, or with a lawn ferti-lizer spreader.

Wettable powders and emulsifiable concentrates are used in sprays. Mix the purchased product with water, and apply the spray with a sprinkling can, a garden-type compressed-air sprayer, or a knapsack sprayer. The quantity of water to use depends on the type of sprayer you have. Usually you will need 2 or more gallons of water. If a wettable powder is used, frequent agitation of the mixture is necessary.

A quart jar attachment for a garden hose will provide good distribution of an insecticide on a lawn. Use an attachment that delivers a coarse spray and large volume of water. Usually a quart jar full of an insecticide mixture will cover about 500 square feet of lawn.

Baits are usually purchased ready-mixed, but a bait for controlling slugs and snails may be prepared.

Apply insecticides at any time except when the ground is frozen. Spring or fall is the best time to control grubs.

To control underground lawn pests, apply an insecticide and, immediately afterward, sprinkle the lawn thoroughly. One application may control the pests for several years. Control of soil insects is slow, and it may be a month or more before the insecticide becomes fully effective.

To control aboveground lawn pests, apply an insecticide to the grass. Sprinkle lightly with water to wash the insecticide down around the crowns of the plants. Do not water again for a few days; then sprinkle the grass thoroughly to wash off the insecticide. One application may control the pests for several weeks. Repeat the application if they become numerous.

Do not apply pesticides to a lawn when people or animals are on it. Do not allow pesticides to drift to an area where they might injure people and animals and contaminate food, feed, or water.

After a pesticide has been applied, do not permit children and pets on the lawn until the pesticide has been

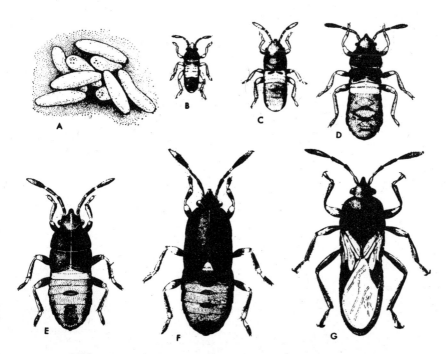

Chinch bug. A. Eggs; B–F. Nymphs in different stages; G. Adult.

PESTICIDES FOR CONTROLLING LAWN DISEASES AND INSECTS

Disease	Chemical	Ounces recommended per 1,000 sq. ft.	Where and when to apply
Helminthosporium leaf and crown disease.	Acti-dione-thiram	4	Spray lawn with fungicide when disease symptoms first appear and repeat at 7–14-day intervals as needed.
	Captan	5–7	
	Dyrene	4–6	
	Ortho lawn and turf fungicide.	4–6	
	PMA	1–2 of 10% soln.	
Brown patch	Mercury-containing fungicides.	Manufacturer's directions.	Do.
	Dyrene	4–6	Do.
	Ortho lawn and turf fungicide.	4–6	Do.
	Tersan OM	5	Do.
Dollar spot	Cadmium-containing fungicides.	Manufacturer's directions.	Do.
	Dyrene	4–6	Do.
	Ortho lawn and turf fungicide.	4	Do.
	Tersan OM	5	Do.
Rusts	Acti-dione-thiram	4	Do.
	Zineb	2–4	Do.
Pythium diseases	Dexon	2	Do.
	Zineb	2–4	Do.
Snow mold	Dyrene	4–6	Treat before lasting snow.
	Mercury-containing fungicides.	Manufacturer's directions.	
	Ortho lawn and turf fungicide.	4	Do.
Mushrooms and fairy rings.	Mercury-containing fungicides.	Manufacturer's directions.	Treat affected areas only.
Slime molds	Any good garden or turf fungicide.	....do	Do.
Nematode injury	Nemagon	....do	Drench with nematocide when soil temperature is at least 65° F.
	Fumazone	....do	
	V–C 13	....do	
Ants	Aldrin	1	To entire area or to individual nests. Sprinkle thoroughly after application so insecticide reaches nests.
	Chlordane	4	
	Dieldrin	1	
	Heptachlor	1	
Armyworms	Chlordane	2	As soon as infestation appears.
	Dieldrin	1	
	Heptachlor	1	While worms are small.
Chinch bugs	Chlordane	4	As soon as damage occurs. A second application may be needed in 7–10 days.
	DDT	4	
	Diazinon	3	
	Dieldrin	1	
	V–C 13	9	
Cutworms	Chlordane	2	In late afternoon.
	Dieldrin	1	Do.
	Heptachlor	1	Do.
Grubs	Aldrin	1	When examination shows grubs are present. Usually in early fall.
	Chlordane	4	
	Dieldrin	1	
	Heptachlor	1	
Sod webworms	Aldrin	1	In late afternoon or evening. A second application may be necessary.
	Chlordane	2	
	DDT	2	
	Dieldrin	1	
	Heptachlor	1	Do.
	Toxaphene	2	Do.

washed off by sprinkling and the grass has dried completely.

Note.—You can use a tablespoon or cup to measure emulsifiable concentrates.

1 fluid ounce = 2 tablespoons.
8 fluid ounces = 1 cup.
1 pint = 2 cups.
Dry formulations vary in weight.

HOME VEGETABLE GARDENING

THERE ARE four good reasons why a householder may want to devote some of his garden space and energy to growing vegetables.

The reasons: To save some money; to have a pleasant hobby; to enjoy the perfection of quality that is possible from one's own garden, without reference to cost; to get the satisfaction of digging and sweating and producing a home-grown product.

Few gardeners would wish to devote all their space to vegetables at the expense of ornamentals, however, nor should they.

If soil, light, and climate are favorable, a few salad vegetables and greens may well be included in the general garden plan, and sometimes utilitarian plants, including vegetables, can be

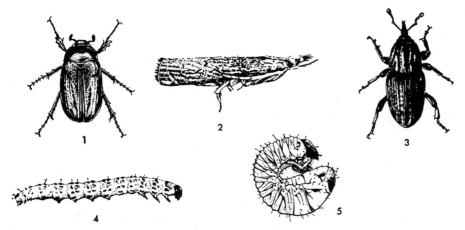

1. *Adult May beetle.*   2. *Adult sod webworm.*   3. *Adult billbug.*   4. *Larva of sod webworm.*
5. *A white grub, the larva of a May beetle.*

grown as "ornamentals." Runnerless strawberries, the French *fraisiers de Bois,* for example, make an attractive border. Small-fruited peppers, thyme and tarragon and other herbs, frilly lettuce or mustard, endive, carrots, red-leaved Swiss chard, and a few plants of parsley are at home among flowers.

ASSUME THAT, like most urban and suburban householders, you have but a very small plot (say, up to 400 or 500 square feet) that is suitable or that you wish to grow vegetables on. What should you grow?

First, choose a few kinds that require little space for growing the amounts you may want. Generally, under such conditions, you would not grow such things as pumpkins, melons, sweet corn, and potatoes.

Next, among the kinds that require little space, choose those you and your family enjoy most, especially those that product a high dollar value per unit of land or that on the market may have disappointing quality.

Among the vegetables for use fresh, tomatoes probably are foremost. Other good fresh salad vegetables and greens are sweet peppers, tender varieties of lettuce, endive, green onions, radishes, spinach, turnip greens, mustard, collards or kale, and parsley and chives (a few plants of each). You may want a few plants of other herbs for flavoring soup and salads.

You may have no place available for vegetables but strips around boundaries or along walks in the backyard. You can grow tomatoes on stakes in the back of such narrow beds and have low-growing flowers on the sunny side of the rows, if you wish. Or low-growing vegetables can be grown on the sunny side, or very quick-growing early vegetables (such as green onions, radishes, and leaf lettuce) on either side of the row.

Cucumbers and pole beans can be trained up on the sunny side of a high wire fence. Low-growing vegetables or flowers can be planted to the sunny side of them. The few plants of parsley and flavoring herbs you need can be put at some inconspicuous place in a flower border or mass.

You can transplant a few parsley plants into big flower pots in the fall, trim them back close to the crown, and keep them in sunny windows in the house for continuing harvests of leaves during the winter.

Now SUPPOSE you have space for a small garden in a compact plot, say 1,200 to 1,500 square feet.

You could still use some of the devices mentioned, if you wish, to save space in this larger plot, in which you profitably could grow larger amounts of the several items.

Also, you would be justified in growing additional kinds, including some that require more space to produce significant amounts, or that have lower money value. Examples are cabbage, broccoli, bush squash, and snap beans.

The principles are the same for growing on the very small scale mentioned in preceding paragraphs as for growing on a larger scale. On very small areas you grow only a few plants, usually of small-growing kinds.

Growing sweet corn, melons, potatoes, and sweetpotatoes in a garden of 1,500 square feet is not recommended. If, however, you prefer to use the space for such items, and sacrifice something else, go ahead and do it. After all, tastes and desires differ. Keep in mind, however, that the items take a lot of space and may crowd you out of growing small amounts of many other desirable things.

If you have a garden area approaching one-fourth acre (say, 10 thousand square feet) with ample water, you can grow all the fresh vegetables an average family needs during the growing season and probably a lot more.

A half acre of good soil in a good climate can produce all the fresh vegetables a large family needs with considerable quantities for canning and freezing. Do not, however, grow such quantities for your own use unless you have ample help and facilities for processing and for proper storage of root and tuber crops.

Do NOT PLANT more of one thing at one time than you can enjoy using before it is past the proper harvest stage. Planting too much at once is a common error of the beginner. You learn by experience how much is enough for your needs.

Remember that a single planting of many vegetables is "good" for harvest for very few days. You can use but little from some plantings before the product becomes poor in quality or useless.

For example, radishes are ready to harvest in 3 to 4 weeks from planting and are "good" hardly a week. Sow only 3 or 4 feet of row per person who will eat them, every 5 to 7 days up to early summer.

Many new varieties of snap beans tend to bear for only a short season, but they produce an abundance of pods of high quality. At first, plant 5 to 10 feet of row per person about every 2 weeks for as long as you want fresh beans and there is time to grow them before frost. If you want a big yield at one time for canning or freezing, plant more, but do not overdo it. A good crop of Tendercrop, for example, will yield a bushel (32 pounds) or more per 100 feet of row, of which about half can be obtained at the first harvest.

A half-dozen plants of one variety of cabbage is enough for the average family to plant at one time if it is to be used fresh. Plant a half-dozen plants of each of three or four varieties that will reach harvest over a period of weeks, if you want cabbage over a period of weeks.

If you grow spinach and peas, do not try to get a spread of harvests by successive plantings in the spring. These plants are very sensitive to hot weather. They must be planted very early. Delayed planting causes serious reduction in yield and quality. Get some spread of harvest by planting varieties that have different times of maturity.

Many other vegetables are sensitive to hot weather. Study the planting time-tables and get your local recommendations.

If you have a large enough garden for supplying sweet corn from successive harvests, plant 3 or 4 short sections of rows side by side at intervals of 5 to 7 days. When plants of one planting date stand close together in short multiple rows, pollination often is better than if the plants are in a single long row. Plant at one time no more than you will use in 3 or 4 days. One planting of a single kind yields ears of good quality for only 2 or 3 days. Mixed seed of two hybrids that mature 2 days apart gives a better spread of harvest from a single planting date than does seed of a single hybrid.

Six tomato plants of indeterminate habit (not "self-topping") and medium or later maturity can supply enough fresh tomatoes for one person. Plant a few plants of one of the very early small-vined varieties to harvest before the later varieties start ripening. A half-dozen to a dozen sweet pepper plants can supply enough peppers for salads

and an occasional cooked dish, for the average family, for the season.

Here is a rough and conservative estimate of the yield to be expected from 50 feet of row—not that 50 feet is the amount you necessarily should plant:

Asparagus, 13 pounds; shelled lima beans, 7; snap bush beans, 12; beets, 40; sprouting broccoli, 17; cabbage, 62; cantaloups, 76; carrots, 38; sweet corn, 22; slicing cucumbers, 55; eggplant, 47; escarole, 30; kale, 17; lettuce, 29; mature onions, 40; green shelled peas, 4; green peppers, 50; potatoes, 67; spinach, 13; sweetpotatoes, 25; tomatoes, 79; watermelons, 83.

You may want more, or less, or none of these. The figures are based in part on the average yields per acre of the several crops as grown commercially in this country. Good yields by good gardeners may be two to three times as much. Some may be less.

Again, you will have to learn from experience what yields you can expect from your various crops; assuming you have enough space, how much you need to plant at one time and in one season to satisfy your requirements; or, conversely, what you can expect to produce on a small space available to you.

HERE ARE SOME TIPS on management.

• Protect your soil. Loose, dry, bare soil can blow away in a high wind. Newly planted seeds and very small plants can be blown out of such soil, and small plants can be damaged by blowing particles or covered by them.

• Try to keep the soil moist, covered with plants or mulch, or protected by windbreaks to keep it from blowing. Leaving the surface between the rows a bit rough and trashy with organic matter will help.

• Sloping soil can be washed away easily by rainstorms or runoff from rapidly melting snow. Do not let that happen. Keep the surface covered with plants or mulch to retard runoff.

• Work organic matter into the soil to increase penetration of water. Run the rows on the level instead of up and down the slope, even if you have to curve the rows to do so.

• Do not let water from higher ground flood across your garden. Divert it into drainways where it will do no harm.

• Keep your garden space at work for you throughout the season.

• Plan your plantings, if possible, so that as soon as one crop is all harvested you can plant another in its place. Quick-growing crops should be planted together so that after harvest, convenient space for others is available.

• It is often feasible to plant small, quick-maturing things between the rows of large, slow-growing ones (or close to one side) and harvest the quick-maturing things before there is any serious interference.

• Sometimes, after a rather long-growing, spring-planted crop, you will have time to plant a quick-growing crop for autumn harvest.

• Do not overlook possibilities of late summer or early fall plantings for harvest in autumn, and (in the South) during the winter.

• Remember to watch for the first signs of plant diseases and insect infestation.

FLOWERBED FEATURES

PUT A FLOWERBED in the right place, choose plants of good colors, and give it and them the care they deserve, and you have a thing of beauty and a joy forever, wherever you are and however small the space you can use for flowers.

First, choose a site where the garden will complement the general landscape effect.

It may be a border along the side or across the back of a property line, along a driveway or in a triangle at a corner of the property, in an ell between house and garage, along a walk or path, or just a spot directly opposite a picture window, terrace, or patio.

It may even be confined to large planters, strategically placed and massed with cascading petunias.

A circular bed in the middle of a lawn panel is rarely, if ever, good.

Your time and energy for maintenace should dictate its size. Better to have a small, neat, well-cared-for garden than a long, rambling border that you must always apologize for.

THE SECOND STEP is to select the plants that are appropriate for the place.

The amount of sun or shade, the nature of the soil (heavy clay, loam, or light sandy soil), drainage, and existing windbreaks or shrub borders are some of the determining factors.

If the spot is next to a terrace or patio, you may choose low-growing plants, many in the white-yellow range to pick up the highlights of early evening hours.

If the garden is in front of a high hedge at the back of a property, taller plants, bolder in their effect, would predominate.

Problems of steep changes in grade sometimes are solved by making a rock garden on the slope or by constructing a dry rock wall, in which low-growing, rock-garden types of plants are set in the spaces between the rocks.

For the average flower garden, a border about 6 feet wide permits a variety of plants. The tallest plants are put in the background, the intermediate ones go in the middle area, and the lowest plants grow in the foreground.

FLOWERBEDS may contain only annuals (which live only one season) or only perennials (which live over more than one winter), but it may be well to have some of each.

If you have a newly built home, you may wish to concentrate on annuals for immediate effect the first year and gradually add perennials for more permanent plantings.

Regardless of the type of plant material, the best effect is usually created by massing. Avoid a single row of zinnias spaced 18 inches apart. Instead, plant them 12 inches apart in groups. A thin line of dwarf marigolds is pathetic, but the same number of plants grouped together is effective.

For most perennials, a clump of three is a minimum. If space permits, five or six may be better.

Large specimen plants, such as peonies, hostas, and oriental poppies, need not be set in groups but are better spaced throughout the planting.

Solid plantings of a single genus of perennials, such as peonies or iris or oriental poppies, usually are to be avoided because before and after their burst of bloom there is nothing but foliage, but you can relieve the monotony of such a planting by adding annuals for all-season color.

Roses should be segregated in an area by themselves. They lose much of their effectiveness if they are planted among annuals and perennials.

The smaller the garden, the greater is the need to choose plants that are in flower for a long time in order to have continuous color.

Among the perennials in this classification are golden marguerite (Anthemis), coreopsis, gaillardia, coralbells (Heuchera), *Campanula carpatica,* Shasta daisies, summer flowering phlox; and the tufted pansy (*Viola cornuta*).

As you enlarge the bed, you can add plants with a shorter period of bloom.

If you are away all summer, perhaps a combination of spring flowering bulbs and chrysanthemums or hardy asters that bloom in the fall may suffice. Otherwise, select the plants that will give you the most color throughout the growing season.

To insure a succession of bloom from early spring to late fall, the backbone of many gardens over much of this country, in order of bloom, consists of spring flowering bulbs, such as narcissus and tulips, and these perennials: Iris, peonies, summer flowering phlox, and chrysanthemums or hardy asters. To this skeleton, annuals, biennials, additional spring and summer flowering bulbs, and other perennials could be added.

The chief purpose of the spring-flowering bulbs, such as crocus, narcissus, hyacinths, and tulips, is to extend the period of bloom of a garden, as most of them provide a striking mass of early color.

They are a versatile group and are satisfactory in borders, along walks, around pools, and in front of foundation plantings or shrub borders. They may be spotted in groups throughout perennial beds. Many, except hyacinths and tulips, can be naturalized.

Many of the dwarf and miniature bulbs also are appropriate for rock gardens.

If you plant solid beds of bulbs for mass effect in the spring, you can use annuals in the same bed for color during the rest of the season without disturbing the bulbs.

Summer flowering bulbs, such as lilies, are specimen plants that enhance any planting. The common species combined with new hybrids make it possible to have one lily or another in flower from early summer until late frosts. Their many colors, heights, flower forms, and season of bloom can improve every garden.

Tender bulbous material, such as tigridias, acidantheras, and gladiolus, and tuberous material, such as dahlias and tuberous begonias, require more care, because they must be dug and stored yearly. Gladioli often are lined out in rows in a separate area, as they do not usually blend in with a miscellaneous planting. The others can be included in a general flowerbed.

ANNUALS, which are grown each year from seed or cuttings to produce a good show of color during the current season, provide the quickest results, are relatively inexpensive, and present few cultural difficulties.

They can be planted directly over beds of spring flowering bulbs. Many are useful in planters or window boxes.

Annual vines offer many possibilities for screen plantings.

Because of their transient nature, annuals provide versatility for temporary gardens. They enable you to correct any mistakes in design, color combination, or placement because of habit or height the following year.

SEEDS of most annuals can be sown directly in the garden, but quicker and better results are achieved if you set out plants started by amateur or professional growers in frames or greenhouses. The plants often are in bud or in flower when they are set out after danger of frosts and give an immediate effect.

Petunias, zinnias, dwarf marigolds, and ageratum are among the annuals that provide colorful plants all season.

Lobelia, impatiens, and bedding begonias are excellent choices for shaded areas. Portulaca requires full sun.

If you are interested in color but not flowers, many plants, which are treated as annuals, have variegated or multicolored foliage. Among them are coleus, variegated geraniums, purple leaf basil, alternantheras, bloodleaf, and (in the tender bulbous group) caladiums.

Taller annuals, such as cleome, cosmos, some sunflowers, and gloriosa daisies, add interest as background.

PERENNIALS provide the greatest range of material. For any given location, very likely you will find some perennials that are appropriate.

They range in height from creeping bugleweed (Ajuga) and the six-inch crested iris to towering monkshood (Aconitum) and foxtail lilies (Eremurus). Some, like the vertical foxgloves and delphiniums, are erect. Some are an airy mass like baby'sbreath Gypsophila) and sea-lavender (Limonium). Candytuft (Iberis) is low, compact, and moundlike.

Gardeners interested in texture may choose among the coarse-leaved hostas, the delicate foliage of blue flax (Linum), the huge, coarse flowers of hibiscus, and delicate columbines.

Adaptability to various locations recommends primulas, monardas, bleedingheart, and hostas for the shade; rudbeckias, helianthus, and heliopsis for the sun; cardinal flower (Lobelia), for the wet area; artemisias where it is dry; and german iris and dianthus where the soil is somewhat alkaline.

Lythrums, hemerocallis, and spiderworts seemingly do well anyplace.

The Christmas rose (Helleborus) flowers under the snow. Leopardsbane (Doronicum) blooms before the tulips fade, and the last chrysanthemum flowers will be finished off by late frosts.

Because most species of perennials are in bloom about a month, you should have a variety of material to obtain a sequence of bloom if you use only perennials. Some species have early- and late-flowering varieties that can be combined to extend the flower interest of any one type.

Some genera, such as the hostas and veronicas, contain some species that flower early in the season, others at midseason, and still others that are late flowering.

Hemerocallis (daylilies) comprise an almost foolproof group. They do well in almost any situation and require practically no maintenance. A selection of varieties makes it possible to have one or another in bloom at any time of the season. Their colors range through the various shades and tints of cream, yellow, orange, and red and maroon.

BIENNIALS are grown from seed, produce a rosette of leaves the first year, flower the second year, and are then discarded. Among the commoner ones are sweet-william, hollyhock, foxglove, and Canterbury-bells. They may self-sow in the garden, but the seedlings that result often revert to ordinary or undesirable colors. It is recommended therefore that you buy new seed regularly.

As TO COLOR in the garden, the important point is that you have what you enjoy.

You may prefer a riot of color and find bright, clashing colors stimulating. Or you may want only pale pastels in your garden. Again, you may like, as many do, a garden with all flowers of one color—white, for example, or red. Have what you like. If you tire of it, change.

Temperature, humidity, amount of rainfall, soils, and length of growing season vary so greatly over the United

States that no blanket recommendations can be given for the selection of plants. It is not hard for you to get lists and suggestions applicable to your locality, though—from your neighbors who garden, nearby nurserymen, county extension workers, and books.

Remember this: A flower garden is a dynamic project. It is never static. Over the years, you change what you do not like, eliminate some, add new types or varieties, and try different combinations.

One final tip to keep in mind: You can double the life of cut flowers by cutting their stems at a long slant. Add a lump of sugar or camphor or a couple of aspirin tablets to the water. The flowers will keep fresh longer if the leaves below the water are removed.

ELIMINATE PESTS AMONG YOUR FLOWERS

PREVENTION is a watchword for the flower garden. Keep the plants growing vigorously, and you will have fewer troubles with pests and diseases.

Too much fertilization, which seems commoner than underfertilization, often kills or injures plants and makes them more susceptible to diseases and pests.

Too much of one fertilizer element can cause an imbalance of another element and produce a yellowing of leaves and other symptoms.

Too little fertilizer may produce stunted, unhealthy plants.

Deep cultivation and too much mulch (leaves, compost, peat moss) can be detrimental, particularly to such shallow-rooted plants as azaleas. Injury caused by careless cultivation to roots, the crown, and stem offers points for disease organisms to enter the plant.

When you select plants, consider their needs for moisture, temperature, shade, soil acidity, and other environmental factors.

Leaf spot organisms, crown-attacking fungi, and flower-blighting organisms may attack plants spaced so closely that air circulation around them is poor. You can reduce the chances of pests and diseases if you keep weeds in check, for weeds may cause crowding, harbor disease organisms and pests, and compete with other plants for water and nutrients.

Another way to keep disease organisms and pests out is to select healthy plants, seeds, and bulbs or treat them to eliminate the disease organism or pest before you plant. Preventing entry into a garden often is easier than other control measures.

Buy plant materials from reputable dealers.

Avoid plants that show root-knot nematode galls or root decay.

Dusting seeds lightly before planting with a fungicide, such as thiram, ferban, or captan, eliminates many seed-rotting or damping-off organisms.

Lily bulbs are dipped with ferbam plus pentachloronitrobenzene to reduce bulb and root rots.

Many disease organisms and nematodes enter the garden in infested soils. The camellia flower blight fungus may be brought into a blight-free garden in the soil ball, which harbors the resting stage of the fungus, or on flowers.

DISEASE ORGANISMS and pests that do become established despite your careful management should be eradicated.

Often it is advisable to remove and destroy the plants or plant parts that are affected by such diseases as root-knot, lily fleck, aster wilt, and southern blight.

The spread of aster wilt and southern blight and other diseases involving damping off, crown and root rots, and stem cankers can be reduced by removing the affected plants and drenching the place they grew. A general-purpose drench consists of captan plus either thiram or pentachloronitrobenzene (1 tablespoonful of each per gallon of water). Apply it at the rate of one-half gallon per square foot.

The removal of cankers on trees or shrubs also may be advisable to prevent infection in the other parts. Make the cut into healthy wood and, as in normal pruning, make it flush against a larger limb or just above a leafbud to induce faster healing. On larger cuts, use a wound dressing, which you can buy at seedstores.

Destroy the diseased plants or plant parts you remove and weeds that can harbor pests. Camellia flower blight often is reduced in severity by destroying old flowers. Powdery mildews and a few other diseases can be eradicated by spraying or dusting with recommended fungicides.

Rotation is another aspect of prevention. Move your planting area after 3 or 4 years. Thereby you can aid in control of some soilborne diseases and pests, as wilts, crown rots, and root rots. Some rotation can be practiced even in a small flower garden.

The soil in which plants are to be grown can be treated to reduce or eliminate soilborne organisms.

You can do this in the seed flat by baking moist (but not wet) soil in an oven until a potato placed in the soil is cooked.

For a larger area, methyl bromide (1 to 3 pounds per 100 square feet) may be released under a plastic covering. The soil should be loose, with enough moisture for seed germination and above 50° F.

Other general-purpose fumigants you can use without a plastic covering are formulations of dichloropropene-dichloropropane mixture plus methyl isothiocyanate (DD+MENCS) or sodium methyl dithiocarbamate.

To control nematodes, products containing ethylene dibromide (EDB), dichloropropene-dichloropropane (DD), dibromochloropropane (DBCP), or other recommended materials can be used as preplanting treatments.

The manufacturers' directions should be followed carefully. Be careful lest these poisons harm or kill people, pets, trees, shrubs, and other plants that have roots in or near the treated area.

Allow ample time for the fumigant to dissipate from the soil before you plant it.

Another nematocide that can be used directly around many plants is dibromochloropropane (DBCP).

PROTECTIVE BARRIERS placed between the susceptible plant part and the attacking disease organism or pest are helpful. Usually they are chemical sprays or dusts. To be effective for disease control, the sprays and dusts must be applied before the disease appears or before it becomes well established.

Insect pests can be killed by an insecticide after the pests attack the plant, but by then they may have disfigured the plant.

Insecticides, which kill by contact or upon being eaten, should be applied when they will be on the plant for at least several hours.

Sprays or dusts for control of disease are more effective when applied before rains, heavy dews, fogs, or watering because infection occurs when moisture is present or the humidity is high. Thus a spray or dust applied after a rainy period to control black spot of roses may be too late to prevent some infection.

For black spot and many other diseases for which sprays or dusts are used, repeated applications are necessary. The interval depends on the life cycle of the organism, the weather, and sometimes the plant. Applications of zineb or thiram, for example, to control azalea petal blight should be made two or three times a week (rather than once a week), while new flowers are opening and developing to the susceptible stage.

Some systemic insecticides, as demeton, schradan, and phorate, which plants absorb, kill many sucking insects when the insects suck the toxic agent from the plant. Liquid forms for foliage application and granular forms for soil application are available. Growers of Easter lily bulbs have used systemic insecticides to control aphids capable of carrying viruses that cause fleck disease by soaking the bulbs before planting, spraying the plant, or applying them to the soil. These insecticides can be absorbed through the skin of humans, so all precautions must be taken when you handle them.

Apply sprays uniformly as a fine mist from the top of the plant down and from the bottom up until the spray just begins to run off the foliage. Keep the spray nozzle moving. The sprayer, unless it has a mechanical agitator, should be shaken often to prevent settling of the chemical.

Dusts should be forced through the foliage to give an even, light coating to both leaf surfaces. Apply them when the air is still, preferably early in the morning or at dusk.

Either dusts or sprays can be used satisfactorily in the flower garden.

Dusts are usually more expensive, but the dusters cost less than comparable sprayers and are more convenient and easier to use.

Sprays are less difficult to handle in windy weather.

Plunger-type dusters are the smallest kind and can do a fair job for a few plants. A small bellows or rotary fan duster will give better coverage for a small garden. Larger rotary dusters and power dusters can be used on larger gardens for better distribution.

Household sprayers that hold up to 4 quarts can do a reasonably good job of spraying if they deliver a continuous fine spray or mist.

Compressed-air sprayers that hold 1 to 5 gallons are satisfactory for garden use. Larger sprayers with a continuously operated hand or motor pump are needed in larger gardens.

Clean sprayers thoroughly after use and allow them to dry.

Ready-to-use sprays in pressurized cans are useful on house plants or a few plants in a garden. They may be expensive.

You may like the hose-proportioner sprayers, in which the chemical is placed in a jar and mixed with the water at the hose nozzle. They are convenient, but more chemical is used than with a conventional sprayer, and the proportioners vary in distribution of spray material.

AVAILABLE general purpose sprays or dusts will eliminate the need for mixing several control materials. Better, cheaper results can usually be had by using a material specifically recommended for a particular disease or pest. Recommendations should be followed closely in all cases.

CHOOSE, whenever possible, varieties that withstand a disease. Examples are rust-resistant snapdragons, wilt-resistant asters, and wilt-resistant mimosas.

Resistance does not always mean that the disease will not develop. Sometimes it does develop, frequently because the disease organisms also have many varieties or strains, and a plant resistant to one disease strain may fall prey to another.

PROTECTING TREES

MOST SHRUBS and ornamental and fruit trees are attacked by relatively few insects and diseases, which leave only minor troubles if they are controlled.

The insects are of two general types—those that chew the plant parts and leave holes or some other evidence of their presence and those that suck plant juices.

Beetles and caterpillars are examples of chewing insects.

Aphids (plant lice), leafhoppers, and scale insects are among the sucking insects.

Plant disease—which may be considered as any deviation from normal—may be caused by fungi, bacteria, virus, mineral deficiency, or even some abnormal physiological condition brought about by drought.

All of them may be of major importance, and your ability to recognize the cause of the trouble is the basis of your campaign against them.

Most of the time you will be dealing with fungi, bacteria, or some environmental condition as the cause of your trouble.

Fungi are low forms of plantlife that lack the green color (chlorophyll) of higher plants. Because they lack chlorophyll, they cannot make their own food and have to live on dead organic matter (saprophytes) or on living organisms (parasites).

We are concerned primarily with the parasites because they often cause disease in living plants.

The fungi include mildews, rusts, smuts, molds, mushrooms, puffballs, and allied forms.

Bacteria are one-celled microscopic organisms, which also lack chlorophyll and mostly are saprophytic or parasitic. The parasitic types cause blights, cankers, leaf spots, and galls on their host plants.

IT IS IMPORTANT to keep your shrubs and trees healthy, because often the weak ones are most susceptible to attack.

Trees and shrubs may be weakened by malnutrition, drought, whipping by wind, sunscald, mechanical injury, poor drainage, and transplanting at the wrong time of year.

Your plants will suffer from malnutrition when they cannot get the major elements (nitrogen, phosphorus, potassium), and sometimes some of the minor elements (sulfur, calcium, magnesium, iron, and several others).

It is best to apply a complete commercial fertilizer in the spring before the buds break. Drill holes in the ground 8 to 10 inches deep and fill with fertilizer. The holes should be about 2 or 3 feet apart and distributed out as far as the branches extend.

The amount of fertilizer (10-6-4) to use for a tree you can calculate quickly. Use 2 pounds per inch of trunk diameter, measured 3 feet above the soil surface.

Never let your plants suffer from lack of water. If you are away from home for long periods during the dry season, arrange with your neighbor to water your plants, because extensive damage can occur during this time.

Wind whipping can be corrected by a few guy wires.

Wrapping a tree trunk with heavy paper or burlap will prevent sunscald. The paper or burlap should be sprayed or treated with a DDT suspension (2 tablespoons of 50 percent DDT wettable powder per gallon of water) to prevent borers from getting into the trunk.

Mechanical injury can be prevented if you are careful while working with mower or tools around the tree trunk.

WHEN YOU PLANT shrubs and trees, inquire if disease- or insect-resistant varieties or species are available. Even though they are more costly, you may save yourself many troubles by planting them.

A few varieties of trees have been bred that show some degree of resistance to certain diseases. Among these are mimosa (wilt), chestnut (blight), apple or flowering crabapple (scab and powdery mildew), pear (fire blight), and American elm (phloem necrosis).

Do not plant trees or shrubs with galls on the roots or stems.

CLEANLINESS is the first commandment in a control program.

Prune out diseased or dead branches and destroy them and all trash, because they may harbor insects and disease-causing organisms. If you do not do so, no matter how good a spray program you follow, the plants may be reinfested with insects or reinfected with disease organisms.

Paint pruning wounds with an asphaltum base tree-wound dressing to prevent invasion by secondary wood-rot organisms.

If you follow those practices, you have solved many problems. The remaining problems very likely will be those caused by insects and diseases and usually can be corrected by applying fungicides and insecticides.

Most chemical control programs for fruit trees are based mainly on protective sprays or dusts.

Sprays are more effective and last longer. Sprays protect the plant by a thin layer of chemical. In time, the layer loses its effectiveness and must be replenished or renewed. As the plant grows, the new growth must be covered with chemical.

A thorough and complete spray schedule is needed for fruit trees. It is important to cover both surfaces of all leaves completely, as well as the fruit, with a fine, mist-type spray.

CHERRY LEAF SPOT

BROWN ROT ON PEACH

FRUIT SPOT OF PEAR

PEACH SCAB

POWDERY MILDEW

APPLE SCAB ON FRUIT AND LEAF

In most parts of the country one simply cannot get effective control with two or three applications. The reason for failure usually is that the gardener sprays only once or twice during the growing season.

The climate and other environmental conditions in your part of the country usually determine the number of applications needed for effective control. Some sections require 10 or more applications, although 7 or 8 may be the average.

Applications on fruit trees should begin when a small amount of color (prepink) is visible in the blossoms.

Make the second application just before the blossoms open (the pink stage).

Make a third application when most of the petals have fallen.

Subsequent applications (fruit-cover sprays) should be applied at intervals of 10 to 20 days, depending on the weather.

Because the chemical barrier is worn away rapidly during rainy periods, the shorter interval should be maintained, but the spray interval can be lengthened when the weather is hot and dry.

Besides the sprays during the growing season, about every 2 to 3 years during the dormant season you should apply an oil spray to control scale insects. This spray may also kill some eggs of aphids and mites.

It is suggested that backyard gardeners use mixtures of the fungicides and insecticides that are needed to control the main diseases and insects of fruit trees. Such formulations are called all-purpose fruit sprays.

They usually contain captan, dodine, or ferbam as the fungicide or a combination of those chemicals. Applied according to directions, those fungicides control organisms that cause scab (apple, pear), leaf spot (cherry), and brown rot (peach, cherry, plum).

Fungicides, such as wettable sulfur or Karathane, sometimes are included in all-purpose formulations to control powdery mildew. Sulfur also is included usually in peach sprays to control scab.

Insecticides usually included with the fungicides are DDT, methoxychlor, carbaryl (Sevin), and malathion. They control one or more insects, such as plum curculio, apple maggot, codling moth, and aphids. Malathion sometimes is also included to control small spider-like animals (Arachnids), called mites or spider mites.

Do NOT USE COPPER in any form on peaches during the growing season. Copper compounds often cause peaches to lose their leaves.

Copper-containing compounds, however, sometimes can be applied to other fruit trees without serious damage. In fact, although various copper formulations under certain conditions may produce some degree of russeting on apple and pear fruit, fixed coppers or bordeaux (copper sulfate plus lime) mixtures are the only effective materials that can be recommended to backyard gardeners for control of the bacterial disease fire blight. The antibiotic streptomycin sometimes is used commercially to control this disease, but in most parts of the country its use is limited to the prebloom or bloom period.

USUALLY it is not necessary to keep a protective deposit of insecticide and fungicide on shrubs and ornamental trees as it is on fruit trees.

The chemical is applied during the season when a certain disease or insect usually makes its appearance or when a small amount of damage is observed.

After one lives in a locality for a few years, he learns when to expect a certain disease or insect and applies the proper materials at that time. In this way he keeps damage to a minimum. The Japanese beetle is an example of an insect that usually makes its appearance in the northeastern part of the country about the same time each year.

Some insects that cause trouble on certain plants are Japanese beetles, cankerworms, bagworms, leaf miners, aphids, bark beetles, lacebugs, borers, pine shoot moth, juniper webworm, and scale insects. Spider mites also may be serious on some trees and shrubs.

In general, malathion is a good all-round insecticide, which controls many chewing and sucking insects as well as some of the spider mites.

Malathion, however, tends to have a short residual life and sometimes requires frequent applications.

Methoxychlor, DDT, and carbaryl (Sevin) normally give much better control of chewing insects than sucking insects and usually last 2 to 3 weeks.

Mildew, leaf spot, blight, rust, and other diseases attack certain shrubs and ornamental trees. A variety of fungicides, such as sulfur, dodine, zineb, maneb, captan, thiram, and copper, may be suggested as controls.

HOW TO STOP WEEDS

WE HAVE COME a long way in our struggles with weeds.

We know that we will have fewer weeds in lawns and gardens if we plant weed-free seeds.

We know the value of controlling weeds in fence rows, roadways, and other marginal places.

Good cultural practices, such as control of insects and the plant diseases, balanced and regular fertilization, routine mowing, pruning, and irrigation provide good conditions so that vigorously growing plants will crowd out weeds.

We have new chemicals to eradicate weeds.

We give some suggestions for the use of new methods for the control of weeds around the home. Which of the alternative methods you choose will depend on your individual problem and situation.

Herbicides must be used and stored with care.

CONTROL crabgrass, chickweed, lambsquarters, pigweed, and many other broad-leaved weeds and weed grasses in patios and along the margins of walks, roads, and flowerbeds with carefully directed sprays of Stoddard solvent drycleaning fluid.

Use full strength in a hand sprayer. Thoroughly wet the foliage with the solvent. It kills foliage on contact.

Repeat the treatment as new weeds appear. Three to four treatments usually control the weeds for the growing season.

Do not let the solvent touch the foliage or stalks of wanted plants, which it also will kill. Carefully direct the spray, therefore, and use a low pressure that reduces drift of the spray.

Weeds die the day of treatment in hot weather. The solvent evaporates quickly and does not leave a chemical residue.

AGAINST WEEDS in woody ornamental and tree plantings, use Stoddard solvent as a carefully directed spray.

Keep the solvent away from the bark and foliage of valuable plants.

Repeat the treatments as new weeds appear.

Black polyethylene film may be placed in strips, squares, or circles when you make new plantings to control many germinating annual weeds and conserve moisture.

To protect established plantings, place the film carefully around the bases of plants after cultivation or spraying to remove growing weeds.

DCPA, used in spray or granular form, controls germinating grasses and some broad-leaved weeds without injuring many woody ornamentals and trees.

WEEDS in annual vegetable gardens can be controlled most effectively by a treatment with SMDC, DMTT, or methyl bromide before planting.

These herbicides are called soil fumigants. They control most annual and perennial weeds. They dissipate rapidly.

A short time after treatment, vegetables or ornamentals may be planted without injurious effects.

Apply SMDC and DMTT on newly worked soil followed by sprinkling to form a soil-crust seal to hold the vapors in the soil. Wait 2 to 3 weeks between treatment and planting.

Methyl bromide is applied under a polyethylene film on newly worked soil. Planting may be done 48 hours after removal of the cover.

Methyl bromide is a deadly poison. Prevent children and pets from being exposed to it. Never release it in a closed room.

Many germinating weeds, including annual grasses in flowerbeds, can be controlled with DCPA.

In general, the soil fumigants should not be used in flowerbeds in lawn areas, although they may be used effectively when the plantings are isolated from lawns or woody ornamentals.

SPECIAL TREATMENTS are needed for some weeds, including dodder, mugwort, and poison-ivy.

Dodder has become increasingly bad among herbaceous annual and perennial ornamentals, apparently because of the wider use of animal manures that contain dodder seed.

Dodder is controlled by soil treatments with DCPA. Apply in the early spring immediately after transplanting the ornamentals and before the weeds come up. Most established ornamentals are tolerant of DCPA.

Mugwort, a perennial weed, sometimes mistakenly is called wild chrysanthemum because of resemblance of its foliage to cultivated chrysanthemums. It is spread by seed, the transport of roots in soil accompanying ornamental plants, and creeping root stocks. It is difficult to control. You may have to sacrifice some ornamental plantings in order to control mugwort with herbicides, although the loss can be minimized by carefully localized treatments.

Directed spot treatments with amitrole are effective if you repeat them two or three times at monthly intervals during the growing season. Wet the foliage thoroughly with the spray.

Brush plants, such as oak, elm, cherry, sassafras seedlings, honey-suckle, Virginia-creeper, poison-ivy, and others in wooded areas also can be killed with amitrole.

If ornamental plantings are not near, 2,4,5-T may be used for the woody weeds.

The resprouting of trees after cutting can be stopped by the use of am-mate herbicide applied in liquid or crystalline form to the stump.

Bamboo may be a problem in places where the climate is warm. It can be controlled with repeated treatments with dalapon, beginning when the plants are 18 inches to 2 feet tall.

Ragweed and goldenrod often grow in fence rows and other marginal areas. Spraying with 2,4-D controls them and minimizes the allergic reactions they may cause in some persons.

WEEDS occur in lawns where the grass is thinned by heavy use, diseases, and insects; in disturbed areas; and along borders.

Most weeds are a minor problem if the lawn grass is dense and vigorous.

Lawn management practices recommended in another chapter should accompany the weed control methods recommended here.

Broadleaf weeds—dandelion, buckhorn, other plantains, moneywort, pennywort, and others—are controlled by a single spraying of 2,4-D in the spring or fall and when the plants are making rapid growth. The rates of application are given on the label.

Nutsedge is hard to control. 2,4-D at about double the normal rate for broadleaf weeds every 6 weeks for two or three growing seasons will greatly thin stands of nutsedge.

Control wild garlic with repeated annual treatments in the early spring with 2,4-D. Use the rate suggested for nutsedge. Add a teaspoon of liquid household detergent to each gallon of spray.

Silvex is more effective than 2,4-D for control of chickweed, ground-ivy, yellow woodsorrel, knotweed, and mat spurge. For greatest effectiveness, spray in spring while the plants are small and growing actively. Many of these weeds can be controlled at any season as long as they are growing well.

Red sorrel is not well controlled by sprays of 2,4-D or silvex. Dicamba is effective, but it must be used only at the rate of one-half pound per acre, because it may be absorbed by roots of

HERBICIDE SUMMARY CHART FOR WEED CONTROL AROUND THE HOME [1]

Weed	Lawns		Woody ornamentals and shade trees	Herbaceous perennial ornamentals	Wooded and marginal areas
	General	*Spot treatments*			
Nutsedge	2,4-D, repeated heavy rates.	2,4-D, methyl bromide, SMDC, DMTT.			
Bermudagrass	dalapon	dalapon, methyl bromide.	dalapon		dalapon.
Crabgrass	DCPA, DMPA, R–4461, trifluralin.		DCPA, DMPA.		
Goosegrass	DMPA, R–4461	Stoddard solvent, DSMA.	DCPA, DMPA.		
Dallisgrass	DSMA	DMPA.	Stoddard solvent spot treatment.		
Nimblewill	DMPA, repeated heavy rates.	DMPA.			
Plantain	2,4-D	2,4-D			
Dandelion	2,4-D	2,4-D			
Ground-ivy, Chickweed, Henbit, and Knotweed	silvex	silvex			silvex.
Pigweed	2,4-D	2,4-D	DCPA, sesone, DNBP.	DCPA, sesone.	
Lambsquarters	2,4-D	2,4-D	do.	do.	
Dodder				DCPA, CIPC.	
Wild garlic	2,4-D	2,4-D			
Purslane			DNBP, CIPC.	DNBP, CIPC.	
Red sorrel	dicamba	dicamba.			dicamba.
Spotted spurge	silvex	silvex			
Mugwort			amitrole	amitrole	
Poison-ivy	2,4,5-T	amitrole	amitrole, ammate.		2,4,5-T, amitrole, ammate.
Virginia-creeper			do.		Do.
Honeysuckle	2,4-D	2,4-D	do.		amitrole, ammate, 2,4-D.
Hardwood seedlings	2,4,5-T	2,4,5-T.	amitrole		amitrole, 2,4,5-T.
Orchardgrass, Tall fescue, Timothy, and Broomsedge		Stoddard solvent.			
Woodsorrel	silvex	silvex			silvex.
Ragweed	2,4-D	2,4-D			2,4-D.

[1] Home vegetable gardens: Preplanting treatments with SMDC, DMTT, methyl bromide control most annual and perennial weeds. Black polyethylene plastic may be used. Annual ornamental plantings: Preplanting as for vegetable gardens.

Common chickweed.

Nutsedge.

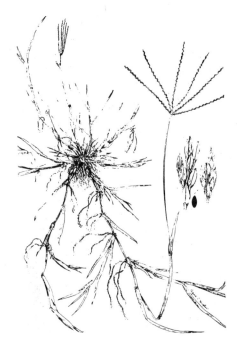

Large crabgrass.

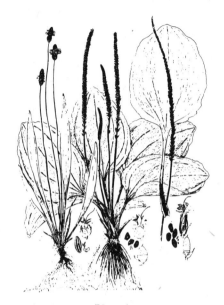

Plantains.

Ground-ivy.

Bermudagrass.

Lambsquarters. 484

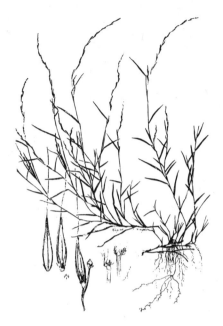

Nimblewill.

Red sorrel.   *Common purslane.*

trees and shrubs if it is used at higher rates.

Red sorrel likes acid soils. Therefore apply lime if your soil needs lime.

Many organic herbicides control such annual grasses as crabgrass, foxtail, goosegrass, barnyard grass, and annual bluegrass if the chemicals are applied before their seeds germinate. Trifluralin, DMPA, DCPA, and R–4461 prevent infestations of crabgrass and foxtail.

DMPA and R–4461 are moderately effective on goosegrass when it is applied in the spring and on annual bluegrass if it is applied early in the fall before it germinates.

Lawn grasses should not be seeded for several months after you use these herbicides.

Dallisgrass and related *Paspalum* species are perennial plants that can be controlled by spraying the foliage with DSMA. Repeatedly spraying the foliage with DSMA every 7 to 10 days for two or three treatments effectively controls crabgrass, foxtail, goosegrass, and sandbur.

Occasional plants of coarse perennial grasses, such as orchardgrass, tall fescue, timothy, redtop, velvetgrass, and broomsedge, are unsightly in lawns. They may be spot-treated with Stoddard solvent. Repeated treatment will be necessary.

Nimblewill and bentgrass often are undesirable and difficult to eliminate from lawns.

Silvex applied repeatedly at about double the usual rate of treatment will reduce the stand of bentgrass. Spraying should start early in the spring.

Nimblewill stands are reduced by spraying DMPA at heavy rates in May or June. A second treatment should be applied about a month later.

Such aggressive perennials as bermudagrass and quackgrass cannot be killed in lawns without hurting other plants. Effective herbicides kill all the grasses, and reseeding the area is necessary.

Only methyl bromide, a fumigant released under an airtight cover that is kept in place 24 to 48 hours, will kill all these weeds in a single treatment. Special application equipment is required.

Treated areas may be reseeded within 48 hours after removal of the cover.

Repeated treatments of dalapon, SMDC, and DMTT control bermudagrass and quackgrass. Start the treatments in July on actively growing grass; irrigate the lawn about a week before treatment if necessary to encourage growth. Water the area after treatment if necessary to encourage the growth of dormant, unkilled buds. Make a second treatment 4 to 6 weeks later to kill any regrowth.

If it does not rain, irrigate every 7 to 10 days after the second treatment for 3 to 5 weeks to help dissipate the herbicide from the soil. Seed lawn grasses late in September.

ADVICE ON HOUSE PLANTS

TWO GROUND RULES for selecting and maintaining house plants are:

Select the right plant for the conditions in your house.

Water the plants to maintain them rather than to grow them.

Many types of plants may be used as house plants. Some of them are:

Iron-clad plants, which are useful under many conditions: Aglaonema, aspidistra, ciccus rhombifolia, crassula (Jade), dieffenbachia, ficus, philodendron, sansevieria, schefflera, scindapsus, and syngonium.

Tough plants, which are useful for extremely dry conditions: Bromeliads, cacti, peperomia, sansevieria, scindapsus, and zebrina.

Plants for large tubs: Dieffenbachia, dracaena, fatshedera, ficus elastica, ficus panduranta, palms, pandanus, philodendron, and schefflera.

Plants for low temperature (50° to 60° at night): Bromeliads, cineraria, cyclamen, English ivy, Germany ivy, Jerusalem cherry, kalanchoe, and primrose.

Plants for medium temperature (60° to 65° at night): Christmas cactus, chrysanthemum, gardenia, grape ivy, palms, pilea, peperomia, ti plant (*Cordyline terminalis*), tuberous begonia, wax begonia.

Plants for high temperature (65° to 70° at night): African violet, aglaonema, croton, dracaena, ficus, gloxinia, philodendron, scindapsus, schefflera, cacti and succulents, caladium, and syngonium.

Many other plants are grown in the home, but they require much more attention than the ones listed.

Most flowering plants do not grow and flower well in the home unless supplemental fluorescent light is used. African violets, gloxinias, begonias, geraniums, primulas, and bulbs require this special care.

Grow your plants in individual pots or in a planter.

Here are some tips that make it easy to maintain plants in individual pots in a window garden.

• Plastic pots are good because water is not evaporated through them. Their use means you need not water the plants so often.

• Glass wicks inserted in the bottom of the pot conduct water from a reservoir.

• Put a sheet of vinyl film, matching or contrasting with the plants, under the pots to protect the window sill from water.

• Turn the plants every week toward the sun to encourage symmetrical development.

• Fluorescent lamps, controlled by a timeclock, supplement sunlight for a 16-hour day (6 a.m. to 10 p.m.). The plants thus are lighted for evening display. A combination of cool white and lavender (Gro-Lux) lamps enhance the color of plants and furnishings.

• Night temperatures that are comfortable for people are good for plants —65° to 75° F.

• Trays containing gravel and water increase the humidity around the plants.

• A planter that is easy to care for has an outer shell of plywood, painted to match walls, or of wood veneer, stained or oiled to match the furniture. The planters may be put on platforms or rollers to make handling easier.

• The inner shell is a watertight, galvanized tin liner, painted with asphalt to retard rusting. Heavy polyethylene film stapled into the outer shell may serve as a temporary liner.

• A layer of gravel in the bottom of the planter provides airspaces.

• To have all plants and pots at the same level, put small pots on top of larger ones; use unmilled sphagnum moss or pea-size marbles or granite chips to fill the space between pots.

• You may wish to use fluorescent lamps to supplement sunlight for the planters.

• Plants should be grown in individual clay pots, never planted directly.

START TO ADJUST the plants to the new conditions of the home as soon as you get them.

The soil ball, clay pots (if that is the kind you use), and the material you use in big pots should be watered to saturation, but not to excess.

Allow the whole area of the soil ball and the planter to dry until the plant is near wilting. Detect wilting by a change in leaf color from green to gray-green, a drooping of the foliage, and wrinkling of the stem.

Water again thoroughly to saturation. Allow the excess water to moisten the soil ball and the surrounding moss or stone chips in the planter.

Some of the oldest leaves may turn yellow at this time. Wash the foliage with warm, soapy water; remove the yellow foliage; and stake the plants.

Water thoroughly each time, but lengthen the number of days between waterings to the maximum.

Each time you water, try to increase the number of days over the previous number of days for watering. Watering on a regular schedule often kills house plants because no judgment is involved.

A successful watering procedure is based on constant observation—to observe that the soil ball is dry and the first signs of wilting are evident. One then waters to saturation. Again, the time of observing—waiting until the first signs of wilting are evident again.

The number of days between watering should gradually increase, and so you have the plant trained to maintain itself without extensive growth, the whole root system continues to function, and care is at a minimum, but you continue to observe it.

If you do not water enough each time, part of the roots will die from lack of water, and eventually the whole plant will die. Thorough watering keeps the entire root system functioning.

If you have many sizes of pots in the planter, you may have to water different plants at different times.

A planter should not be static—the same plants in the same place.

Introduce new plants, even potted flowering plants, to give a seasonal look to the planter—chrysanthemums in the fall, poinsettias at Christmas, azaleas and hydrangeas in the spring, and gloxinias and tuberous rooted begonias in the summer.

Plan to replace them; do not try to carry them over to the next season.

The planter in the home is a poor place to grow flowering plants. The many sizes of pots will require special watering consideration—flowering plants will require much more water than foliage plants. Avoid overwatering the planter so that the foliage plants will not receive too much water.

A plastic funnel may be used as an aid in watering to saturation. The size of the funnel depends on the size of the

pot. The diameter of the funnel should be at least half the diameter of the clay pot. Insert the neck of the funnel into the soil in the pot and fill the funnel with water. Continue to add water to the funnel until saturation, then remove the funnel.

The soil should be watered thoroughly but never to excess. The poor aeration that results from overwatering will kill the roots. Watering to saturation at longer intervals keeps the roots active and lengthens the life of plants.

APPLY water-soluble fertilizers through the top of the pots every 4 weeks while the plants are in active growth. Use the concentration the manufacturer prescribes, but use one-fourth strength when you add water to the subirrigation pans or funnels.

Fertilize only when the plants are in active growth. Withhold fertilizers from resting plants.

Sparing but continuous feeding is desirable for most house plants. It helps keep all foliage green.

A good rule is to feed by adding a water-soluble fertilizer each time a new leaf emerges on a large-leaved house plant. Unless the fertilizer is added, the oldest leaf on the plant will turn yellow at the time a new leaf develops.

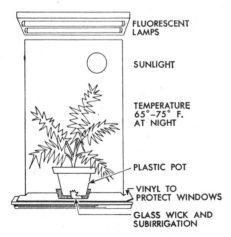

Easy maintenance of individual pots in a window garden.

A cross section of an easy maintenance planter.

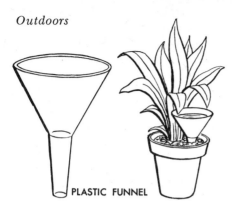

Plastic funnel may be used as aid in watering to saturation.

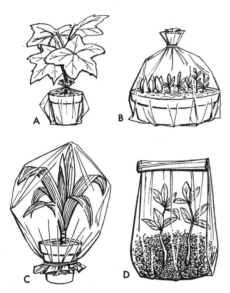

Use of polyethylene films. A. Cover clay pot of well-watered plant with polyethylene film. B. Cover propagation pan to keep humidity high around rooting cutting. C. Cover recently rooted, air-layered plant to retard water loss from foliage. D. Wrap unrooted cuttings in sphagnum moss and cover with perforated polyethylene film.

Dry fertilizers seldom are successful for house plants, because a great part may remain in the soil, and repeated use may kill the roots in time.

Remove any white deposit that accumulates on the surface of the soil and replace it with new soil.

When clay pots turn white or crusty, they are loaded with insoluble, unused fertilizers—primarily phosphorous compounds (calcium phosphates), which are toxic to root development.

You should replace old pots as they become useless. Many people feel that they can wash or soak the fertilizer out, but that is impossible. Throw the pots away. They are not even useful as broken pieces in the bottom of another pot. For best culture, use a new clay pot.

For potting soil, mix equal parts of garden soil, sand or perlite, and peat moss. To each gallon of mixture, add a tablespoon of rock phosphate and one of limestone if the soil is acid. Bagged soil mixtures that are available generally duplicate that mixture.

If the mixture holds a great deal of water, add one-third perlite to increase the aeration.

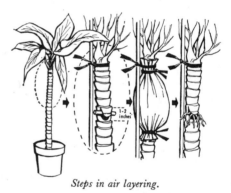

Steps in air layering.

These soil mixes should be sterilized (pasteurized) before they are used as a medium for potting plants. The commercial soil mixtures generally are pasteurized. For the home mix, place the soil in a shallow pan; set it in an oven held at 250° F. Hold it until a potato put in it bakes. Many people lose house plants from rot organisms found in home-prepared mixes.

YOU CAN MAKE good use of polyethylene film in several ways.

Use it to cover the clay pot after you have watered the plant well. Thus some plants can be left unattended for many weeks before they require additional water.

Cover a propagation pan to keep a high humidity around rooting cuttings. Place the pan in indirect light to avoid overheating by the sun. Remove the film as the cuttings start to root.

Cover recently rooted, air-layered plants to retard water loss from the foliage. Open the film gradually to establish the plant in air.

Wrap unrooted cuttings in sphagnum moss and cover them with perforated polyethylene film. The cuttings may be shipped or held several days before they are inserted in the rooting media.

To PROPAGATE PLANTS, you may wish to try air layering, which is the only way for plants that have stiff or woody stems and eventually grow too tall to be attractive.

Do it this way: Attach the stem securely to a stake. Make an upward cut into the stem, separating the bark with a small stick. Cover the cut area with a ball of moist (but not soggy) sphagnum moss. Reduce the water loss by covering the area with polyethylene film. Continue to grow the mother plant in the usual way. When you can see the roots in the moss, cut the rooted top off the mother plant and plant it in a pot. Continue to grow the mother plant; new lateral branches often develop down the stem. You can air-layer the same mother plant many times.

INDEX

THE EDITOR AND HIS BOOK

PAUL McKENNA FARGIS was born in New York City in 1939, the son of George B. Fargis, an attorney and Elizabeth H. McKenna. He and his three brothers and four sisters were raised in New Rochelle, New York. Mr. Fargis received his Bachelor's degree from Fairfield University in 1961 and, under a scholarship, earned his Master of Arts degree from the New York University Graduate Institute of Book Publishing in 1962. While studying in the Masters program, he served as a publishing apprentice for Prentice-Hall, Inc. He enlisted in New York's 107th Regiment—the famed "Silk Stocking" Regiment—and after a brief tour of duty, joined Hawthorn Books as an Assistant Editor. In his years at Hawthorn he has successively been Editor and Managing Editor and is now Assistant Vice President. He and his wife and son reside in Mount Vernon, New York.

This book was set in type by Spartan, Div. of Argus-Greenwood Inc., Hackensack, New Jersey; printed by Mahony and Roese, Inc., New York City and bound by American Book-Stratford Press, New York City. The text is set in Baskerville, a face designed by John Baskerville in 1750. The first modern version of this face was produced by Stanley Morison in 1923.

A HAWTHORN BOOK